DOWN AND OUT

IN EIGHTEENTH-CENTURY LONDON

Down and Out
in Eighteenth-Century London

Tim Hitchcock

hambledon
continuum

Hambledon Continuum
A Continuum imprint

The Tower Building
11 York Road
London, SE1 7NX
UK

80 Maiden Lane
Suite 704
New York, NY 10038
USA

First published 2004 in hardback
This edition published 2007 in paperback

ISBN 1 85285 281 X (hardback)
ISBN 1 85285 552 5 (paperback)

Typeset by Carnegie Publishing, Lancaster
and printed in Great Britain by MPG Books, Cornwall.

Contents

Illustrations

Dedicated to

Sonia Constantinou

with all my love,
respect, friendship and admiration

Acknowledgements

The origins of this book lie in a youth spent hoping that living poor would purchase real freedom – that if I could just restrict what I spent to as close to zero as possible, I could avoid the ever slavering maw of work and responsibility. I did not succeed. But for the years between 1973 and 1983 I hitchhiked everywhere, tens of thousands of miles on two continents, frequently slept rough, and occasionally went hungry. In the longer term I failed to eschew consumption and desire, but the experience was wonderful, and it kindled in me a profound respect for the kindness, intelligence and resourcefulness of most people in most circumstances. The assumptions and expectations that inform my research on London's poor were created from the unthinking small kindnesses I received from hundreds of different hands, seemingly whenever I asked. It is also informed by my few, largely unsuccessful, attempts at outright street begging. My first debt of gratitude is to all the people who gave me lifts, meals, and a place to sleep when I needed them, and also to those who turned me down – forcing me to think hard about what I was doing, and why.

In more recent years my debts have become easier to quantify if no less numerous. I first met Robert Shoemaker over twenty years ago in the grubby basement of London's County Hall. He is the kind of historian I have always aspired to be. He is intellectually bold, and frighteningly careful. More than this, he is the most moral person I have ever met, and the best friend. His support and enthusiasm has helped midwife this book in to the world. Penelope Corfield has been a constant and unflagging supporter for almost as long – she has made more contributions to this book than she knows. The Long Eighteenth-Century Seminar at the Institute of Historical Research has provided a context in which to think about the past, and a social arena in which to enjoy it. I am particularly indebted to Arthur Burns and Julian Hoppitt, who have always been willing to entertain my more fanciful views, while restraining me from publicising my more absurd ones. The people who have attended this seminar over the years and contributed to this book through their questions and seminar presentations are too numerous to name, but I would like to particularly mention Louise Falcini, Susan Whyman, Margaret Hunt, Amanda Goodrich, Kevin Siena, Nicola Pullin,

Tanya Evans and Karen Harvey. These are the kinds of friends that make scholarship possible and enjoyable.

The many people who have worked to make Old Bailey Online a reality (www.oldbaileyonline.org) have also contributed to this book in innumerable ways. In particular Mary Clayton's hard slog in the archives of London provided many insights and examples which have since been incorporated into this text, but as importantly, her constant good humour and enthusiasm in the face of a difficult job, was an inspiration. The staff at both the Higher Education Digitisation Service at Hertfordshire and at the Humanities Research Institute at Sheffield, have also contributed more than they realize. I would particularly like to thank Simon Tanner, Geoff Laycock, Mark Greengrass, Jamie McLaughlin, Louise Henson, Edwina Newman, Kay O'Flaherty, Gwen Smithson, Christine Meckseper, Martin Shephard and Andrew Prescott. Patrick Mannix's generosity in providing high resolution scans of eighteenth-century maps has ensured that I never entirely lost my way on the backstreets of London. The support of the AHRB and the New Opportunities Fund has also been instrumental.

My students at both the University of North London and the University of Hertfordshire, many of whom have become colleagues and friends, have also made more contributions than I can list. I would particularly like to thank Stuart Hogarth, Dr Heather Shore, Dr John Black, Dr David Price, Ian O'Neil, Mark Latham, Janice Turner and Dianne Payne. My colleagues at both institutions have also been immensely important. This book would not have been finished without their help. In particular I would like to thank Kathy Castle, John Tosh, Matthew Cragoe, Laura Gowing, John Broad, Lien Luu, Tony Shaw, Owen Davies, Nigel Goose, Alan Thomson, Helen Boak, Sarah Lloyd and Graham Holderness. The staff at the archives and libraries of London have never failed me. I thank them for their help.

Beyond these debts, I owe more than I can say to friends whose historical expertise I have shamelessly drawn upon. I would particularly like to thank Rowan McWilliam, Kelly Boyd, Wendy Bracewell, Deborah Valenze, Lisa Forman Cody, Tim Wales, Nick Rogers, Jo Innes, Mark Jenner and John Styles. Tony Morris and Martin Sheppard at Hambledon and London have been endlessly supportive of this project, and have helped gently to push it in the right direction.

Finally, I would like to thank Nicholas Hitchcock for continually reminding me that the world did not end in 1800, and Sonia Constantinou for her constant and uncomplaining support and help and presence. She has read every word of this book, and contributed more than anyone to it.

Abbreviations

BL	British Library
CLRO	Corporation of London Records Office
GL	Guildhall Library
LMA	London Metropolitan Archives
NA	National Archives
OBP	*Old Bailey Proceedings*: consulted at www.oldbaileyonline.org prior to 1 February 2004
WAC	City of Westminster Archives Centre
WAM	Westminster Abbey Muniment Room

Introduction

William McNamee, or just 'Mac' as he was known to his family, was a beggar:

> In height he was upwards of six feet, and as perpendicular as the gable-end of a house; his bones were so poorly protected with anything in the shape of muscle, that he looked like the frame of a man being set up ... He wore buckskin smalls (a part of the uniform of the foot guards); [and] wore his [hair] hanging down upon his shoulders; the colour was that of a dark chestnut, and it hung in graceful natural curls ... He had but one failing, but this one followed by a thousand others; if he once tasted intoxicating liquors he had no power to close the safety-valve until he either became prostrated, or his finances were exhausted.

From the secure perspective of an economically successful mid nineteenth-century family man, Mac's stepson, James Dawson Burn, recalled a journey to London in around 1810, when Burn was only eight or ten years old, and Mac was in his forties. They went out begging together on the streets of London.

> When all other resources failed for raising money, he used to make charity sign-posts of himself and the other two boys, along with me. Human sympathy is a strange thing – it binds men of all ages, countries and conditions, in the god-like bonds of universal love. To those who have not got occasion to think upon the subject, it would be a matter of surprise to learn the amount of real charity which exists in London. If [Mac] had taken care of the money he had given him during his begging campaign in London, I am satisfied that he could have gone in to some business, by which means he would have been enabled to have rubbed the vagrant rust off his character, and become a respectable member of society.[1]

This book is about the beggars and the beggarly poor of eighteenth-century London. It is about who they were and where they slept. It is about how they kept body and soul together with little money and few connections. It is about how, by combining begging on the streets with selling ballads or their bodies, by working as shoe blacks and chimney sweeps, cinder sifters and errand boys, as criers and hawkers, sellers of mackerel and cabbage nets, poor women, men and children constructed a life in this million person city. It will demonstrate, as Mac discovered, that when the poor threw themselves on the kindness of strangers, they were frequently caught. It will suggest that the beggars and beggarly poor of eighteenth-century London were the very people who made the economy of this great city work. That it was the labour of the out-of-luck and the out-of-place, given in exchange for casual charity, that helped to drive this economic success story that was London.

The eighteenth-century metropolitan poor have always been seen as a problem to be solved – a population suffering through drink and illness, who had no where to turn, and no hope of salvation. They are part of that dystopia of social disorder found in the works of Daniel Defoe, William Hogarth and Henry Fielding, and reproduced by historians of London ever since. They are the pus at the heart of the 'Great Wen'. They are the degraded and suffering poor, against whom the respectable working class of the next century is so frequently measured. But by looking at how the poor used social policy, how they exploited the resources of the capital, and how they deployed the rhetoric of suffering – by exploring what eighteenth-century London looked like from the poor's perspective – this book redraws that image and reshapes that comparison.

It suggests that eighteenth-century London was more welcoming and more charitable, more orderly and more forgiving, than historians have allowed. It also suggests that the eighteenth-century poor were creative and imaginative actors in their own lives, and in the life of this metropolis. They were smart, resilient and flexible, and in the process of surviving, forced many of the changes which contributed to the creation of this newly modern city.

1

The Streets of London

London's widespread reputation for generosity to the beggarly poor was frequently bemoaned by more censorious commentators. Writing in 1751, Henry Fielding complained bitterly about the open-handed charity of his fellow citizens. They:

> are so forward to relieve the appearance of distress in their fellow-creatures, that every beggar, who can but moderately well personate misery, is sure to find relief and encouragement; and this, though the giver must have great reason to doubt the reality of the distress, and when he can scarce be ignorant that his bounty is illegal, and that he is encouraging a nuisance.[1]

A few years later William Hutton, who himself regularly gave small change to both beggars and street sellers, made a similar complaint:

> The city abounds with beggars (this is December!) which shews a defect in the police. It is hardly possible to travel the streets of London, and keep money in one's pocket; not because it is picked out, but drawn by our own consent … This kind of mistaken charity, however necessary, defeats its own intent, by encouraging the beggar in his practice.[2]

Most others, however, were more forgiving, and saw casual charity in the light of good citizenship, hospitality and Christianity. Joseph Addison seems moved to real admiration in the *Spectator*, when he depicts his gentlemanly creation, Sir Roger De Coverly, the epitome of eighteenth-century Tory goodness, relieve a common beggar in Gray's Inn Walks:

> I was touched with a secret joy at the sight of the good old man, who before he saw me was engaged in conversation with a beggar man that had asked an alms of him. I cou'd hear my friend chide him for not finding out some work; but at the same time saw him put his hand in his pocket and give him six pence.[3]

Addison and Steele have another correspondent complain:

> As for my part, who don't pretend to more humanity than my neighbours, I have oftentimes gone from my chambers with money in my pocket and

returned to them not only pennyless but destitute of a farthing, without bestowing of it any other way than on these seeming objects of pity.[4]

Nor was it just between the leather-bound covers of eighteenth-century advice literature that casual charity can be found. It was probably for the purpose of almsgiving that William Matthews, a gentleman down to his very undergarments, had about him three separate hoards of cash when he went out riding in Hyde Park on a Friday morning in the spring of 1770. In his right-hand waistcoat pocket, next to his body linen, he had a substantial amount, 1 guinea, 5 shillings and 3 pence, tied up in a small yellow bag, as befitted a gentleman out for a ride. In his left-hand breeches pocket, handy but not readily accessible, he kept 8 shillings, probably to pay for a drink or the common expenses of the day. But, in his right-hand coat pocket, the pocket most easily reached, was squirreled his small change, along with his gloves, a clasp knife and a pocket book. This was the pocket in which he kept those items he would need most frequently throughout the day. The money was always ready to give out to any beggar who caught his fancy.[5]

It was not solely gentlemen who gave to the poor. Erasmus Jones in his cutting 1737 guide to urban etiquette, *The Man of Manners: or Plebeian Polished*, was careful to advise his rough middling-sort audience on the correct manner of giving charity. He observed that he had:

Seen some people as they have pass'd open-handed enough; but then they dispensed their charities with so unhandsome a grace, that methought they did ill in doing good, and refus'd an alms while they gave one. They seemed to insult over a poor creature's misery and seldom open'd their purse till they had vented their gall. This is not to relieve the indigent, but to throw shame upon want and confusion upon necessity; 'tis to hang weight to their burthen and to fret poverty with contempt ...

He went on to advise:

There cannot be a greater mark of ignorance and ill manners than to gape at a person worn down in a consumption, afflicted with a jaundice, or labouring under any other visible infirmity, as they pass along, and to stare at 'em as at a statuary shop at Hyde Park Corner; because it oftentimes gives too great a shock to low spirits, and has been attended with very ill consequences to the unhappy sufferer.

Instead, in Jones's view, you should always give, and give alms with, 'A kind compassionate look, [which] oftentimes refreshes more than a crown ...'[6]

Even beggars themselves recognised the demands of a universal compassion. When Mary Howell was eleven years old she ran away from her

London home. It was the spring of 1749/1750 and she 'travelled for several days, without any other food than what the hedges afforded', until:

> One night, I crept under a hovel for shelter, and there came an old beggar-man to lie down; seeing a child by herself, he asked me where I came from? I forget what I told him: I fear some lie ... Poor as he was he had pity on me; and gave me a piece of fat bacon, which I ate, without bread, as greedily as if it had been the finest food.[7]

And when George Parker, an itinerant actor, almost a beggar himself, came across a woman and her five children, 'sorrow and despair ... painted in her countenance', he did not hesitate to give her what money he had. 'I could relieve them – I did, and purchased pleasure at the cheapest rate I had ever bought it for money.'[8] For eighteenth-century Londoners of all classes, relieving beggers on the street was a normal part of everyday life. Children relished their first charitable acts, and adults calculated the cost of the small coins they distributed daily to ragged individuals.

The people who asked for and received relief on the streets were a mixed lot. At the very end of the eighteenth century, in a remarkably impressive piece of early social science, Matthew Martin surveyed the street beggars of London. In 1796 he set up the Mendicity Enquiry Office at no. 190 Piccadilly in the centre of the West End. He

> caused tickets to be printed, and about 6000 were disposed of to myself and others, at the price of 3d. each [in packets of ten, twenty or thirty],[9] for the purpose of being distributed to beggars, who were admitted to the office in consequence of their shewing such tickets, and received the value and frequently more. Thus a small fund was raised of which the paupers had the benefit in return for the accounts of themselves; and the tickets being lettered and numbered, and registered when disposed of, served as clues in particular cases where required, to assist the donors in tracing the history of the parties on whom they were bestowed ...[10]

In little over seven months Martin filled forty volumes with examinations of the beggars who came through his door, detailing the life histories of some two thousand adults and over three thousand dependent children. Six hundred people were excluded by Martin because, 'though paupers, did not confess themselves to be beggars'.[11] He published statistical tables of the content of these examinations, and the result is the most comprehensive survey of street beggars produced prior to the late nineteenth century. In methodological terms, Martin's survey is a more robust source of information than many of its twentieth-century equivalents. Martin himself thought 'it improbable, though the circulation of tickets was extensive, that more than one third (if so many) of the beggars of the Metropolis should have applied at the office in so short a space of time as seven months'.[12]

Of the two thousand adult and self-identified beggars who made their way to the Mendicity Office, 192 of them were men, of whom forty-five were single, a hundred were married and forty-seven widowed. Among these were twenty-one military men and fourteen seamen. The most striking thing, however, was the number of women and children. There were 1808 women in this sample – 127 of whom were single, 1100 married and 581 widowed. Of this number some 240 had a military connection as the wife or widow of a soldier or sailor. And with these women came a further 3096 children.

In other words, London's beggars were predominantly women, and married or widowed women with children at that, with only a relatively small number of adult male beggars. Martin concluded that:

> Men are stronger than women, have more resources, and are better able to provide for themselves than women are; and single women are more eligible for service than married, and have usually only themselves to maintain. The greater number of widows may in some measure be accounted for by their being frequently more advanced in life, and having in many cases, children to provide for.[13]

The perhaps typical figure to emerge from his examinations is someone like Margaret King, who claimed to be the wife of John King, and who had 'two small children, and [was] ... big with another'. Although Margaret claimed that John was the father of all three of her children, they did not live together, and there is no evidence he provided any financial support. She and the children shared a room with Mary Granville, who 'carries chips about to sell', and who had a sideline in casual prostitution. Mary paid 6d. per week in rent and Margaret 9d. for a small room, with a fire and a rudimentary bed. On Wednesday, 9 April 1760, she was 'out all that day ... with my two small children', and had earned 'two shillings and eleven-pence halfpenny, which she said she had laboured hard for'. She described her work as 'begging'.[14]

It is certain that most of London's beggars were women, and yet other sources concentrate on male beggars, and in particular on adult male beggars. Criminal records and novels, newspaper reports and artistic images all reflect the greater visibility of male beggars. When John T. Smith wrote his unique account of the picturesque beggars of London in 1817, *Vagabondiana*, he included forty-seven images of beggars and the beggarly self-employed, many of whom he claimed had worked the streets of London for over thirty years. Among this ragged crew were the blind, and the crippled, ballad sellers and singers, crossing sweepers and grubbers, but only two women.[15] Almost all of Smith's beggars were adult men. In a very real way, adult male beggars were seen as a problem, and are recorded as such, while Martin's thousands of female beggars were simply a fact of life – the acceptable face of metropolitan begging. There were adult male beggars on the streets, but they were only the most visible portion of the beggarly poor.

Martin's figures, however, tell us more than a familiar tale of patriarchal inequality in which female suffering is hidden behind male representation. He also broke down his sample according to the settlement status of each individual interviewed. Every English and Welsh person had a parish of settlement, by birth, marriage, apprenticeship or a period in service, or as a result of renting a tenement of over £10 per year in value. For most paupers their settlement was closely guarded and frequently discussed. It was a 'right' which the English and Welsh poor felt gave them a claim on their parish of origin (or else the parishes of origin of their parents or husbands). It was also an issue that struck at the root of class relations in the eighteenth century. Elite writers continually sought to undermine the right to a settlement. Adam Smith, for instance, disingenuously claimed that 'There is scarce a poor man in England of forty years of age, I will venture to say, who has not in some part of his life felt himself most cruelly oppressed by this ill-contrived law of settlements'.[16] At the same time, the poor knew that this 'ill-contrived law' was the closest thing they were ever likely to have to an old age pension and unemployment insurance. As a result, settlement information was something the poor valued and cared about, and something they deployed with remarkable accuracy and fulsome detail.[17] For some, in a world where sudden death and abandonment were common, a settlement examination was their only connection to family and friends. Susannah Brady, for instance, was examined by the overseers of St Botolph without Aldgate on 9 January 1779. A cold, sharp wind was blowing out of the south east.[18] She explained how, in her infancy, she and her brother and sister had been 'found in a house', and how many years later, she had stood by as Samuel Batman, the vestry clerk for St George Hanover Square, had read out her father's examination from the parish book. She had memorised its every detail, and it formed her only knowledge of and connection to the parents who abandoned her as a child.[19] When Robert Blincoe, a parish orphan, discovered that the overseers of St Pancras had failed to preserve his parent's settlement examination, he was devastated. With bitter tears in his eyes he explained, 'I am worse off than a child reared in the Foundling Hospital. Those orphans have a name given them by the heads of that institution, at the time of baptism ... But I have no name I can call my own'.[20] For Blincoe his settlement and his identity were irretrievably intertwined.

The statistics Martin collected on the settlement of his examinees suggests that, as well as being female and being encumbered with children, the beggars of London were also largely Londoners. Like Susannah Brady, 750 of Martin's beggars had a settlement in London and Middlesex, while only 336 were from distant English parishes. Only sixty-five were from Scotland, and thirty from abroad. Indeed there was only one category of beggar who matched the home-grown variety in numbers. Martin noted down 679 Irish beggars among his total of two thousand.[21]

These figures, however, come from an unusual period of economic distress during which many more beggars, and Irish beggars in particular, were drawn to London through the military. The 1790s combined political crises with harvest failure to throw many men and women in to poverty. But earlier evidence suggests that Martin's statistics represent an older pattern. Between 1738 to 1742 the Lord Mayors of London decided to crack down on beggars. Of a sample of 153 individuals apprehended for begging and loitering in the City of London over half were adult women; a further 8 per cent were children. Adult men made up only around 40 per cent of the total – a percentage certainly inflated by the perception that male beggars needed to be policed, their bodies arrested and their names recorded, in a way that women, and women with children in particular, were not. And if we look at the settlement of these people, almost half, seventy-five, had a legal settlement in the metropolitan London area.[22] For a very brief period in October 1705 the Governors of the Poor for London recorded the place of settlement of everyone apprehended for vagrancy, and whether or not they were in receipt of a parish pension. The results again confirm Martin's findings. Of twenty-nine individuals apprehended, fifteen of them were adult women, seven were men and seven were children. Thirteen of this twenty-nine had a recorded settlement in London, and only two had settlements outside the capital. Perhaps more surprising, six of them were in receipt of parish pensions at the time of their incarceration. They were people like Katherine Archer, a fifty-year-old resident of Whitechapel, who was arrested for begging by the Warder of Bishopsgate. She was in receipt of 12d. a week from her parish. Or William Stephenson, a forty-three-year-old blind man who lived in St Martins-in-the-Fields, who was arrested with his wife Katherine 'idle and begging [in] Tower Ward'. He and his wife received 1s. 6d. a week from their parish.[23]

In part, the shape of this pauper population was a result of a changing history of migration. From late seventeenth century long-distance migration became less frequent, while short-distance and migration within London became more common.[24] The poor population of London gradually became both less likely to live in their parish of birth and probable settlement and, at the same time, more likely to have relatives, connections, friends and a parish of settlement within a reasonable distance. With the notable exceptions of Irish migrants, who figured largely among the population of beggars, and groups such as the black poor from the 1780s, most beggars were Londoners born and bred.

The question remains why the individuals who made up this population of the desperate were forced on to the casual charity of Londoners. We can certainly generalise about the roles of illness and illegitimacy, of family breakdown and of alcohol, but it is impossible to measure the impact of these factors directly. The forty volumes that made up Matthew Martin's body of evidence have not survived.[25] And although other sources allow tantalising glimpses of the world of eighteenth-century beggarly poor, the details of their poverty and homelessness seem to sit just below the surface of the text – always out of reach.[26] The vagrancy examination of Catherine Jones, for instance, who was examined by Samuel Bever in September of 1756, is an exercise in frustration. She patiently explained to the justice:

> that she is the wife of William Jones, an in-pensioner in the Royal Hospital in Chelsea, who is very old and utterly unable to provide for her. And the legal settlement of the said William is not to be found. This examinant says that she was born in Kinsale and was also married about thirty-three or thirty-four years past ... in St Maltess Kinsale in the kingdom of Ireland. That she is now very infirm and hath no lodging or place of abode.[27]

The best evidence we have for why people were forced on to the charity of others comes from the voluminous records of the dozens of workhouses that filled the back alleys of the capital. These do not detail the lives of street beggars, although many workhouse inmates begged the streets and, on occasion, were even encouraged to do so by the parochial authorities. But they do give us detailed life histories of that subset of the very poor who could rely on a parish of settlement for some relief, and who could use workhouse relief as a single component in a broader and more complex survival strategy. So although, the population of London's workhouses was made up almost exclusively of those who could claim a settlement, this does not sharply divide these men, women and children from the broader population of the beggarly poor. Some professional beggars felt contempt for the relief the settled poor could claim from the parish. Samuel Badham, for instance, came home one day to find his common law wife wearing a 'parish gown'. He said, 'Sukey, there's no body that ever belonged to me ever wore a parish gown'. And immediately 'went out and asked charity, and with what I got I bought her another gown, and got the other made in to a petticoat for her'.[28] Nevertheless, viewed as a group, workhouse inmates shared many characteristics with Matthew Martin's sample of street beggars.

At the workhouse belonging to St Luke's Chelsea, at the western edge of urban London, around half of all inmates were adult women. Many of these also brought with them dependent children, while only around a fifth of inmates were adult men. Workhouse inmates were also relatively young, with women between the ages of about twenty and sixty forming the greatest number.[29] The inmates at Chelsea were there as a result of personal crises and likely to make use of the house only once or twice.[30] The large workhouse register filled with the names and ages, and reasons for entry and exit from the house, tell thousands of stories which collectively reflect a gendered and episodic form of poverty. Elizabeth Bullock can stand in place for hundreds of others. Born in 1731, she was married to a soldier named William. At the start of the Seven Years War William was ordered abroad and she was left with no money or place to live, and with three children to care for, a girl and a boy aged four and two, and a babe in arms named Thomas, two months old. In the first instance she was sent with a vagrant's pass to her husband's place of settlement in Wolverhampton. She begged her way for several hundred miles through rural England, being passed from overseer to overseer. Once she arrived, however, her welcome was far from enthusiastic. The parish in Wolverhampton, where her husband had served his apprenticeship, appealed against the removal order, and she was sent back to Chelsea. Again she begged her way down the length of the country before ending up in Chelsea's workhouse, sick, with two of her children in tow (the youngest, Thomas, probably died en route). Like almost half of all parish children, the second youngest child, William, died in the house within a few months,[31] while Elizabeth, the elder girl, lived in the house for the next seven years, before being sent out to service at the age of twelve.[32]

Like Elizabeth Bullock, most women ended up in the workhouse as a result of illness and desertion.[33] A fifth of all women were there because they were 'ill', temporarily in need of care and medicine, others because they were 'infirm', permanently unable to walk or work. They were there because they were pregnant, or lunatic, or suffering from venereal disease and in search of an expensive mercurial cure. Others were there simply because they were 'poor'. As with Matthew Martin's beggars, most brought children with them.

The relatively small number of men who ended up in the Chelsea workhouse were more likely to be old and past work than were the women, and many were in their sixties and seventies. They also entered the house in more desperate circumstances than did women. Even more men than women were ill when they entered the house, and a larger percentage were likely to die there than were their female contemporaries.

Like workhouse inmates, the beggars and street sellers of London were primarily women, and women with children. They were deserted and infirm, ill and desperate. The relatively few men on the streets were older and obviously disabled. The workhouse material also suggests that men and women experienced poverty and approached begging in different ways. Women had a perhaps readier claim on charity, and certainly seem to have been able to make better use of institutions such as workhouses. They were also more thoroughly enmeshed in an economic network which, when it collapsed through desertion or unemployment, rapidly led to complete pauperisation. Men had more opportunities to make a living on the street, even if it was poor one, and were almost certainly more able to move in to and out of the 'pauper professions' of the capital. Their relative absence from Martin's figures, and from the Chelsea workhouse, suggests that they could generally eke out a living at the margins of London's economy, as long as they could maintain at least a semblance of health.[34] At the same time, their much greater visibility in other types of sources, in fiction and criminal records, suggests that begging by men was seen in a particularly censorious light.

Although London's beggers fit a common pattern, they would have thought of themselves as a much more varied crew. Accent and age, neighbourhood and occupation (whether practised or not) divided beggers, just as much as these factors divided the rest of the population. For the very poor, their neighbourhoods, and the sense of belonging that flowed from them, was likely to be found in the penumbra of parishes that circled the City and bordered the river, providing cheap accommodation and casual employment for the beggarly poor. The character of these neighbourhoods, and those along the river in particular, is captured in Alexander Pope's 'The Alley':

> In ev'ry town where Thamis rolls his tide,
> A narrow pass there is, with houses low.
> Where ever and anon the stream is eyed,
>
> ...
>
> There oft are heard the notes of infant woe,
> The short thick sob, loud scream and shriller squall:
> Some play, some eat, some cack against the wall,
> And as they crouchen low for bread and butter call.
>
> And on the broken pavement, here and there,
> Doth many a stinking sprat and herring lie;

> A brandy and tobacco shop is near.
> And hens, and dogs, and hogs are feeding by;
> And here a sailor's jacket hangs to dry.
> At ev'ry door are sunburnt matrons seen
>
> ...
>
> Scolds answer foul-mouthed scolds; bad neighbourhood I ween.[35]

Poor neighbourhoods were packed into the jerry-built and unhealthy back streets of St Giles-in-the-Fields and around Rosemary Lane and St Catherine's Lane in the East End, and in a host of smaller pockets of desperation in the adjacent parishes. Even outside London's identifiably poor neighbourhoods housing was haphazard and squalid. Up until at least the passage of the London Building Act of 1774, many suburban developments were the work of speculators – mainly poor carpenters and bricklayers, employing even poorer materials. During periodic depressions in the building industry, houses put up in hope of attracting middling sort and rich occupants were let out room by room to the very poor. House collapses occasionally crushed whole families in their beds. At the same time new types of street lighting, of paving and water supply evolved to a remarkably high standard in the West End and in those parts of the City rebuilt after the Great Fire, while a remarkably low standard could still be found in many other areas. In most poor neighbourhoods ground water from public wells was the only source, and mud filled the unimproved roads for much of the year.

James Dawson Burn recounted his time in the poorer neighbourhoods of London. St Giles-in-the-Fields, with 'huge sufferings, savage lives, and innumerable crimes' came first in his recollection, closely followed by St Catherine's:

> St Catherine's was another of these dark spots in the wilderness of London, where vice and crime flourished in tropical luxuriance. I have often been taken through Swan Alley [just south of East Smithfield], which was ... looked upon as being one of the most consummate sinks of iniquity in London ... Tower Hill was honoured with the title of Rag Fair, and the traffic of dilapidated garments ... was divided between the Jews of the stock of Jacob and those of St Patrick ... Tower Moat then lay stagnant and green, sending up its sweet effluvia ...[36]

Between them, the neighbourhoods of St Catherine's and of St Giles-in-the-Fields formed the two most densely inhabited slums of eighteenth-century London. Along with the parishes of Southwark, the 'Borough' south of the river, they housed perhaps half of all 'poor' Irish men, women and children – a group the 1815 Committee on Mendicity in the Metropolis claimed included a high proportion of beggars. St Giles-in-the-Fields had over two thousand poor Irish inhabitants, comprising 17 per cent of the poor Irish population of London.[37] Many commentators believed that these districts were peopled largely by thieves and prostitutes, but most of them were simply poor, and many were simply beggars, or at the least practitioners of the begging professions. The accommodation available to the inhabitants of these districts is described in the evidence given by William Droyre to the court at the Old Bailey in 1787:

> The place that I did lodge in, there is neither a bolt, nor yet a latch to the door; the last that goes out, takes a bit of a padlock, and locks the door, and takes the key down, and hangs it in the kitchen; several people lodge in the same room; there are three beds all occupied, and there was one woman drunk in bed when they came there, that was a ballad singing woman; my wife and I went out to sell some cabbage nets, and white rags ...[38]

Droyre and his wife lived in Hampshire Hog Yard, just off Broad Street in the heart of St Giles.

If the very poor were restricted to the cheapest and worst accommodation, if they were forced to live in the areas that would in the nineteenth century become the infamous rookeries of Victorian London, they did not beg there.[39] Instead, they chose sites that could supply a ready stream of the financially secure. For women, the kitchen doors of the City and the more prosperous suburbs were the best bet. For men, it was the busy streets of the central districts of London that supplied the most profitable pitches.

Joseph Price, a common beggar, said he chose to beg at the 'corners of streets' because he could be assured of finding large numbers of people, and because he could employ himself as a sweeper.[40] The author of *A Trip Through Town* was accosted in the Strand and in Covent Garden. Lincoln's Inns Field was a particularly noted location in which to beg. Thomas Brown suggested that beggars had already begun to take up their positions in Lincoln's Inn by seven in the morning; while Steele in the *Spectator* described a beggar he dubbed 'Scarecrow' as a regular inhabitant there. John Gay warned that urban pedestrians should beware of crossing Lincoln's Inn at night for fear they would be knocked down with the crutches of beggars who had spent the day soliciting charity. The Royal Exchange was similarly full of '. . . Mumpers, the halt, the blind, the lame, your vendors of trash, apples, plumbs, your raggamuffins, rakeshames, and wenches [who] have justled the greater number of [merchants] out of the place'. Likewise, John Sharp, one of the City of London's most active vagrant-catchers, regularly patrolled London Bridge in search of beggars. Beyond these locations, beggars, both male and female, could be found in the Haymarket, Temple Bar, Smithfield and at the City gates. They could be found at both Mew's Gate and Warwick Street in Charing Cross, at St Paul's and on Tower Hill, in Gray's Inn Walks, at Temple Stairs and in Westminster Hall.[41] In other words, they could be found in most of the 'public' streets and major thoroughfares of the centre of the capital.

From the perspective of the beggar soliciting alms from unknown pedestrians and from the occupants of coaches as they alighted, these sites provided the perfect venue. All of them were locations where the pedestrian traffic was likely to be thick and to contain a reasonable variety of social classes. These sites also formed a natural corridor, and were part of the traditional processional route that had helped to define ritual London for centuries. Before the Embankment changed the shape of pedestrian London, walking from the Royal Exchange to St Paul's and on to Temple Bar, the Strand and Covent Garden, and finally Charing Cross provided one of the few alternatives to an expensive trip by river. Beggars soliciting farthings and halfpence on these streets knew they would have a reasonable selection of consciences to work upon. At the same time Lincoln's Inn Fields, perhaps the most frequently mentioned site for begging, was conveniently located on the walking route between the prosperous suburbs of the north west of town, and the courts. These were not the backwaters of St Giles's or Rag Fair, these were not the areas in which the poor actually lived; instead they were positions from which a man or woman in rags, with a story to tell, or a ballad to sing, could make a living. Even parish authorities recognised the importance of choosing the right location at which to beg. In 1748 one commentator complained bitterly that overseers of the poor ordered parish paupers

> such as the blind and lame [to sit] begging at gates in the highways and other places where huts are ... erected for them ... where they attend to receive that charity from passengers which they ought to receive from the parishes to which they belong.[42]

Together, the back alleys and slums, and the public thoroughfares of London, inhabited and navigated by London's beggars and the beggarly poor each day, formed the largest city in Europe. More than anyone else, it was the poor who tied the two halves of the city in to a single whole, but the façade London presented to the world, and that historians have inherited, was still schizophrenic. No topic divided eighteenth-century commentators more thoroughly than did London. It was either a sink of vice or a beacon of sociability. It was both the pinnacle and the nadir of British and European culture; both the most elegant capital of the Enlightenment, better lit than any other city in Europe, and, at the same time, the most squalid. To understand the lives of the men and women who begged and lived on London's streets, we need to first explore how our image of those streets has been created. Eighteenth-century art fully reflects the choices that contemporaries made, and historians have reproduced, when deciding how to depict this patchwork quilt of urban life.[43]

Painters like Canaletto and Samuel Scott depicted London as a city of monumental buildings and wide, clean avenues, peopled with the leisured and the well dressed. Yet, during the same decades that Canaletto and Scott made London their own, William Hogarth was creating an equally compelling vision. His London, the canvas upon which he painted his reforming and moralising tales, was a veritable hell of cramped and crowded streets, full of business and disorder, the poor and the disabled. Somewhere between these extremes lay artists like Paul Sandby and, slightly later, Thomas Rowlandson. A single location, Charing Cross, and its treatment by each of these artists, reflects the extreme perceptions of a perhaps mundane reality. Between these varied images, the London experienced by the poor and the beggarly is exposed.

Charing Cross was at the western end of the traditional procession route through London, and one of the city's most important public spaces. It was here that many riots began, and criminals, particularly men accused of homosexuality, were punished on the pillory and exposed to the wrath of the crowd. If you wanted to walk from the City to Whitehall or to the growing suburbs of the West End, or from the western reaches of London back to the City, you would almost necessarily go through Charing Cross. Early in the nineteenth century Francis Place, sitting at his window overlooking Charing Cross, remarked on the sheer energy of the scene below, 'which cannot be witnessed in any other country in the whole world, and perhaps at no other place in the world than at Charing Cross'. At 2 p.m. on one late November afternoon he counted 119 horses, and forty-two carriages, 'not including several small carts with donkeys ...'[44] He also recollected the Charing Cross of his childhood in the 1770s and 1780s. To his censorious eye it was full of pornography, prostitution and cheap food:

> the wall was covered with ballads and pictures ... miserable daubs ... of the grossest nature ... At night there were a set of prostitutes ... horribly ragged, dirty and disgusting ... These miserable wretches used to take any customer who would pay them twopence, behind the wall ... [And] at noon every day two very large stalls were set up for the sale of 'Bow Wow pie' ... A small plate of this pie was sold for three-halfpence, and was usually eaten on the spot, by what sort of people and amidst what sort of language [only] they who have known what low life is may comprehend ...[45]

A few years earlier the more forgiving Samuel Johnson claimed simply that 'the full tide of human existence is at Charing Cross'.[46] It was also a favourite pitch for beggars, shoe blacks and hawkers. By six in the evening, during the mackerel season, fish 'just come up with the tide, which will not keep till the ensuing day' was sold in 'great quantities very cheap among the crowds of people [at] Charing Cross'.[47] And John Gay, in Trivia, places his mock-heroic shoe black 'where branching streets from Charing Cross divide'.[48] At its centre was Herbert Le Suer's imposing equestrian statue of Charles I, which Hackney coachmen used as a convenient stand and which formed an important practical and cultural landmark.

After Trafalgar Square was carved from the Royal Mews, Green Mews and the odoriferous Dunghill Mews in the early nineteenth century, the statue, and Charing Cross itself, lost much of its significance to the new square. But throughout the eighteenth century it remained an all important social space, and its statue an iconic image that attracted the attention of all the artists mentioned of above, of Canaletto and Hogarth, Sandby and Rowlandson.

In Canaletto's 'London: Northumberland House', of 1752, – his busiest and most comprehensively urban London scene – the expanse of Charing Cross is seen bathed in late afternoon sunshine. The rich façade of the Northumberland House, with its lion and towers in the background, looks down benevolently on the people below. At the same time, the impression created of this most vibrant and occasionally disorderly of urban spaces is of one that is somehow empty of life. There are no pornographic prints or Bow Wow pie in evidence. The carefully chosen perspective allows some dirt, and building work, some workers, beggars and street sellers, but pushes them to the corners of the scene, and makes them small and inconsequential by comparison to the architecture. Where Francis Place had looked down with eyes only for the people who filled the roadway, Canaletto minimises the bustle and the filth. And although the scene that Canaletto depicts is a real one, drawn with great accuracy, it obscures the life that existed between the buildings. It faithfully renders much of what he saw, but what he chose to record was a clean and modern city, peopled by clean and modern individuals. The figures he includes seem to exist on the cityscape rather than in it. They wander and promenade, they chat and flirt, they stare fixedly from the canvas, but seem oddly purposeless. Even the coaches he includes are stationary. In part this impression is a legacy of Canaletto's painting technique. He almost certainly used a camera obscura and traced the precise outline of both the buildings and figures, upside down in a darkened, first floor room on the north side of the roadway, before turning the image over and copying it onto canvas. As a result, people, carts and carriages, things that moved too quickly to be recorded, were simply left out.[49]

1. Zuane Antonio Canal (Canaletto), 'London: Northumberland House' (1752).

The image that remained is of a cityscape devoid of the hustle and bustle, the life and energy, which almost all commentators, in prose and verse, agreed was the most compelling aspect of this particular location.

In contrast, when William Hogarth chose to depict this urban landscape he crammed ever more people on to his canvas. At the right hand edge of Canaletto's 'Northumberland House', Le Suer's bronze equestrian statue prances out of eyeshot towards Whitehall, and directly in to William Hogarth's 1738 scene 'The Night', from his 'The Four Times of the Day'.

Although Hogarth's scene is set on an imagined street, just a dozen yards from Canaletto's urban idyll, it could not be further away. It is full of disorder and distress. The coach to Salisbury is overturned, its horse frightened by a bonfire. Apprentices, armed with sticks and wooden swords, possibly celebrating Guy Fawke's Night, menace and harass the frightened passengers. A homeless family sleeps beneath the bulk of a barber's shop, while an unlucky victim squeezes the arm of his chair against the pain inflicted by a cack-handed barber-surgeon. The keeper of the New Bagnio, or bathhouse, waters down his wine in the background. From a window above, a woman's hand pours the contents of a chamber pot on to the head of the Justice of the Peace, Thomas DeVeil, drunk and in Masonic regalia, impervious to the disorder around him, being escorted home by a watchman.[50] This image is part of a quartet full of classical references, designed as a manifesto for a new sort of English art, both moral and comic. As the final scene of four, it is intended to be the most disorderly and criminal, the nadir to which London could fall.[51] But it is also peopled with recognisable individuals, the presence of whom reflected contemporary concerns and perceptions. Thomas De Veil, for instance, spent the 1730s and 1740s striving to reform the policing of Westminster, establishing a more professional night watch. His central position, surrounded by evidence of his many failures, reflects the anxieties and concerns of Londoners. The image also brings together everyday phenomenon with which the inhabitants of London would be familiar. Link boys and rough sleepers, traffic accidents, and the smells and filth of a city's waste, the fear and pain of everyday life, and the apparent disinterest of the authorities, can all be found in contemporary records. Hogarth, and many historians, have simply concentrated London's many problems, boiling them down to a single powerful image. But, just as Canaletto's painting obscures the life between the buildings; Hogarth's overdraws and overstates. While Canaletto gives only the smallest corner of his canvas to the beggars and hawkers whom he could certainly see in the lens of his camera obscura, Hogarth brings the poor centre stage, but more to mock them, than in empathy.

This same urban space, Charing Cross, and the same statue of Charles I,

2. William Hogarth, 'The Four Times of the Day', plate iv, 'The Night' (May 1738).

can also be found in other depictions of the capital. Thomas Rowlandson painted Charing Cross in 1808 for the *Microcosm of London*. For him, the architecture and the crowds seem more in balance than for either Canaletto or Hogarth. Northumberland House is lost to one side, and the focus of the picture is the crowd surrounding two men in the pillory. To Rowlandson's eye London is full of people and disorder but lacks the sense of social crisis so much to the fore in Hogarth's vision. Francis Place was living in Charing Cross when this picture was painted, and later described the scene:

> Charing Cross was the most usual place for 'pilloring' those who were sentenced to punishment for offences committed in the metropolis on the north of the Thames and without the City of London ... As it was always well known that such an exhibition was to take place at a certain time, a large mob always assembled, a considerable portion of which consisted of the lowest vagabonds, men and women, girls and boys, that St Giles and Tothill fields could furnish ... Some of these people brought with them on donkeys and in bushels, rotten eggs which they procured from the egg warehouses, decayed cabbages etc, etc the refuse of Covent Garden market ... Near the pillory were two stands for hackney coaches under these there was a quantity of hay, dung and urine trampled into a mass by the feet of the horses, this was collected, soaked in the mud in the kennels and then handed to the women to pelt the man in the pillory ... The shoutings of the mob exhilirated the pelters, and induced many who came as spectators to join in the mischief ...[52]

What Rowlandson suggests is an alternative to both Hogarth and Canaletto. For him, and for Place, Charing Cross was a simple and vibrant echo of a flawed, but much loved city. It both possessed the problems so much to the fore in Hogarth's work, and the elegant lines of Canaletto. And while there is disorder in Rowlandson's image, it is the disorder of a community gathered together to punish one of its own.

The individuals who people this crowded scene are neither mocked nor ridiculed. But, at the same time, they are not brought into focus either. To see further in to the crowd, to stare in to the eyes of one of the individuals who peopled Charing Cross and the other public streets of London, we need to turn to Paul Sandby. Sandby was a near contemporary of both Canaletto and Hogarth, and used the same statue and location as the backdrop to his *c.* 1759 'Sock Vendor', but this time the underlying message is both more sympathetic and less dogmatic than Hogarth and more humane than Canaletto.[53]

Sandby's sock vendor stares from the picture, challenging both the viewer and buyer. His shaded eyes glower from beneath his hat and his mouth frowns. He is neither funny nor subservient, but he seems to capture the

3. Augustus Pugin and Thomas Rowlandson, 'The Pillory', from Rudolph Ackerman, *The Microcosm of London* (1808).

4. Paul Sandby, 'Sock Vendor', *c.* 1759. (*Nottingham Castle*)

difficult choices made by the London poor, and the sense of self-worth they were nevertheless able to maintain. He is certainly better dressed than most of London's beggarly poor. His clothes are well maintained, and he appears well fed. At the same time, he represents the more economically secure and successful end of a social continuum that stretched to link-boys and ballad-sellers, to chars and cinder-sifters, and finally to the street beggars of London.

Sandby was familiar with the work of both William Hogarth and Canaletto. He was an early and regular critic of Hogarth and his work. In 1753 and 1754 Sandby produced a series of eight etchings satirising the intellectual pretensions of Hogarth's 'Analysis of Beauty', while Sandby's 'Asylum for the Deaf' (c. 1760), was a direct and unflattering commentary on Hogarth's much earlier 'The Enraged Musician' (1741). At the same time, he also studied Canaletto. Sandby produced two massive watercolours, his 'View to the West from the Gardens of Somerset House', and his 'View to the East from the Gardens of Somerset House' that clearly reflect his familiarity with Canaletto's works on the same theme, which would have been available for Sandby to view in the Royal Collection from 1763.[54] In the 'Sock Vendor', two boys play on Herbert Le Suer's statue while to the left, in the direction of the side street Hogarth uses in the 'Night', a man in the pillory is pelted by the crowd. Sandby published the first part of his set of 'Cries' as *Twelve London Cries Drawn from Life* in 1759, and during the same period painted a large number of watercolour studies. In the end, his published 'Cries' were a commercial failure, but he and his brother Thomas did reuse several of these figures in more ambitious paintings.[55] Collectively, Paul Sanby's Cries form the most individualised and humane depictions of the poor of London ever created. Paul Sandby never painted a large-scale image of Charing Cross, but what he has left us is a compelling image of the people in Rowlandson's crowd, the people Hogarth caricatured and whom Canaletto simply ignored. His 'Sock Vendor' may have been more successful than the more ragged street traders and beggars with whom he shared Charing Cross, but with them, he possesses a humanity and sense of purpose that is missing from the London created by Hogarth and Canaletto and from the work of many historians ever since.

This book is about William McNamee and Paul Sandby's sock vendor, and the women who, despite the greater prominence given to male beggars in criminal and literary records, formed the majority of London's poor. It is about the shoe-blacks, the prostitutes, crossing-sweepers and cabbage net sellers. It is about women who sold mackerel, and beggars who used mistletoe and holly at Christmas to justify their presence on the streets. It is about the errand boys and pickpockets of eighteenth-century London. It is an attempt to recover the lives of the individuals who struggled, and frequently failed, to make a living on the street. It is an attempt to see eighteenth-century London through their eyes, and to understand their rationality, their decisions, their options.

2

Sleeping Rough

At forty years old and dressed in 'clean britches and waistcoat and my brown coat' and selling stockings about the streets of London, John Harrower could easily have been the model for Paul Sandby's 'Sock Vendor'. He grew up in Lerwick in the Shetland Isles. He was fit and, while his education was rudimentary, he could read, write and keep accounts. On Monday 6 December 1773 he was forced to leave behind his much-loved wife and small child to seek work. With just eight and a half pence clinking in his pocket, and a bundle of stockings worth £3 on his shoulder, he set off for Leith. His journey was frustrating, but uneventful. From Leith he travelled first to Newcastle then on to Portsmouth, begging free passage on a coastal collier, and constantly enquiring after work. He subsisted on a monotonous diet of bread, cheese, broth, and a bit of meat and ale. For food and to pay for his accommodation when not on shipboard, he sold pair after pair of stockings. On 5 January he recorded, 'This day snowing very hard ... At 9 a.m. went out to see if I cou'd sell any stockings, but returned again at 10 a.m. without selling any ...' Later the same day, he 'travelled the town until 2 p.m. in which time I sold three pair of stockings for four shillings and four pence, which was eight pence less than they cost me ... '.

From Portsmouth Harrower tramped up to London, passing through Petersfield, Godalming and Wandsworth. On the first day he made four miles, carrying his box and bundle on his shoulder, and managing to sell two pair of stockings for 4s. 6d. to a man he joined on the road. Three days later, on Tuesday 18 January 1774, he was in London:

> This day I got to London and was like a blind man without a guide, not knowing where to go being freindless [sic] and having no more money but fifteen shillings and eight pence farthing a small sum to enter London with; but I trust in the mercys of God who is a rich provider and am hopefull before it is done some way will cast up for me.

His trust in God was perhaps misplaced. His first challenge was to find a place to sleep. He made his way down to the docks in Wapping, and secured accommodation at the Old Ship Tavern in Little Hermitage Street, just east of Hermitage docks and north of the river. He was hoping to find a berth as a book-keeper or clerk to a merchant, and he chose his lodging to be close to London's shipping. With food, his accommodation cost him 1s. 2d. per night. And although the innkeeper was in prison for debt, it was a relatively well-run establishment. For a little over a week he tramped about London seeing the sights, selling his stockings and seeking a place. He wrote letters to merchants and sea captains asking after work. He answered advertisements in the daily press. He made what use he could of the tenuous connections he had in London, but soon, his supply of stockings exhausted, he was forced to admit defeat. He refused to beg on the streets, although in his own words, 'many good people are begging', but he was left with few alternatives. On Wednesday 26 January:

> Reduced to the last shilling I had was obliged to engage to go to Virginia for four years as a school-master for bedd, board, washing and five pound during the whole time [I] had only left [home] about three weeks before.[1]

In order to avoid begging, he sold himself into temporary slavery.

That journey of hope and despair, travelled by John Harrower, was familiar to tens of thousands of eighteenth-century people – men, women and children. They came to London from Scotland and Ireland, Wales and the West Country. They came from Africa, the West Indies, France, Germany and the Netherlands.[2] Some of them had money in their pockets and friends to call upon. But most did not. Like Harrower, but with even fewer choices, the poor were forced to find charity and accommodation in a city that baffled even Londoners.[3] Harrower was an intelligent and experienced man, in full health, and yet London was a landscape in which he could not navigate, in which he was unable to find a place, a berth, a job. For the less well supplied, for children and women, for the ill and the desperate, London was an even greater challenge. It was an environment that required the poor to use every cultural and imaginative resource at their disposal. In the words of Ann Candler, who was abandoned to her fate by her alcoholic husband at the start of the Gordon Riots, in a city she knew not at all, migrants to London were 'exposed to the horrors of extreme poverty in the midst of strangers'.[4] The remarkable thing is that unlike John Harrower, most of them survived, most of them found a place, a niche, in the complex world of London. Very few of them died on the streets or were forcibly removed by overseers and constables. Instead, they slept in barns, and in the sheep pens at Smithfield. They found warmth in the annealing yards of the glass houses, and food among the cast offs of Covent Garden and Billingsgate. They begged for broken food and casual labour at kitchen doors. They went 'on charity' into the homes of the middling sort, and formed the army of porters and sweepers, errand boys and charwomen who made London work.

Londoners' frequently complained about their city:

> Houses, churches, mixed together,
> Streets unpleasant in all weather;
> Prisons, palaces contiguous,
> Gates, a bridge, the Thames irriguous.[5]

Despite this carping, London was a well ordered city – perhaps one of the most beautiful, and beautifully maintained, cities in Europe. By the 1740s it was the best-lit city in the world, and the view from the top of St Paul's left many visitors speechless.[6] César de Saussure, normally so informative of the details of London life, simply gave up:

> From this elevation on a fine day, when the atmosphere is clear, you can see the whole of London and also the Thames and the pastures around. This is one of the finest views in the world, and my words cannot give you any real idea of its beauty ...[7]

It was also a city of stables, barns, outhouses, bog-houses and kitchens, tucked away but still accessible. There were over eighty-five stables and stable yards listed on John Rocque's 1746 map of the capital.[8] There were also abandoned houses and half-built ones. It was a city in which the streets were constantly being repaired and buildings were constantly being reconstructed.[9] More than an elegant expression of Enlightenment values, or a disastrous social failure, London was a city full of opportunities for the poor.

A cheap, but essentially respectable lodging in an alehouse cost from 6d. per night, without food, and twice that if food was included,[10] but if you were willing to seek a bed in the rougher parts of town you could find a place for three pence. Certainly when, on a 'dark, dull cloudy, cold ... and damp' evening in December 1782, William Jones was forced to seek lodging in a house in Black Boy Alley, one of the most disreputable addresses in the City, he paid just 3d.[11] Having said this, the conditions were not pleasant. A couple of years earlier William Blizard, having toured the low lodging houses of Chick Lane, Field Lane and Black Boy Alley, described what he found:

> The houses are divided from top to bottom, into many apartments with doors of communication amongst them all, and also with the adjacent houses, some have two, others three, nay four doors opening into different alleys ... In many of the rooms, five, six, seven, eight, nine and ten men in bed, in one loft into which we were obliged to creep through a trap door, were eight men.[12]

Nevertheless, you needed a steady income in order to afford even this kind of accommodation. There were alternatives.

The most unsettled of inhabitants could find a place to sleep if they were desperate. In 1785 James Wilson returned from two and a half years at sea. With the money he received on his discharge at Chatham, he made his way to town. For over a year he, 'followed no business or labour' and lay 'sometimes in one place, sometimes another'.[13] Barns and hay lofts were by far the favourite home of these unsettled poor.[14] On one cold and clear Tuesday evening in October 1761,[15] James Peck surreptitiously crept into the stable at the Bull Inn in Bishopsgate Street – a coaching inn noted for its hearty toasts and heavy drinking[16] – and snuggled in to the straw for the night. He was only disturbed when the constable, Robert Bradley, made his rounds at midnight and arrested him.[17]

It was far better to seek the permission of the owner before settling down. William Border slept for over a year in the hay loft belonging to John Lock of St James's Market. He rapidly became well known to the local community, and garnered the nickname of 'the Doctor'. He was given beer at local inns, and the fact that he (and at least one person before him) regularly slept in the stable formed part of the insider knowledge accumulated by the local night watchman, Robert Gardner.[18]

Thomas Shaw was able to carve a bit of free accommodation from the fabric of the city as well. During the early 1780s he worked as a porter at the King's Arms Inn, near Holborn Bridge, and by 1786 had moved to the Peacock in the Minories.[19] He was an alcoholic and eventually lost his job and his home, ending up begging about the streets. But for two years, during the early 1790s, he haunted the neighbourhood of Holborn, sleeping in the stables belonging to his first employer, warmed by the breath and sweat of the horses. When he fell ill, the innkeeper, Robert Hughes, gave him gin and tried to see that he did not freeze on the street. In fact, he died sitting before a warm fire, wrapped in a thick rug, at the New Compter.[20]

The great inns and the low alehouses of London were made up of a plethora of rooms and outhouses. The Star Inn on Fish Street Hill at the northern end of London Bridge, for instance, contained three stables, a hostelry, a coal house and coal hole, besides several warehouses, a kitchen and a buttery.[21]

Of course, you had to be careful whom you asked. Thomas Shaw's master, John Granger at the Peacock in the Minories, probably stopped allowing ex-servants to sleep in his outhouses and barns after 1786. In that year his wife, Rebecca, gave an ex-servant, John Peazy (Black Jack or John as he was called), permission to sleep in their 'back kitchen'. Rebecca was probably carrying on an affair with Peazy. She had certainly given him money and gin on several occasions, and walked out with him on four succeeding Sundays without her husband's knowledge or permission. On the night of 15 January,

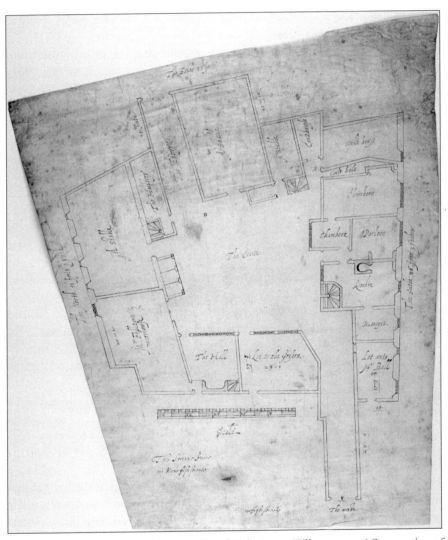

5. Plan of the Star Inn on the east side of Fish Street Hill, *c.* 1700. (*Corporation of the City of London*)

while the temperature hovered a few degrees above freezing, Jack slept in the back kitchen and in the morning was given a large tot of gin and most of the cash in the till by Rebecca. John Granger discovered the gift, argued with his wife, and then sought Jack out at a neighbouring alehouse. Jack was committed to the New Compter and tried for his life at the Old Bailey. He was lucky to be found not guilty.[22]

The conditions suffered by men and women sleeping in outhouses and barns were not pleasant, but the filth and squalor was commonplace. Popular attitudes to sleeping rough are reflected in the ballad of 'Brick Dust Nan', sung about the streets to great laughter in the last quarter of the eighteenth century:

> By the side of a green stagnant pool, brick dust Nan stood scratching her head.
> Her matted locks all over her skull, like the bristles of the hedge hog were
>   spread;
> But the wind blew her tatters abroad, and her arse and brown beauties
>   revealed,
> When a link boy through the mud, bare footed scampered over the field,
> With his lid lod lid lod etc.
>
> Oh! My dear tho' I can't so well draw, for the playing at the house ant' begun,
> No tobacco ant' so sweet to my jaw as a kiss from the lips of my Nan;
> Running up to her straightway he gave her such rib squeezing hugs,
> I could douse in a dusthouse with thee, tho bit by the blood sucking bugs.
> With his lid lod lid lod etc.
>
> A courting they sat in the rain for the space of a quarter of an hour,
> Then their wedding to keep in the dry, to a hog sty they instantly did scour,
> Where the rats, hungry round them explor'd, yet undauntedly, they took their
>   repose
> All night in the litter they dossed, and got up in the morning to louse.
> With their lid lod lid lod etc.[23]

Filth, rats and lice were the everyday and inevitable enemies of those sleeping rough. Despite these problems it remained the preferred option for some. James Lackington describes how one female resident of St James' workhouse 'had a great aversion to sleeping in a bed, and at bed-time would often run away to a field in the neighbourhood called the Priory, where she slept in the cow-sheds'.[24]

In general, however, women on their own seem to have found the hay, clean or otherwise, of the capital's barns and stables more difficult to make use of than did men. Beggarly women were frequently seen as sexually available and sleeping in a barn left them particularly exposed. It was perhaps fear of sexual assault that led Grace Powell to seek a night's lodging at Samuel Pate's. She had just come out of the St Martin-in-the-Fields work-house and had very little money. She later described the situation: 'That Samuel Pate letts two-penny Lodgings, and entertains Black-shoe-fellows, and sells Drams ... and the House used to be full of People, Men and Women, all lie together in the same Room'.[25]

Women could sometimes find more suitable accommodation for less than the 2d. demanded by Pate. In late February 1765 Jane Austin found her-self in an awful situation. She was relatively new to the city, and had lost her lodging in White Hart Yard, when the man she was living with, John Dug-gin, beat her and threw her out. Homeless and friendless on the streets of London, she was suffering from both the beating and a long-standing chest complaint. Her first response was to apply to the overseer of the poor of the parish of St Martin-in-the-Fields for admission to their workhouse. Her set-tlement was enquired into, and she was found to possess none. As a result she was turned back onto the street. For three days she wandered up and down the Strand and in Covent Garden, sleeping in doorways at night, but by the third day she had become desperate. The weather that week was cold and stormy. The temperature ranged between a freezing 29 degrees Fahren-heit and a still bone-chilling high of 43 degrees.[26] She was also starving and the wound in her side from the beating continued to plague her. At noon on the third day she knocked at the door of Elizabeth Stewart's apartment in a low lodging house belonging to Ann James in New Bedford Court, a tiny enclave off the Strand.[27] Several women were working in the room, and Jane begged to be allowed to sit by the fire. She was invited in and sat for the rest of the afternoon, while more fortunate women – poor but employed – worked around her. In the evening she shared a pint of purl (hot beer, herbs and gin mixed together) and at ten, when Elizabeth Stewart returned from an errand, she asked to be allowed to sleep in front of the fire for the night.

For that night at least Jane had a warm place to sleep. By the next day, Elizabeth Stewart had tired of dispensing charity and asked the lodger upstairs, a black man named Michael Reading, to escort Jane out of the house. He took her by the arm and led her to the door and down the stairs. She fell, and he grabbed her around the waist, and together they ended up on the doorstep in confusion. Two minutes later Jane was dead, the victim of a beating, or of hunger or cold, or her final tumble down stairs.[28]

The innumerable abandoned and tumbled-down houses of the metropolis also created at least temporary and insecure accommodation for many women. In one 1749 pamphlet the anonymous author suggested by mid-night:

> Houses which are left open, and are running to ruin, [are] fill'd with beggars, some of whom are asleep, while others are pulling down the timber and packing it up, to sell for firing to washerwomen and clear starchers about that neighbourhood.[29]

Ironically, one 'old woman' actually took up residence in the abandoned workhouse belonging to the parish of St Pancras. Her occupation of the house was of such a long standing that the Bow Street runners nearly dismissed a light shining in the house as belonging to her. In fact it was the crucial evidence that would lead to the arrest of five footpads using the abandoned workhouse as a base from which to commit highway robbery in 1782.[30] During the same year, Simon Edy, a familiar beggar who regularly stationed himself outside St Giles's Churchyard, slept with his dog in his arms, 'under a staircase in an old shattered building called "rat's castle" in Dyot street'.[31]

In 1763 a prospective buyer was looking over a house in Stonecutters Street, which ran between Fleet Market and Shoe Lane, just north of St Bride's Churchyard. London was full of abandoned and half-completed houses at this time, and squatting was commonplace. In this instance the buyer found the emaciated bodies of three almost naked women on the ground floor, while in the garret he found two women and a girl, alive, but on the verge of starvation. Two of the bodies were of women who had worked as casual porters in Fleet Market, just a few yards down the road, both of whom were known by the name of 'Bet'. In the garret a woman named Pattent had established herself over a long period. She was an out-of-place servant, who had gone to the Fleet Market to look for work and had been told by one of the 'Bets' that the house on Stonecutters Street was empty. In the succeeding months, she lived in the garret as best she could, taking what employment she could – sleeping in the house at night, and working in a cookshop in King Street, Westminster, in exchange for food, during the day. The girl, Elizabeth Surman, was only sixteen. Her father had been a jeweller and had lived in Bell Alley, off Coleman Street in the City. John Strype described the alley as 'pretty broad and indifferent well built and inhabited', with 'some good houses, especially on the East side'.[32] But Elizabeth's parents died, leaving her to be apprenticed very young to the pauper trade of silk winding in the much less salubrious Spitalfields. She did not last long at this, and spent the next six years working for a washerwoman as a children's nurse. When she fell ill, her mistress discharged her. With nowhere to go, she slept on the streets for weeks before finding a bit of shelter in the house. When she was strong enough, she went out begging, coming back to Stonecutters Street at night. A couple of days before they were discovered, Pattent had pawned her apron for 6*d.*, which they spent on food.[33]

The death and malnutrition of the women on Stonecutter Street shocked eighteenth-century sensibilities, but their ability to live for months and years as squatters reflects the extent to which it was possible to find shelter from the weather – if not from the harsh winds of economic depression. Nor should we assume that their experience of squatting (as opposed to starving to death) was unusual. It was simply one end of a continuum of housing arrangements that sheltered the poor. Even if you were paying a weekly rent, the conditions under which you lived were likely to be very basic and very crowded. In 1792, two houses collapsed in Haughton Street, one of the cramped turnings between Clare Market and the Strand, east of Covent Garden. Almost a hundred years earlier John Strype had described Houghton Street as 'well built and inhabited', but by the end of the eighteenth century it had become little more than a slum.[34] Each house contained just two rooms per floor, including a front and back garret under the eaves. At No. 8, the larger of the two houses, consisting of four stories, lived some eighteen people, and seven separate families. At No. 7, which was only three stories high, seventeen individuals were crammed into the dilapidated building. A Mr Higgins and his four children rented the two ground floor rooms, while above them, at the front of the house, were Mr and Mrs Gibbons and their two children. At the back on the first floor, again in a single room, were Mr and Mrs Brussell and Mrs Remmington. And in the garret, at the front, lived Mr and Mrs Mills and their two children, while at the back lived Margaret Kirby, on her own. The fronts of the houses collapsed without warning at 8.30 a.m. on a warm and cloudy Saturday morning, 27 June.[35] Most of the men were already out at work, but one man, four women and two children were killed outright, while the body of a boy, whose name was never discovered, was found among the ruins.[36]

As a young, married journeyman in the 1790s, Francis Place rented a furnished room at 'a coalshed at the back of St Clement's Church' and paid 3*s.* 6*d.* for the privilege of living there, out of a weekly income of around fourteen shillings.[37] Later in life, he described the house:

The house in which we lived was very old and … was very narrow, it was a continuance of Butcher Row to Wych Street. Our landlord kept a coal-shed, i.e. sold coals in a shop, the house was very dark and dirty. The houses in Butcher Row … had overhanging fronts each of the three or four stories projecting beyond the story underneath, many of the windows were casements as all of them had been, and, like all such places, they were dirty, and filled with rats, mice and bugs.[38]

Crowded, dirty courts and alleys, with shared privies and no privacy, were the commonplace for working Londoners. They were both squalid and unhealthy. Whole families, however large, frequently shared a single room and a single bed. But they were also homely. Neighbours looked after you and your children. While people moved frequently, they also formed close communities. Mary Flarty, for instance, felt safe leaving her son Jerry to play with the neighbour children in Pipemakers Alley on a cool and cloudy Saturday afternoon in April 1762.[39] The alley, just north of Tothill Fields and east of the Artillery Ground, was a tiny, quiet turning off a quiet street. While Jerry was only two or three years old, five-year-old Ann Ellison was on hand to keep him safe. Indeed, the whole alley seemed perfectly organised for children. Even the shared privy had a special low seat for toddlers. On this occasion, a bit of play on the street ended in tragedy when Jerry fell down the privy and drowned in its noisome contents. Ann Ellison raised the alarm, yelling up to an open window, 'Mrs fflarty, Jerry is down':

> immediately she alarmed the neighbourhood and she was informed by a person who looked on his watch that it was just ten minutes from the time of Ellison's crying out to the time of the deceased being taken up. Says she was not by when he was taken up, but he was brought to her directly and was then dead.[40]

Francis Place later ascribed much of the 'improvement' in manners and behaviour he perceived among working people during his lifetime to the gradual decline in whole families living and working in a single room. From the perspective of the very poor, however, the crowded and cramped nature of London's housing was both a boon and a bane. Crowding just one more person in to an already heaving bed or house seems to have caused little comment and less anxiety. The arrangements were seldom permanent, and many people, having been given one or two night's respite from the streets by charitable neighbours, would find themselves back sleeping rough as soon as the weather improved, or the temper of their host declined.

London in the winter was cold and wet by turns. Rain and sleet was followed by rain and snow, and to survive you needed to be able to keep dry and warm, but for much of the year it was possible to survive with more rudimentary shelter. The grand jury for the City of London regularly complained that the unsettled poor 'assemble and lye together whole nights upon shop bulks and at the doors of empty houses'.[41] And while the sinful anti-hero of one anonymous Religious Tract Society production complained bitterly that 'every bone in my body aches with lying on the ground at nights without a ... covering',[42] there were times when sleeping rough was the sensible alternative. In 1749 Mary Howell was eleven years old. On 2 February of that year there was a grand fireworks display in St James's Park, to celebrate the coming of peace. Mary was determined to see it, and ran away from home in order to do so. When her father finally caught up with her, he dragged her back and chained her to a bedpost for three days, feeding her on dried bread. In revenge for this treatment, she spoiled her father's work, tearing the silk he wove and ruining the quills she was set to wind. He locked her up, chaining her by the leg to a heavy log. In her own words:

> When I got my liberty, I quickly found means to run away; for soon after, my father sent me on an errand, and gave me a shilling and a plate to hold what I was to purchase. Being careless about pleasing him, I lost my time in catching flies on the rails as I went along; but in the midst of my sport I lost the shilling, and whilst I stood crying and looking for it, I dropt the plate and broke that. Now, I durst not think of returning, but ran farther and farther from home. Oh what a scene of distress, sorrow and trouble, did I bring myself into by this unguarded action! For several nights that I staid in town, I was forced to creep under bulks or any where, to hide myself from the watchmen; and as soon as day broke, I went in to the markets, to pick up rotten apples, or cabbage-stalks; as I had nothing else to support nature.[43]

Bulks were the wooden shelves that stuck out over the pavement in front of most shops. During the day they groaned under the weight of the new and fashionable goods streaming into this commercial heart of the British economy. But at night, cleared and disregarded, the bulks formed a convenient shelter for the homeless, an almost traditional prerequisite of the poor.[44] Certainly, Samuel Stainton thought so in 1792. He was a night watchman, one of the thousands of local policemen who watched over London's midnight streets. On many occasions watchmen arrested vagrants sleeping rough, but on the evening of Thursday 13 June Samuel Stainton defended one woman's right to do so. It was relatively warm, and was probably raining, as Stainton patrolled Lime Street, a small thoroughfare between Leadenhall and Fenchurch streets just west of the Tower.[45] A gentleman, a Mr Sinclair Gordon, spotted a 'poor woman lying under a bulk' and insisted that Stainton arrest and remove her. When Stainton refused, Gordon 'laid hold of his coat ... and a struggle ensued'. In the end Stainton was forced to apologise to the 'gentleman', but the anonymous woman was allowed her night's sleep.[46]

Hogarth included three figures – perhaps a family, the child asleep in its mother's arms – beneath a bulk in his 'The Night' of 1738. And John Smith turned the noun into a verb in his 'Solitary Canto to Chloris the Disdainful',

6. Detail from William Hogarth, 'The Four Times of the Day', plate iv, 'The Night' (May 1738).

when he has his young lover, refused entry to a sweetheart's bed, decide: 'To bulk it, or use the hard ground for a pillow'.[47] John Gay saw in the bulks the metaphorical home of all of London's street urchins. In his *Trivia* he spends some sixty lines describing in loving detail the origins of the shoe black from the coupling of the goddess Cloacina, in the form of a cinder-wench, and a beshat scavenger.

> When the pale moon had nine Times fill'd her Space,
> The pregnant Goddess (cautious of Disgrace)
> Descends to Earth; but sought no Midwife's Aid,
> Nor midst her Anguish to Lucina pray'd;
> No cheerful Gossip wish'd the Mother Joy,
> Alone, beneath a Bulk she dropt the Boy.[48]

In 1749, the anonymous author of *Low-Life: or One Half of the World Knows Not How the Other Half Live* thought that by three or four in the morning:

> The bulks of tradesmen's houses [are] crowded with vagabonds who have been picking pockets, carrying links, fetching whores for spendthrifts to taverns, and beating drunken men, who are now got drunk themselves and gone to sleep.[49]

But much more than a literary home, the bulks were a ready refuge from the rain and the intrusive gaze of the nightwatchman.

In the cool of October in 1701 Margaret Rouse was sent to Bridewell, 'for being an idle vagrant and found under a bulk'.[50] In November of 1735 Elizabeth Roach and Mary Vizage were arrested for a similar offence, 'for being found ... frequently lying at doors and on bulks and loitering up and down the streets all night and being disorderly idle persons'.[51] And in 1742 John Cock was apprehended 'for being an idle disorderly person loytering about ... [Honey Lane] Market and lying in stalls and bulks there and neglecting and refusing to give any account of himself'.[52]

With the evolution of glass window displays and more sophisticated shop design, the bulks gradually disappeared from the streets of London. They survived outside some specialist stores, such as second-hand book shops, but by the early nineteenth century had ceased to be an ubiquitous piece of urban street furniture and comfort to the homeless. Just as new systems for policing became more searching, the classic hiding place for the beggar and vagrant, the runaway child and homeless pauper, was pulled down and replaced with twinkling displays that could do no more than reinforce the sense of exclusion experienced by the poor.

Bulks were not the only quiet corner a homeless pauper could escape to. The markets, wharves and quays also provided a number of hiding places from the biting wind and searching light of the night watchman. At the quayside women such as Susanna Jones could find both a place to sleep and the means to keep body and soul together. She lived at Botolph Wharf in the early 1740s, 'She is a woman that lies thereabouts constantly, she is an old offender', and made a slim living pilfering tobacco.[53] The markets were if anything more popular, with the markets at Fleet, Leadenhall, Smithfield and Billingsgate providing favoured accommodation.[54]

We have already seen that the porters of Fleet Market occasionally squatted in the vacant houses in the area, but the market itself also attracted a pool of the economically marginal and homeless. A general meat and vegetable market, it was built to replace the older Stocks Market, demolished in the early 1730s. It consisted of two rows of single-story shops connected by a covered walkway with skylights, with a clock tower overlooking the whole scene. Designed by George Dean, it was built on the covered over northern reaches of Fleet Ditch. The market was located just west of the notorious debtor's prison of the same name, in an area famous for its sponging houses – private lodgings where debtors were incarcerated until their bills were paid. It was also just north of the still open sewer of the Fleet leading in to the Thames, on the shores of which Bridewell – that prison for the poor – proudly stood. James Sharp, 'The Flying Pie Man' could frequently be heard to yell his wares, 'One a penny, A slice, Hot!' at the market during the 1750s.[55] And George Parker claimed in 1781 that:

> If you have a mind to have a ballad on a treasonable subject, or one which injures the peace of society, you … may hear it sung … from … the corner of Fleet Market.[56]

Ann Glassborough was caught 'lying about the Fleet market' on a cold and cloudy night in early February 1757, while four years later, on a cloudy but pleasantly warm Tuesday in May, the constables picked up Ann Kettlewell and Mary Willis 'wandering abroad and lodging in the open air in Fleet market'.[57] Dennis Shee and William Andrews were similarly picked up on a Wednesday in early January, 'lying about Fleet Market and not giving any good account of themselves'. The weather was stormy that week, and the temperature hovered just a few degrees above freezing, so the protection of the covered market would have been welcome.[58] They were sent to sea for their trouble. And Mary Robinson, 'found sleeping in the open air in Fleet Market' on a cool Tuesday night in Spring 1763, was sent to the London workhouse.[59]

The location of the Fleet Market in the centre of one of London's most disreputable quarters no doubt encouraged the homeless and the disreputable. Peter Campbell claimed Francis Philpot attempted to sodomise him

in Fleet Market in 1785;[60] while on 14 October 1741 John Piper was stabbed
to death by John Woolford in the middle of the market, encouraged by the
taunts of local boys.[61] It was almost certainly the opportunities for casual
labour as basket women and porters, the possibility of garnering free food
at the end of the day, and the absence of householders to oversee the space
after the stalls had been closed down, that attracted paupers such as the
woman Charles Maxwell found in the market in mid December 1799. No
one knew her name, but about ten o'clock on a Thursday night, Maxwell
found her:

> Lying upon her hands and knees on the pavement in the middle of the mar-
> ket ... her cloaths were very ragged torn and dirty, and she appeared quite
> insensible. [Maxwell] moved her and placed her in a sitting posture against the
> door of one of the Butcher's shops.

He returned to see how she was doing a couple of more times during the
course of the night, and finally around 2 a.m. took her to the local watchhouse. By six the next morning she was dead.[62]

Leadenhall Market was similarly attractive. Located just north of London
Bridge in a corner of London defined by Gracechurch Street and Leadenhall Street, the market was a complex array of three different areas,
specialising in beef and hides, poultry and pork, and in green vegetables.[63]
Better policed than Fleet Market, Leadenhall attracted the poor more
because of the food available and the protection it offered from inclement
weather than because of its location. César de Saussure was particularly
impressed by Leadenhall:

> Nowhere can you see finer markets than in London, especially those of Lead-
> enhall, of Stock Market and several others; they are vast, covered and shut in,
> and in them you can find every kind of butchers' meat, the finest in all the
> world, and kept with the greatest cleanliness.[64]

Of course, the poor could not afford to buy this meat, 'the finest in all the
world'. Many of them stole it instead. In 1722 the governors of Bridewell
complained of Leadenhall Market that, 'the butchers meat is frequently
stolen away'.[65] In the same year Benjamin Hewett and Timothy Goree were:

> Taken about 2 o'clock in the night in Leadenhall Market, giving no account of
> themselves but suspected to be run away from their friends. The first known
> to be a companion of John Burroughs, lately committed for pilfering pork.[66]

A month or two later, John Smith was similarly taken up for 'lurking in
Leadenhall'.[67] And on a clear and cold Wednesday night in November 1769,
while the faint trail of a comet could still be observed in the sky, James Neale

was taken up for 'lodging in the open air in Leadenhall Market and not giving a good account of himself'. He was bound out to a fisherman from Greenwich by the Marine Society.[68]

If the Fleet attracted the poor because it was poorly policed, and if Leadenhall's fine foods explains its appeal, the smelly, agricultural warmth of Smithfield was its greatest attraction. During the daytime, the sound of lowing cows and squealing pigs, full of fear generated by the smell and sound of butchery and death, filled the market and its environs. After the killing had been done, the blood let and the carcasses hung, the market settled down.[69] Just west of the main square, the vast sheep pens, containing hundreds of animals driven through the streets to their eventual deaths, steamed with animal warmth on a cold night. This is perhaps what attracted Jonathan Files, Thomas Aston and Jonathan Jossett to the pens in 1718. They were found asleep there at midnight, 'all pretending to be just come to town'.[70] Similarly, in 1696, Edward Hewitt and Elizabeth Pierson were arrested because they 'lye about the sheep pens in Smithfield and can give no good account of themselves'.[71]

Covent Garden Market, Billingsgate, Newgate, St James's, Queenhithe, Hungerford and Clare Markets were all sites in which the poor slept rough.[72] These were busy open spaces whose very purpose was to bring strangers together. As a result, they were difficult to police. They were also familiar public landmarks at which a pauper might hope to find a bit of casual work, or broken food, or, if necessary, from which they might steal a few of the necessaries of life. Even the mentally retarded and physically disabled could find a casual home in the markets. Richard Aldridge was a 'poor foolish fellow' who lived in St James's Market. He was treated brutally by the other boys, who 'black his face, and carry him about in a basket, and then throw him out into a kennel to wash him'. But during the late 1720s and early 1730s he was able to make a living as a basketman or casual porter, and to earn the affection and concern of the market's stall holders. When Albridge stabbed and killed one of the boys who had persecuted him, and who was attempting to steal a piece of buttered bread, several stall holders trooped to the Old Bailey to give evidence in his defence and to save him from the gallows.[73]

The bulks and the markets were ordered areas in a less orderly environment. The bulks, in particular, were almost a traditional prerequisite for the poor. But London was also full of temporary hiding places. Every building site, fire and house collapse created an opportunity to gain shelter from both the prying eyes of the nightwatchman, and from the rain and wind of a northern climate. In sixteenth- and seventeenth-century London every hoarding or fence erected around a building site had to be registered with the City. In 1653, for instance, ten hoardings were recorded within the confines of the old City. By the eighteenth century, only a small proportion of hoardings were being recorded in this way, but the licences granted by the Corporation still reflect a city in which a person could hide themselves for the night. In 1730 Jonathan Wheeler, for instance, was granted permission:

> to enclose with boards etc ... ground in the Poultry before his house for ye space of 35 feet from east to west and 20 feet from north to south and to continue ye same for three months provided it be no hindrance to passengers nor offence to ye neighbours.[74]

At one house still under construction in Great George Street, in 1767, two men decided to sleep on the site, secure that the nightwatchmen would not bother them. John Bampton had slept there for several nights, 'about a quarter of an hour after nine o'clock [he] prepared the [wood] shavings for himself and [Edward Allen] to lye on ...'[75]

Ruins and fires were even more useful – if only because a pauper's morning's rest was unlikely to be disturbed by the arrival of workmen at daybreak. Of course sometimes being disturbed was a godsend in disguise. Certainly the unknown pauper who crawled under an archway in the ruins at Round Court off Maiden Lane, just south of Covent Garden, on a 'cloudy, raw' evening in December 1777 would perhaps have survived if a workman had found him a bit earlier. Instead, it was two or three in the afternoon before a couple of children discovered his frozen body.[76]

Besides being unregulated, ruins and fires were also full of opportunities for the poor. Francis Place recalls, with unalloyed joy, his gang's youthful ownership of a particularly large site just south of Holywell Street, off the Strand:

> Owing to some particular cause ... the ruins were not dug out by the Fire Insurance Offices, and a large quantity of iron and lead remained in them. A hoard was put up and in this state the [ruins] were left for a long time. To these ruins an entrance was soon made at one corner between two posts through which a stout boy could squeeze himself ... And out of sight and hearing of all but ourselves we went ... digging and selling the iron and lead we obtained ...[77]

Simply to list the number and variety of places in which the poor slept rough is to give a sense of the variety of resources an urban landscape could provide. Besides the bulks and markets, sheds and barns, besides the beds of friends, squats and ruins, they could be found on dunghills for their warmth, in blacksmiths' shops, in dark houses and in cellars, in Moorfields and in dust tubs, sheltering under the cranes at the quayside, and in the boghouses that serviced the courts and alleys of the capital.

If rough sleepers were a common part of the London landscape, there was one place in the capital, and one group of the homeless, that Londoners struggled to contain and to understand, the Black Guard youth: children sleeping in the glass houses of the Minories. Accused of pickpocketing and pilfering, of stealing from the quays and markets, the Black Guard was an object of both high-level social policy and literary invention. They formed the subject of one of Daniel Defoe's less frequently read novels, and were the inspiration behind the re-establishment of the London Workhouse in 1698. In one of his social policy pamphlets, Defoe describes the life and frequent death of Black Guard children:

> 'Tis scarce credible what a black throng they are ... many of them indeed perish young, and dye miserable, before they may be said to look into life; some are starv'd with hunger, some with cold, many are found frozen in the streets and fields, some drowned before they are old enough to be hang'd.[78]

In many respects the Black Guard were imaginary: a product of the paranoia of London life. But, there was a group of young men and women, boys and girls who fitted the description and came to revel in their notoriety. They did pilfer and steal, and they did sleep rough in the filthy warmth of the annealing yards associated with the glass manufactory, where newly-made bottles were set to cool. The reality of their lives was more mundane, more vicious and more tragic than most printed sources allow.

In 1698, Ned Ward in his *London Spy* gave an affectionate and sympathetic account of meeting the Black Guard on their way to the Minories:

> a very young crew of diminutive vagabonds, who march'd along in rank and file ... we salut'd them after this manner: 'Pray what are you for a congregation of ragged sprites, and whither are you marching?' 'We masters, reply'd one of the pert frontiers, are the City Black-Guard marching to our winter quarters in the glass-house in the Minories. Lord bless you, Masters, give us a penny or a halfpenny amongst us, and you shall hear any of us if you please say the Lord's Prayer backwards; swear the compass round; give a new curse to every step in the Monument; call a whore as many proper names as a peer has titles.'
>
> I find, said I, you are a parcel of hopeful sprouts. However, we gave the poor wretches a penny, and away they troop'd with a thousand 'God Blee-ye's', as ragged as old stocking mops and I'll warrant you as hungry as so many cat-a-mountains [leopards]; yet they seemed as merry as they were poor, and as contented as they were miserable ...

'They are poor wretches', says my friend, 'that are drop'd here by gypsies and country beggars when they are so little they can give no account of parents or place of nativity, and the parishes (not caring to bring a charge upon themselves) suffer them to beg about in the daytime and at night sleep at doors, and in holes and corners about the streets till they are ... harden'd in this sort of misery ...'[79]

The most detailed treatment of the Black Guard is in Daniel Defoe's 1722 *History and Remarkable Life of the Truly Honourable Colonel Jack*. The eponymous hero of this novel is the bastard child of a gentleman put out to a nurse for a small fee. When the nurse dies, Jack, aged ten, is left with two other boys to the mercies of the street. He ends up 'a dirty Glass-Bottle House Boy, sleeping in the Ashes ... a *Black your Shoes your Honour*, a Beggar Boy, a Black-Guard Boy'.[80] Jack and his two childhood friends beg and pilfer a living on the streets, 'the People in *Rosemary-Lane*, and *Ratcliff*, and that way, knowing us pretty well, we got victuals easily enough, and without much begging.'[81] In the summer the three boys lie 'about the watch-houses, and on bulk-heads, and shop-doors, where we were known', and in the winter, 'we got into the ash-holes, and the nealing-arches in the glass-house, call'd *Dallows*'s glass-house, near *Rosemary-Lane*, or at another glass-house in *Ratcliff-high-way*'.[82] Jack describes the conditions:

> Those who know the position of the glass-houses, and the arches where they neal the bottles after they are made, know that those places where the ashes are cast, and where the poor boys lye, are caveties in the brick-work, perfectly close, except at the entrance, and consequently warm as the Dressing-room of a *bagnio*; that it is impossible they can feel any cold there, were it in *Greenland* ... and that therefore the boys lye not only safe, but very comfortably, the ashes excepted, which are no grievance at all to them.[83]

For a bed 'sometimes a little straw, or upon the warm ashes'.[84]

Colonel Jack becomes more and more mired in crime and beggary. His friends either end on the gallows or are transported to North America. Jack himself is eventually kidnapped and spirited to Maryland as an indentured servant. He later becomes a slave-owner, returning wealthy and secure to London. Published just four years after the City of London lobbied for the passage of the 1718 Transportation Act, *Colonel Jack* can be read as an advertisement for the efficacy of a newly popular punishment, and a condemnation of the more brutal aspects of slavery. But it also contains shards and fragments of the reality of many young children's lives.

A group of four boys were taken up in a glass house in January 1748, 'at an unreasonable time of night loytering and misbehaving and having no visible way of living'. One, John Evans, was a runaway barber's apprentice from Whitechapel; two others, Thomas Cooper and John Dumbleton, were parish children, almost certainly orphans; and a fourth, Richard Silvester, had run away from his father.[85] The rough charity of the area around Rag Fair and Rosemary Lane, lovingly recreated in *Colonel Jack*, also had its reflection in the conditions on the street. Rag Fair, the used clothing market held on Rosemary Lane and the streets around it, was one of the most disorderly of London districts. It had an unsavoury connection with stolen goods – handkerchiefs and hatbands could be sold at the fair with impunity. The City authorities tried unsuccessfully to suppress it on several occasions. In 1737 the Lord Mayor, Thomas Barnard, proclaimed on behalf of the Common Council, 'in or near Little Tower-Hill, leading towards Rosemary Lane ... continues a sort of market or fair for the buying and selling of old rags and clothes ... the ill got effects of thieves and robbers ... this court to use their power and authority to remove this great and dangerous nussiance ...'[86] In fact, Rag Fair was not finally closed down until the beginning of the twentieth century.[87] It was increasingly associated with London's Jewish community, adding a new sense of exoticism to its shops and hawkers, but even before this gradual development, starting around 1700, Rag Fair and the streets around Ratcliff Highway and Rosemary Lane, Glass House Yard and Salt Petre Bank was a world of it own. In the latter decades of the eighteenth century Francis Place warned that it was:

> a dangerous place for any decent person to have gone into, he would assuredly have been robbed, and the fear of being robbed and otherwise ill used would ... prevent most people who knew the place ... from venturing to go through it.[88]

Dominated by female traders, Place went on to recall his youthful experiences in the area in the 1780s and 1790s, and in particular the fashions of the women:

> At that time they wore long quartered shoes and large buckles, most of them had clean stockings and shoes, because it was to them the fashion to be flashy about the heels, but ... many at that time wore no stays, their gowns were low round the neck and open in front ... Drunkenness was common to them all ... Fighting among themselves as well as with the men was common and black eyes might be seen in a great many.[89]

Amongst this dirty and disorderly crew there were certainly ragged and homeless boys and girls, sleeping rough and picking pockets. There is some evidence that these children did develop a sense of self-identity, that they did see themselves as the City's 'Black Guard', with all the traditional and medieval implications of those words. Mary Pewterer, for instance, clearly saw herself as a member of the Black Guard. She 'us'd to lie in the Glass-house in the Minories (as many more in the Winter-time use to do) and was call'd the Queen of the Glass-house'. Her behaviour also reflects the more unpleasant side of Black Guard life. In 1716 she enticed a nine- or ten-year-old girl, Phillis Delpeck, to an alehouse. Once there, Mary Pewterer, this 'Queen of the Glass-house', held Phillis down while a man raped her, giving her syphilis in the process. Two nurses at St Thomas' Hospital later testified that 'they never saw a Person more afflicted with that Disease than she had been'.[90]

It is important to remember, however, that while the warmth of the annealing yards allowed poor children to survive on the winter streets, it did not make for a comfortable life. Most of these children wore rags and went barefoot. This was not a problem when sleeping on the warm ashes, but they still had to go out to make a living. It was also a lifestyle that could not be supported in the longer term. Poor food, lack of medical care, simple neglect, meant that most children either died, or were forced to seek a more comfortable and stable situation, even if that stability was purchased at the cost of crime and the risk of death on the scaffold.

The casual desperation, the occasional financial success, and the personal insecurity that underpinned the experience of these Black Guard children is illustrated by Thomas Coleman and his friends. Coleman was a young orphan when he was sent to live with an aunt in Salt Petre Bank in the late 1720s. She was either uninterested in looking after him or simply unable to do so. When he wasn't sleeping in the annealing yards, he found a place in a neighbour's garret. Soon he was living with Katherine Collins and at least thirteen other boys, just next to Glass House Yard. According to his deposition, given before Justice George Welham on the eve of Guy Fawkes Night, 1730, Collins:

> harbours theeves and buys stolen goods, who inticed [him] to goe a theeving which he did for about a year last past in company with Andrew Knowland, Daniel Smith, George Scott, Edward Perkins, Joseph Paternoster, Joseph Darvan, Nice Noddy, Little Tom, Dick Wools, Halfe Thumb, Abey Gibson, Robert Shelton [and] George the sailor, who all lodge in her house, whom she orders to goe out at night and steale any thing they could meet with and accordingly they did ...

Like Charles Dickens's nineteenth-century fence and thief, Fagin and the Artful Dodger, Collins and her boys stole whatever came to hand. They went pickpocketing at Bartholomew Fair and stole two dowlas shirts that had been left to dry in the sun on a bush on Battersea Common. They took shoes

7. Thomas Rowlandson, 'Miseries of London' (1807). (*Corporation of the City of London*)

from the window of a shoemaker in Leadenhall Street, and two blue aprons 'out of a yard between White Chappell Turnpike and Hackney'. But for the most part they dealt in the most basic of foodstuffs. They

> brought home to her Cheese and sold it for two pence a pound, likewise butter, bread, shoes and severall other things which she, the said Katherine Collins bought of them, and when they came home without anything she shut them out of doors and they went to the Glass House near there and lay together.[91]

The fate of the fourteen boys named in Coleman's deposition gives a clue to the desperation of children such as these, and the range of their activities. It also reflects the risks abandoned children were forced to take in order to secure a roof over their heads. It reflects the lives of the hundreds of boys and girls, with no homes to go to, forced to sleep rough and to make hard decisions about how to survive. When they could not beg, they stole; and when they could not steal, they starved. In the end most of the boys named by Coleman, boys just like the Black Guard youth depicted by Defoe in *Colonel Jack*, were caught for some crime or other, transported or hanged.

Fifteen-year-old John Collins, Katherine Collins's son, and John Wheeler were tried at the Old Bailey in the summer before Thomas Coleman turned king's evidence. They had stolen 'two yards and a half of printed linen' that hung out of a shop window for display, giving a local shopkeeper 'saucy language' in to the bargain. Later, having escaped with the cloth, it was 'sold in Rag-Fair'.[92] Wheeler and Collins were found guilty and sentenced to transportation. Along with the conviction and transportation of Bristow Will, Cow, Cornish and Corkeye, this was the beginning of a disastrous period for this particular Black Guard gang.[93] In February 1731 Andrew Knowland or Noland, along with John Allright was indicted for 'stealing a piece of flannel'. Knowland was probably related to a notorious fence, Mary Callicant, who later accused Joseph Paternoster and Joseph Darvan of burglary in order to save her own neck.[94] Richard Collier confessed to the offence, but succeeded only in ensuring that all three boys were sentenced to transportation.[95] Daniel Smith was luckier. In June of 1731, he was named as an accomplice in the theft of a gold-headed-cane. Three years later, still at large, he was accused of involvement in the theft of '55 yards of printed Linen, value £10'.[96]

George Scott had been named by Coleman, but enjoyed a full eighteen months of freedom living in St Leonard's Foster-Lane. In the early spring of 1732, however, he too was indicted, along with Henry Whitesides, for the theft of 'a hat, value 10*s*. and a hatband, value 1*s*., the goods [of] Paul Fellows ...' Despite his protestations that he had only gone in to the shop 'to ask what was a clock', he and Whitesides were both sentenced to transportation.[97] Edward Perkins was named along with his old friend from Katherine Collins's garret, Daniel Smith, as accomplices in the theft of a cane which they attempted to sell at the 'Sign of the George in Rosemary-Lane'. He was acquitted only because the witnesses failed to show up at court.[98] He was back, however, at the next sessions in July 1731. This time he was accused of stealing two gold rings, worth some 23s., from the unconscious body of Dismore Brown. Brown fell on his way home through the Minories, just west of Rag Fair, and felt Perkins's hands in his pockets as he recovered. In his defence, Perkins appears to have turned king's evidence against two of his companions. He 'pleaded that he had the rings to sell for two other boys that said they had found them in the Minories, which appearing probable, by some circumstances depos'd in Court, the Jury acquitted him'.[99]

The list of crimes, criminals and punishments continued. 'Joseph Paterson, alias Peterson, alias Paternoster, and Joseph Darvan', who was listed as Durvell in Coleman's deposition, were tried for housebreaking in December of 1731. Mary Callicant, alias Nowland, Noland or Knowland, had been arrested for selling stolen goods. While being held in the Surrey gaol she gave up Paternoster and Durvan to the authorities.

> Go, says she, to the Three Cranes in Castle Lane, Westminster, and enquire where Mrs Ram lives. Paternoster and Darvan lodge up one pair of stairs in her house. If you don't find 'em there, go to the Horse Shoe behind Green's Free school, and if you miss of 'em there too, desire the people of the house to tell you where Mr Morris the shoemaker lives, for they often meet at his house. Paternoster is a young man with a bald head, he wears a fair wig, an outside light drab coat, with a great cape. His under clothes are snuff colour, and sometimes blue grey turn'd up with black, a silver watch with a crimson string. Darvan is a young lad near 19 years of age, pretty well set. [He] wears a light wig, a new hat with a silver loop and button, a blue grey coat, and a work'd waistcoat; and sometimes an olive-colour'd suit. Each of 'em wears a small diamond ring.

Despite their protestations, Paternoster and Darvan were arrested and their drawers and boxes ransacked. Among their goods all the paraphernalia of thievery was discovered. The constables found a long wire, with a hook on the end, designed to 'draw goods out at a window, when they lie too far within a room', and seven waistcoats marked with a 'GR' at the top – the monograms partially picked out.[100] After three full trials for different crimes, including burglary, all conducted at the December 1731 sessions, after several failed attempts to pin the crimes on their landlady and to establish credible alibis, Paternoster and Darvan were finally convicted and sentenced to transportation.[101]

Thomas Coleman's special partner in crime was nicknamed Yarmouth, an alias for John Crotch. Despite being named by Coleman, Yarmouth remained out of prison until April 1732, when, like almost all his companions from Salt Petre Bank, he was arrested for theft. His very presence on the street aroused suspicion. On 9 April he and a friend were standing outside Pewterer's Hall Gate, on Lyme Street, just south of Leadenhall market, humming a tune. John Maxey 'look'ed at 'em by the Light of a Lamp, and did not like 'em'. Maxey later testified that they followed him into Fenchurch Street, where 'one of 'em took hold of me, and clapp'd his hand to my mouth, and then ... snatch'd off my hat and wig and went off ...' Yarmouth was found guilty and sentenced to transportation.[102] As for Thomas Coleman himself, he was tried for the theft of 'two pair of shoes', in January 1731, and was acquitted. But someone of the same name was convicted and transported for the theft of two wrought-iron boxes eight years later.[103]

Of course not all the boys named by Coleman were caught or convicted, and some, like Colonel Jack, might hope for a more promising future. Whatever their fates, they were paupers who, at least for a time, successfully carved out a niche for themselves in the rich environment of the city. They probably would not have envied Nicholas Randall, but both of them were seeking a home and shelter from the weather. In the long run it was perhaps Randall who was more successful. He was an old man and 'a beggar', who regularly stationed himself at the 'pissing place going to Brentford', but by 1759 he had also created for himself a small house and garden at Turnham Green that he was willing to defend at the cost of his own life. By the side of the highway there, he 'has a little house ... and a garden a little distance from it', with 'two pear-trees, a damson tree, and two or three apple trees in it'. On a warm and overcast Sunday in mid-August a group of twelve boys from the neighbouring village, around fourteen or fifteen years old, were hanging around Randall's garden.[104] One yelled 'knock the old son of a bitch down'. Randall, took a gun, loaded it with shot, and proceeded to fire at the boys, blinding one of them. At his trial, he railed against the dishonesty of his neighbours, who refused to confirm the depredations the boys had caused to his garden, and was himself sentenced to death.[105] Clearly, despite the tragic conclusion to Nicholas Randall's life, it was possible to create a home from the disregarded corners of greater London.

3

Pauper Professions

The visceral proximity between the rich and the poor in eighteenth-century London struck even its own inhabitants. In *Humphry Clinker*, Tobias Smollett voiced the complaints of many through his upright, country-loving squire Matthew Bramble. Writing of his stay in London, Bramble complains:

> It must be owned that Covent Garden affords some good fruit; which, however ... is distributed by such filthy hands, as I cannot look at without loathing. It was but yesterday that I saw a dirty barrow-bunter in the street, cleaning her dusty fruit with her own spittle; and who knows but some fine lady of St James's parish might admit into her delicate mouth those very cherries, which had been rolled and moistened between the filthy, and perhaps ulcerated chops of a St Giles's huckster ...[1]

It was through the pauper professions, through those innumerable tasks which combined begging and service that these two Londons, the city of the rich and that of the poor, the well established and the newly arrived, confronted each other face to face. Labour was given in exchange for charity, and charity bestowed in response to deference. In the process, large numbers of hard working Londoners were forced to accept charity as a form of payment – to beg for their rightful wages.

To make a living on the streets of London the poor needed an excuse to be there, a justification that kept the heavy hand of the constable and watchman from fingering their ragged collars. A basket, tripod and bottle of oil, a few laces, a mackerel, or some cabbage nets, were both a means of making money in themselves, sold to whomever would buy, and a badge that proclaimed a purpose to a beggar's wanderings.

Israel R. Potter was the most bigoted and complaining of American residents of eighteenth-century London, but even he was overcome by the sheer level of activity he found on London's streets:

> When I first entered the city of London, I was almost stunned, while my curiosity was not a little excited by what is termed the 'cries of London' – the

streets were thronged by persons of both sexes and of every age, crying each
the various articles which they were exposing for sale, or for jobs of work at
their various occupations ...[2]

Francis Place was similarly struck by the vibrancy of London's street life. He
occasionally sat at his window, at No. 16 Charing Cross, looking out over
the street. On one July morning recorded how:

> The people in the street were variously garlanded; workmen – market people
> with baskets of fruits and flowers on their heads, or on their donkeys, or in
> their small carts, numbers of them with vegetables, newsmen and boys run-
> ning about to sell their papers to the coach passengers at least a dozen of which
> leave the Golden Cross or pass it about 7 o'clock, gave a *coup d'oeil* which
> cannot be witnessed in any other country in the whole world ...[3]

For others the scene was humorous. Tom Brown ignored the hard work of
street sellers and emphasised their absurdity instead:

> One tinker knocks, another bawls, 'Have you brass pot, iron pot, kettle, skil-
> let, or a frying-pan to mend': Whilst another son of a whore yells louder than
> Homer's Stentor, 'Two a groat, and four for six pence mackarel'. One draws
> her mouth up to her ears and howls out, 'Buy my flawnders', and is followed
> by an old burly drab that screams out the sale of her *maids* and her *sole* at the
> same instant.[4]

Others were even more scathing. Jonathan Swift complained bitterly:

> A restless dog, crying cabbages and savoys, plagues me every morning about
> this time; he is at it now. I wish his largest cabbage was sticking in his throat.[5]

For all their charms, many of the men and women who cried their wares
and services through the streets were desperate as well as picturesque. The
more lucrative professions were monopolised by freemen and the well established. Unloading ships and carrying merchandise through the streets was
the province of the ticket porters (marked for all to see by a lead badge on
their lapel).[6] Fellowship porters engrossed the work centred on Billingsgate
Market, while Hackney coachmen both jealously guarded their role on the
streets, and were tightly regulated from the seventeenth century onwards.[7]
Licences and badges were readily displayed to prove *bona fides*, and steep
charges on entrants were imposed to support the system. But this still left a
host of employments that ranged from the illegal occupations of prostitution and barrow gambling to the necessary and valued ones of chimney
sweep and milkmaid, with a myriad of others in between. What all these
essentially unregulated occupations had in common was their use of the

public streets, and the abject poverty of the vast majority of the men and
women who laboured hard to make a living at them. What they also shared
was a beggarly element. When no one would buy their mackerel and their
ballads, they traded in pity and compassion. One street seller described the
workings of this relationship:

> Such indeed was sometimes our miserable appearance, clad in tattered gar-
> ments, that while engaged in our employment in crying for old chairs to mend,
> we not only attracted the notice of many, but there were instances in which a
> few half pennies unsolicited were bestowed on us in charity – an instance of
> this happened one day as I was passing through Threadneedle Street; a gentle-
> man perceiving by the appearance of the shoes that I wore, that they were
> about to quit me, put a half crown in my hand and bid me go and cry 'Old
> shoes to mend!'.[8]

Ambiguity always clung to the beggarly end of street selling. William
Marshall Craig, for example, was certain that the matches hawked from
door to door disguised a more beggarly intent:

> The criers of this convenient article are very numerous, and among the poor-
> est inhabitants of the metropolis, subsisting more on the waste meats they
> receive from the kitchens, where they sell their matches at six bunches per
> penny, than on the profits arising from their sale. Old women, crippled men,
> or a mother followed by three or four ragged children and offering their
> matches to sale, excite compassion, and are often relieved, when the importu-
> nity of the mere beggar is rejected.[9]

Robert Blincoe, a parish orphan living in St Pancras workhouse in the 1790s,
envied the freedom of street urchins, but recognised the beggarly nature of
their employment. He later recalled his envy of

> the poorest of poor children, whom, from the upper windows of the work-
> house, he had seen begging from door to door, or, as a subterfuge, offering
> matches for sale.[10]

This same ambiguity, observed by both William Marshall Craig and Robert
Blincoe, the diminutive parish orphan, seems to have also existed in the
mind of Sarah Spiller. Called as a character witness for Mary Shepherd when
she was tried for theft in 1783, she became confused when asked about Shepherd's occupation: 'I knew her from a child, she used to sell water cresses,
and go out a begging along with her mother, her mother is a beggar ... If
her mother was a beggar, what was she? – I do not know ...'[11]

A certain entrepreneurial approach, a willingness to take advantage of
whatever opportunities arose, was a necessary characteristic of the street

merchants of London. In part, it was a simple matter of changing one's wares with the seasons. The sellers of food, and to a lesser extent services, had to move swiftly from selling one commodity to another, as the year grew older. Each season had its trade, and changing circumstances brought their own opportunities. The mackerel sellers came out in the winter and spring, and the pedlars set off in spring and summer. Gay reflected this pattern in his *Trivia*:

> Successive Crys the Season's Change declare,
> And mark the Monthly Progressive of the Year.
> Hark how the Streets with treble Voices ring,
> To sell the bounteous Product of the Spring!
> Sweet smelling Flo'ers and Elder's early Bud
> With Nettle's tender Shoots, to cleanse the Blood:
> And when June's Thunder cools the sultry Skies
> Ev'n *Sundays* are prophan'd by Mackrell Cries.
>
> Walnuts the Fruit'rer's Hand in Autumn, stain
> Blue Plumbs, and juicy Pears augment his Gain;
> Next Oranges the longing Boys entice,
> To trust their Copper Fortunes to the Dice.
>
> When Rosemary and Bays, the Poet's Crown
> Are bawl'd, in frequent Cries, through all the Town,
> Then judge the festival of *Christmas* near ...[12]

But more than a seasonal rhythm, shoeblacks and ballad-sellers, hawkers and prostitutes needed to adopt a promiscuous approach to their work. They had to treat the streets as a resource to be exploited, as well as a shop front for their wares. Some writers tried to turn this aspect of working the streets in to a discreet profession. The author of *Low Life* (1749) described how, between two and three in the morning:

> The whole company of finders (a sort of people who get their bread by the hurry and negligence of sleepy tradesmen) are marching towards all the markets in London, Westminster, and Southwark, to make a seizure of all the butchers, poulterers, green grocers and other market people left behind them at their stalls and shambles when they went away.[13]

Combining scavenging and begging with selling was more typical. Whether crying oysters or cabbage nets, selling laces or mending pots and pans, the assumption was always that begging was a part of these activities; that any spare food or old clothing, any spare cash or spare kind, would be picked up and reused. If the streets of London were clean and well ordered, this was largely down to the beggarly poor who recycled and reused any item casually dropped upon them. Israel Potter, for instance, cried 'old chairs to mend' about the streets, but as he did so he also 'collected all the old rags, bits of paper, nails and broken glass which I could find in the streets, and which I deposited in a bag, which I carried with me for that purpose ...' [14] As a child in the 1770s Francis Place similarly exploited the London environment:

> On one occasion I raked the kennel of a street at the back of my father's house (Water Street) which led down to the Thames. The old iron I found [came to] half a crown, the largest sum I had ever possessed ...[15]

Place was wealthy enough to be able to spend the money on a kite, but for others resources such as this contributed to their daily diet and physical well-being. Cinder sifting, for instance, was a regular occupation for poor women. During the autumn of 1766 Elizabeth Collman made a precarious living 'upon the hill of ashes in the field at Pimlico with several other women ...';[16] while in the same year James Jeffreys, a boy about Place's age, spent his evenings collecting coals on the foreshore of the Thames. With John King he was 'in a barge which was floating upon the River Thames and gathering coals in a tin kettle'. It was a warm clear Tuesday evening, with the temperature in the high 60s, and in just five minutes he collected two full loads of coal.[17] 'Mudlarking' in this way became a clearly established 'job' only at the very end of the eighteenth century, but it is certain that there was a ready market for the fuel collected. On one cool evening in the early Spring 1796 a boy named Slein was arrested in Moorfields with a bag of coals.[18] In his defence, 'he said he found 'em at waterside ... says he gathered them at low water, is a mudlark. Was going to sell them to a woman who is to be produced by him tomorrow'.[19] Broken glass and ashes, wrought iron, rags and waste paper, horse manure and its human equivalent all had a value and could frequently be collected for free. Rotten eggs and old vegetables could be gathered from Covent Garden and sold on to the crowds around the pillories:

> As soon as ... the offenders began to move round, the constables permitted a number of women to pass between them, into the open space round the pillory. These women were supplied with the materials for offence from the bushels of those who brought them, the bystanders giving them money for their 'wares'.[20]

The masters of this economy of makeshift were the shoeblacks and linkboys, the crossing sweepers and runners of casual errands. Shoeblacks, in particular, were emblematic of eighteenth-century London street life. Their employment was only created as a discrete occupation at the end of the seventeenth century, at the same time as early trade cards suggest that shoe polish began to be sold in the form of pre-prepared balls. But polishing the shoes of London's pedestrian throngs provided a perfect excuse for being on the street and for approaching passers-by.[21] Some residents avoided the need to deal with shoeblacks by having their shoes cleaned by weekly contract. In the early 1780s Carl Phillip Moritz claimed to have his shoes cleaned, 'by a person in the neighbourhood, whose trade it is; who fetches them every morning, and brings them back cleaned; for which she receives weekly so much'.[22] Paul Sandby, in his mid eighteenth-century 'Cries of London', also depicts an adult woman cleaning shoes.[23] In most instances, however, and certainly in the public imagination, the shoeblack was a young boy of the sort Gay depicts in his 'Trivia', who worked the streets:

> The Child through various Risques in Years improv'd,
> At first a beggar's Brat, Compassion mov'd;
> His Infant Tongue soon learnt the canting Art,
> Knew all the Pray'rs and whines to touch the Heart.

Until, that is, his goddess mother takes pity on him, and provides the tools of his new trade:

> The Youth strait chose his Post; the Labour ply'd
> Where branching Streets from Charing Cross divide;
> His treble Voice resounds along the Meuse,
> And White-hall echoes – Clean your Honour's Shoes.[24]

The insecurity and near-begging nature of the shoeblacks' occupation is probably better caught in the records of the criminal justice system. In 1720 the high constable of Holborn reported:

> That several boys wandering about the streets under pretence of cleaning shoes, have been apprehended & carried before several of his Majesty's Justices of the Peace, who have dealt with them as they in their wisdom have thought fit.[25]

A couple of years later, in 1722, two young boys, Nathaniel Bear and William Walker, were tried as vagrants at the Court of Bridewell for 'being very ... idle and disorderly fellows pestering the streets by blacking shoes ...'[26] The attempts to suppress shoeblacking, and its inclusion as a vagrant occupation, along with the fact that there are only two instances in the Bridewell records of it being prosecuted, reflects both the legitimacy of street begging under the pretence of blacking, and its clear association with mendicity. The treatment of boys like Nathaniel Bear and William Walker reinforce Daniel DeFoe's easy elision between '. . . a *black your shoes your honour*, a beggar

8. Detail from William Hogarth, 'The Rake's Progress', plate iv, 'Arrested for Debt' (June 1735).

boy, a black-guard boy, or what you please, despicable and miserable, to the last degree'.[27] Hogarth's use of a group of young shoeblacks to point up the dangers of gambling in 'The Rakes Progress' is similarly indicative.

Crossing-sweepers were if anything more beggarly than shoeblacks, although contemporaries frequently thought they worked hand in hand:

> When waggish Boys the stunted Beesom play,
> To rid the slabby Pavement; pass not by
> E'er thou has held their Hands; some heedless Flirt
> Will overspread thy Calves with spatt'ring Dirt.[28]

Requiring, of course, the attentions of a shoeblack. Unlike shoeblacks, crossing-sweepers had to rely on the generosity of the well-off to make a living. In the words of William Whitehead, while shoeblacks were 'vain pensioners, and placemen of the crowd!', crossing sweepers 'pour your blessings on mankind':

> Uncertain of reward, bid kennels know
> Their wonted bounds, remove the bord'ring filth,
> And give th' obstructed ordure where to glide.[29]

In other words they ensured that the bright red heels of London's well-to-do were preserved from the filth and rubbish that naturally collected in the open gutters, hoping for payment rather than demanding it. In the process, they also acted as beggars, and as collectors of the very filth they swept. Ned Ward, who could see real economic opportunities for a hard-working crossing-sweeper, recounts one such almost certainly spurious story in his *London Spy*:

> When he came first to town, he had but threepence in the world, which he prudently laid out in a new broom that might sweep clean. This he very dexterously applied, with his utmost labour, to the dirty wharf, without anybody's bidding; but he had sense enough to consider it belonged to somebody, who would at least give him thanks, if not recompense for his trouble. The master of the wharf happening to espy him at his task, give him some small encouragement to continue his cleanliness. This he practised daily ... [till] he is now become a man of a great estate and considerable authority.[30]

Sweeping the filth from popular crossings required less energy than blacking shoes, and also allowed a certain ownership over the public street. Unlike Ned Ward's upwardly mobile sweeper, most seem to have been elderly or disabled. The author of *Low Life* thought most crossing sweepers were 'poor women and lame men',[31] while Isaac Bickerstaff has Ambrose Gwinett 'the lame beggar: who for a long time swept the way at the Mew's

146 You *are clean* Fair Lady *but our* Ways *and* Means *are* Dirty.

9. Anon, 'You are clean Fair Lady' (1791). Note the hat held in a 'begging way'. (*Corporation of the City of London*)

Gate, Charing Cross' describe how, after a life of adventures: 'Though not an old man, I was so enfeebled by hardships, that I was unable to work; and being without any manner of support, I could think of no way of getting my living but by begging'.[32]

The sense of ownership and community, the sense in which an individual could make themselves part of an urban landscape by acting as a sweeper is perhaps best caught in the behaviour of an anonymous 'grubber' at Cow Cross. Standing by her post, she overheard Archibald Gilchrist discuss the theft of a silver spoon and his suspicion that 'Newgate Nan' was involved. The sweeper immediately volunteered the information that Nan could be found at a local brandy shop. Gilchrist did not find her there, but went back to the sweeper for more information. In the end, her local knowledge of the comings and goings of Nan and her common law husband, John Turner, resulted in Turner's arrest and his eventual conviction and transportation for theft.[33] In other words, sweeping provided an opportunity to claim a particular spot in the urban landscape as one's own, it allowed the development of a complex knowledge of the locale, and offered an excuse to beg from passers-by. Their stationary pitch and local authority also gave them a claim to charity that, according to John Gay at least, made their requests difficult to refuse:

> Where the labourious Beggar sweeps the Road.
> Whate'er you give, give ever at Demand,
> Nor let old-age long stretch his palsy'd Hand.
> Those who give late, are importun'd each Day,
> And still are teaz'd, because they still delay.[34]

The legitimacy of sweeping as begging is reflected in the almost complete absence of any criminal prosecutions under the vagrancy laws of men and women making their living in this way. In 1703 Christopher Perkins was arrested and charged at the Court of the Governors of the Poor for 'sweeping kennells', but his case is unique.[35]

Acting as a crossing-sweeper was also largely restricted to the paved centre of town. Beyond an ever-changing boundary of paved streets, both the sweeper and the shoeblack became redundant.[36] In the areas where the poor actually lived there were few opportunities to keep your shoes and stockings clean. At the poverty-soaked end of her life, Charlotte Charke found herself living in such an area:

> Her habitation was a wretched thatched hovel, situated on the way to Islington in the purlieus of Clerkenwell Bridewell, not very distant from the New River Head, where at that time it was usual for the scavengers to leave the cleanings of the streets ...

The night preceding a heavy rain had fallen, which rendered this [place] nearly inaccessible, so that in our approach, we got our stockings enveloped with mud up to the very calves, which furnished an appearance much in the present fashionable style of half-boots.[37]

At the same time, the poorly policed and unpaved backstreets of London provided a justification and employment opportunity for link-boys, who were themselves frequently equated with begging. By the 1740s London was perhaps the best-lit city in Europe. In the early 1780s Carl Philipp Moritz positively gushed over the dazzling display afforded by many London streets. 'I was astonished at the admirable manner in which the streets are lighted up ... The lamps ... are so near each other, that even on the most ordinary and common nights, the city has the appearance of a festive illumination.'[38] One ironic result of this night-time splendour was a commensurate growth in night life, which in turn created a demand for link-boys who could light travellers home from their late night revels.[39] This new, or at least a newly vibrant, demand was readily satisfied by London's beggarly poor. One author suggested that as the evening progressed:

> Link-boys who have been asking charity all the preceding day, and have money sufficient to buy a torch, [take] their stands at Temple Bar, London-Bridge, Lincoln's Inn Fields, Smithfield and the City Gates ...[40]

Operating at the edge of the more salubrious parts of the city, link-boys gave a sense of security to the midnight pedestrians fearful of footpads and prostitutes. Their role on the streets is perhaps best captured by the experience of William Burton who, late on a rainy night in September 1744, chose not to employ a link-boy:

> between the hours of one and two at night, I was going to my lodging in Covent Garden; but it raining very hard. I was obliged to stand up, and got upon the steps of a night cellar in the Strand; the woman of the cellar (as I supposed her to be) asked me what I wanted? I said, I only stood up for the rain; but thinking she expected I should call for something, I said, bring me a pint of beer, and then I shall give you no offence: she would have pulled me down stairs, but I did not care to go down. The pint of beer was brought, I called a watchman and gave it to him, and he called a link-boy to drink with him, and asked me if I did not want a link. I said I did not want a link: the watchman said you are very safe, you may step down and stay till the rain is over. I believe I went down two or three steps, and staid about five minutes; I found the rain ceased, and went homeward. About three or four perch from the place I met [Elizabeth Andrews and Sarah Page] and they said, Sir, where are you going? I said, I don't want any thing with you; they laid hold of me, and began to pull

me and hustle me, and riot me to pieces; in the struggle I missed my stock and clasp, said I, You damned jades what do you rob me of my stock? ... I put my hand up to my hat and wig to secure them, and called out watch ...

For Burton a light homewards was perceived as an unnecessary expense, but the scene also reflects the link-boy's secure position on the midnight streets, called over by the night watchman, whose job among other things was to arrest vagrants, to share Burton's casual charity. For others, link-boys retained a certain romance. Restoration playwrights occasionally associated link-boys with sodomy, while there is clear evidence in the eighteenth-century Molly House trials that link-boys were among their regular clientele.[41] Indeed, there is an association between link-boys and shoeblacks and homosexual prostitution. One ballad collected by James Boswell, entitled *The Ladies Whim Wham*, implies as much through a full range of double entrendres. The ballad describes 'two frolick-some gentlemen', who meet a boy and offer him a guinea bet:

> And so with his catcher they both went to play
> The boy who was master indeed of the game
> He tossed it, and catched it without any pain.[42]

Perhaps because of the sexualised nature of their occupation, many link-boys were possessed of a certain charm. Charlotte Charke clearly thought so. For a brief period in the 1730s she ran a chandler's shop and supplied link-boys with the tools of their trade:

I remember, in particular, one of those nocturnal illuminators, who are the necessary conductors for those who don't chuse chairs or coaches, came every night just before candle-time, which is the dusky part of the evening, the most convenient light for perpetrating a wicked intent ... As I dealt in spiritous liquors, [I] treated him with a dram ... The arch villain smiled, and expressed great satisfaction that even, in his poor way, he had power of serving his good mistress. He bow'd, and I curtsey'd; 'till, walking backwards out of my shop, he had complemented me out of every brass weight I had in it.[43]

Whatever their romance, it is also clear that plying the streets as a link-boy was an act of desperation. Even Charke characterised them as 'the sooty colour'd youth'.[44] Frequently, link-boys were on the street precisely because they had nowhere else to go. The author of the *Midnight Rambler*, for instance, suggests that in the small hours of the night the market sheds and bulks: 'Were covered with vagrants, that had been picking pockets, carrying links, or skulking about in quest of any thing they could lay their hands upon ...'[45]

The poverty and desperation of the life of people attempting to make a living from carrying a link is caught forcefully in the experience of Daniel Maccartey, who was accused with several others of murdering Alexander Innys. Maccartey explained how:

> I was a hackney-coachman, but being reduc'd to poverty, I carried a link. Towards Charing Cross the Gentleman ply'd me, and I was to light him to Fleet Ditch; when we came there he said he had no small money, and bid me go about my business. I said it was very hard; and told him, I had never seen him before; upon that he struck at me with his cane, and dropped it; I took it up, and every body said, keep the cane, poor man, keep it, and the gentleman cry'd, d – n the cane, 'tis not worth three-pence.[46]

In the end Maccartey was acquitted of the murder that followed this incident, but only after a long and harrowing trial.

By the last quarter of the eighteenth-century, link-boys were becoming more picturesque than pitiable. In 1774 Joshua Reynolds painted his 'Cupid as a Link-Boy', marking perhaps the saccharine beginnings of a newly romantic vision of street children. And by the 1790s the City decided that the real children who worked the streets at night should be driven out. Jonathan Count, for instance, was charged at Guildhall Justice Room in January 1791, 'as a link-boy, which class of people the beadle was ordered to suppress ...' But, he 'returning after driven away. His sister [undertook] to prevent his future attendance'.[47]

The kind of life suffered by shoeblacks, crossing sweepers and link-boys was inherently insecure. A spell of bad weather, ill luck, illness, or the end of a war, with its discharged soldiers, could turn economic sense into nonsense. As a result, these were the sorts of job that young men, and occasionally women, undertook in desperation and old men took up in despair. They were only three of the tens of different strategies that the poor could adopt, each of which had its own measure of success. For shoeblacks and crossing-sweepers, the ability to carve a space for oneself on the streets was almost sufficient. For others, ambitions were both higher and more mundane. For ballad singers, real financial rewards were possible; while charwomen could hope to find secure employment in a middling sort house.

Charwomen were perhaps the most common, and least discussed, of the beggarly professions. On most days the more salubrious parts of town were frequented by women going from door to door asking first and foremost for a bit of work in exchange for some food, and accepting casual charity when their supplications went unanswered. Mary North, for instance, was a char. She 'was one that used to go a chairing and being a poor woman and destitute of a lodging, as we had a spare bed in our garret, we let her lie there out of charity'.[48] So was Ruth Child. On a cold and miserable Wednesday, 14 February 1759, she 'Stood at my door for charity, she had neither shoes nor hardly any thing else that could be call'd apparel; I used to take pity on her, and gave her some cold victuals, and an old petticoat, and an old curtain to make a gown, and other things, and sometimes money, and in return she wash'd my door down ...'[49]

'Broken victuals' were claimed by servants as a prerequisite, and were frequently used by them to bring in chars to lighten their domestic labour. For many chars this simply provided a meal when nothing else was available, but this recycled food also had a financial value. Rag Fair in Rosemary Lane, just beyond the eastern edge of the City, was well known for its casual trade in old clothes and broken food, in which no real money needed to change hands: 'The chief customers were mumpers and people as ragged as themselves, who came to barter scraps for patches ... it was a very currant swop, to change food for rayment'.[50]

With the revolution in domestic architecture following the Great Fire, the relationship between the char at the door and the workings of London's households became more difficult. The development of a separate floor for the kitchen and services, and the arrival of the 'area' with its stairs and wrought iron, meant that charwomen frequently found themselves dealing with more established servants, rather than the master or mistress.[51] In the seventeenth century the parish poor were commonly sent from house to house to beg for broken food, and to do whatever work was asked of them. In St Martin-in-the-Fields the vestry sanctioned this kind of begging in 1677 on condition that the poor identify themselves with a badge: 'Who thereby have liberty to aske and received broken meate only ... and the hours of asking at doores allowed are from one to foure in the afternoone and noe longer ...'[52] By the eighteenth century this kind of begging had become more problematic. The ambiguity of the situation is caught perfectly in the difficult advice meted out to young servants by Eliza Haywood, in her 1771 *New Present for a Servant Maid.* Under giving away victuals, she says, 'charity and compassion for the wants of our fellow creatures are very amiable virtues', but that servants needed the permission of their mistress before the dole was given. In other words, she essentially approved of charity in kind distributed at the kitchen door. On the issue of charwomen, she was more censorious and suggested that the common practice of giving 'them victuals for helping you' would lead to all kinds of problems, as well as introducing the possibility of theft.[53] In the end, it is clear that charring made foggy and indistinct the boundary between begging and service, neighbourliness and vagrancy.[54]

For charwomen, begging at kitchen doors offered the possibility of a more secure employment. Indeed, the sheer numbers of women employed in this way suggests that the strategy worked. Of one sample of 1436 women who gave evidence before the London church courts between 1695 and 1725, 11.5 per cent gave their employment as 'charring' or laundry work.[55] But it is the ambiguity of their position that emerges most clearly. Jane Chalk was accused of conspiring with Katherine Field, an established servant, to steal jewellery, towels and plate from the house where Field was employed and where Jane occasionally worked as a char. Having been found with the plates in her own home, Chalk claimed in her defence: 'she being a poor woman, used to assist Field sometimes in the office of Chairwoman, and had the Plates home with some broken Victuals, and did intend to return them ...'[56] It was a likely enough story, and the jury acquitted her. This same sense of the ambiguous involvement of charwomen in the working of a household is also present in the evidence Elianor Coote gave against another established servant, Elizabeth Vickars:

> I have gone ... through the kitchen and seen Elizabeth and a charwoman that assisted in the house sit together at a little table therein and she did dine and sup with the charwoman and with my maid and such servants as had attended their masters or mistresses ...[57]

There is a palpable sense of an unstated social boundary clearly offended against.

Charring both allowed charity to be given and cheap labour to be supplied. It was one of those grey areas that ensured even the most disreputable members of London society could hope to find a place. Sexual misconduct, becoming pregnant outside of marriage, for example, was not a complete impediment. Rebecca Portore was found guilty of stealing £5 11s. 6d. worth of goods from the home of Bridget Murphy in 1748. Murphy related how Portore had come to be employed as a casual char in her house:

> The prisoner's aunt recommended her to me as a very good hand at washing, and I took her into my house; for I thought she had been set in scorn by her friends, on account of her having a sweetheart, and the first or second of June she lay at my house. I ordered my maid to let her have some victuals, and go to bed. I talked to her a good deal, and spoke very simpathizing to her; and I said, if she had done a fault, she was not a thief ...

Both Murphy and the court concluded otherwise in the end, and Portore was transported.[58]

Sarah Churchill came begging at the door of Frances Norris in October 1722. She had just come out of the Marshelsea, where she had been imprisoned for debt, and appealed for work as a char. She was given a night's accommodation, before leaving the next day with several items not belonging to her, carefully concealed about her person. Similarly, in April 1744 Elizabeth Edwards (alias Lareman) was employed for about three weeks as a char by Elizabeth Brooks. She was employed 'out of compassion, till she could get a better place'.[59]

Chars were seldom paid in ready money, and it is clear that even the women who employed them saw them in the ambivalent light of both servant and beggar. As a result, chars exemplify a series of chimerical employments that seem to disappear the more closely they are examined. They were like the men and boys who hung around inns hoping to earn a few pence running errands; men like John, who for several years just prior to 1794 stationed himself 'upon the foot pavement on the south side of Lower Thames Street' as an 'errand man'. Though no one could remember his surname, both a local ironmonger and the beadle for Billingsgate, Nathaniel Tibbs, knew him by sight.[60] Or like the women who laid claim to the job of washing the steps of the houses on a particular street; women like Susannah Hart, who swept 'the doors before gentlemen's houses in Rathbone Place' throughout the 1730s. Her common law husband was a street beggar; and by comparison her employment was more secure, but it still partook fully of the character of begging.[61]

These were employments that relied on the condescension of the middling sort – the casual recognition of a right to be there, to claim a particular job and its wages. The men and women who worked hard for their alms in these laborious positions hoped to turn casual pity in to the more substantial coin of a master-servant relationship. For many the strategy worked. Or, at least, there is good evidence that large numbers of men and women living for years in the middling-sort households of London, 'on charity'; secure from the uncertainty of the street, even if they never became fully-fledged servants.[62]

The value of a 'place', a role, even if it was a lowly one, is perhaps best captured in the experience of individuals like Hester Sunderland. Hester was a servant to Ann Dyson and by 8 December 1768 had lived in this capacity for nine months. There is no evidence that she was ever paid anything more substantial than the dubious comforts of poor food and a shared bed, but nevertheless she remained with her mistress. In rapid succession, Hester's mistress Ann Dyson lost her lodgings in Northumberland Court, when she failed to pay the rent, and became violently ill. In early December, on a cold, clear night, with the temperature just above freezing, Dyson and Hester Sunderland found themselves together, homeless and begging, in Poultney Court in St James.[63] The two of them were taken in by a Mrs Brown and allowed to sleep with the family in the Brown's single bed in a damp green cellar. Dyson later died, but, at the coroner's inquest held a few days later, Hester Sunderland still described herself as Dyson's servant.[64] Despite begging on the streets together, Hester clung to her role as a dependant.

This sense of a relationship that had value for the servant, and obligations for the master or mistress, is even more tragically evident in the case of William Urin. Urin was a servant to Lewis Watters, who took a house in Pimlico in 1771 at half a guinea a week. Watters rapidly fell in to arrears with the rent, and was forced to sell his furniture and move out of the house. A few weeks later one of the neighbours noticed the door was ajar, and on investigation found William Urin, who 'said that his master told him if he did not chuse to lye there, he must go out of doors, says that ... he was very bad and ... had been afflicted with the foul disease for some time ...' Urin's body was later found in the house, 'lying down upon a bed on the floor without any bedstead ... dead, and appeared to be very much wasted having very little flesh upon his bones ...' The coroner concluded that Urin had died of starvation, of 'want of proper care and necessaries'.[65] In effect, he had died as a result of his abandonment by his master.

Not all the beggarly professions aspired to this kind of master-servant relationship, or the social integration it implied. Ballad-singers appear to have been much more independent, and recalcitrant. Ballad-singers were both much appreciated and much derided inhabitants of London's streets. They were associated with commercial sex and with cap-in-hand begging, and were accused of being in league with pickpockets and of seducing apprentices. Some sang bawdy songs, with even bawdier gestures, while others appealed to religious feelings through hymns and chants. Defamatory ballads could be commissioned and paupers paid to sing them about the streets. George Parker, for instance, claimed:

> If a man has an enmity to a particular person or family there is a house of call where a set of men are ready to write on any subject ... Apply to this house with seven and six pence, and you may hear it sung in the course of three hours from your time of payment in St Paul's Churchyard ...[66]

Collectively ballad-singers formed a large and very visible outpost of the begging professions, and again reflected that ambiguous relationship between begging and working. They seem to have built on the insecurity and excitement of the street, rather than trying to escape from it. In good weather, and in good times, being a ballad-singer could provide a regular (if meagre) wage and inexpensive entertainment for pedestrian London that was enjoyed by all classes. Looking back from the late 1810s, Francis Place estimated that 'There were probably a hundred ballad-singers then [the

1770s] for one now'.[67] Even the middling sort and elite would occasionally stop in their tracks to listen to a tuneful voice or to stare at a pretty song-ster. Richard Steele, for instance, complained: 'my unhappy curiosity is such, that I find it always in my interest to take a coach, for some odd adventure among beggars, ballad singers or the like, detains and throws me into expense'.[68]

John Reeve must have felt even more aggrieved. On Whitsun Eve, 12 May 1722, he stopped 'to hear the ballad singers in St Paul's Church Yard, between 9 and 10 at night ...', and only later discovered that his peruke, worth seven pounds, had been stolen from the wig box under his arm.[69] Others did not even have to leave their homes to find themselves a part of a singer's audience. One 'cloudy, damp and raw' day in August 1775 Samuel Curwen decided to stay home and write a letter to his wife. Even here, how-ever, he 'was accosted by a Girl who placing herself before my window on a leathern stool which a younger attendant brought along with her and uncas-ing her fiddle played several tunes accompanying them with her voice'.[70] But it was working people and servants who made up most of the crowds who gathered round to hear. These were the servants Eliza Haywood warned off: 'Another great fault I have observed in many of you is staying when you are sent on an errand; ... a crowd gathered about ... a ballad-singer has the power to detain too many of you ...'[71]

A more sympathetic account of the attractions of ballad singers was recorded by Francis Place. Although Place was always willing to condemn the excesses of his youth, his clear memory of the lyrics suggests that he numbered himself among the idlers eager for a rendition of the outrageously sexual, 'Bawl Away':

> which I remember was sung by two women at the end of Swan Yard opposite Somerset House in the Strand, every evening ... There was always a consider-able crowd of fools, idlers and pickpockets to hear them. There were many such groups in different parts of London in proportion to the vileness of the songs and the flash manner of singing, there was the applause the singers received.

One can easily imagine the gestures that accompanied the lines:

> My smock's above my knee she did say, she did say
> My smock's above my knee she did say.
> My smock's above my knee and you may plainly see
> You may have a smack at me. Bawl away, Bawl away.[72]

Or the laughter heard in Clare Market in response to the sexual innuendo of 'A Hole to Put Poor Robin in':

> A bed and blanket I have got
> A dish, a kettle and a pot
> Besides a charming pretty thing
> A hole to put poor robin in.[73]

Some ballads were much more explicit even than this. 'Morgan Rattler', for instance, with its violent imagery of sex as a military assault, or 'Dadabum Doo' which gave a fond, if explicit, description of female anatomy:

> Its rough and hairy and furry too
> And goes by the name of Dadabum Doo.[74]

Place assiduously recorded the more sexual ballads, and the songs that celebrated the adventures of highwaymen and thieves, but it is also clear that many ballad-singers specialised in religious hymns and songs. Ned Ward describes walking past the cast iron palings that encircled St Paul's Cathedral, and finding:

> a melancholy multitude drawn into a circle, giving very serious attention to a blind ballad-singer, who was mournfully setting forth the wonderful usefulness of a godly broadside proper to be stuck up in all righteous and sober families ... After he had prepared the ears of his congregation with a tedious preamble in commendation of his divine poem, he mounted upon a stone, above his blue-apron auditory, and began with an audible voice to lyric it over in a psalm tune. This greatly satisfy'd the penitent assembly, who sigh'd and sob'd, shook their heads and cry'd ... Many charitable Christians bought his religious sonnets because he made 'em himself, wondering how a blind man should see to pen such marvellous things, and remember to sing them by heart without the help of his eyesight.[75]

The functions of ballad-singing in popular and religious culture were legion, but what is also clear is the extent to which ballad-singing formed a type of begging. There were occasional attempts by the authorities to clear ballad-singers from the street. In October 1705, for instance, the Court of the President and Governors for the Poor ordered, 'that all the ballad-singers that are in the streets be taken up and sent into the workhouse'.[76] And in the late 1710s and 1720s, a concerted effort was made to prosecute ballad-sellers and singers who retailed Jacobite and anti-Hanoverian songs.[77] Similarly, in the late 1760s, obscene ballads momentarily garnered the attention the officers of the Court of Bridewell. Mary Radcliffe was charged with 'singing very indecent songs' in late April 1769, while in June, Emelia Perrott and Sarah Lewley were charged for 'singing inflamatory ballads in St Paul's Church Yard and raising a great mob there'.[78]

These prosecutions reflect the insecure position of ballad-singers, but the poverty and desperation of many is better caught in John James Bezer's account of his early nineteenth-century attempt to earn a living singing hymns on the streets of London. A recently married shoemaker and porter, Bezer was a devout Methodist. When his luck ran out he determined to 'sing a hymn or two for bread and wife and child'. The internal struggle his poverty caused him is heart-rending. Having determined to begin, he went through the city:

> stepped into Thomas Street for that purpose, and then stepped out again; and thus I acted in several streets along the Borough. However, I would commence, that I would ... But no, courage failed again, and on I travelled. – I will not weary my reader as I was wearied by recounting my repeated trials, and my repeated failures, till I got right on to Brixton ... Here goes – 'God moves' – begin again – 'God moves in a' out with it, and so I did, almost choking, 'God moves in a mysterious way, His wonders to perform'. Just before I had concluded singing the hymn, a penny piece was thrown out ...'[79]

Bezer's approach to singing on the street reflected a genuine and heart-felt appeal to Christian charity, while his emotional stage fright, his inability to commit himself to the act of begging, reflects the extent to which the role of the beggar was fundamentally at odds with his image of himself as a man; but, in terms of the profession of ballad-singing, it is also clear that Bezer considered his musical employment to be literally begging. Bezer's account of how he learned to present himself with appropriate humility, how to avoid being arrested, how to avoid coming in to conflict with other beggars, is a powerful example of the ways in which the very poor needed real expertise in order to live on the streets. And if Bezer's account of his experience is unusual, his poverty was far from unique.

In 1780 Samuel Curwen gave an account of one ballad-singer, named Selby, who 'gets a wretched livelihood by begging and selling ballads':

> a man whose haggard looks, and tattered garment denoted variety of wretchedness, having a long squalid grisly beard, his face dirty and wrinkled, his hair through which, in appearance a comb had not passed for many years, his garment of every possible colour and shade, each piece of the bigness of ones palm tackt together by thread of a different colour and in stretches half as long as one's thumb, the length of this partly coloured garment scarce down to his knees ...[80]

Even Selby was fortunate by comparison to many. In late March 1796 one man, whose name no one could remember, set out to sell 'last dying speeches' on the streets of the City of London. The temperature was in the low 40s Fahrenheit, and he was barefoot and starving.[81] By one or two in the morning, he had collapsed. The watchmen took him up and brought him to the Poultry Compter, the local prison, and asked that he be given a bed for the night. The turnkey, Rueben Balden, a young man with a lame arm, who claimed to know the man, said, 'he was an imposter' and refused him entry. With nowhere else to go, the watchmen left the man slumped against a wall in a neighbouring parish, where he died the following morning, by the 'inclemency of the weather'. When his body was searched at six in the morning by John Fenner, he, 'found five pence, farthing in copper, about two ounces worth of bread, a comb and some printed papers of dying speeches ...'[82] His body was never claimed. Nor was it just male ballad-singers and sellers who suffered in this way. When, in 1745, Henry Juratt claimed, 'I have seen many a ballad singer, and I never saw one with two aprons' he was certainly referring to female singers.[83]

For many, singing on the streets was in itself an act of desperation. It was an easy occupation to take up, even if the rewards were less than certain. Mary Saxby became a ballad-singer almost by accident around 1750:

> I now wandered from town to town, till I met with a poor travelling woman, who had three daughters ... Her youngest daughter was about my age, and with her I soon contracted an intimacy. As we both had pretty good voices, we agreed to go about together, singing ballads ... Ah, did young, inexperienced persons, know what misery awaited them ...

For the next few months the two young girls made a living 'singing in alehouses, at feasts and fairs, for a few pence and a little drink'.[84]

This beggarly character probably contributed to the contempt with which ballad-singers were held by the authorities. At the Old Bailey in 1744, Joseph Haughton attempted to provide a 'character' for Sarah Lowther, who was charged with counterfeiting a will. His credibility as a witness, however, was fatally undermined when someone in the courtroom yelled out that he was a 'ballad-singer'. Haughton had to admit that he 'cannot say I never did sing', but absolutely denied having done so in the previous week. Nevertheless, his respectability punctured, Lowther was found guilty. She was only saved from the gallows by pleading her belly.[85] John Slevin used the same accusation to smear two witnesses who appeared against Jenny Smerk in April 1745:

> As to these people who appear against her, they are ballad singers, and vile persons ... one is called Bet, and the other Suck: but as to their surnames, I never heard them. They took me into a house, I believe it was an unlawful house,

and that scenes of iniquity have been acted there. I believe they would not stick to swear any thing.[86]

Again, the accusation was at least partially successful, and Smerk was acquitted of at least one of the two charges against her.

Like shoeblacks and link-boys, ballad-singers were just on the edge of beggary. They may have entertained the crowds, or moved the religious with their songs, but first and foremost they were beggars. Many were blind and disabled, and many others simply desperate. Some must have turned to ballad-selling and singing when all other forms of employment were closed to them. These were people like 'Philip in the Tub', a severely disabled man who dragged himself through the streets of London in the 1740s, selling ballads, who Hogarth immortalised in his 1747, 'Industrious 'Prentice out of his Time and Married to his Masters' Daughter':[87]

During the 1710s and 20s, when seditious anti-Hanoverian and Jacobite ballads were cried through the streets, and when the justices in London made a special effort to control their activities, the women who were caught up and imprisoned were the poorest of London's poor. They were people with names like 'Blind Fanny', 'Irish Nan' and 'Lame Cassie', women whose nicknames at least suggest that they were on the very edge of London life.[88] Many were illiterate and many others were old and infirm. Elizabeth Scales was arrested in 1716. Her petition for relief, written for her by the turnkey, related that she was, 'aged about eighty years, lives now very ill in the Gatehouse', where 'she is in a very distressed and deplorable condition ...'[89] And while Marcellus Laroon could depict his late seventeenth-century ballad-seller as well dressed, and attractive, the reality for most people was certainly closer to Hogarth's eighteenth-century depiction of a ragged woman, a child in her arms, bawling out a ballad of female ruin for all she is worth.

At the same time, and despite their poverty and their beggary, it is also clear that at least some ballad-singers were able to maintain a sense of self-worth and independence. Mary Cut-and-Come-Again went to the gallows in 1745. She was a ballad singer and was arrested on 27 March in Monmouth Street for stealing an apron from Elizabeth Turner. Mary's response to her arrest reflects of a deep, if destructive, self-confidence:

> she said, she would not be taken away till a proper officer came: she pulled her breasts out, and spurted the milk in the fellows' faces, and said, d – n your eyes, what do you want to take my life away? She licked the prosecutrix before the justice, and said, she longed for it; and she said, she would spit upon the justice's seat, and she did so. The justice said, he would send her to Newgate, she

10. Detail from William Hogarth, 'Industry and Idleness', plate vi, 'The Industrious
'Prentice Out of his Time, and Married to his Master's Daughter' (1747).

11. Marcellus Laroon, 'A Merry New Song', from *Cryes of the City of London Drawn from Life* (1687).

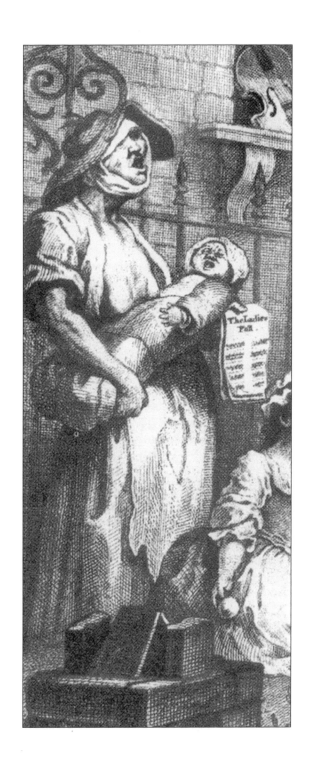

12. Detail from William Hogarth, 'The Enraged Musician' (1741).

said, d – n my eyes then I shall have a ride for the money. Then the justice ordered her to be fettered and handcuffed; and she said, if he would take the handcuffs off, she would tell him her right name, otherwise she would not.

The handcuffs staid on, and Mary went to her death under the pseudonym, Mary Cut-and-Come-Again.[90]

The beggarly professions of eighteenth-century London provided economic opportunities, however meagre the rewards, for the most insecure and marginal of individuals. At the same time, they also provided the services and products needed by the middling sort and elite. They were a fundamental part of the economy of London. And while the authorities occasionally attempted to restrict their activities, to round up those street urchins who had offended against one morality or another, it was only in the twentieth century, with new forms of entertainment, and new networks for retail distribution, that these casual employments were destroyed.

For the poor these occupations were at least in part about claiming a place on the street, about being recognised as part of the environment. The practitioners of these pauper professions usually succeeded in making a clear distinction between themselves and the objects of opprobrium the vagrancy laws were meant to sweep from the pavements. When Jonathan Swift wanted to remind his Stella of their lodgings in London, he wrote to her: 'We have abundance of our old criers still hereabouts. I hear every morning your woman with the old sattin and taffata, etc., the fellow with old coats, suits, or cloaks',[91] giving her an aural reminder of their time together that spoke powerfully of a single location. These beggarly street traders made themselves a defining part of London life. By combining the authority of a beggar's plea with the mechanics of rational exchange, they transformed both the nature of charity and the essence of economics. And if any single phenomenon tied the very poor to the middling sort and elite and helped to contain the ongoing violent struggle between smug riches and hungry desperation, it was these professions. The ability of new immigrants and old outcasts to take up these laborious forms of begging helped to ensure that each new group, each new set of immigrants, could gradually integrate themselves in to the distinctly ragged and patched social fabric of London.

4

Menaces and Promises

On 7 April 1740 John Collet went out begging on the road leading from London to Hampstead. He 'had a wife who lay-in, and was starving' and 'had neither eat nor drank that day'. Approaching Mary Curtis, who was walking home through the fields, he asked 'for some money'. Mary 'told him, I have but a shilling to pay my coach hire, and I pulled out a shilling, and a halfpenny at the same time, which I gave him, and then he went off'. She later explained that she 'was frightened because I was alone, and had a guinea about me and more shillings: but he did not threaten me with any words, nor did he lay hands on me'. But when William Staples, who was driving a cart through the same field and who knew Mary Curtis, rushed up and asked 'her if the man had robb'd her? She said, yes'. Collet was run down by Staples and a couple of other men, and arrested and charged with highway robbery. When Curtis saw Collet at a nearby public house, she 'swoon'd away several times at the sight of him'; and, although she freely admitted to having given Collet the shilling in charity, he found himself on trial for his life at the Old Bailey. He was acquitted, but his experience reflects the ambivalent character of begging; the extent to which a request for relief could be misinterpreted as a threat, or a promise. The fact that a snuff-box in the shape of a gun and an unsheathed knife were found in Collet's pocket when he was searched, also reflects the extent to which begging could be used very self-consciously as a mask for other, more illegal activities.[1]

For many writers the elision of begging, theft and criminality gave point and grist to their dyspeptic social diatribes. For Henry Fielding there was no distinction between a beggar and a thief:

> all the thieves in general are vagabonds in the true sense of the word, being wanderers from their lawful place of abode ... These various vagabonds do indeed get their livelihood by thieving, and not as petty beggars or petty chapmen ...[2]

But for beggars and prostitutes, the boundary was also illusory. The offer of sex could wring a few extra pence, the threat of violence a few more, while the promise of being repaid twice over opened many uncharitable purses.

By rights, beggars were supposed to cringe and supplicate; to hold their bodies in an attitude of submission, and to pitch their voices in a whining powerless note, what John Gay refers to as a 'begging tone'.[3] Indeed, an inability to play this role could create a real problem. Daniel Defoe's Colonel Jack, for instance, was forced to turn thief precisely because he was:

> a surly, ill-look'd, rough boy ... if he beg'd, he did it with so ill a tone, rather like bidding folks give him victuals, than entreating them, that one man of whom he had something given, and knew him, told him one day ... thou are but an awkward, ugly sort of a beggar ...[4]

The tone and physical self-presentation of beggars was a constant, and constantly distrusted, claim to powerlessness. The extent to which this persona could be adopted and then thrown off was frequently recognised by eighteenth-century commentators. In *Trivia*, John Gay warned:

> Where Lincoln's Inn's wide space is rail'd round,
> Cross not with vent'rous step; there oft' is found
> The lurking Thief, who while the day-light shone,
> Made the Walls echo with his begging tone:
> That crutch which late compassion mov'd, shall wound
> Thy bleeding head, and fell thee to the ground.[5]

And one anonymous mid-century commentator asked bitterly:

> How frequently do we meet with instances of beggars who come in the most suppliant manner, make out a long, compassionate case, but when they find that ... they are not likely to gain their ends, turn the rough side of their tongues, and ... take another way of being supplied, that is, by force take from you what your discretion thought proper to deny?[6]

This ambiguity, this sense of real physical threat lurking beneath the rags and self-deprecating body language of the very poor did not exist merely in the minds of the middling sort. Begging with menaces was a common activity whenever it was likely to result in success. Chimney-sweeps used the threat of their own dirtiness to encourage almsgiving on May Day. Certainly the man who begged a shilling from Carl Moritz as he walked towards Windsor in 1782 seems to have been aware of the impact of his threatening physical presence. He asked Moritz,

> for a halfpenny to buy, as he said, some bread, as he had eat nothing that day. I felt in my pocket and found that I had no halfpence; no nor even a sixpence in short nothing but shillings. I told him the circumstance which I hoped would excuse me: on which he said with an air and manner the drift of which I could not understand, 'God bless my soul?'. This drew my attention still

closer to the huge brawny fist, which grasped his stick; and that closer attention determined me immediately to put my hand in my pocket and give him
a shilling.[7]

The behaviour of many poor men and women during the explosion of
anti-Catholic violence of early June 1780, the Gordon Riots, reflects the
extent to which a threat underlay many claims for relief even more clearly.
Throughout the week of disorder, gangs of young men and women shouted
'No Popery!' and demanded 'contributions which they called mob-money
from everyone they met'.[8] Francis Places later described them as, 'Gangs of
ruffians with iron bars in their hands' who 'went from house to house
demanding money'. 'No one ventured to refuse them.'[9]

Others claimed an 'alms' for the 'poor prisoners' released on Tuesday 6
June, when Newgate was burned. 'Everyone gave half-crowns and some
more.' Reports circulated that the men demanding money in this way were
chalking symbols of the sort long associated with beggars on doors as they
passed – a silent indicator that the house had given relief or refused, should
be visited again or burned to the ground. An **O** indicated that the inhabitants had made a small and unsatisfactory contribution; an **Ȯ** meant that the
alms had been refused; a ✔ indicated a generous alms; while ⦿⦿ that a lone
woman was in the house.[10]

The sense of excitement and threat experienced by the beggarly poor, and
rich householders is evident in the deposition of James Mahon:

> My boy said, Sir, they are coming for money. I went down and opened the
> shop door. I saw a little dirty ragged boy at the door, with a blue cockade in
> his hat: he said, God bless your honour, remember the poor mob. I said go
> along, you little impudent rascal, or I will kick your backside ... He immedi-
> ately turned away from me, and said, then I will go and fetch my captain ...
> The mob came from Mr Eades's house to mine ... led by the boy who came
> to demand money of me before, and ... a vast crowd followed him; there
> might be a hundred ... The boy said, Now I have brought my captain, Sir ...
> I said, ... How much, Sir? Half a crown Sir, says he. I ... put two shillings and
> sixpence into his hand. He looked at it some time ... They then gave me three
> cheers and went to the next house ...
>
> What did he do with the money? – I believe he put it into his pocket. I was
> in too much terror to take notice of that.[11]

Unlike this particular 'dirty ragged boy', George Banton did not have a
mob to back him up. He spent the week of the Gordon Riots drunk. Banton
was a porter in Newgate Street whose wife took in laundry. On the morning
of Thursday, 8 June (a full week after the riots had begun), he went to the

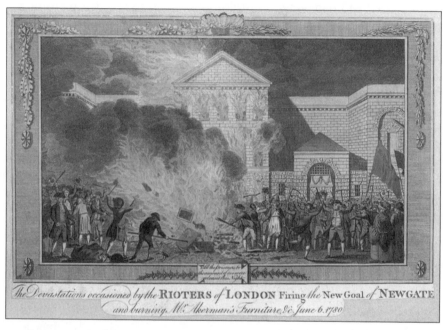

The Devastations occasioned by the RIOTERS of LONDON Firing the New Goal of NEWGATE and burning Mr. Akerman's Furniture, &c June 6.1780

13. 'Newgate Gaol being set alight during the Gordon Riots' (1780). (*London Metropolitan Archives*)

Bell Savage Inn to collect some linen for his wife. It was hot, and temperatures reached the mid 70s.[12] 'I staid drinking till about twelve o'clock, and
got in liquor. Then I went to the Magpye and had some more liquor.' He
continued drinking until all his money was gone. At the Featherstone Buildings in Holborn he knocked at the door of a Mr Walford, and spoke to Walford's apprentice, Richard Stone. Stone later recalled, 'he pull[ed] off his hat
in a begging way' and said '"pray remember the Protestant religion" ... and
I put twopence into it. Then he said he must have sixpence ... he must and
would have it'. From here Banton went next door to Richard Rowton's
house. Having knocked on the door, he again 'pulled off his hat and desired
me to remember the Protestant religion'. But in this case neither the appeal
nor the threat of the iron bar Banton held in his other hand was sufficient to
prise some cash from Rowton. Instead, he refused to give him anything,
threatening to call a constable. At this Banton threatened Rowton with
his iron bar and said, 'if I did not give him something he would break my
windows'. Eventually Rowton was persuaded to give Banton 3*d*.; even so
Banton was later arrested and eventually tried for assault. Whether Banton
thought of himself as a rioter or a beggar is unclear. The outstretched hat,
held 'in a begging way', suggests the latter, while the iron bar, held in his
other hand, seems to suggest a more active role. The jury found him guilty
of assault, but it is clear they viewed him more in the light of a beggar than
an assailant. Despite finding him guilty of a capital charge, they specifically
recommended him to 'His Majesty's Mercy'.[13]

The 'mob' was a powerful force in eighteenth-century London. On holidays and in political crises, it regularly enforced its views on householders.
A candle in the front window was a common sign of support for whichever
side of a political question was currently in control of the streets. During
one of the Wilkite riots in 1768, one observer claimed, 'there were candles
in every window in all the houses, some out of fear, and some perhaps out
of respect'.[14] Windows without the required candle were likely to be broken,
and a shilling or two could justifiably be demanded by way of an earnest
from any pedestrian who found himself in the wrong place. Drink was a
constant but expensive handmaiden to popular politics and one whose price
needed to be paid. George Banton was undoubtedly very unlucky to be
prosecuted for demanding what many of his contemporaries asked for and
received without cavil.

Using menaces to encourage the charity of contributors was not, however,
restricted to the carefully scripted political crises of the eighteenth century.
The role of violence in begging was ambiguous enough to form a basis for
a defence offered by the uniquely pompous and successful early advocate at
the Old Bailey, William Garrow. He was engaged as defence lawyer by James

Rook and James Jordan in 1785 when they were charged with highway robbery. Rook and Jordan had violently assaulted James Stewart, grabbing him by the lapels of his jacket and saying 'money we want, money we must have'. William Garrow addressed the jury:

> Now I need not state to the jury that that expression is perfectly equivocal, it is the language of threat, of menace, or the language of supplication, of indigence in the mouth of a beggar; there is no ... indication on the part of the person asking, that he intended to distinguish his application from that of a beggar; a man earnest for a bit of bread, might address the person of whom he sought relief by laying his hand on any part of the body, and most naturally on the shoulder of such person ...[15]

The jury were not entirely convinced, and condemned Rook and Jordan to seven years' transportation, but it is clear that Garrow thought the strategy was worth a try.[16]

In 1719 Thomas Paven was charged by one of the constables of St Stephen Coleman Street with:

> Begging, frequently pretending to fall in to fitts, at other times attempting with a broom stick to break heads when not relieved and known to be a very disorderly, idle person.[17]

And on 30 September 1744, William Burke was arrested for 'wandering and begging about the street and particularly for abusing Phil Gill, glover, the corner of the Old Change for refusing to relieve, and threatening him with a pistol'.[18] In other words, while Defoe's fictional account of being attacked by a disabled beggar was indeed fictional, it nevertheless reflected one facet of street begging:

> Being come out into Gracechurch Street, I observ'd a man follow'd me, with one of his legs tied up in a string, and hopping along with the other, and two crutches; he begg'd for a farthing, but I inclining not to give him any thing, the fellow follow'd me still, till I came to a court, when I answer'd hastily to him, I have not for you, pray don't be so troublesome; with which words he knock'd me down with one of his crutches.[19]

As the account of the encounter between Mary Curtis and John Collet that began this chapter demonstrates, beggars could stir real fear in the hearts of many more timid Londoners, especially women, and on occasion could also represent real danger.

A more common companion to begging than violence was simple and surreptitious theft. Every shoeblack and ballad-singer was tempted by the opportunities for subtle and illegal pilfering presented by a life on the streets. Mary Saxby, for instance, knew this temptation well. As a young runaway she begged her way around London: 'I had many temptations to steal, but could not as yet break through my former convictions'.[20] The very poor were surrounded by material goods that could be readily exchanged for cash: by clothes hung out to dry, and goods set out to entice. Driven by need, or simply by desire, in a world that, despite the warnings of the pop- ular press, left material goods readily to hand, and which largely trusted everyone to respect private property,[21] many beggars could not resist. Mary Richardson, alias Ann Hammond, lived very poor indeed. In 1715 she was prosecuted for stealing 'a leg of pork, value 4s. 6d. out of the shop of Andrew King'. She was found guilty and sentenced to be whipped.[22] Two years later she was convicted of stealing several items of clothing from Elizabeth Thom- son and branded on the hand.[23] On 11 June 1717 she went out begging, and approached the house of the Reverend Dr Thomas Bennet at eight in the morning, hoping to be relieved with a mug of small beer. The door was open, and she made her way into the house, and to Bennet's study, where she found two damask table clothes and five napkins. She slipped these into the basket she carried, and quietly complied when Bennet, 'bid her go out of doors', 'thinking her a very bold beggar to come through the house and into his study'.[24] Some paupers actively justified theft on religious grounds. When in 1752 Rebecca Hart was arrested for stealing coals, she declared, 'It was no sin in the poor to rob the rich; and that if it was, J— C— had died to procure the pardon of all such sinners'.[25]

The pressures that led to theft, and the ability of some beggars to resist those same pressures, are reflected in the case of Margaret Davis. She was a widow and 'used to work with my needle'. Friday 25 April 1755 was cloud- less and warm, and having been south of the river to visit a friend, Margaret was walking home when James Hudson accosted her:

> he said, let me go home with you, I said, I never took any body home with me, but he much desired it, so I let him. We went into my room, he took his buck- les out of his shoes and gave them to me, and he pulled off his shirt for fear of vermin, and laid that and his cloaths upon a chest, and unfortunately I got up and went away with them.

Hudson's fear of vermin speaks eloquently of Davis's poverty, and it is clear that the temptation to casual prostitution and theft were too much for her to refuse. More striking is what happened next. She approached 'two beg- gar-men going up Highgate-hill', 'and said, she had got a prize'. They immediately arrested her, assuming she had stolen the shoe buckles, along with a silver watch and a pair of crystal 'sleeve-buttons' she also had about her, and marched her to the nearest constable, Thomas Beal. They charged her with theft, and she was eventually found guilty at the Old Bailey and transported for seven years.[26]

Not many beggars could resist the temptations of theft, as these two beggarly men appear to have done, and most were probably forced and enticed to step over the line between an 'economy of makeshift', which included collecting the detritus of this world city, and outright criminality. The petty and beggarly nature of their crimes, however, is fully reflected in the items they stole. Just to list the 'objects of desire' that enticed the men, women and children caught thieving in the City of London and tried at the Court of Bridewell for a single month in 1744, gives a powerful sense of the desperation and poverty of these 'criminals'. They stole ham from a shop, old iron, a handkerchief, a napkin, ribbon and brush, old books, sugar on Bear Key, two loaves of bread, an apron, asparagus, an old gown from a washerwoman, a silver thimble, a thousand tin tacks and a pair of old stays.[27] These were the thefts of the beggarly poor – people who took advantage of the opportunities that presented themselves, and overstepped the bounds of legality.

Theft brought with it a real danger of judicial retribution. It was also something that sat awkwardly with eighteenth-century popular culture. Although highwaymen frequently became popular heroes, and, while pilfering from the docks as part of employment there was an everyday expectation, this was also a society in which honesty and fair-dealing was highly prized by the poor as well as the middling sort and elite. The biblical injunction against theft, and oaths made on the Bible, were treated with profound respect. As a result, while theft could not always be resisted, many of the beggarly poor sought other ways of gaining a livelihood – perhaps equally illegal, but nevertheless morally more acceptable. An appeal to greed, to 'conditional promises of future returns, with an interest extraordinary, beyond the statue of usury, tho' out of the reach of it', was one such strategy.[28]

Rigged dice, mock auctions, games with three thimbles and pricking at the garter were just a few of the activities that allowed begging to be reformulated as games of chance and advantage. Gay lists some of these in his 'Trivia':

> Who can the various City Frauds recite,
> With all the petty Rapines of the Night?
> Who now the Guinea-Dropper's Bait regards,
> Trick'd by the Sharper's Dice, or Juggler's Cards?

Who shou'd I warn thee ne'er to join the Fray,
Where the sham-quarrel interrupts the Way?

...

Careful observers, studious of the town,
Shun the misfortunes that disgrace the clown.
Untempted, they contemn the jugglers' feats,
Pass by the Meuse, nor try the thimble's cheats[29]

In part, the dangers of the street listed by Gay and his contemporaries reflect a literary tradition rather than the real behaviour of the poor. He is listing the 'Tricks of the Town' for both an unwary provincial audience and a knowing urban one, but there were real opportunities for subtle fraud and the poor of London were not backwards in pursuing them. Some of these 'tricks' came under the direct auspices of the vagrancy laws. On a Thursday or Friday in late January 1725/6, for instance, Rowland Davis was intrigued enough to follow John Jones into a public house with the promise of 'tricks with balls'. But he became angry when Jones started 'asking him for money for the same ... and endeavoured to cheat him of his clothes'. The Court of the Governors of Bridewell decided that Jones could be 'esteemed a juggler [and] therefore a vagrant idle person'. Jugglers, along with actors and pedlars were among the rag-tag list of paupers whose titles filled eighteenth-century legislation.[30]

Perhaps the classic urban 'trick' was 'money dropping', and its variant 'ring dropping'. An early nineteenth-century account of money dropping (also known as guinea dropping) which claimed that the practice had been much more common in earlier times, gives a flavour of both the literary tradition of the 'Tricks of the Town', and the reality of some people's experience of the frauds of London:

'What is this?' says the dropper; 'my wiggy! If this is not a leather purse with money! Ha! ha! ha! Let's have a look at it.' While he unfolds its contents, his companion comes up, and claims his title to a share. 'Not you, indeed! Replies the finder, this gentleman was next me; was not you, Sir?' To which the countryman assenting, or, perhaps, insisting upon his priority, the finder declares himself no churl in the business, offers to divide it into three parts and points out a public house at which they may share the contents, and drink over their good luck: talks as they go of his once sharing in a much larger sum, with a 'stranger, who was honourable: – nothing like honour!' The found money is counterfeit, or screens, or else Fleet notes ... They drink, and fill their grog again ... the draught board, or cards, constantly exhibit the means of staking the easily acquired property so lately found, but which they cannot divide just now for want of change. The countryman bets, and if he loses, is called upon to pay; if he wins 'tis added to what is coming to him out of the purse.[31]

Money dropping was not an exclusively literary phenomenon. Henry Sweetingham, a journeyman, had lived in London for at least a few years prior to Monday, 19 May 1735. 'He came home that afternoon almost frighted out of his Wits.' He 'cry'd and stamp'd and was ready to tear [his] Hair off for Vexation'. The cause of his misery was a variant of this same classic ruse. He later told the court at the Old Bailey:

> Between two and three in the afternoon, in St Paul's Churchyard, a man stoop'd down and pick'd up a shilling, and told me, I should be welcome to drink it out with him. Accordingly we went to the Black-Spread Eagle in Paternoster Row, and met [John Boswell]. They two went to cutting of cards for six pence a time. I told them I'd go six pence with them. I presently lost 3s. 6d. which was all the money I had. The prisoner said he would give four guineas for my watch. I took it out and laid it on the table; but instead of offering me money, he said he would play for it, at two guineas, a cut. I cut once and lost two guineas, and then I said I would cut no more. The other man swore if I would not, he would, for his money was at stake as well as my watch. So as he was going to cut, the prisoner catch'd up my watch and run away with it, and the other after him. All this was done in less than half an hour.

In a knowing urbane way, the judge instructed the jury that 'A gambler is one of the modern cant names for a money dropper'.[32]

Joseph Millikin was similarly duped by William Wilson in the spring of 1750. Millikin was a stranger in town, and possessed of a broad provincial accent that marked him out every time he opened his mouth. Even the short-hand recorder at the Old Bailey could not resist making fun of his accent, recording his speech phonetically: ''thou art the mon that robbed me'. Millikin was 'walking in the Fleet Market ... about four in the afternoon' on Monday 18 June, looking for the house of a Mr Clarke. A young boy approached him and offered to take him to the address he was seeking. The boy took him 'into Ann Glover's house in Chick-lane' and soon after:

> came in a pretty lusty man and [William Wilson]: they set to gaming at something, they called it pricking at the belt; the prisoner first lost a shilling, then a guinea, upon which he asked me to change a five pound, or a 5 guinea piece. I had got a silver watch in my pocket that I had received in lieu of some money, that was above my gold. I took that out and laid it down upon the table, there was £3 12s., two 36s. pieces and three moidores; I took them out and laid them on the table, upon which, said he, I think you have got a gold watch, I have let mine run down, please to let me regulate mine by yours; said I, it is but a

pinchbeck one. So I took it out; then the lusty man got up and turned me a little about, and carried me out of the door; going out I looked back and saw Wilson clap his handkerchief over the gold and watches, and pull'd them to that side of the table he was on. When I came in again the watches and gold were gone ...

Wilson was a tallow chandler down on his luck and a few weeks before this incident was caught pilfering a basket of game containing six pigeons and one hare from the back of the Ailesbury coach.[33] Pricking the girdle or belt involved coiling a long piece of rope and piercing it with a nail or knife. Bets were then placed on whether it was fixed to the table beneath.

Robbing less sophisticated visitors to London and gambling in general seem to have played central roles in the culture of London's poor. Indeed gambling was thought to be so ubiquitous that in 1737 Erasmus Jones felt confident in claiming that 'there is more money expended in wagers among the people in low life, concerning the fate of thieves and robbers, in one year, than is plunder'd by private felows from the publick in three ...'[34] While William Hogarth's choice of gambling as one of the central themes in his story of Tom Idle's downward spiral to the scaffold, reflects again its centrality to eighteenth-century life.

Even the poorest of London's inhabitants were expected to play games of chance. In mid January 1768 Thomas Turner was lodging at Mr Bavis's cook shop, earning a living by hawking a basket of sausages or 'polonies' through the alehouses of St James's. It was a cold, clear Saturday night when he found himself at the Thistle and Crown in Swallow Street where Abraham Javelleaue was a lodger, and entered the taproom, calling out his polonies to the assembled crowd.[35] Javelleaue challenged him to toss for a polony. Despite Turner's evident poverty, he seems to have willingly agreed and lost two sausages as a result. In the subsequent disagreement, several of the polonies fell to the floor, and Javelleaue stole several more. In the end, another customer, Thomas Tinderbox, took up Turner's cause and fought Javelleaue in the alehouse yard. But what is remarkable is that Turner agreed to the wager in the first place.[36]

In many respects casual gambling of this sort was simply an expected and accepted part of the everyday lives of Londoners. It encompassed a series of behaviours that the beggarly poor, working people and the well-to-do all found useful and enjoyable – at least when they won. There were, however, several circumstances in which gambling became both unacceptable in itself and where it was perceived as a form of vagrancy. Certainly, the governors of the Court of Bridewell were keen to prosecute games such as 'pricking at the garter', false dice and, most especially, wheelbarrow gambling. In January 1745/6 Henry Howard was discovered 'keeping false dice' and

The IDLE 'PRENTICE at Play in the Church Yard, during Divine Service.

Proverbs CH:XIX Vc:29.
Judgements are prepar'd for Scorners
& Stripes for the back of Fools.

14. William Hogarth, 'Industry and Idleness', plate iii, 'The Idle 'Prentice at Play in the Church Yard, during Divine Service', (1747).

playing 'unlawfull games in a wheelbarrow in Moorfields'; while in the same month James Mills was accused of defrauding Robert Fryer of 23 shillings at 'pricking at the garter'.[37] Wheelbarrow gambling involved either a game with a ball and three cups or a simple game of dice, but it was always frowned upon and was subject to regular proclamations from the Common Council, Lord Mayor and the Middlesex Sessions. The Lord Mayor and Common Council, for instance, issued a proclamation in 1796 declaring:

> This court considering the real obstructions, hindrances, dangers and injuries that frequently do happen ... by the great numbers of unruly and disorderly persons that oftentimes assemble and meet together ... about illegal sports and pastimes and particularly with wheelbarrows, or other things for playing with dice ... command that no person or persons whatsoever ... throw at any cock or cocks, or meet or assemble in the said streets, lanes, publick passages or places, about any such unlawful sports or pastimes whatsoever, either by throwing at cocks, or gaming upon wheelbarrows, or otherwise howsoever ... to the pestering thereof ... upon pain of being prosecuted as rioters and breakers of his majesty's peace ...[38]

At the same time it is also clear that many of the beggarly poor were more than willing to try their hands at this kind of trick. The role of illegal games of chance in the construction of a pauper 'economy of makeshift' is clearly reflected in the many proclamations against wheelbarrows. In 1707, for instance, the Middlesex Sessions issued an order directed against everyone who sold 'Oysters, Oranges, Decayed cheese, Apples, Nuts, Gingerbread etc' from wheelbarrows, claiming that they all 'carry with them dice and encourage unwary passengers and children to play with their said dice for some of such their goods ...'[39] Sarah Bland spent much of her youth as a prostitute working the streets of the West End. She and her cousin, Mary Maurice, worked as a team in St Martin's Lane in the early 1740s. She had spent time in St Martin's workhouse, and was one of the twenty-four women who suffered in the Roundhouse disaster of 1743. Within eight years of watching her cousin die of heat prostration in her arms, at the hands of William Bird and the parochial authorities of Westminster, she was 'wandering abroad and using unlawfull games with dice in a wheelbarrow'.[40] A generation earlier, in January 1714/5, Elizabeth Brown was arrested for 'seducing and corrupting' a young apprentice, Samuel Petter, and 'for driving a wheel barrow in the streets with fruit and dice'.[41]

Most games of chance required at least a little capital. Reasonably respectable clothing was also necessary if the unwary were to be fleeced in games of this sort, as the possibility of large rewards depended on the impression that all the participants possessed at least some money. Without the right clothes, or the wherewithal to buy or borrow a wheelbarrow, the chance of successfully perpetrating games and tricks on less worldly Londoners was limited. At the same time, however, it was possible to perpetrate beggarly tricks without a lot of cash. In September 1731 James Northall and Thomas Haycock worked up a sham petition against the 'Pot Act' and went from alehouse to alehouse 'extorting money', perhaps suggesting that they would report the publican for serving short measure if they were not given some contribution. The Pot Act regulated the measures used in the sale of alcohol, and one can only imagine the mixture of fear and uncertainty Northall and Haycock provoked in the minds of alehouse keepers keen to both avoid unwelcome attention and to unburden themselves of an onerous layer of regulation.[42] A decade later, on 25 February 1740/1, Daniel Hawks knocked on the door of the Reverend Mr William Rayner with a heavy bundle. Hawks claimed it was a parcel just arrived on the Oxford coach, and demanded payment for its delivery. In fact the bundle contained only three bricks.[43]

The 'Tricks of the Town' relied on greed. They promised a quick return and easy profit, but they nevertheless acted as one of the mechanisms through which money was redistributed from the relatively well off to the very poor. While fraud and begging were clearly differentiated in the minds of both victims and perpetrators, it is also clear that many of the beggarly poor were happy to trick strangers and countrymen if they came across an opportunity, if they could afford a carefully filed pair of dice, or were quick-handed enough to play a successful game of ball and three cups.

If greed and sleight of hand were useful to the beggarly poor, lust was even more useful, and frequently easier and cheaper to generate. Prostitution is generally seen in terms of the history of sexuality. The frisson of the erotic has always coloured the historical analysis of commercial sex. Yet it is clear that most prostitutes were desperately poor, and were using the one commodity they had, their bodies, to elicit a few pence for food and warmth. At the beginning of the eighteenth century John Gay depicts prostitutes as bedraggled and desperate:

> 'Tis she who nightly strowls with saunt'ring Pace,
> No stubborn Stays her yielding shape embrace;
> Beneath the lamp her tawdry ribbons glare,
> The new-scower'd Manteau, and the slattern Air;
> High-draggled petticoats her travels show,
> With falt'ring sounds she sooths the cred'lous Ear,
> My Noble Captain! Charmer! Love! My Dear![44]

In many cases prostitutes were beggars who added the allure of sex to the claims of charity. The language of both body and voice used by most prostitutes – a gentle (or not so gentle) tug on the sleeve, with a 'Ah country-man, give us a Dram',[45] or 'How do you do, Countryman; Will you give me a Pint of Wine?' – was at least superficially a plea for charity. Even when these pleas were prefaced by 'My Noble Captain! Charmer! Love! My Dear!', the language used by prostitutes seems more akin to the 'Kind Christian Gentleman, wont you relieve my suffering?' used by beggars than it does to any sexual chat-up line.

On a cool evening in late April 1781, John Downs, a black man living in Fleet Street, was having a quiet drink at the Sir John Falstaff. Sarah Robinson approached him:

> she asked me to drink and said she was very hungry: I gave her three-pence to get something to eat; she was very ragged; I asked her if she had no better clothes than those on her back; she said her clothes were in pawn; I gave her some money to get them out; she took me to her lodgings at Mr James's in St Giles's; I paid her very fair; I staid all night.[46]

Sarah Cooper 'had lately come out of the workhouse, and ... was very distressed' when she met John Craig coming down the Strand. First she asked him to give 'her something to drink, and [then] asked him for two shillings first, and he said he would give me two shillings after I had obliged him ...'[47] Mary Long accosted Christopher Hall in Drury Lane on 5 December 1717 with a 'How do you do, countryman; will you give me a pint of wine'. She and her companion were dressed in rags and went with Hall to a private room at the Fountain Tavern. A third women, equally ragged, joined them there. Hall sat at one end of the room, bought drinks for all three women, and eventually allowed, or encouraged, Mary Long to come close enough to masturbate him to orgasm. The literally arms' length relationship between Mary Long and Christopher Hall speaks strongly about the cultural, as well as the physical, distance between the two. Like Sarah Robinson and Sarah Cooper, Mary and her companions were essentially ragged beggars, performing a service in exchange for the gift of a small amount of alcohol.[48]

The apparent poverty and raggedness of Mary Long and her companions was not unusual. Late in life, Francis Place recollected the state of the young women who worked the streets in Limehouse, St Catherine's Lane and Rosemary Lane in the East End towards the close of the eighteenth century:

> many had ragged dirty shoes and stockings and some no stockings at all ... numbers wore no handkerchiefs at all in warm weather, and the breasts of

many hung down in a most disgusting manner, their hair among the generality was straight and 'swung in rat tails' over their eyes and it was filled with lice …[49]

Margery Stanton was a prostitute and a thief who worked the alleys and passages around Bond Street. Her face was heavily marked with smallpox, but, perhaps the clearest reflection of her desperation and poverty was her nickname, 'Ruggety Madge'. At her trial, just before she was sentenced to death, she declared, 'I have not a half-penny to save me.'[50]

Of course, not all prostitutes were entirely destitute. Sarah Knight, for instance, was a common streetwalker who worked the lanes near Union Street in Westminster with Mary Mills, the wife of a carpenter. Knight had lodged in the same building for over three years and appears to have had a relatively stable existence. On a cool and clear Saturday night, 10 September 1774, she spent a long evening 'sauntering' up and down, plying for custom.[51] Her mother had died the previous week and, in her grief, she drank heavily. Elizabeth Gregory, a fellow prostitute and the wife of a Chelsea Pensioner, described how she 'appeared to be much concerned and cryed' for the loss of her mother. She was not entirely broke, however, as she had 'two shillings to pay for her liquor and had four or five more in her pocket'. Later that night she was picked up by the watch and forced to spend her first evening ever in a watchhouse cell. Between the death of her mother and the experience of imprisonment, she decided she could stand no more. She took the expensive white silk ribbon she wore to attract customers, tied a sliding knot in it, and hanged herself from the door post of her watch house cell.[52]

The ragged appearance of many street walkers is all the more striking given the role of fine clothing, of the small promise of luxury and cleanliness represented by a single white silk ribbon, in attracting customers. Indeed, it was a recognition of the function of finery in prostitution that encouraged the Governors of the London Workhouse in January 1704/5 to order 'that all nightwalkers that are and that hereafter shall be brot into the workhouse be made to work in the same dress they are brought in'.[53] Gillray's harrowing portrait of a prostitute down on her luck makes a similarly tragic connection between clothing, poverty and prostitution.[54]

Nor is it difficult to locate real women for whom prostitution formed just one stop in an ever downward cycle of poverty. Martha Tilman claimed to be 'a poor girl come up from Scarborough in order to get a service'. But Elizabeth Honour claimed, 'she gets her bread by street walking, so do I', and that they shared a bed in a common lodging house. On the night Martha was accused of having stolen a pair of stays from Elizabeth Honour at least three other people were asleep in the same room, 'There were a

15. James Gilray, 'The Whore's Last Shift' (1779).
(*British Museum*)

woman and two children lay in that other bed, but they were beggars'.[55] From service to prostitution to beggary were two very short steps indeed.

Sarah Spiller was examined by the parochial officers of the small City parish of St Dionis Backchurch in the spring of 1777. By this point in her life she was being maintained by the parish in a contract workhouse run by John Hughes and William Phillips at Hoxton – a place described by one fellow inmate as 'a slaughter house for poor human bodies'.[56] Sarah described the circumstances of her life, and the almost casual place of prostitution in it:

> She went away from Pauls Head Court at 5 years of age with her father and lived with her grandmother after that several years. At ten years of age she went to service to take care of a child in Spitalfields where she lived 2 months and then 6 or 7 months out of place. Then she went to live at Baptist Head, St John Street where she lived about 7 or 8 months. From thence she went to Islington and lived at the Crown Alehouse in Laser Street. Lived there about 8 months and then lived in Tash Street at ye Coach and Horses. Lived there about 4 or 5 months, then lived at No. 10 Lambs Buildings Bunhill Row and lived there about 7 months. After that Justice Spiller, her cousin, put her to a place to learn to sew [and she] was about 9 or 10 months there and then went to a cousin's, Isindike, in George Street Spittlefields. [She] was there about a year and half and had no wages only victuals and drink for her work and was then near 3 years on the Town and then went to live at the 2 Sugar Loaves, King Street and lived there about 8 months, where she fell sick. From thence went to a lodging about a fortnight and thence to St Giles's workhouse.[57]

In the early 1760s Mary Brown and Rebecca Dean worked the streets around Fleet market, picking up men.[58] They formed one of the ubiquitous pairs of women who gave areas such as Fleet Market such a bad reputation. It could well have been this pair who found the fifteen-year-old Ann Hook, 'quite a stranger and very poor and destitute' on the streets. Whatever their names, Hook

> was closely applied to by some girls of the town, who was by and belongs to one Fanny Finley, who keeps a house of ill fame in Fleet Market, next door to the Bull and Garter, there to go live with her. That one night being in company with them, she was prevail'd upon to go home with them, when after pressing her to drink very freely of Liquor the said Fanny Finley found means to extort a promise from her to live with her promising to find her with meat, drink, cloaths, washing and lodging for 15s. a week, which was the method she took with the rest of the girls there, and that they were to earn this money by walking the streets and bringing men and bad company to her house ...[59]

In Ann Hook's case desperation and begging clearly led directly to prostitution. In this instance, the relative security of a 'bawdy house' provided a real, if temporary, refuge from the street. For others, prostitution was a more casual and contested affair. Mary Price, the twenty-three year-old wife of a tallow chandler in St Martin-in-the-Fields, combined begging in the western reaches of London with casual prostitution. She told a local gardener how her financial and sexual relationship with the improbably named local notable Francis Gotobed had saved her from starvation: 'she had had many a shilling and sixpence of him and had it not been for him she should have been half starved'.[60] The beggar-woman whom John Nicholls, himself a pauper, entertained in his almshouse in Aldenham in 1731 was also clearly willing to combine begging with prostitution. Only an anonymous tip-off to the governors of the almshouse put a stop to their regular arrangement.[61]

This same equation between begging, poverty and prostitution can also be found in the attitudes of the authorities and of men in general. William Hutton, that always enthusiastic Birmingham 'countryman', was struck both by the beauty and fine clothing of London's prostitutes and by their poverty:

> These transitory meteors rise, like the stars, in the evening; are nearly as numerous; and, like them, shine in their only suit. They hawk their charms to a crowded market, where the purchasers are few. – Many attempts are made for one customer gained. They cling to ones arms like the Lilliputian ships to the girdle of Gulliver.
>
> Some of the finest women I saw in London were of this class. I conversed with many of them. – they could all swear, talk indecently and drink gin. Most of them assured me they had not a penny in the world. I considered them as objects of pity more than of punishment; and would gladly have given a trifle to each, but found it could not be done for less than ten thousand shillings.[62]

In other words, the women who tried to wrest a living from the lust of male Londoners were, at least in Hutton's view, objects of charity. A careful observer could not help but notice their beggarly characteristics. And while historians have tended to connive at the depiction of prostitution as a distinct and well-defined process (even a profession) it is clear that commercial sex was more an outpost of poverty than anything else.[63]

It was not just in the uneven scales that measured the financial circumstances of poor women that begging and sexuality were linked. Quite simply, young women forced to beg for a living were assumed to be sexually available. In part, this was a small fragment of a broader misogyny and culture of exploitation.[64] Every female domestic was at risk of assault,[65] while vicious public attacks on prostitution frequently poured from London's presses:

> The bane of vertue, and the bawd of vice,
> Pander to hell, is this she cockatrice:
> She's like the devil, seeking every hour,
> Whom she may first decoy, and then devour.
> Let every thinking mortal, then beware,
> Least he be caught in her damn'd cunning snare: ...
> Your body to the pox and soul to hell.[66]

Even beyond this sort of bile and vitriol, a clear assumption of sexual availability can be discerned. Even the slight defence of a child on one's back did not preclude men of all classes simply assuming that they could purchase sex from a beggar. William King, in his 1709 poem 'The Beggar Woman', tells the story of a gentleman out riding who comes across a woman with an infant tied to her back:

> A beggar by her trade; yet not so mean
> But that her cheeks were fresh and linen clean ...
> She needed not much courtship to be kind ...

The beggar-woman leads the gentleman into the woods in search of a secluded spot, 'little Bobby to her shoulder bound ...' In this instance, before the gentleman can satisfy his desires, the female beggar manages to foist her infant on to him, trussing him up in a cloth with the child. Running off, she cries:

> 'Sir, goodbye; be not angry that we part,
> I trust the child to you with all my heart:
> But, ere you get another, 'ti'n't not amiss
> To try a year or two how you'll keep this.[67]

Despite the trick, the rider's clear assumption is that any beggar would have sex in exchange for money. This same assumption was clearly in the mind of Felix Donnelly when he attempted to have sex with Margaret King on 9 April 1760 just off Rosemary Lane. King, a beggar, described the situation on that chill Wednesday to the court at the Old Bailey:[68]

I had been a begging all that day. This other woman carries chips about to sell [and] she came home and had lost the heel of her shoe. She asked me to be so good as to lend her my shoes. I lent them to her. She met Sarah Tisham and this man [Felix Donnelly] coming together. They called me to bring a light ... Said she, I have got an acquaintance [and] she insisted upon my going to an

alehouse, but I would not ... When I came up with the pot of beer, I found
him and the two women close together ... I said, what are you about? One of
them said, hold your tongue, or I'll run this knife to your heart. He wanted to
lie with Mary Granvile, and the other woman said she had got the pox. He said
he liked his country women better. He took me and used me very odiously,
too bad to be spoke of; he put me in fear, and wanted to be rude with me, and
gave the old woman a shilling for the bed, desiring she would coax me to lie
with him ... I was barefooted and bare leg'd.[69]

Even women engaged in the entirely legal pauper professions were
assumed to be sexually available. William Woty's 1770, 'A Mock Invitation
to Genius' assumes that all street sellers are essentially prostitutes, and
expresses a preference for them over his own more discriminating muse:

> Or sooner would I seek relief from Nell,
> Town-tramping, oyster-laden – or from thee,
> Soap-lathering Bess, the chief of all thy train,
> Great mistress of the washing-tub, well-skilled
> In friction ambidextrous. Ye, my fair!
> Ye first should have my vows, green-vendent Peg!
> (Than whom none sooner decks the verdant stall
> With fruit cucumerous) and shrimp-crowned Doll,
> In alehouse well-agnized, with brawny Jane,
> Who constant plies the market, basket-armed.
> Nor less doth deep-mouthed, piscatory Kate
> (Whose voice is melody through all the realm
> Of Billingsgate, admired for flow of words
> And well-timed oratory, far beyond ...)
> Or brick-dust Nan attract my due regard.[70]

In some cases this assumption of the sexual availability of poor women
led to a tragic outcome. Sarah Griffin was begging her way from London to
Worcestershire, with a pass and two pence and three farthings in her pocket,
when on 7 September 1740 she asked a young man, William Duell, 'to shew
her a lodging'. He directed her to a barn in Horn Lane in Acton owned by
a Mr Life, and very helpfully 'opened a truss of hay for her to lie on'. Sarah
was obviously nervous, as she specifically asked Duell 'not to tell any body
that she was there'. Later that night Duell came back with five or six other
young men including George Curtis, alias Tug-mutton, who himself normally slept rough in a local barn. When Tug-mutton accosted Sarah asking
'who was there?', she answered 'A poor soul! Don't meddle with me', claiming that she was poxed. He attacked her anyway, putting his hands up her

dress and declaring, 'pox'd, or pox'd not, by God I will'. With this the boys held her down while first Curtis and then John Davis, then Henry Richards, followed by John James, alias Jack at the Captains, then John Wolfe and finally William Duell all raped her. She struggled and cried murder. Having finished, the boys went to the Star alehouse in Acton and drank away Sarah Griffin's last few pence, leaving her to die slowly in the barn.[71]

Perhaps the ambiguity of the relationship between begging and prostitution is best captured in the experience of Elizabeth Burroughs. On Wednesday 4 August 1736 she was 'coming up Drury Lane about 9 o'clock at night, and at the Corner of Princess Street', she was stopped by an American, William Orr. They agreed to go to the Hamburgh Coffee House, where Orr secured a private room and a quartern of brandy. Burroughs later recounted their conversation: 'Then he told me if I would have some concerns with him, he would make me a present'. After a fair amount of drinking and sex, Orr refused to pay Burroughs the sum she expected and she took up his silver watch in lieu. Orr, 'contested with the girl, in order to have [the] watch again'. But Burroughs 'desired money before she'd give it [up], first half a guinea, then a crown, then charity because she was poor'. For Elizabeth Burroughs the boundaries between prostitution and begging, between theft, trickery and the pleas of absolute poverty, were illusory. Each formed a small fragment of a broader relationship to a society filled with people more powerful than herself.[72] Just as with the blackguard youth who pilfered and stole around the quays while accepting victuals at neighbour's doors, and the desperate men who fingered iron bars with one hand and proffered hats 'in a begging way' with the other, the easy divisions between charity and theft, begging and prostitution made by modern historians, and indeed eighteenth-century commentators, seems to melt away in the face of the hard decisions and desperate needs of the very poor. For them, begging, theft and prostitution were just minor variations on a well-worn theme.

5

The Rhetoric of Rags

In the late 1720s the Swiss traveller César de Saussure was living in London. In letters home he related in admiring tones the magnificence and liberality of the major charities of the metropolis and how poor relief was distributed by the parishes. At the same time he complained that 'Notwithstanding all this, quantities of beggars are continually to be seen asking for alms in all the streets and highways of London'. By way of explanation for this apparent contradiction, he related a story told to him 'by a lady', assuring his reader 'one can believe all she says'.

> This lady was much attached to a pretty servant-maid she had, being very well satisfied with her services. A young man became acquainted with the girl, and, falling in love with her, asked her to marry him. She replied that she would accept him with pleasure, but ... first wished to know his trade and means of sustenance ... Her lover at once produced a purse containing at least one hundred golden guineas, and said that his trade brought him in much gain, but that he could not possibly divulge it to her before the marriage. Quite dazzled by the sight of the gold, the girl made no more difficulties, and they were married. A few days later the husband told his wife that it was time she learnt his trade, which was that of simulating a cripple, and he added that she on her side must do the same. For a long time the poor girl resisted her husband's orders, but he personally inflicted such barbarous treatment on her that her head appeared to be attacked by cancer. In that state, and dressed in rags, she took up her station in Leicesterfield Square [just a few streets north of Charing Cross] near the Prince of Wales's palace, where passers-by gave her charity.

A couple of years later, the lady received a visit from her old servant, who was in good health, but deep mourning for her now deceased husband. He had died leaving her around £1000 in cash:

> all amassed by begging and by saving; for he had been so avaricious that he never spent one penny, but lived on the remains of bread and meat begged from rich people's houses.[1]

The significance of this story lies not in the existence of professional cheats and charlatans. We can even give a name to at least one professional beggar who haunted Leicester Fields. In the early 1770s 'Foolish Sam', dressed in rags, was 'well known about Leicester Fields'.[2] Instead, what is important is the assumptions de Saussure makes about beggars in general. He believed the beggar woman's scars and bruises were real, as was the couple's beggarly lifestyle – the broken victuals and poverty – and yet they were still fakes, still making a pretence of their suffering.[3] Almsgivers and the broader population of the eighteenth-century London assumed that beggars were masters of the art of self-presentation – that beggars knew what to wear, and where to wear it, and that this was true both of the genuinely impoverished and the skilful professional. Richard Steele, writing in the *Tatler*, brought an expert eye to his assessment of two beggars he came across in 1709. He compared their techniques and relative success:

> Going through an alley the other day, I observed a noisy impudent beggar bawl out, that he was wounded in a merchantman, that he had lost his poor limbs, and showed a leg clouted up. All that passed by made what haste they could out of sight and hearing. But a poor fellow at the end of the passage, with a rusty coat, a melancholy air, and a soft voice, desired them to look upon a man not used to beg. The latter received the charity of almost every one that went by. The strings of the heart, which are to be touched to give us compassion, are not so played on but by the finest hand.[4]

Steele and his fellow Londoners believed they recognised the strategies of self-presentation employed by beggars, but at the same time they also looked carefully for those signs of suffering, of filth, rags and disability, lice and bruises, that could assure them of the deserving poverty of the supplicants they grudgingly relieved. One anonymous poet gave voice to the meaning his contemporaries hoped to find in a beggar's rags:

> These tatter'd cloaths my poverty bespeak,
> These hoary locks proclaim my lengthen'd years;
> And many a furrow in my grief-worn cheek,
> Has been the channel to a stream of tears.[5]

More than perhaps at any time before or since, clothes made the man or woman in eighteenth-century London.[6] Lace and frills, velvets and brocades marked out the very rich from their humbler contemporaries. For the poor, however, the significant item of clothing was always their body linen – that complex set of shirts, stockings and shifts that lay next to the skin, and acted as underwear, vest and socks.[7] It both protected the wearer from the coarse fabrics and dirt of everyday life and labour, and saved expensive outer garments from the stains and smells of the human body. Clean linen, washed once a week, was the absolute marker of decency and a necessary prerequisite for making the complex system of clothing worn in the eighteenth century work properly. It was all the more important because many outer garments were never washed. Francis Place recalled the filthy state of the clothes worn by artisans during his eighteenth-century childhood:

> since I can remember the wives and daughters of journeymen tradesmen and shopkeepers, either wore leather stays or what were called full boned stays, and these latter sort were worn by women of all ranks. These were never washed, altho worn day by day for years ... petticoats of camblet, lined with dyed linen, stuffed with wool or horsehair and quilted, these were also worn day by day until they were rotten, and never were washed.[8]

Leather breeches, of the kind worn by most working men, needed to be cleaned by a tailor at a cost of around 1s. 6d. per time. Even the better off did not consider undertaking this expense more frequently than once a month.[9] The almost unavoidable dirtiness of most outer garments made the possession of clean linen next to the skin all the more significant, while the dual role of shirts and shifts as both vest and underwear simply added a significant layer of meaning to clean collars and cuffs. Soiled linen was a sure indicator that it was not simply hands and face that needed washing. As a result the poor went to great lengths in order to hide any deficiency in their linen. In 1740 John Loppenburg was a poor servant, but he recognised the importance of keeping his linen clean. He regularly went to the ponds in Paddington, near Tyburn, to wash his shirts out of the sight of the censorious eyes of a washerwomen. On Saturday 26 April he set out:

> in order to wash a coarse dirty shirt; I was ashamed to be seen doing it by any body, because it was torn and ragged. I went to one pond, and saw people there, so I went to another ... I hung my shirt up to dry, and walked to and fro while it was drying, and saw two men walking about; I threw the shirt from me least they should laugh at me ...[10]

Elizabeth Beck certainly felt the same shame experienced by Loppenburg. She had breakfast with Prudence Wilson on a warm and hazy Thursday morning, 29 April 1762, at her apartment in Strutton Ground.[11] They had known each other since Elizabeth was a child, but in recent months Beck had fallen on bad times and taken to drink. 'She was very bare of cloaths and appeared to be in very bad circumstances'. Unable to face her financial problems, Elizabeth went home after breakfast and hanged herself in her garret room in Duck Lane.[12] The shame felt by both Loppenburg and Beck was based in the certain knowledge that ragged and dirty linen would mark them out in their poverty. The prosecutor at the 1789 trial of Mary Wade and Jane Whiting put it succinctly when he asked of one witness whether the perpetrator of the crime, 'Was it a decent person, or a ragged person?'[13]

George Parker was an itinerant actor who made money where he could. At one point in his travels he attempted to pass himself off as a university lecturer to a provincial audience. He rented a substantial hall and employed a bill sticker to advertise his lectures. In the process he ran up substantial debts. But the debt that was to prove his undoing was owed to the washer-woman. His charade came to an abrupt end when she demanded payment:

> Where is this lecturing man? ... I will be paid. Damn him ... does he think I pay nothing for my soap and starch? I thought by his linen he was a vagabond, and I never should be paid. I wonder how the fellow gets it on; he must do it by piece-meal; a sleeve in one tub, a collar in another, and a wristband in a third.[14]

Even parish paupers demanded fresh linen every week, and its provision formed one of the most substantial prerequisites of domestic service.[15] A parish apprentice, for instance, could expect to be given a number of shifts as a matter of course, and to have them washed regularly. Ann Nailor was thirteen years old when she was starved to death and murdered by Sarah Metyard, but it was made perfectly clear at the subsequent trial that, while Ann was starved, she was provided with clean linen. One of her fellow apprentices was carefully questioned on just this point:

Q.   How many shifts had the girl?

[A.]   We had all three a piece; her shifts were all marked No. 4. She had three new ones and one very ragged one; she had one of her new ones on [when she ran away] ...

Q.   How often had you clean shifts?

[A.]   Once a week, and sometimes once a fortnight.

Q.   What day of the week did you put them on?

[A.]   On the Monday morning.[16]

Both men and women were expected to wash their hands and faces daily, and their feet at least once a week, and to pull a fine-toothed comb through their hair (or to shave it off completely and wear a wig) as a protection against lice. All workhouse inmates above the age of four at St Olave Hart Street in the City were expected to be: 'up, have their hands and faces wash'd, and their heads combed with small tooth'd combs ... by six in Summer and eight in Winter'. This ritual was then followed by morning prayer:

we bless thee for this comfortable provision that is made for us, that we who were naked; that we who were scattered and solitary are settled in one family, trained up to order and industry and taught to know and to serve thee our God …[17]

The good order and industry for which these paupers were forced to thank God and the parish was founded on a strict regime of cleanliness – for good reason. The alternative to a regular change of body linen, and daily washing, was the indignity and discomfort brought by lice and fleas, which in their train brought social disgrace. After over three weeks on the road, John Harrower, an itinerant stocking-seller and soon to be an indentured servant, arrived in London and could not resist recording his first change of clothes in almost a month:

> This day I shifted my cloaths and put on a clean … shirt, clean britches and waistcoat and my brown coat. I not having any other cloaths on ever since I left Lerwick but my blew jacket and bigg coat above it and a plain shirt.[18]

His relief at actually wearing something clean is palpable, but perhaps as telling is his willingness to wait three weeks before changing his clothes, certain that he would need to present a respectable figure once he arrived in London.

Most beggars did not possess clean linen, and its absence forms one of the clear and distinguishing marks that spoke most eloquently of their real need. The addition of ragged outer garments was equally significant. Simon Edy's outfit, while substantial and cumbersome, also spoke powerfully of homelessness and need. He normally stationed himself outside St Giles's Churchyard and had the nickname of 'Old Simon':

> He wore several hats, at the same time suffered his beard to grow, which was of a dirty yellow-white … He had several waistcoats and as many coats, increasing in size, so that he was enabled by the extent of the uppermost garment to cover the greater part of the bundles containing rags of various colours; and distinct parcels with which he was girded about …[19]

John Webb was not so well established. He begged about Grosvenor Gate to Hyde Park throughout June 1762. The gatekeeper warned him that, 'he must not continue longer there, on account of his being offensive and stunck very much, having no cloaths or linen to shift himself'. He probably went to the pond near the cheese-cake house on Tuesday 11 July in order to wash himself and his clothes, and perhaps to earn himself a reprieve. The air in London that day was very bad, and the temperature was in the low 60s.[20] Unfortunately, John Webb fell into the pond and drowned.[21] These same rags also spoke to real need in a different way.[22] Mary Ann Lawless was taken up by Edward Hammond in early July 1748, 'with a little child in her arms, and by the child's having good things on, and she was in a ragged condition, I did not think it was her child'. Lawless was found guilty of the theft of the child's clothing and sentenced to transportation.[23]

The considerable expense of maintaining a full set of clothes, and its importance in preserving an independent life, is well captured in the experience of Elizabeth Wood and her two children. She was a parishioner and sometime workhouse inmate at St Helen's within Bishopsgate. Her clothes were in such a tattered condition that she did not even feel she could address the workhouse committee in person, and was forced to write.

> Sir I must beg ye favour of you to stand my friend and plead for me ... for I cannot come and I am in graite want of all necessers for I am quite a shamed to appear before any ...

Some time later she wrote again, explaining, 'I am so bare of clothing I shall be forced to leev my place having not enough to keep me cleen'. Eventually the parish took her in to their workhouse and clothed her and her family at the cost of £1 19s. 9d. Elizabeth herself received '1 under coat, 2 shifts, 2 aprons, 2 hancher, 1 capp, 1 pair shoes, 2 yards 1/4 long ells, 12s. 9d.'[24]

Joseph Barker knew this same shame at not having sufficient clothing to cover his body and the sense of distance it created between himself and other working people. Looking back to his beggarly childhood at the very beginning of the nineteenth century, he recalled:

> It was a great trial to me to be unable to obtain sufficient clothing to cover me properly. I felt it a great humiliation when I had to mingle with a crowd of others ... At that time my trowsers besides being sadly out of repair in other respects, had got torn from the bottom quite up to the thigh. I fastened several parts together as well as I could with some thorns from the hedges and in that plight trudged along ...[25]

But, just as his ragged trousers created what seemed to him unbridgeable distance between himself and other boys his age, it is also clear that ragged clothes and a lack of linen made a powerful case for real poverty. A basic lack of clothing could move even the most hardened of hearts. John Brown was committed to Bridewell on Wednesday 11 September 1745 for 'wandering about this city with a pass and pretending to have a wife and eight children'. Two months later on 22 November he was arrested again, being this time described as a 'common vagrant'. Despite the clear belief on the part of the governors of Bridewell that he was an undeserving case, they ordered 'the steward to give him a pair of stockings and a shirt'.[26] By 1792 the City of London was spending over £1057 per year clothing vagrants arrested and referred on to St Thomas's and St Bartholomew's hospitals as a result of their poor health.[27]

If ragged clothes contributed to a powerful case for the reality of poverty, it was not only beggars who were forced to wear clothes past their best. In a pre-industrial society in which every inch of fabric was created only at the cost of the hard physical labour of spinners and weavers, fullers and dyers, a full set of clothing in good condition was prohibitively expensive. When, as an escaped prisoner of war, Israel Potter was on the run from the authorities and attempting to make his way to London in the late 1770s, he exchanged his sailor's garb for the best clothes owned by a labourer:

> The first garment presented by the poor old man, of his best, or 'church suit', as he termed it, was a coat of very coarse cloth, and containing a number of patches of almost every colour but that of which it was originally made – the next was a waistcoat and a pair of small cloathes, which appeared each to have received a bountiful supply of patches to correspond with the coat ...

As telling was the old man's response to the clothes he received in exchange. He 'apeared very much pleased with his bargain, and represented to his wife that he could now accompany her to church much more decently ...'[28]

The eponymous hero in Daniel Defoe's *Colonel Jack* is described as a member of 'the ragged regiment', and his fellows as 'a gang of naked, ragged rogues'. On his first substantial success as a thief he immediately buys some food, accompanied by some beer 'begg'd' from a 'good woman' to go with it. But the second thing Colonel Jack does is to visit a 'broker's shop, over against the church, where they sold old cloths, for I had nothing on but the worst of rags', where comments on his lack of cleanliness and ragged appearance burn hot in his ears.[29] In a similar way, when James Lackington, an impoverished shoemaker, first arrived in London and began to make a bit of money, he measured his success in clothing:

> In a month I saved money sufficient to bring up my wife, and she had a pretty tolerable state of health; of my master I obtained some stuff-shoes for her to bind, and nearly as much as she could do, and as we had plenty of work and higher wages, we were tolerably easy in our circumstances, more so than we ever had been, so that we soon procured a few cloaths.

His next extravagance was a great coat purchased for 10s. from a used clothing store in Rosemary Lane, next to Rag Fair.[30]

Many of the men and women who cried their wares on the streets of London combined selling cheap goods and services with begging, and were dressed in rags that encouraged casual charity. The woman crying 'Last

Dying Speeches' at Tyburn in Paul Sandby's 1759 watercolour is wearing
what appears more a collection of rags than a set of garments. And even
allowing for artistic licence and the desire to depict the poor as raggedly
picturesque, this image speaks powerfully to the state of clothing worn by
many Londoners.[31]

If the men and women who made their living through the beggarly professions were characterised by the poor state of their clothing, beggars
themselves were even less well dressed. A woman, whose name was never
discovered, collapsed on Thames Street early in the evening of Thursday 25
April 1793. 'She appeared to be a distressed woman in a dirty mean dress'.[32]
A few years later another woman was discovered, 'halloeing out in the end
of Fleet Market Next Holborn Hill'. 'Her cloaths were very ragged, torn and
dirty and she appeared quite insensible.' She died later that night and was
listed in the coroner's inquest as, 'A Woman Unknown'.[33]

Charles Allen discovered the body of a beggar just before eight in the
morning on a cold Friday in December 1792. The temperature that day never
rose above 37 degrees Fahrenheit, and the beggar, whose name was never
discovered, was found lying on the pavement in Shoe Lane near Holborn
Hill:[34]

> He had not shoes on, his stockings very much torn ... his breeches were very
> much torn, that he had no hat on, that he appeared very ragged and poor, that
> what cloaths he had on were very wet and dirty as if he had been in the dirt ...[35]

For people like Jonathan Swift who could afford a full set of clothes, a
beggar's rags were simply one of the tools of his trade:

> neither do they much regard cloaths, unless to sell them; for, their rags are part
> of their tools with which they work: They want only ale, brandy and other
> strong liquors, which cannot be had without money; and money, as they
> conceive, always abounds in the metropolis.[36]

Addison and Steele agreed, they have Sir Andrew Freeport express the
commonplace Whig view of beggars and their clothing:

> The other day, as soon as we were got into his Chariot, two or three beggars
> on each side hung upon the doors, and solicited our charity with the usual
> rhetorick of a sick wife or husband at home, three or four helpless little chil-
> dren all starving with cold and hunger. We were forc'd to part with some
> money to get rid of their Importunity ...
>   'Well then', says Sir Andrew, 'we go off with the prayers and good wishes of
> the beggars ... But how few ounces of wooll do we see upon the backs of those
> poor creatures? And when they shall next fall in our way, they will hardly be

16. Paul Sandby, 'Last Dying Speeches' (1759). (*Paul Mellon Collection, Yale Centre for British Art/Bridgeman Art Library*)

better drest; they must always live in rags to look like objects of compassion. If their families too are such as they are represented, 'tis certain they cannot be better cloathed, and must be a great deal worse fed ...'[37]

But if beggars, and to a lesser extent the poor of London, really were dirty and ragged, it was at a terrible cost. A forty-year-old beggar found shelter from the cold and the rain on Monday 5 November 1793 in White Coop Street in the City. The barometer had been falling all that week, and the temperature on Monday night was only 43 degrees Fahrenheit.[38] John Robertson, an apothecary, later examined his body:

> He appeard to be about forty years of age, his apparel very mean and scanty, his body covered with a course piece of linen rag, very black and over it an old crown coat without any linen. He appeared as if he had not been shaved some months. His stomach and bowel were depressed and empty, his flesh exceedingly dirty and bloody ... Inside of his coat were covered with innumberable quantity of lice still living ... His death might have arisen from cold, filth and poverty and for want of the common necessaries of life.[39]

Of all the suffering and disadvantages experienced by beggars as a result of their rags, and lack of clean linen, it was probably the depredations of lice which pained them most.[40] With his tongue firmly in his cheek, but possessed of a clear memory of his youthful discomfort, James Dawson Burn recalled his early experience with lice:

> no young urchin could possibly have a better suit for ventilation, and what was more, I had numerous live stock on my body with the addition of the itch to keep me warm.[41]

A bitter dispute arose in 1731 as a result of the death of Mary Whistle in the workhouse belonging to St Gile's in the Fields:

> There for Eleven Weeks poor soul she lay.
> Half starved, eat up with Vermin (as they say)
> Holes in her Legs, her Arms, her hips and Thighs,
> The Vermin eat and in her head likewise,
>
> Her Hair was matted with the Vermin so,
> The like before no one did ever know,
> A filthy sight alas, for to be seen,
> What misiry must this Poor Soule die in.[42]

Twelve years earlier Richard Hutton, the steward of the Quaker Workhouse at Clerkenwell recorded at length a quack recipe for dealing with fleas and lice:

Take of the highest rectified spirit of wine (viz. Camp spirits that will burn all away dry, and leave not the least moisture behind) half a pint; newly distilled oil or spirit of turpentine, half a pint; mix them together and break into it, in small bits, half an ounce of camphor, which will dissolve in it in a few minutes. Shake them well together, and with a sponge, or a brush dipped in some of it, wet very well the bed or furniture wherein those vermin harbour or breed, and it will infallibly kill and destroy both them and their nits, although they swarm ever so much ... The quantity here ordered of this curious, neat, white mixture (which costs about a shilling) will rid any one bed whatsoever, though it swarms with bugs.[43]

A shilling would house and feed someone for a day or two. Hutton's willingness to spend this amount to fumigate one bed reflects the importance he placed on keeping his workhouse vermin free.

Ned Ward turned one beggar's forlorn attempt to deal with the problem of vermin into a theatrical joke, another facet of the elaborate pantomime of begging. He has one denizen of his 'beggars' club':

Halting about the room, cap in hand as if he was at the arse of a miserable alderman, then biting his nails and shaking his head, as if he curs'd him in his heart because he had not charity enough to reward his prayers with a loose half penny; then suddenly as if attackt by his eight legg'd enemies ... fingers his collar, conveying the little prisoners between his finger and thumb from his neck to his mouth in order to bite the biters ...[44]

The visceral disgust felt for lice and the extent to which they signified social exclusion and real poverty, is perhaps best caught, however, by Jonathan Swift in his description of Gulliver's reaction to the public beggars of Brobdingnag:

the beggars watching their opportunity, crouded to the sides of the coach and gave me the most horrible spectacles that ever an ... eye beheld. There was a woman with a cancer in her breast ... full of holes ... There was a fellow with a wen in his neck ... And another with a couple of wooden legs ... But the most hateful sight of all was the lice crawling upon their cloaths ... It perfectly turned my stomach.[45]

In the process it also helped turn out his pockets.

Filth, a lack of linen, rags and lice were characteristics that beggars both experienced along with their poor contemporaries and which marked them out. They provided the visual clues that allowed middling sort and elite men and women to reassure themselves about the real need and desperation of the recipients of their casual charity. At the same time they were experiences shared with many other poor Londoners. The inclusion of a ragged beggar, as the six of diamonds, amongst fifty-one other more fully employed street criers in a 1754 pack of cards, reflects the extent to which ragged beggars were part of this broader community.[46] Francis Place's recollection of the lice tolerated by men and women of the artisan classes in his childhood, reinforces this continuity:

> The children of tradesmen and other persons keeping good houses in the Strand for instance and the streets north and south of the Strand, were all of them when I was a boy infected with vermin that is had lice in their hair, they used to be combed once a week with a small tooth comb, on to the bellows or into a sheet of paper in the lap of the mother ... the larger number by far of the youth of both sexes had vermin in their hair, and many grown people were not free from them.[47]

The life histories of the men who gathered in the parlour belonging to Simon Place in the 1770s and 1780s, further suggests the extent to which both the experience of begging, their suffering, their rags and lice, was an integral part of many lives:

> Duke a tailor ... his busines decayed, and being nearly ruined he sold his niece whom he had brought up, to a rich man who came from the East Indies and lodged in his house, he contrived to live upon them for some time. His niece was a pretty modest girl, who pined herself to death and Duke became destitute. Soon after this his wife died and he became a beggar about the streets.[48]

A more distinctive claim to real poverty than rags and lice, and an experience that was both shared with many working people, and which set the beggarly poor apart from other Londoners was disability.[49] Withered limbs, blindness, deafness, epilepsy, idiocy and insanity both forced many Londoners to beg on the streets and, at the same time, formed a powerful claim on the pockets of the physically whole. Many of the images we posses of eighteenth-century beggars depict them as crippled and damaged. 'The Lame Crew', an anonymous late seventeenth-century image makes this connection explicit.

The verse accompanying this image is a metaphorical treatment of the state of religion, but the range of disabilities depicted above is real enough.

> What a lame Crew's here, what a strange sight,
> Among so many there's none that walks upright.[50]

We have no clear measure of the numbers of eighteenth-century men,

Prnted & sould by P. Stent

The Lame Crew

What a lame Crew is here what a strang sight   Of blind & most decreped sectaries
Amongso many theres none that walkes upright   Seducing Jesuites & Incendiaries
It is not Beggers Bush that can display   And many sectes besides Religion
So many beggers halt a seuerall way   Till now neuer was so distracted known
Yet the vnhappy dayes aboue all other   So much disfigured that we cannot tell
A stranger weaknes farr in us discouer   of what religion we are very well
Euenen in Religion we grow lame and halk   Nor what to be of Nothing so much tryes
None walke vpright none Truth striue to exalt   The chusers Iudgments as Varietyes
We are full of putrefaction lameness all
Religions now become an Hospitall

17.   'The Lame Crew' (*c.* 1660). (*Corporation of the City of London*)

women and children who were disabled in some way. Among the primarily male beggars who managed to remain on the streets for decades, and to elbow their way in to elite literature, a high proportion were severely hand-icapped. John T. Smith dedicated a whole section of his *Vagabondiana* (1817) to men he termed 'Go-Cart, Billies in bowls, or sledge-beggars'. In his world of picturesque beggars, men such as Samuel Horsey loomed large. According to Smith, Horsey begged on the streets of London for over thirty years, starting around 1785, when he lost his legs to the surgeon's knife at St Bartholomew's Hospital. He normally begged either at Charing Cross or in front of Coutt's bank in the Strand.[51]

Poverty and disability went hand in hand. For the vast majority of peo-ple, their livelihood depended on their ability to do hard physical work. When that ability was removed, poverty haunted their lives and destroyed their hopes. The vast majority of workhouse inmates, for instance, found themselves constrained to apply for relief because they were ill or infirm.[52] Contemporaries also believed that London itself attracted disabled beggars from around the country. Joshua Gee, in his 1729 *Trade and Navigation of Great-Britain Considered*, suggested that the beggars of London were more likely to be disabled than their country cousins:

> If any person is born with an defect or deformity, or maimed by fire, or any other casualty, or by any inveterate distemper, which renders them miserable objects, their way is open to London; where they have free Liberty of shewing their nauseaous sights to terrify people, and force them to give money to get rid of them; and those vagrants have for many years past, removed out of sev-eral parts of the three kingdoms, and taken their stations in the metropolis, to the interruption of conversation and business.[53]

At the same time, it was claimed that even the most obvious disabilities were faked. With make-up and a complex superstructure of straps and crutches, with vermin-ridden hair and theatrical rags, apparently disabled beggars played the ultimate urban confidence trick on the better off. Ned Ward, in his 1709 *History of London Clubs* depicts the scene at the beggars' club, after its members had retired from their curbside posts for the night:

> where by the vertue of sound tipple, the pretenders to the dark are restor'd instantly to their sight, those afflicted with feign'd sickness, recover perfect health, and others that halt before they are lame, stretch their legs without their crutches ... their dirty handkerchiefs and night caps are slipt into their pock-ets, their crippled legs and arms taken out of their slings and return'd from their cramping postures to their ease and liberty ...[54]

Every now and then a false beggar, faking disability, was discovered. These

London Published as the Act directs April 30 1816 by J. T. Smith Nº 4 Chandos Sᵗ Covent Garden.

18. Samuel Horsey, from John T. Smith, *Vagabondiana* (1817).

were people like Henry Goodwin who found himself before the Court of Bridewell on 8 April 1742, charged 'for being a loose disorderly person wandring abroad and begging disguised by a long beard and pretending to be lame', or Isaac Fairbrother, charged the same day 'pretending to be an old woman and begging'.[55] Goodwin in particular was a professional beggar who was familiar with the ways of London. He had been apprenticed to a wood turner in Distaff Lane in the City, and supported a wife and child from his begging.[56] In 1702 the President and Governors of the Poor of London gleefully recorded their discovery of Richard Alegil:

> a boy of eleven years of age, who pretended himself lame of both his legs, so that he used to go shoving himself along on his breeches; they ordered him to be taken into their workhouse, intending to make him a tailor, upon which he confessed that his brother, a boy seven years of age, about four years ago, by the advice of other beggars, contracted his legs and turned them backwards, so that he never used them from that time to this, but followed the trade of begging; that he usually got five shillings a day, sometimes ten shillings; that he hath been all over the West of England, where his brother carried him on a horse, and pretended that he was born so, and cut out of his mother's womb. He hath also given an account that he knows of other beggars that pretend to be dumb and lame, and some that tie their arms in their breeches, and wear a wooden stump in their sleeve.[57]

But, if some entrepreneurial beggars faked their physical form, a much larger number of beggars on the streets of London were in fact disabled in some way. They were missing limbs, blind, ill, idiotic or simply insane.[58]

Wounds and disabilities were self-consciously deployed by the poor in order to excite compassion. They were important signifiers, which when combined with a humble aspect and a pleading tone, denoted real need. Whether those signs of poverty were faked or real is unimportant. Certainly, for many eighteenth-century commentators, the boundary was much more subtle and immaterial than a modern perception might suggest.

> We say that when nature is deficient in one part, she makes amends in another, and the observation is no where so true as in the beggars ... for when she sends a creature from the womb legg-less, and of consequence a dependent upon the next turner's shop for deputy supporters, she ever supplies him with much brown for a natural cushion, as knowing him more inclinable to the sedentary than the peripatetick philosophy. If she puts out his eyes, she enlarges the sense of feeling, and makes him an acute distinguisher between brass and silver. If she chops off his arms, she in return stretches the wind-pipe, dilates

the thorax and makes him capable of talking longer, and more to the purpose than a female scold.[59]

Faced with the necessity of making a living from charity excited by sympathy the truly disabled were forced to expose their broken bodies to the horrified gaze of pedestrian London, while the physically whole used what strategies they could to give the impression of both disability and poverty.

The motive force driving this behaviour was the effectiveness of physical infirmity in wringing charity from the tightly-closed purses of the well-to-do. More effective even than rags and lice, exposed wounds and missing limbs worked:

> When sores are very bad, or seem otherwise afflicting in an extraordinary manner, and the beggar can bear to have them exposed to the cold air, it is very shocking to some people; 'tis a shame they cry such sights shou'd be suffer'd: the main reason is, it touches their pity feelingly, at the same time they are resolv'd, either because they are covetous, or count it an idle expense, to give nothing, which makes them more uneasy. They turn their eyes, and where the cries are dismal, some would willingly stop their ears, mend their pace, and be very angry in their hearts, that beggars shou'd be about streets.[60]

Begging has always required its practitioners to deploy a complex language and visual rhetoric. You need to cajole without threatening, and draw attention to yourself without attracting the wrong sort of attention. You need to present a compelling case for charity in the split second during which a walker's eyes slide over the one aspect of your being that cannot be reduced or denied, your physical presence.

For the London poor who inhabited a visceral world in which the body's products, its phlegm and milk, shit and piss, had a meaning and power that we have since lost, using these visual clues came naturally.[61] Long before Adam Smith used the subtle tricks of political economy to turn human beings (or at least poor human beings) into mere ciphers for physical labour, the beggars and paupers of London had been obliged to learn the trick of thinking of their own bodies as a resource to be used and expended. They both sold their bodies for whatever price they could get, and at the same time maintained a strong sense of emotional and personal 'self-hood'. A clear mind-body duality was a resource the poor could not afford to live without. Not based on some high-flown Cartesian model, this pauper duality was the price they paid every single day in their efforts to wrest a living from the streets.

The accident, the tragedy that marked the beginnings of a life on streets, effectively forced beggars to look to the one resource they had left, their body. In around 1732 Samuel Badham fell ill. His feet became infected, and he could no longer wear shoes. In response to these events, to the decay of his feet, he went begging, 'a thick bundle of rags tyed under the soles of his feet, and with a stick in each hand'. For the next eight years his life fell in to a regular pattern, with an established route through London, allowing him to show his ragged appendages and wave his crutches at a new audience each day.[62]

In part, the power of disability to claim charity from the physically whole rested on fear. Pregnant women provided at least the excuse for commentators' opprobrium. Civicus, writing in the *London Journal* in 1731, thought crippled beggars: 'ought not to be suffer'd to wander the streets, exposing their distorted limbs, and filthy sores, such sights being frequently attended with the worst consequences to women with child'.[63] Joshua Gee agreed:

> As to those creatures that go about the streets to show their maim'd limbs, nauseous sores, stump hands, or feet, or any other deformity, I am of opinion, that they are by no means objects fit to go abroad ... considering the frights and pernicious impressions which such horrid sights have given to pregnant women (and sometimes even to the disfiguring of infants in the womb) ...[64]

Despite these concerns, the number of people begging on the streets of the capital with the transparent semaphore of a missing limb simply increased. In part this was the result of the changing nature of warfare, along with the absurd adventurism of the new 'fiscal-military' state. More and more soldiers and sailors, in particular, were faced with the limited possibilities open to a damaged man in this most physical of worlds. For well-to-do victims, for the Nelsons of the world, there was at least the consolation of beautifully crafted false arms and legs. For them, the services of Gavin Wilson of Canongate were readily available. In the words of George Galloway:

> Thank heav'n! I'm safely landed frae Ostend,
> My broken ribs and shattered arms to mend
> By famous Wilson of Canongate;
> These wings of my poor trunk he'll reinstate.
>
> ...
>
> Legs, thighs an' arms, to equip our battered hulls
> Toes, fingers, noses he must bring bushels.[65]

For most people, this reconstructive fantasy was not possible. The poor were faced with the stark choice of begging or starving. This was certainly the choice that Thomas Dargaval confronted in 1780 when he lost his arm to canister shot, and the surgeon's knife, while serving before the mast on the *Vigilant*. His response was to craft the story of his lost arm into a compelling military narrative, and to ask the ship's carpenter to help create a prop – a small wooden model of the ship. Armed with the story, his empty sleeve and the ship, he made a living on the streets of London.[66] Most disabled beggars had to make do with the less elaborate prop of a crutch.

If the empty sleeves and missing limbs of London's beggars formed a self-evident case for charity, and a clear resource from the beggar's perspective, these most obvious wounds were just one fragment of a larger repertory of physical representation. Blindness was perhaps the next most used disability. The *Blind Beggar of Bethnal Green* was an irritatingly saccharine play that was reprinted regularly throughout the century. More importantly, it reflects the equation in popular imagination between begging, and legitimate begging at that, and blindness.[67] Workhouses and hospitals, even the Foundling Hospital, regularly trained blind children in music, frequently in how to play the violin.[68] The prominence given to the blind cellist and disabled violinist and hautboy player in Paul Sandby's 1760 image 'The Asylum for the Deaf', simply reinforces this equation of begging, music and disability.

The expectation was that the disabled children and adults would support themselves through public begging, justified with a tune. The extent to which blindness both justified begging, and disarmed criticism can be measured by the case of Thomas Cooper. Charged with theft in May 1755, he claimed:

> The prosecutor wanted me to go into divers parts of the kingdom, to shew how the roads lay to the French; I was to lead about a blind man, but to enter into the French service at the same time; and he wanted me to go to the priest about it, but I would not ...[69]

That a blind beggar could be conceived as a cover for spying is a measure of the power of blindness in constructing a beggar persona. Equally revealing were the acts of wilful blinding committed by Anne Martin, alias Chapney. In 1761 she was committed to two years in Newgate Prison for 'putting out the eyes of children, with whom she went a begging about the country'.[70]

Of course, the other thing about blindness is that it is was one disability (along with deafness and the inability to speak) that could be readily faked. In 1705 Thomas Newby was arrested 'for binding up his hand pretending to be lame and his eyes blind'.[71] And in 1730 Samuel Gold was prosecuted 'for being an imposture and pretending to be blind when he hath [been seen] to play at cards ...'[72]

For men, in particular, these obvious signs of tragedy were important

19. Paul Sandby, 'The Asylum for the Deaf' (*c.* 1760). (*Victoria and Albert Museum*)

visual claims to legitimate relief. For women, pregnancy and the presence of children formed an equally compelling assault on the limited charity of passers-by. Ann Fretwell, alias Davis, was arrested in Newgate Street, 'pretending to be with child and imposing upon people thereby with intent to move compassion ...'[73] Many more women begged the streets with an all too real child on the way. The significant thing is that drawing attention to their condition formed a powerful begging strategy.

Babies, once born, continued to have a valuable role in begging. Elizabeth Evans's defence when she was tried for infanticide in the spring of 1740 was that 'she found [the baby] dead, and therefore laid it away from her; and before she would have killed it, she would have gone a-begging with it'.[74] There are very few images of ballad sellers, or female hawkers, or indeed female beggars, that do not include a baby, swaddled and slung across its mother's back. There are even real examples of women borrowing children for the purpose of begging. In 1760 Julian Harrington was arrested, 'wandering about the streets and receiving alms under colour of a pass pretending to be the mother of a boy she had with her who did not belong to her ...'[75]

The power of an infant child to wrest reluctant alms from the well-to-do can be more effectively measured in the frequent claims that beggars rented out small children from parish nurses and, more fancifully, from fully organised baby rental agencies. The anonymous author of the 1744 *A Trip from St James's to the Royal Exchange* recorded how he rambled:

> into the heart of the good parish of St Giles in the Fields ... At length I came to a place call'd the Infant Office, where young children stand at livery, and are let out by the day to the town mendicants. The first scene that presented was a little vilain of about seven years old, who, upon my asking him some questions, told me that his father had been a house carpenter in Dublin, where he broke his neck by a fall from a scaffold in repairing a cellar window, and died about seven years before he was born. A woman above fifty would needs hire a baby that was sucking at the breast; and another who had a complexion as sallow as a Portuguese sailor, must forsooth be accommodated with a child as fair as a smock-faced parson. One woman hired no less than four for the day, two she pack'd up behind her like a Scotch pedlar's budget, the third was to run by her side bawling out for victuals; and the fourth she held in her arms, like a tuneable instrument to be set to musick, when she came in the view of any seemingly well-disposed people ... A beggar woman, who was vastly in arrears for the lett of children, being refused any longer credit [threw] an old ragged riding-hood over her shoulders, cursing 'em for a parcel of unchristian old B – tches, in forcing her to tell the town ten thousand lyes, by saying she had three poor infants sick at home.[76]

20. Detail from William Hogarth, 'Industry and Idleness', plate vi, 'The Industrious 'Prentice Out of his Time, and Married to his Master's Daughter' (1747).

Many women with small children used them to deflect the accusations and expectations of prostitution. Mothers with children also had the great advantage that they were essentially able-bodied. They could follow a likely almsgiver down the street, and encourage their children to use, 'pray's and whines to touch the heart';[77] and to reward any benefaction with 'blessings and acclamations'.[78] Being able to move, even if encumbered with children, meant that people coming out of coaches could be more easily approached; while the ebb and flow of the city crowd could be allowed to dictate which squares and corners should be targeted at particular times of day. The power of children to touch the compassion of passers-by is reflected in George Parker's description of his encounter with a beggar woman and her five children:

> I came up with a poor woman and five children. The marks of a heart alive alone to sorrow and despair were painted in her countenance. I asked her 'how far she was going with those children on the road?' her answer was – 'The soldiers killed him!' – 'Killed whom?' – 'My husband and those infant's father. – We are perishing. – My husband murdered. I have no home – my children famished – no covering for my head but the clouds and the Overseers quarrelling about poor Sam's parish.' – She was jaded, faint and squalid. The children hung round the miserable parent, and exhibited an awful, a shocking picture of human wretchedness! I could relieve them – I did and purchased pleasure at the cheapest rate I had ever bought it for money.[79]

As with disability, children and poverty went together. The absurd claims to the existence of a 'Infant Office' in St Giles, reflects the distrust felt by the better off for even this most clearly poverty-stricken group, while George Parker's unalloyed joy at being able to relieve a woman with her five children reflects the power children could exercise over the hearts of the better off.

Regardless of their rags and disability, despite the hungry children in their train, at the end of the day beggars had to ask for relief. Commentators waxed eloquent on the tone of voice and language used. The author of the 1735 *Trip Through Town*, described the process as follows:

> a beggar asks you to exert [your pity] for Jesus Christ's sake ... He represents to your view the worst side of his ailments and bodily infirmities; in chosen words he gives an epitome of his calamities, real or fictitious; and while he seems to pray to God, that he will open your heart, he is actually at work upon your ears; the greatest profligate of them flies to religion for aid, and assists his cant with a doleful tone and a study'd dismality of gestures: but he trusts not

to one passion only, he flatters your pride, with titles and names of honour and distinction, your avarice he sooths with often repeating to you the smallness of the gift he sues for and conditional promises of future returns ... People not used to great cities, being thus attached on all sides are commonly forc'd to yield and cannot help giving something tho' they can hardly spare it themselves.[80]

Perhaps the most common variety of language recorded in the mouths of beggars was that of religion. And as the *Trip Through Town* suggests, even the self-conscious and dissembling used 'a great many scripture words' with great success,[81] appealing to a tradition of Christian charity in formulating their requests. At the same time it is also clear that many poor men and women in desperate circumstances felt their own sincerely-held religious beliefs helped to justify their appeals to the benevolence of their co-religionists. Certainly, James Dawson Burn remembered with real admiration the sincere religiosity of his otherwise drunken, beggarly and improvident stepfather, William McNamee, in his *Autobiography of a Beggar Boy*:

whether McNamee was drunk or sober, he never forgot to pray, morning and evening: and it was an amiable trait in his character that, whether in prosperity or adversity, he never let any of us forget the duty we owed to God.[82]

For most beggars the use of 'scripture words', the appeals to God and Christian charity, were simply a normal language of supplication to which no substantial meaning can be attached.

Other languages and strategies included humour and self-deprecation. Richard Steele records one episode in which humour gives the beggar authority over his erstwhile social superior:

at the corner of Warwick-Street, as I was listning to a new ballad, a ragged rascal, a beggar who knew me, came up to me, and began to turn the eyes of the good company upon me, by telling me he was extreme poor, and should die in the streets for want of drink, except I immediately would have the charity to give him six pence to go in the next alehouse and save his life. He urged, with a melancholy face, that all his family had died of thirst. All the mob have humour, and two or three began to take the jest; by which Mr Sturdy carried his point ...[83]

Steele was sixpence the poorer, and immediately quit the scene in a hackney carriage, but the sympathy of this crowd of Londoners was clearly with the alcoholic beggar. What 'Mr Sturdy' had done was use humour to claim the authority of good fellowship, to present himself as a good fellow, rather than a beggarly stereotype.

Soldiers and sailors combined an unique appeal to both their valour and their sacrifice. John Thomas Smith recorded one early nineteenth-century street beggar asking for alms in the following terms: 'My worthy heart, stow a copper in Jack's locker – for poor Jack has not had a quid to-day'.[84] Others still relied on perseverance to encourage almsgiving:

> The only thing the industrious Beggar has left ... if he can walk either with or without crutches, is to follow close and with uninterrupted noise teaze and importune them, to try if he can make them buy their peace.[85]

These same appeals could work as well for women as men. In the case of appeals to military valour, women needed to explain their husband's military connection, but it is nevertheless clear that such a connection helped to justify begging. Women also used the language of seduction and desertion with powerful affect. William Hogarth depicts a female ballad-singer bawling out a piece entitled 'The Ladies Fall' below the enraged musician's window, suggesting just how these facts of eighteenth-century life fitted into the narratives told by beggars.[86] Over the course of the eighteenth century narratives of seduction became more and more important to the popular culture of London's poor, and would come to dominate that culture in the nineteenth century. The petitions submitted to the Foundling Hospital for both the abandonment and retrieval of babies frequently feature seduction and abandonment. The growing habit of prostitutes to describe themselves as 'unfortunate' and 'misfortunate' speaks to the same development.[87]

Besides the content of the language, there was also the question of accent and vocabulary. An Irish accent bespoke poverty, but militated against a friendly reception. Different parts of London were also characterised by different vocabularies and accents. In St Giles, 'you had the blackguard slang of landsmen of all nations, mixed up with the technicalities of prigs and professional beggars ...' And in St Catherines, in the East End, 'you had the benefit of the jargon of salt junk and the fo'-castle, refined with coal-dust and the elegant vocabulary of Billingsgate'.[88] John Fielding described this part of London as 'another country. Their manner of living, speaking, acting, dressing and behaving are so very peculiar to themselves'.[89]

A beggar needed to hold his or her body in the correct attitude of supplication. Hogarth depicts a female beggar, a child strapped to her back, kneeling in grateful obeisance at the door of his virtuous apprentice on his wedding day. But most people stood in a more forthright attitude. Indeed, Henri Misson, in his late seventeenth-century memoir, complained that in London: 'Among the customs of those gentlemen [beggars] it is one with them to knock at peoples' doors as boldly as if they were the masters of the house, when they beg alms.' He goes on to suggest that beggars should follow the French custom of 'never giving above one knock and that a soft one, at the doors of a superior'.[90] There is even some evidence that London beggars took up Misson's advice. The *Tatler* describes a demonstration of door-knocking technique:

> he fixed one of his knockers to my parlour door. He then gave me a complete set of knocks, from the solitary rap of the dun and beggar to the thunderings of the saucy footman of quality, with several flourishes and rattlings never yet performed. He likewise played over some private notes, distinguishing the familiar friend or relation from the most modish visitor ...[91]

More typical than a knock on the door, and more generally understood, was to stand 'in a begging way', with a hand outstretched. If you were a man, you would be expected to proffer your hat to receive any alms. How you held your hat, whether it was in supplication or in threat, could mean the difference between life and death.

One final signifier of poverty, and one that could not be easily impersonated, was race. Throughout the eighteenth-century, but more particularly from the end of the Seven Years' War, London possessed a growing population of African and Black Caribbean men and women.[92] The vast majority of this community was integrated in to London's plebeian neighbourhoods and occupations, but there remained a highly visible group of men who became known as the 'Black poor'. After the American War many Black Loyalists, ex-slaves promised freedom and support in Britain in exchange for military service, found themselves largely abandoned by the British state on the streets of London. One group of six petitioners pleaded with the Commission for American Claims that their situation: 'leaves us, dark coloured Men, the unemployed, unprotected, and homeless objects of poverty, want and wretchedness'. Few received any substantial compensation from the Commission.[93] Besides the complex issue of race, many Black Londoners were also disadvantaged by the system of parish settlement and the Old Poor Law. Few could claim a parish, and this gave greater point and urgency to their claims for relief on the streets. The last quarter of the eighteenth century was also a time when the issue of the slave trade, slavery and its abolition was taking a stronger hold on the British imagination. When John Clare visited London and came across a 'poor African', silently begging near St Paul's, his response spoke strongly of the power of race.

> The sincerity of his distress spoke plainer than words. I felt my pockets but I had only four pence in all and I felt almost ashamed to receive the poor creature's thanks for so worthless a pittance ... I determined the next day to

get my pocket recruited if possible and give him a shilling and my first walk was to St Paul's, but the poor African was gone and I never saw him again.[94]

The claims of race on the alms of Londoners was such that a more organised attempt to provide relief, the Committee for the Relief of the Black Poor, quickly developed. As a result many Black Londoners were shipped off to the disastrous Sierra Leone settlement in 1787. Nevertheless, a small number of black beggars remained on the streets of London. In 1817, thirty years after the Sierra Leone disaster took the lives of so many, John T. Smith devoted several pages of his *Vagabondiana* to images and an account of the lives Joseph Johnson and Charles McGee. Smith observed, 'Black people, as well as those destitute of sight, seldom fail to excite compassion'.[95]

The practice of begging was difficult. People did it because they had to, because poverty and disability, alcoholism and desperation forced them to raise a hand, to expose a wound, to cry for help. The broader meanings attached to these beggarly characteristics cannot hide the real suffering that underpinned the behaviour of the poor on the streets. To present yourself as dirty, or disabled, as overburdened with children; to appeal to religious sensibilities or patriotism; to cringe and supplicate, to make yourself small and insignificant in the hopes that some more fortunate person would notice, does not change the real suffering involved. The usefulness of losing a leg, of being blind, of going naked and unclean, of allowing oneself to be eaten by lice, does not make these conditions less tragic. James Dawson Burn was a beggar boy who could not afford shoes even if his begging life would allow him to wear them:

> During the winter my feet were hacked in innumerable fissures from which blood was continually starting, when I washed them at night before going to bed (which was as seldom as possible) my sufferings were intense, added to this, my heels were [elongated] with the action of the frost, which caused me either continual pain or an itching, which was nearly as bad to bear.[96]

This reflects the tiniest fragment of the real human suffering, of the pain, death and distress experienced daily by the beggars of London – the physical cost of deploying a rhetoric of rags.

6

Begging from the Parish

On a warm and cloudy Thursday, 8 May 1766, Richard James, Henry Newton, Jason Herbert, Francis Leech and William Kippax, the overseers and churchwardens of the parish of St Dionis Backchurch in the heart of the City, went out for a meal to celebrate Ascension Day.[1] At Walter Stanisford's tavern they sat down to an asparagus salad, with radishes and spinach; they had veal and fowl, they ate six lobsters and three turbot, dipped in a butter sauce and gravy. They followed this with cheese and oranges, lemons and sugar. For pudding they had cakes and pastry, and to wash it all down, they drank gallons of beer, Madeira and punch. They spent over two pounds on wine alone, and the final bill came to £12 16s. – twice the annual wage of a female domestic servant. Afterwards, as they sat drinking strong beer and smoking the two shillings' worth of tobacco supplied by the tavern, the conversation might well have turned to the case of Paul Patrick Kearney.[2] A couple of years earlier, while the cold breath of winter clung to the streets and alleys of the City, Kearney, 'with the most sensibly heart felt grief and shame, blushing with sorrow, humbly applied to one ... of the churchwardens ... for common necessaries of life, as one of the poor ... who insolently refused him the same ...' This was the beginning of a seven year long struggle between Kearney and these well fed, but not uncharitable, parish officers of St Dionis Backchurch. Their struggle exemplifies the power and authority wielded by both the most desperate pauper and the most dyspeptic of parish officers.[3] It reflects the wide variety of strategies the poor might adopt, and the impressive range of resources they could hope to gain access to.

Kearney was well educated, possessed of a practised tongue and a fraudulent past. In 1728 he was tried and found guilty of forgery at the Old Bailey and sentenced to stand in the pillory at the gate of the Royal Exchange. He was also condemned to prison until he could pay a fine of £50.[4] A few years later, in the late 1720s or early 1730s, he fell in with Mark McCarty, a respected merchant shipwright, and set up a partnership in Fenchurch Street. It was this partnership that would later form the basis for his claim to a settlement in the parish of St Dionis Backchurch, but it also embroiled him in a positively Dickensesque case in Chancery. Mark McCarty died in 1738, leaving Kearney with power of attorney over his three orphaned grandchildren and their inheritance. The widow of one of these children later accused Kearney of falsifying his identity, forging both the power of attorney and the will of one of the grandchildren and of stealing money meant for their support. In submissions to Chancery verbose enough to require a small flock of sheep to supply the parchment, accusation and counter-accusation grew ever more bitter. Dead children back from the grave, elopements and false marriages, accusations of forgery and perjury resulted in a great deal of heat, but very little light.[5] The case finally collapsed in 1743 when, according to Kearney, Charles Kemp and Nathaniel Dealtry broke in to Kearney's home and stole his books and papers, leaving him 'so much impoverished and afflicted in body and ... ruined thereby' that he was driven to the edge of sanity.[6] By the late 1740s Kearney was writing to members of the government with dire warnings about Jacobite plots. In 1748, well after the Duke of Cumberland had earned his title of butcher of the Highlands, Kearney warned that three or four thousand Scottish men were ready to rise up at any moment. Lieutenant General Bland was sanguine enough to advise that the letter could be safely ignored, as 'the contents ... are so inconsistent with common sense'.[7]

If Kearney had suffered at the hands of the law both at the Old Bailey and at Chancery, and been treated with contempt by ministers of the crown, his most challenging entanglement with the British state was yet to come. Over the course of the 1750s and early 1760s his condition became worse. He was 'afflicted with a complication of distempers which disable him from work or labour without great pain and uneasiness of body, whereby he has been ... reduced to very great poverty and distress and want of food, apparel, lodging, furniture, advice, physick, nursing and accommodation'.[8] By the winter of 1764, barefoot and ragged he had reached rock bottom.

The parish he applied to for relief was a rich inner-city community, snaking its way eastward from the Royal Exchange along Fenchurch Street. Kearney approached Thomas Pope, the churchwarden, sometime in the winter of 1764, and was refused. Nevertheless, Kearney managed to raise a shilling's worth of charity from a Mr Read 'which saved [him] from perishing in the streets that winter night'. The next day he approached William Kippax, the churchwarden, and was refused again.[9] Kearney's next step was open to any pauper in the City of London. He appealed to the Lord Mayor sitting as a magistrate in the Mansion House Justice Room.[10] Outside of the City, local justices of the peace performed the same function as the Lord Mayor, and could and frequently did countermand the decisions of churchwardens and overseers.[11] In 1764 the Lord Mayor was William Bridgen, Esquire. Bridgen probably knew the churchwarden, William Kippax, as the two of them had sat together for three days at the Old Bailey in January that year, Bridgen as judge and Kippax as juryman. Kippax was also brought back in February to sit on a specially empanelled jury, again with Bridgen sitting as judge.[12] Nevertheless, at Kearney's request the Lord Mayor summoned Kippax to appear before him at the Mansion House. According to Kearney, 'Mr Kippax ... vindictively attempted to shew cause to his Lordship why ... [he] should not be relieved [and] told his Lordship several untruths ...' In response Kearney 'justly and truly contradicted' the claims and demanded that Kippax swear an oath supporting them. Kippax refused, and in response was given short shrift from the Lord Mayor, who declared, the 'parish can get no credit by giving this [man] such treatment ... and ordered [him] to be ... relieved'. 'Kippax then and there promised his Lordship to relieve [Kearney, and gave him] a note in his ... own handwriting directed to one Richard Birch in Rose Lane ...'[13]

From 1761 to 1767 the parish contracted out its poor relief to a 'pauper farm' or private workhouse run by Birch at the eastern approaches to the City.[14] To Kearney's horror he was sent outside of the parish and more ominously, outside the jurisdiction of the Lord Mayor. In Kearney's words the note he received:

> instead of being an order for [his] relief was a warrant of commitment of [his] body to imprisonment, labour or work in an infected filthy dungeon called a workhouse kept by ... Richard Birch, containing near one hundred poor victims to parish cruelty, but not capacious enough healthily to hold forty ...[15]

Nevertheless, Kearney was forced to move in to the workhouse in Rose Lane.

The conditions in contract workhouses were notoriously bad, but there is good reason to think Kearney overstated his case. From the beginning of St Dionis Backchurch's contractual relationship with Richard Birch and his pauper farm, the churchwardens regularly inspected conditions at the house, giving out six pence to each of the poor on the occasion of their monthly visits, and later providing every adult householder with an extra shilling a week in cash to spend as they chose.[16] On Thursday 11 June 1761 they:

> called the poor severally and inquired into their state – had no complaints. A motion was made to allow a pint of porter to each person in the house on the first Tuesday of each month and likewise to agree with Mr Birch to let them have a joint of roast meat on the same day instead of their usual dinner.

There is also some evidence to suggest the existence of a real sense of care and duty for the poor on the part of parish officers. Charlotte Dionis was a foundling named after the parish. In January 1762, the churchwardens:

> Gave Richard Roberts, Margaret Morgan and Elizabeth Thomas 12d. each on account of their standing gossips for Charlotte Dionis, and 1s. to Ann

Woolnorth for her care in nursing her ... The child wasting, ordered a nurse with a breast of milk.

Unlike many parish foundlings Charlotte survived to be weaned and fostered with a Nurse Collap at three shillings a week. And while complaints about conditions in the house were probably not especially welcome, this did not prevent the poor making them, or the overseers responding to them. In June, six months after standing gossip for Charlotte Dionis, Elizabeth Thomas spoke up for all the poor and demanded more beer be served on meat days. And when, two months later, Richard Birch struck Hannah Morris on the head, the overseers made a detailed enquiry and found

> that her refractory behaviour on her coming home drunk was the reason of Mr Birch using some severity towards her, but thinking Mr Birch had done wrong to strike her; after properly reprimanding them both, dismissed them ...[17]

Despite the relatively careful management of the house (at least by contemporary standards), Kearney was less than impressed and immediately set about forcing the parish to maintain him outside of the workhouse. A few years later he described his experience, and how he had been kept at demeaning and inappropriate labour to the damage of his health:

> Birch grossly insulted and abused and ordered [me] to work at emptying the soil out of vaults that pass in drains or sewers through under or in the said mock work house which so over came [me, that I] fainted and fell sick and was in that condition forced into a nasty bed ... swarmed with lice and the itch, mange and a malignant or pocky leprosy ...[18]

His obvious willingness to complain ensured that he very soon found himself back on the streets of London. After just three weeks and three days at the Rose Lane workhouse, on a cold and clear Monday in late May, he was discharged back on to the streets with a new great coat, hat and waistcoats worth some £1 1s.[19] During the next two months he received further items of clothing from the parish – a double cap, a pair of yarn hose, a single cap, until on 7 August he gained admission, at parish expense, to Guy's Hospital. Here, in his own words, he was put 'under the care of an eminent physician surgeon and apothecary who did all they could to cure him'.[20]

By early November Kearney had fully ingratiated himself with the steward at Guy's, William Robinson. Robinson wrote to the churchwardens at Kearney's behest, asking for 'some allowance towards washing his body linen', and suggesting that he 'is civil and good, and I have not had any complaint of him ...' By early December, however, Robinson's tone had changed. In a letter dripping with sarcasm, he wrote to the parish to inform the officers that 'the Great Paul Patrick Kearney was discharged ... yesterday much dissatisfied with the sister of the ward about washing money for his body linen, which he wanted her to pay him'. The parish had supplied two shillings for two months' worth of washing, with the expectation that the linen would be put out to an independent washerwoman. Instead, Kearney 'would not let her put his linen out to wash ... but would have the money himself'. William Robinson concluded that Kearney was 'a very singular man indeed', and promptly landed the parish with a bill of £2 2s. for his care at Guy's.[21]

In the spring of 1767 William Kippax had been replaced by John Haydon and William Lem as churchwardens for St Dionis Backchurch. For most of that year, Kearney was able to squeeze regular relief from the parish. Kearney later claimed that during this period he was 'often reduced to the want of every necessary of life and applied to [the churchwardens] who ever refused him relief ...',[22] but the parish accounts suggest a rather different story. From the spring of 1767 his name appears regularly against notes of expenditure amongst the parish vouchers. He received a weekly pension of between 2s. 6d. and 2s. 10d. The parish also paid 12s. for medicine to help cure his several complaints, including a course of balsalmic tincture and balsamic lohock or linctus. He was also given a new great coat, a pair of breeches, and a new pair of shoes.[23] In this one year alone the parish spent over £4 16s. 1d. on medicine and clothing, and at least a similar amount on lodging and a cash pension.

The following spring the identity of the parish officers changed once more. William Lem and John Haydon were replaced by John Green and a Mr Chesson. In the process the institutions of the parish and the City, which had supplied so many of Kearney's needs, turned against him. He later claimed that the churchwardens:

> went unknown and behind [his] back to and by fraud, art and false insinuations to Mr Alderman Turner when Lord Mayor of London [and had him] before his Lordship in custody with their beadle attending as a peace officer of London at the Mansion House ... as a criminal. His Lordship told [him] that he should not be relieved but go to the workhouse ...[24]

In the previous year the parish cancelled its contract with Richard Birch and transferred its poor to one of the larger pauper farms located in Hoxton, run by John Hughes and William Phillips – where, for 4s. per week, several small central London parishes boarded their poor. By this time Hoxton had become a veritable village of pauper farms, almshouses and private madhouses, including the Weavers' and Drapers' Almshouse, the Fullers' Almshouses, the Haberdashers' Hospital, Robertson's Pauper Farm, as well as Tipple's, and Hughes and Phillips'. St Dionis Backchurch transferred thirteen people from Rose Lane to Hoxton in early July 1767.[25]

Despite Kearney's plea to the Lord Mayor that he had never 'had the small pox, and that the ... workhouse was a murdering place', he was given 18d. and an order to present himself at the door of this 'mock workhouse in Islington'. Barefoot, 'near naked, near blind, near deaf and lost his smelling', Kearney walked to Hoxton, arriving too late at night to be admitted. Refusing this indignity, he turned his back on London and for the next two years seems to have begged his way across southern Britain and Ireland. He 'languished a long time at Bath and elsewhere' and 'went to Ireland to take possession of an estate there'. By early 1771, back in London, staying at the Ipswich Arms in Cullum Street, just off Fenchurch Street, Kearney was willing to chance his luck with the Lord Mayor one more time. On a cold and stormy Tuesday, 11 February, he swore an affidavit at the Mansion House before Brass Crosby.[26] He detailed his experience at Richard Birch's Rose Lane workhouse and his treatment by a succession of churchwardens. He claimed that the parish had retained his papers and as a result prevented him from collecting money due to him. He pleaded with the Lord Mayor, and described how, 'he has not had any food since last Tuesday and must have perished of hunger and thirst, cold and misery for want of apparel and lodging'.[27] Having taken the initiative, this time the Lord Mayor issued a printed summons requiring the churchwardens to attend, 'at the Mansion House ... at eleven of the clock in the fore noon, to answer the complaint of Paul Pat Kearney for refusing to relieve him ... Fail not ..., Brass Crosby, Mayor.'[28]

In the event the case was heard by aldermen sitting at the Guildhall the following day, and Kearney was once more sent to the pauper farm at Hoxton; 'into prison to be bodily and unlawfully punished and mentally tortured in a slaughter house for poor human bodies unlawfully kept by John Hughes and William Phillips and their accomplices'. When the churchwardens performed their monthly inspection of the poor in Hoxton, Kearney complained that he:

> was perishing of cold for want of clean, warm apparel and lodging, ill of a complication of the distemper occasioned by the cruelties exercised at ... Birches etc, and that I could not eat half the victuals allowed me because of my illness and their being cold and not warm victuals fit for an ailing person, nor any spoon meat, not even sage tea and but 3 pints of small beer which occasion'd my drinking more water there than beer daily ... I was insulted, tormented, vexed and otherwise constantly abused in so much that my life was a burthen to me there.

He was also threatened with Cope's Madhouse in Bethnal Green.[29] Faced with a stark choice between real incarceration and escape Kearney made one last deal. Although still living in Hoxton, Kearney marshalled the support of George Millar, the keeper of the Ipswich Arms in Cullum Street, where Kearney had lodged two years before, and advertised for work. He described himself as 'an English Protestant who has travel'd and at some of the Courts of Europe, acquired the most polite national as well as courtly and elegant pronunciation of several languages, which he was classically taught at home'. He offered 'Persons of either sex, any country or age' the opportunity to learn how to pronounce foreign languages properly, as well as suggesting he could teach, 'all methods of keeping accompts, at sea or on shore, correspondence, history, natural and moral philosophy, ethics, logic, rhetoric, algebra' and much more. He offered to travel wherever required, as long as 'travelling expences first paid him according to distance from ... Cullum Street, London'.[30]

Some time later, the advertisement generated a response, and he was offered the place of 'secretary, precept or clerk tutor or agent for three or four years out of England' to a Captain Scot. After haggling over the salary, but with Cope's Madhouse still hanging in the air, Kearney wrote one last letter to the churchwardens of St Dionis Backchurch in March 1771. He explained about the prospective position with Captain Scot, and offered the parish a deal, 'that I never would demand, ask or claim any relief of St Dionis's parish if you would furnish me now with about forty shillings to get my things to fit me for that place ...' He signed his note, 'Your afflicted and abused neighbour, P. Kearney'.[31] He does not appear in the parish records again.

To quote William Robinson, Paul Kearney was 'a very singular man indeed', but his relationship with the parish was not that unusual, nor was his ability to force the hand of the churchwardens. With none of Kearney's undoubted eloquence or charm, Catherine Jones, a disabled pauper settled hundreds of miles from St Dionis Backchurch, could be just as effective. In a series of letters stretching across the late 1750s, she forced many of the same parish officers who gave Kearney so much trouble, to treat her rather better. Whereas Kearney stood on his rights as an ex-householder, Jones appealed to both the sympathy of the churchwardens, and to their real fear that she would appear on their doorstep at any moment. An early letter reflects the pattern:

For Mr Piter yrhope in Fan church street London.
September the 2 1758

onerd sir I sent a letter a month ago. I herd no anser. I am very soray to be so trubelsum to you, but I canot help it for I am in gret want of relief from my parch. I have no where else to mack my complements, or i would not be so trublesum to you nor the gentelmen of Sen Deianis back church nor anney were eles … Heir everything is at gret prise but watter. Their is none knows what paines I do baer in my limes and I can not stire sum time for the ruptor, but I do keep my contyenas as well as I can or eles I should be sent to my parch before now. And if the gentlmen will be so good as to send me two guinies the frust oportunity or I must go the ofissers of this parch for I am in sum det heer, and when they will come to knows that I do belong to the parch they will humt me from heer as the did from Wrechame. Then I must come to london. But I do raether have to gunyes heir if you bless to tack the trubel to send me a letter wher the money is payed that I may go and look for it and not then have to such trubble to look for me. I can come to Sosbre in the Cartte that caryes the webes and the flannes to Mr foullns then he my see me and he may satisfy you of my infirmetys. No more from a poor poper Catherine Jones. Deerect for me att William Mories ner llangedweoon Demby Sier, North Walles. I hp to have relife soun from you, then I shall be bund to pray for my frins.

In her next letter she asks for a further £3 3s., and explains that she has since broken both her arms. In later correspondence, she berates the churchwardens for their lack of care, and threatens to put the parish to 'six pound carish, in bringing of me up' to London, praying repeatedly for more and regular relief.[32] Like Kearney, Catherine eventually ended up at Hughes and Phillips' pauper farm in Hoxton – they probably met each other there. Also like Kearney, Catherine was able to make a final deal with the parish:

Hoxton, 2 June 1772.
Catherine Jones applied for leave to return home to Wrexham in Denbighshire upon condition of paying her two guineas in hand and two guineas per annum, which was agreed, to also give her a pair of shoes.[33]

Maintaining Catherine Jones at the pauper farm in Hoxton cost the parish at least £5 8s. per year, so the decision to send her back to Wrexham, where the living costs were lower, where she had friends and some opportunity to earn a living, was a sensible one.

The system of poor relief in eighteenth-century London was extensive, expensive and remarkably comprehensive.[34] For the settled and parish poor, it provided a resource that could not be ignored, while for the unsettled poor and migrant beggars it represented a important component in their economy of makeshift. From the 1720s onwards most of the parishes of the City, Westminster and Middlesex created independent workhouses. By 1776 there were eighty-six workhouses, excluding the dozen or so pauper farms clustered in Hoxton and at Mile End.[35] Over 15,000 paupers were housed and clothed and occasionally set to work. Some of the houses operated by the huge urban parishes of Westminster contained hundreds of paupers. The house belonging to St George Hanover Square could accommodate seven hundred inmates at any one time. Others, like the house at Hampton Wick housed only a half a dozen souls.

The cost of maintaining these institutions was huge. In the same year of 1776, £174,274 1s. 3d. was raised by an equal pound rate on the households of London and spent on the poor.[36] Some commentators, such as Matthew Martin, believed that workhouses actually forced many on to the streets. He argued that the London poor were encouraged to become professional beggars by 'the practice generally prevailing in the metropolis, of refusing relief to paupers out of the workhouse ...'[37] In a similar vein William Blackstone complained that workhouses contributed to the root causes of poverty:

> A work-house tends to destroy all domestic connections (the only felicity of the honest and industrious labourer) and to put the sober and diligent upon a level, in point of their earnings, with those who are dissolute and idle.[38]

In fact, workhouses were simply one of a variety of sources of relief and care the poor needed to create a supportable life. They were not exclusive prison-like institutions of the sort that became commonplace in the mid nineteenth century. Although all eighteenth-century workhouses ran to a timed and structured regimen that meant the poor needed to ask permission to leave, there is little evidence that the adult poor were ever actively restrained, or even discouraged from moving out of the workhouse to alternative housing or employment. Instead, workhouses were general parish institutions that took on the character of emergency wards, and casual night shelters, of crèches and orphanages, almshouses and geriatric wards. They were frequently used for parish meetings, and were often the first port of call for anyone seeking to interact with the parish in any way. They commonly housed the parish fire engine and morgue. Larger houses had a 'workhouse chair', and almost all seem to have possessed a 'shell' or stretcher. These were used throughout the parish as an ambulance to transport accident victims, or to move sick inmates from workhouse to hospital and back again. Larger houses had dedicated wards for lying in, and many women entered London's workhouses only briefly in order to take advantage of this facility. In smaller houses, a collection of clothing and linen was set aside and loaned to women giving birth outside the house. Many workhouses contained dispensaries to treat sick and disabled paupers and the casual poor. And despite Matthew Martin's claim that little relief was available outside of workhouses, it was from the workhouse that weekly pensions were distributed to children and the elderly living independently. In many houses a proportion of the poor continued to live at home, while taking their meals in the house. Elsewhere inmates were encouraged to work outside of the house, and allowed to keep their earnings. Jane Dutton and Amy Holeman, for instance, were paupers dependent on the parish of St Botolph without Aldersgate, they 'go out daily to labour, and go to the work-house to lie'.[39] At the house belonging to St Helen's Bishopsgate the master actually kept a separate account book in which he recorded the weekly earnings of the parish children sent out to weavers as draw boys and to inns and pubs as errand boys. Most of the children at St Helen's earned between 2s. and 2s. 6d. per week; money that was kept aside for them and delivered up on demand.[40]

Some paupers, particularly older men and women, kept their own clothes and goods, and, if married, were allowed private rooms and the trappings of domesticity.[41] The few accounts we possess of life inside a workhouse reflect the porous nature of these institutions, and the existence of a world created by the poor themselves, rather than by administrators and parish officers. It was a world of poverty, loss and frustration, but it was also a world of individuals seeking to create a supportable life. Robert Blincoe, an orphan belonging to the parish of St Pancras, who would later make a name for himself recounting the horrors of life in a northern cotton mill, acknowledged that while a child at the workhouse in the 1790s, 'he was well fed, decently clad, and comfortably lodged, and not at all overdone, as regarded work'. By comparison to his later experience of factory life he looked 'back to Pancras as to an Elysium'.[42]

In September of 1778 ten-year-old Mary Sherwin was living in the workhouse belonging to the parish of St Sepulchre's. Her father worked in Bunhill Row, and Mary was probably left in the workhouse after her mother's death. On Saturday, 5 September the father was sent word that Mary 'was not well', and was 'fretted at not going to Bartholomew Fair'. On the following Monday, Philip Sherwin took the day off work and dropped by the house without any prior notice. In Robert Blincoe's words, 'when the friends, relatives, parents of … children came to visit them … caresses … were … exchanged [and] joy beamed on the faces of those so favoured'.[43] In this instance, Sherwin picked up his daughter and took her to the fair. The weather was pleasant, with high, thin clouds and Philip Sherwin, 'gave her some plumbs [and] a ride round the fair in a coach'. Afterwards Sherwin and Mary went back to his rented room and had tea, before returning to the workhouse.[44] The open nature of the institutions reflected in our few accounts of actual behaviour by workhouse inmates suggests a much more casual institution than published rules imply.

The high point of any week spent in an eighteenth-century workhouse was certainly Sunday afternoon. After church the day was set aside for visiting friends and family. All of the adult poor and most children would rush off to renew their ties to relatives and neighbours. Sunday afternoon also represented an opportunity to beg – to raise a shilling or two for a few luxuries.

Henry Danker fell on hard times in the mid 1750s and in May of 1761 found himself a pensioner in the workhouse belonging to St Martin's-in-the-Fields. According to Henry Smith, one the of servants at the house, he bore his poverty very badly and became increasingly 'melancholy', but his ten months spent in St Martin's Workhouse included a regular weekly visit on Sunday afternoon to his old friend, Paul Chatain, a corn chandler in Castle Street in Leicester Fields. Week in and week out, Danker went to Chatain's house for a drink and to receive a shilling's charity. Most Sundays he also stayed for a meal. In other words, he went begging for just enough money to see him in tobacco or a bit of extra food and strong drink during the upcoming week.

In uniform and with distinctive badges displayed on their sleeves the inmates of London's workhouses must have been a regular site at the kitchen doors of many households on a Sunday afternoon. In his evidence to the 1815 Committee on the State of Mendicity in the Metropolis, Sir Nathaniel Conant, head of the Bow Street police office, claimed that most of the beggars found on London's streets were in fact residents of the capital's workhouses. He divided London's beggars in to three varieties – the lame, the fake and workhouse inmates:

A third and a very numerous one, is those who escape for a short time out of the poor-houses under pretence of seeing friends or going to churches; under the system of the poor-house, there is a liberty of letting them out for churches and so on; and on a Sunday in particular, you will find the beggars whom you see about, quite a different character, older women, decent looking people, who press upon the passengers ...[45]

In the same evidence, Conant also claimed that many of the poor housed in the private pauper farms in Hoxton and at Mile End were allowed the freedom of the streets on several days each week on the understanding that they would beg money for food and drink, saving the contractor a few pence in extra victuals.

It is also clear that the internal discipline of London's many workhouses was far removed from the image painted in the published rules and orders so frequently posted on their walls. In smaller houses, in particular, the working of the institution was dependent on the goodwill of the inmates.

Nursing and cleaning, washing and childcare were done for the poor, by the poor.   The calm and sociable scene in the day room of the house belonging to St James, Westminster depicted by Augustus Pugin and Thomas Rowlandson in 1808 belies the assumptions of cold institutional rigour so frequently associated with workhouses.

In most houses there was a core population, perhaps 50 per cent of inmates, who formed what contemporary administrators called the 'workhouse family'. Made up of older people and children who could live in the house for years, workhouse families contained all the affection and loathing found in any family. There were hierarchies of age and intelligence and relationships that filled the gaps left by abandonment and death.

Around five o'clock on a cloudy Sunday afternoon, 3 July 1755, the half dozen children who did not have parents or friends to visit, were sent to play quietly on the top floor of Aldgate workhouse.[46] Mabell Hughes had been 'appointed to look after the boys ... and see that they did not behave contrary to the rules of the house'. She was 77 years old, and had lived in the workhouse ever since the 'hard winter of 1739'. Mabell was born in Greenwich and was apprenticed as a silk spinner and winder, which background probably explains the decision to appoint her to oversee the children's work at winding silk. In the assessment of the chaplain at Newgate Prison, however, she 'scarce escaped from being an ideot' and was 'as unfit to have management of children as to tame lions'. She regularly 'beat the poor children' under her care, and had a reputation among the other inmates as 'very cross ... to the children'. As a result the children themselves 'would often play tricks with the old woman' and were 'inclined to teize her'.

That Sunday afternoon, Mabell came in to the room where the children were playing and found Alexander Knipe sitting on a chest. Knipe was an orphan, born in the house eleven years before. Hughes knocked him off the chest, and gave him a sharp kick to the groin. Knipe died the next morning, his longstanding hernia ruptured by the kick. Everyone in the house knew Alex, and knew that he had a hernia, and after the kick he sought help from the adult inmates. He went first to John Cox, an older man, and showed him his bruises, and then went to Philip Watson, an elderly man who had lived in the house for a dozen years, crying with the pain. Watson sat by his bedside and tried to comfort him, bidding him to get some sleep.

Late in the night, Alex got up and went down stairs to the women's ward seeking out Mary Primmer. Primmer had helped deliver Alex eleven years earlier – 'the child used to call me mamma'. He came to her door crying for 'mamma Primmer', and saying 'O mamma, I cannot stand ... I am a dying, I shall die'. With Penelope Gilmore, another inmate, she helped him back up to bed and tried to comfort him. Thirteen-year-old John Trevilian

21. Augustus Pugin and Thomas Rowlandson, 'The Day Room at St James's Workhouse', from Rudolph Ackerman, *The Microcosm of London* (1808).

shared a bed with Alex, but on this occasion lay on the floor while the adult inmates sat, powerless, by the bedside. Travailan could not bring himself to let Alex, 'die in my arms'.

The only employee of the parish to appear at the trial that resulted from Alex's death was Sarah Cole, the workhouse mistress. She testified that Alex 'would not hurt a worm', and Judith Cosse added 'he would not hurt a fly, much more a worm'. On the basis of the shared testimony of almost ten workhouse inmates, mainly elderly men and women, Mabell Hughes was found guilty of murder on Wednesday 10 September 1755, and was hanged at Tyburn on the following Monday: 'her body to be dissected and anatomised'.[47] The remarkable thing is not Alexander Knipe's tragic death, but the emotional community of workhouse life exposed to the public gaze at Hughes' trial.

Despite their porous and occasionally homely character, workhouses were frequently loathed by the poorer population of London, particularly by householders. When a parish first opened a workhouse the number of pau- pers willing to enter its doors was regularly a third to a half of the number who had previously received pensions. Riots against workhouses were rela- tively common, and conditions were occasionally the subject of heartfelt outrage. In 1731 a shadowy group, 'the Christian-love poor', whose name at least seems to speak of mid seventeenth-century radicalism, published a pamphlet and ballad attacking the workhouse movement's most active early promoter, Matthew Marriott, and conditions in the workhouse he ran belonging to St Giles's-in-the-Fields. Sung about the streets to the tune of 'Death and the Lady', the ballad claimed that Mary Whistle, an elderly housekeeper in St Giles's, had been forced into the workhouse, and 'put into a dark hold, a place like the condemned hold of Newgate, and there ... upon, till eaten up with lice and perished with hunger ... at the end of eleven weeks, she died in a miserable condition'.[48] The accompanying pam- phlet went on to detail how one woman, dead in the dark hole, had her bones broken in order to squeeze her into the parish coffin, while another woman, dead in childbirth, had her fingers cut off; and a third jumped from an upper window out of desperation; and a fourth had an ear stripped from her head. The pamphlet claimed that it was a common custom for the bod- ies of dead workhouse inmates to be 'carried in sacks by night' and 'made an anatomy of'.[49] There was a judicial enquiry, and Mary Whistle's body was subject to a thorough post-mortem examination that suggested she had been well fed, but suffering from senile dementia, when she died.[50]

The dislike of workhouses expressed in pamphlets such as the *Workhouse Cruelty* was most strongly felt by householders who knew that in old age

they were likely to need parish relief. The wounded pride, snobbery and outrage felt by the anonymous author of the *Workhouse Cruelty* is palpable:

> a poor housekeeper ... brought to so low an ebb of fortune as to be obliged to
> ask relief ... instead of any comfortable relief he shall be then put into a
> workhouse with little or no difference made between the whore, the thief,
> the pickpocket, the chimney sweeper, the japaner, the link boy and this poor
> honest housekeeper ...[51]

For elderly housekeepers the offer of a workhouse place could be heart-
breaking, but for the beggarly poor, for the homeless and the truly
desperate, workhouses formed a suprisingly flexible and useful resource. For
the street beggars of London, for the whores, chimney-sweeps and link-boys,
a workhouse place was something to be valued and sought after rather than
disdained.

As much as workhouses provided a bed, a meal and a warm fire, they
were also the gateway for a wide range of medical and social services. Once
inside a workhouse a beggar, even one who did not have a legal settlement,
could be assured of some medical care, even if they found themselves
removed to another parish in due course. Most houses had originally been
designed on the assumption that the paupers they would contain would be
essentially healthy. Nicholas Hawksmoor's much imitated workhouse design
for St George Hanover Square, commissioned and distributed by the SPCK
in the 1720s, did not contain a separate infirmary.

In fact, the vast majority of adult workhouse inmates were there precisely
because they were disabled, or ill, or pregnant.[52] As a result, and along with
most other London workhouses, the house established by St Sepulchre's was
forced in to a major reorganisation within just a few months of its opening
in 1727: 'that an infirmary be forthwith provided that the unhealthy and
diseased be separated from the others, and the itchy and lousy people be
forthwith removed to the apartment assigned to them ...' As part of the
same process of reorganisation, and in common with most of the other
workhouses of the capital, 'an oven' was provided to bake the clothes of
inmates infested with lice and fleas, and as a public service to the poor living
outside the house.[53]

Like domestic service, time spent in a workhouse ensured that a pauper
would have clean linen, changed once a week, and a robust, if plain, set of
clothes. All institutions ensured that the clothes worn my inmates were
clean and in good repair, and many provided an entirely new set of clothes
to every inmate. The sheer quantity of wearing apparel required to clothe
the poor is reflected in the accounts of the workhouse at St Ann Blackfriars.
A typical male outfit, listed against the name of an inmate named Goodwin,

included a 'coat, waistcoat, breeches, two shirts, two stocks, two pair of stockings and one pair of shoes'; while a Mrs Smith is recorded as having 'A gown, a petticoat, two shifts, two capps, two hankerchiefs, two aprons, two pair of stockings and shoes'. Given the necessarily ragged state of many beggars, these lists represent an impressively complete set of garments. The stock of clothes kept by the same workhouse again reflects the extent to which one of their main functions was to cloth the poor. Besides hundreds of yards of woollen cloth, bayes, serge and linen, the house also held in reserve 'seven pairs of second hand shoes', '6 pair of bodices', '12 pair of childrens stockins' and '17 hankerchiefs for women', not to mention at least three of every conceivable item of clothing needed to outfit a man, woman, boy or girl in the style of a working person.[54]

Perhaps ironically, given the dour and forbidding reputation possessed by all institutions named 'workhouse', the trick was not how to escape, but how to get in. From the 1661 Act of Settlement onwards, every English and Welsh person had a legal settlement in the parish of their birth or apprenticeship, through marriage, domestic service, or by becoming a housekeeper.[55] To gain access to a workhouse you needed to demonstrate that you had a settlement in the parish. At first glance this excluded large numbers of the poor. Irish and Scottish paupers risked being shipped back to Ireland or Scotland, where poor relief was much less generous. Foreigners were similarly left at a disadvantage; although there is no case of a pauper being removed outside of the British Isles. At the same time, and while the workings of the settlement system have been lambasted by more political economists than there were beggars on the streets of London, it is clear the poor used this system to their advantage, or at the least, substantially manipulated it, and that it gave individual paupers a legally defensible claim on a substantial body of resources.

The threat voiced by Catherine Jones – that she would return to St Dionis Backchurch and claim her rights as a parishioner – is just one example of the strategies used by the poor. More imaginative still was that adopted by Mary Brown, a seventeen-year-old prostitute and orphan, when, on a Monday in January 1786 she went into labour. Mary's earliest memories were of living with her father and mother in a furnished room in Featherstone Court off Bunhill Row. In quick succession, when Mary was only three years old, her parents died, and she was sent to her godmother, a washerwoman named Mrs Langley in Rotherhithe, 'to live as one of her own children'. At the age of eleven she ran away from home, and for the next six years earned a living on the street as a prostitute. By 9 January 1786 she was lodging with a Mrs Davies in Jackson's Alley, a small turning connecting Bow Street and

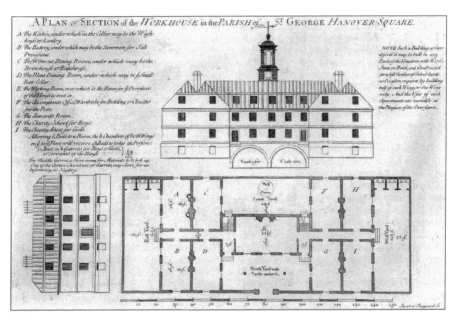

22. Nicholas Hawksmoor's design for the workhouse belonging to St George Hanover Square, built in 1726. BM, Grace Views, Supp. Portfolio xxix, 23. (*British Museum*)

Russell Street, just east of Covent Garden, 'several other young women who are common prostitutes on the town continually lodge there and are encouraged by the said Mrs Davies in the habit of prostitution'. It was a cool, cloudy evening.[56] Pregnant, and in need of help, she asked the advice of her landlady and a long discussion ensued:

> Mrs Davies ordered a coach to be called and told [Mary] that she must not stay there, that if she did she would be lost for want of help, and that it would be the best way for her to go to the workhouse. That she [Mary Brown] then told her that she had no parish, or settlement of her own ... Mrs Davies then said to the several persons about her 'we must send her to some parish, which is the casualty parish? Send her there.' ... She was answered by some of them, St Martins. 'No no' said she, 'St Clements is the best casualty parish, send her there' ... Accordingly Ann Pope, a young woman who also lodged at said Mrs Davies's, came with [Mary] to the end of the court, and ... was conducted to the coach ... She and ... Pope got in [and] the coachman was order'd to drive to St Clements workhouse [where Mary] paid him his fare ... Whilst in the coach [Mary] asked ... Pope what she should say in case any questions were asked her for that she knew St Clements was not her parish ... Pope then told [her] to say she had lived with her (Pope) in Greyhound Court (which this Examinant believes is a court in the said parish of St Clement Danes) and was taken suddenly ill ...

The mistress of the workhouse, confronted with Mary Brown deep in labour, first tried to follow the rules of the workhouse, telling her 'she ought to have obtained an order from the overseers before she could be admitted', but in the end Mary 'was taken so exceedingly bad in labour that the Matron was obliged to order her up stairs to the Lying in Ward where this examinant was afterwards delivered [of] a male bastard child ...' When Mary Brown was later examined, in the full knowledge that admitting to a settlement in another parish would result in her removal, she changed her story, and claimed the one place of birth that would allow her to stay in St Clement's workhouse. She said she 'was born on board ship coming from Ireland'. As a result both Mary and her little boy stayed put in the workhouse and St Clement Danes reinforced its reputation as the best 'casualty parish' in London.[57]

Gaining admittance to a workhouse as an accident victim, in labour or after spending a night in a watch-house was commonplace. Watch-houses, those all-purpose police stations and parish offices of eighteenth-century London, were a particularly important avenue through which the poor could gain admission. Many watchmen sent the obviously ill and desperate to the workhouse door, a note in hand, rather than marching them before a justice, as the law directed. But more common still was a direct appeal to the overseer, the churchwarden, or simply to the workhouse master or mistress. The parish vestries that attempted to draw up rules and regulations for the good management of workhouses continually struggled to keep control of the process of admission. Eighteenth-century parochial records are full of repeated orders on this matter. No pauper was to be admitted to a workhouse without a note from a parish officer, or without appearing before a subcommittee of officers, or even better still before subjecting themselves to a settlement examination in front of a justice of the peace sitting in petty sessions. But, in fact, and as with the internal management of workhouses, these arrangements only occasionally worked.

In 1781 the parish of St Giles-in-the-Fields and St George Bloomsbury published a series of *Hints and Cautions* for the overseers and churchwardens responsible for admitting paupers to their large joint workhouse. The author carefully outlined the ways in which individual men and women might gain access to the house. Each day of the week, except Saturday and Sunday, the parish officers were to attend in rotation at the workhouse at ten in the morning, ready to examine and admit applicants – the beadle standing by to make enquiries as to the truth of the stories retailed by the poor. The casual poor, those without a settlement, or who wanted just a few pence, were particularly directed to the officers sitting in committee.[58] But, most of the *Hints* were taken up with the much more difficult circumstance of officers acting on their own, responding to the poor who came knocking at their doors after the committee had risen. The author warns that the idle poor would 'invent specious tales of distress and put on various false appearances of misery' in order to gain access to the parish workhouse. And suggested that too undiscriminating an approach to relief would result in the vagrant poor resorting to the parish in large numbers as, 'It being their constant practice to enquire in what parishes the poor are best accommodated, and which of the officers are least acquainted with their artifices ...'[59] The officers were cautioned against admitting too many paupers suffering from venereal disease and to take care in dealing with those presenting settlement and vagrancy passes. But the author also recognised the real tensions and difficulties faced by a charitable man confronted by real suffering. He reminded future parish officers that their main role was 'to relieve and protect such of the poor as are infirm and helpless and to see that they are treated with care and humanity'. The pamphlet advised that each parish officer should see

> himself as the friend of the aged and diseased poor, and the parent or guardian
> of those who are in an infant state ... he should be ever ready to alleviate the

misfortunes of the distressed and generally to extend his assistance and protection to those who have none to help them ...[60]

The officers were to view the house as:

an asylum for the aged, for orphans in an infant state, for idiots, lunatics and the lame, blind, sick or otherwise infirm and diseased persons [and] such casual paupers as have not settlement in these parishes, whom it may be necessary to relieve for a time, on account of sudden illness or other calamity ...[61]

For most poor men and women, for the vast majority of beggars, suffering as they were from illness and disability, homelessness and dislocation, the parish officers could be relied on to at least provide casual charity, if not access to the more substantial resources of the tens of parish workhouses that dotted the map of London. They could expect to be treated like Joseph Bowring, who applied to Thomas Edkins, one of the Overseers for St George Hanover Square. Bowring went to Edkins's shop in Davies Street around two in the afternoon on a cold, clear Saturday, 2 December 1797, 'for an order to be admitted into St George's workhouse, and said he was a parishioner'. Edkins made some enquiries while Bowring sat quietly. It didn't take very long, and Edkins happily 'wrote him an order to be admitted into the ... workhouse and gave it to him ...' Unfortunately, Bowring collapsed in a fit and died just as he reached the shop door. 'A shell was brought from the workhouse in to which he was put and conveyed thither'.[62] Even the casual and non-settled poor could reasonably hope for some of the 14s. provided in cash each week to the churchwarden in St Giles Cripplegate, 'to give to casual poor at his own house'.[63]

Without a legal settlement getting past the workhouse door was only a temporary solution. Within a week of their admission most paupers could expect to be examined as to their home parish, and, assuming they were physically able, to be removed and passed. Settlement examinations required the signature of a justice of the peace, and in their written form seem to speak of dull ritual. But the examinations upon which these pauper scripts were based must have been dramatic occasions for the individual giving evidence, whose future hung in the balance. There were specific legal requirements for settlement, and the justice needed to be satisfied about each of them. On a wet and windy Wednesday, 28 June 1780, Elizabeth Gray was examined by churchwarden Bamford for St Helens Bishopsgate, probably in order to determine whether or not a justice needed to be called and a more formal examination drawn up. This would have entailed a shilling's expense for the parish – a charge Bamford was probably hoping to avoid.

He asked her a series of questions of just the sort hundreds of thousands of London's poor had answered since the passage of the Act of Settlement in 1661: 'With whom did Mrs Gray Live? ... At what wages? ... Whether her son and daughter or either of them have ever been at service? ... With whome and how long did they live in their respective places? Whether they ... were at service when she hired herself?' She answered the questions briefly, and Bamford noted that her son was currently in Jamaica, and her daughter had been provided for. He concluded that Elizabeth Gray did have a settlement in the parish 'by service' at the Welch Harp in Carnaby Street, Golden Square, where she had been employed for around eighteen months in the late 1770s.[64] In this instance, no formal legal document was drafted, but in most cases the justice's clerk would have translated his notes into the repetitive language of the law and asked the pauper to sign the statement – with a signature if they could write and a cross if they could not. The justice of the peace would then verify the document with a flourish and add the examination to the parish archive.

Whether you applied for relief, or were apprehended for begging and vagrancy, a similar examination would ensue. Ann Yeats, for instance, was 'apprehended for wandering abroad and begging in the parish of St Gregory in Norwich', in May 1778. Just like Elizabeth Gray she was examined, but in this instance a formal document was produced:

> Ann Yeats ... apprehended by Joseph Harper ... St Gregory, Norwich ... 16 May 1778 ... She is the widow of James Yeates who died seven years and upwards ago without leaving any child. That shortly after his decease she being then a singlewoman was hired to serve Moses Striff of Great St Helen in the City of London as house maid for one whole year from that time. That she accordingly entered upon the said service and served the said Moses Striff one entire year in the said parish of Great St Helen and that she continued more than ten months after the expiration of the said year in the service of the said Moses Skiff at Great St Helen aforesaid. And says that she has not since done any act or thing whatsoever whereby to obtain any other ... settlement ... The mark of Ann Yeats.

She was apprehended and examined on a clear, brisk Saturday afternoon, and legally, should have been imprisoned in the local house of correction for seven days before being whipped and removed.[65] Norwich had a long-established bridewell that John Howard described as 'convenient and ... clean' when he visited in 1776.[66] In the event, she was immediately sent on her way home to London with a copy of the examination and a pass warrant in her pocket, explaining that she had been arrested. Probably on foot, she was forced to set out from Norwich and reached the parish of Cringleford, just a couple of miles from the city walls, that evening. She applied to the constable, Roger Kerrison, who made sure she was fed and given accommodation before he signed and dated the back of her pass. Cringleford had neither a house of correction nor a workhouse, so she was probably put up in the barn of a local inn, or with a pauper family. The next day she would have been given a few pence to see her on her way. From 1740 onwards vagrants and beggars removed to their place of legal settlement were supposed to be passed from one house of correction to the next, day by day. Each night they were to be given food and a place to sleep at the expense of the county rate.[67] Some institutions even took on the character of specialised vagrant way stations. The house of correction at Bedminster in Somerset, for instance, was only saved from closure by a 1749 order of the County Bench that it should specialise in accommodating vagrants and beggars being passed to and from the West Country. This did not result, however, in the creation of a comprehensive network of houses of correction. Some counties actually closed their houses precisely to avoid this new expense of providing nightly accommodation to the vagrant poor.[68]

The next day, Sunday, it was raining and Ann Yeats travelled almost twenty-seven miles to the substantial market town of Thetford. She followed the route of a well-established trunk road and probably rode at least part of the way on a cart or wagon. Here the town gaol doubled as a house of correction, and Ann was almost certainly allowed to sleep in one of the two rooms reserved for 'delinquents'. On arrival she was brought before the mayor, William Holmes, who signed and dated the back of her pass. Assuming the assize court was not in session, when a large number of prisoners awaiting trial would have been housed in the gaol's insalubrious dungeon, she could easily have found herself the only prisoner. When John Howard visited the prison, in December 1774, he found only one prisoner in residence; when he visited again two years later, there were none.[69] On Monday, it was 'rainy and fair by turns', and Ann reached the tiny Suffolk village of Elveden, only three miles down the road and just over the county boundary, where Clement Tookie was the constable. Here there were no institutions of any kind, and Ann would almost certainly have been directed to a local barn. By Tuesday the weather had set fair, and Ann began to make better time. She travelled over seventeen miles and reached All Saints Newmarket that evening, appearing before Jonathan Age, who again endorsed her pass. From here she travelled sixteen and a half miles on to Great Chesterford, where William Gretton probably directed her to the castle, which served as the local gaol. The next day she went eighteenth and a half miles to Bishop's Stortford, in Hertfordshire, and then just under nine miles to Harlow in Essex. Harlow had a workhouse with some twenty residents.[70]

Many workhouses kept a few beds specifically for the casual poor and vagrants, and Ann was probably given one of these. She was now twenty-five miles from home, and finally reached St Helens Bishopsgate on Saturday 23 May. She had travelled some 110 miles in little over a week, and followed an established route.[71] She could confidently expect relief from each parish along the way, and would almost certainly have begged for food at kitchen doors as she went. For the most part the weather had been pleasant, and her pace was determined, but not challenging for a healthy adult.[72]

The authority provided by a pass can be gauged by its limits. Thomas Hardy and his wife overstepped the mark in early December 1732. They were travelling, pass in hand, and approached Thomas Wicks, the churchwarden for St Mary le Bow. First they demanded relief, and then a 'horse carriage to North Britain'. Wicks noticed that St Mary le Bow was 'quite out of the rout of the pass' and had the pair arrested and sent to Bridewell.[73] Nevertheless, their request for 'horse carriage' suggests at least a relatively high level of expectation.

There were different kinds of passes, and it is clear that the law intended the holders of these different slips of paper to be treated differently. Vagrants were theoretically meant to be incarcerated in a house of correction for a week, whipped, and then, in Middlesex at least, delivered by cart to the border of the adjoining county in the direction of their parish of settlement. Parish paupers were passed from overseer to overseer, and were the responsibility of each parish they entered. Soldiers, sailors and their families were simply meant to be relieved and sent on their way. A military pass was particularly valuable because it did not imply that you were necessary travelling to your parish of settlement.[74] From at least the 1770s, London parishes attempted to circumvent the system by using 'friendly passes', which, while having no legal standing, saved both parishes and paupers large amounts of money and trouble. Pre-printed forms for friendly passes took the character of a polite letter:

> To the churchwardens and overseers of the poor of the parish of St Peters Cornhill.
>
> Gentlemen, the bearer, Ann Brown, upon examination appears to belong to your parish. Your taking her without an Order of Removal will much oblige, and the like favour shall at any time be returned by, Gentlemen, St Luke Middlesex, 6 day of June 1772 ... J. White, overseer.[75]

A pass, whether it resulted from a settlement or a vagrancy examination, or had been issued by the War Office, or even informally by a parish, acted as a veritable licence to beg and was highly valued by the poor themselves. Along with apprenticeship indentures and settlement certificates, these legal scripts formed part of an important personal archive. The marks of repeated folds and careful reading on the collection of documents belonging to Rachael Jones and preserved among the papers St Sepulchre's, Middlesex Division, speak powerfully of their role in her life. Her own examination and her long dead husband's carefully preserved apprenticeship indenture provided her with a real claim on the parish.[76] Frequently, passes took the form of a printed document with the blanks filled in, and were regularly forged. There was even a canting phrase, 'Jackman', for someone who forged passes for beggars.[77] Eleanor Clark was arrested on a mild, cloudy Saturday, 19 June 1784, in St Andrew Holborn, 'wandering abroad with sundry passes under different characters and descriptions'.[78] Many more people traipsed the country with legitimate passes, and used them to wrest small sums from overseers and householders. The sheer scale of movement, and the costs involved is reflected in the plea made by the constables of Bridge Ward in 1745. Bridge Ward sits at the northern end of London Bridge on either side of Fish Street, and formed a necessary stopping off point for paupers and vagrants travelling north through London:

> This day the humble petition of John Nettlefold and Edward George, constables of the ward of Bridge was presented unto this court and read setting forth that from the first of June 1744 to the first of April 1745 four hundred and eighty persons have been brought by two hundred and seventy one vagrant passes from Kent, Surry and other parts southward of the Thames to the parish of Saint Magnus London in order to be conveyed through this City in their way to their respective settlements who have been received and conveyed by them ...; that they have been at great expence in providing victuals, carriage and often times lodging for them ...[79]

When paupers and military families are added to the vagrants, thousands must have trudged through the ward, seeking assistance with the help of a pass.

Perhaps the role of passes in the lives of the poor is best captured in the experience of James Dawson Burn. In around 1810 he accompanied his mother to the Mansion House, where she lied to the Lord Mayor in order to obtain a pass:

> My mother took the whole of the children into her charge, and made application at the Mansion House for a pass to Hexham, in Northumberland, as a soldier's widow, which she had no difficulty in obtaining; with this pass we visited nearly all the towns and villages on the east coast of England between

London and Newcastle-upon-Tyne. As my mother preferred taking the journey at her ease, and her own time, she frequently had the benefit of the cash that the overseers would have had to pay for sending us forward in a conveyance, and at the same time she had the advantage of the intermediate relieving officers, who were often glad to get clear of us at the expense of a shilling or two.[80]

A pass allowed the poor to access the very real resources available from parishes along their route. They protected the poor from punishment and legitimated the practice of begging – tying casual charity to the beggar at the door into the heart of England's system of social welfare.

Not everyone could access the resources of the parish, and some positively avoided the dependence such relief implied. Israel Potter, for instance, was both unsuccessful and bitter. He later complained how, towards the end of the eighteenth century:

> I had been driven to the necessity of making application to the overseers of the poor ... for admittance into the almshouse, or for some assistance, but never with any success; having always been put off by them with some evasive answer or frivolous pretence – sometimes charged by them with being an imposter, and that laziness more than debility and real want had induced me to make the application – at other times I was told that being an American born, I had no lawful claim on the government ... I soon found I was addressing one who possessed a heart callous to the feelings of humanity ...[81]

For others parish relief seemed demeaning, something to be avoided if at all possible, but for the vast majority of the beggarly poor parish relief was both available and desirable. Most beggars could rely on a few pence from the overseer, or a night or two in the workhouse, or some clean linen, or medical care and a pass. These were resources that fitted in to the jigsaw puzzle of economics that each beggar needed to complete. And perhaps most importantly, receiving relief did not preclude begging on the street, or moving on to seasonal work, or just moving on. Parish money, with substantial sums raised each year, was just one more facet of a beggarly lifestyle. It made possible the economy of makeshift that so many of the beggarly poor pursued. Neither the parish with its casual and outdoor relief and workhouses, nor casual labour and begging could on their own ensure the survival of the very poor. Together, however, they ensured that few people starved, and most could claim for themselves the common necessaries of life.

7

Charity in Stone

Late on a cold Friday evening in early January 1789 Thomas Perkins reached a new low. He was probably drunk and almost certainly ill, but one thing is clear, he was cold. The night was overcast and the temperature recorded at Greenwich that evening was 27 degrees Fahrenheit, five degrees below freezing, but Perkins was not wearing a shirt and had only one shoe, on his left foot.[1] Around his waist 'he had a sort of trowsers on, and was very indifferently and poorly clothed', and William Rotham, one of the watchmen employed by the rich Westminster parish of St Margaret's thought he was 'very cold and shivery'. At ten that evening Alexander Patterson was doing his rounds on Tothill Street when he saw Perkins collapsed in the doorway of the Rose and Crown alehouse. He called his fellow watchman, John Burton, and told him 'he had got a man there, that was bad' and asked Burton's help in getting Perkins to the watchhouse. Together they lifted Perkins to his feet, and assisted him the couple of hundred yards south to the churchyard, where the watchhouse was located. They sat him near the fire on a chest. Perkins thanked the watchmen for their help and 'hoped he had done nothing amiss'. He referred to himself in the third person as 'poor Jack the sailor', and pleaded, 'God Bless you I hope I shan't be turned out'.

The matter should have ended there, with Perkins spending a perhaps uncomfortable, but warm, night by the fire before being presented to a magistrate and charged with vagrancy the following morning. The magistrate would almost certainly have committed him to seven days in the house of correction before having him removed to his parish of settlement. But, the parish beadle, William Ashden, decided this was not to be. He thought he recognised Perkins, and said:

> 'oh you're an old friend of mine, you have been passed, you shan't stay here', and took hold of [Perkins] by the arm and turned him out at the door. [Perkins] said he hoped he would not turn him out, and Ashden then shut the watchhouse door, [Perkins] on the outside.

About an hour later the constable of the night, a man named Brooks, arrived and ordered William Skirving to go 'out to fetch sixpennyworth of crank' (gin and water) to hurry the evening along. Skirving saw Perkins standing under a tree opposite the watchhouse, and asked him, 'My friend, why are you here?', to which Perkins could only answer, 'Yes, poor Jack'. Skirving left him there, but a few minutes later, after he had returned to the warmth of the watchhouse, Perkins knocked at the door, 'desiring they would let poor Jack in'. Ashden again refused and told him 'he must go about his business, he had been an expense to the parish in being passed'. Nevertheless, Perkins continued knocking, asking again and again to be let in.

Three hours later, two further watchmen, Moore and Mowbray, came across Perkins shivering and naked in the street and brought him back to the watchhouse, saying he 'was a poor distressed man, and he must be there, and put him down by the armed chest near the fire'. Again Ashden threw him out on to the street, 'taking him under the arms, forcing him and shutting the door', while Perkins pleaded that 'he was very cold and wished to be let in'.

By five in the morning Perkins was near death. As the watchmen trooped back to the watchhouse at the end of their night's vigil, several came across Perkins, 'lying on his right side on the ground nearly opposite the watchhouse door'. William Knight, one of the watchmen, accosted Ashden and said, 'here is a poor distressed man, let him in', to which Ashden replied, 'he'd be damned if any patrol or watchman should bring him in there and flew to the door to prevent his being brought in'. Knight pleaded, 'He'll die'. And Ashden replied, 'Let him dye and be damned, and I will be answerable'. An argument ensued with all the watchmen contending against Ashden, and pleading to allow Perkins a space by the fire. Joseph Moone declared, 'he would not have any one die that he could prevent'. It nearly came to blows, and only ended when Ashden, a powerful man, took William Knight 'by the collar, jostling him very much about the watchhouse ... and ... forced him out and was thrown upon' Perkins's prostrate form lying at the watchhouse door.

Eventually, the watchmen convinced Ashden to allow Thomas Perkins to lie in the open cell below the watchhouse. He was sat upon a bench, the door left ajar, to await the morning. By 10.15 a.m. Perkins lay collapsed on the floor, unable to speak coherently. He was rushed to the parish workhouse and 'laid before the kitchen fire', but never regained consciousness.[2]

For the hours of night, between nine in the evening and seven in the morning during winter and ten and five in summer, it was the duty of the thousands of watchmen employed by the cities of London and Westminster, and the urban parishes of Middlesex, to keep order on the streets. And although historians have traditionally seen the night watch through the lens of the criminal justice system, and emphasised its role in arresting pick-pockets and footpads, the watch was also a final court of appeal for the truly desperate.[3] If you were sick and friendless, drunk beyond self-knowledge, or lacking a home on a cold night, the watchhouse was a beacon of warmth and relative safety. More importantly, a night spent in a watchhouse could act as a point of access to the substantial resources available to the very poor in the prisons and hospitals and parishes of the capital.

Every parish in urban Middlesex and Westminster had its own watch-house, while each ward in the City of London could boast a similar establishment. These houses were usually made up of just a few rooms, one frequently stacked upon the other. The cells were normally located on a lower ground floor, with the 'drinking room' above, and perhaps accom-modation for the watchhouse keeper on the top floor. The drinking room was the heart of the watchhouse. It was here that watchmen collected their lanterns and congregated before setting out on their rounds. It was also where prisoners were brought and examined. Food and drink were contin-ually available throughout the night, and its sale formed an important perquisite for the watchhouse keeper.[4]

Many of the sick and indigent used watchhouses to access the parish workhouse. It was a common practice to refer the ill directly to the work-house, rather than put them through the ordeal of an interview with a jus-tice of the peace. A note from the watchhouse keeper, who in this instance acted as a supernumerary parish officer, opened wide the doors of parish institutions to many men and women who had no legal claim. Even being arrested for vagrancy or prostitution and being processed through the crim-inal justice system could form a useful option for the indigent and the hun-gry. When, on a dark and rainy August day in 1782, William Payne, that most unsympathetic and bigoted of reforming constables, arrested three young women for prostitution he was directed to deal with them in a remarkably sympathetic manner. The Lord Mayor acting in his capacity as a justice of the peace ordered that one of them, Sarah Davis, be 'sent to hospital to be cured of a bad leg' (a contemporary euphemism for syphilis). A second woman, Ann Brooks, was simply discharged; while Payne was directed to search out the mother of a third, Mary Ivory.[5] And when Sir John Fielding was confronted by a similar group, he was similarly sympathetic:

> several wretches who had been apprehended the Night before ... were brought
> before Mr Fielding and Mr Errington; when one who was in a dreadful condi-
> tion, being all over covered with the Itch, was recommended to the care of the
> overseers; another who appeared guilty of no other crime but poverty had
> money given her to enable her to follow her trade in the market.[6]

Paid just a few pounds a year, and obliged to sit in their watch boxes or in the front rooms of private houses, and to walk their rounds once an hour, watchmen were the first people to come across the sick and the poor. A drunk asleep on the street, a homeless beggar unable to find a barn to rest in, a baby abandoned to the parish, or a desperate prostitute looking for work in to the small hours of the night were all the business of the watch. The City of London alone employed almost seven hundred watchmen by 1737, while Westminster and the urban parishes of Middlesex employed a similar number. Over the course of the century, as reflected in a slew of local Watch Acts, the night watch became gradually more numerous and more professional.[7]

> In every street [you see a watchman] carrying a stick and a lantern, who, every time the clock strikes, calls out the hour and state of the weather. The first time this man goes on his rounds he pushes the doors of the shops and houses with his stick to ascertain whether they are properly fastened, and if they are not he warns the proprietor.[8]

Watchmen carried sticks and lanterns, and wore visible symbols of their office, but they were not isolated figures of distant authority. They were part of a broader public culture that extended from the watch box all the way to the beggar at his pitch. The watch box itself was a distinctive and commonplace piece of eighteenth-century street furniture and forms a significant precursor to the nineteenth-century police box. The scene recorded by one anonymous early nineteenth-century artist reflects not the watchman's authority over the street, but his participation in its everyday rituals. The chimney sweep, soldier and basket woman, the salop seller and the watchman are all part of the same community.

The inclusion of a watchman, among fifty-one other beggars and streets sellers, as the four of diamonds in a 1754 set of illustrated playing cards, again reflects both the watchman's role in the community and broader social attitudes towards that role.[9]

Eighteenth-century commentators constantly complained about the elderly and ineffectual character of the watch. Henry Fielding held them in contempt:

> I think ... the watchmen in our metropolis; who ... guard our streets by night from thieves and robbers ... are chosen out of those poor, old, decrepit people who are, from their want of bodily strength, rendered incapable of getting a livelihood by work. These men [are] armed only with a pole which some of them are scarce able to lift ...[10]

And it is true that some watchmen were recruited from the poorest of

23. Anon, 'Woman Selling Salop' (1805). (*Corporation of the City of London*)

London's settled inhabitants. Henry Bailey, for instance, was employed as a watchman directly from the parish workhouse belonging to St Giles Cripplegate. In 1745 he was given, 'leave to go to watch for this ward'. His wages were taken by the parish officers, and he was given a penny a night by way of encouragement.[11]

Their sheer numbers, however, and the increasingly stringent regulations they were forced to obey, made the watch a much more effective arm of social and criminal policy than their detractors have allowed.[12] Anyone who was drunk and had a few pence to spare could ask a watchman to escort them home:

> Yet there are watchmen, who with friendly light,
> Will teach thy reeling steps to tread aright;
> For sixpence will support thy helpless arm,
> And home conduct thee, safe from nightly harm [13]

Foundlings frequently owed their survival and their names to the watchmen who discovered them wrapped in rags. When a female child was discovered late at night on 23 April 1741, she was taken from the watchhouse to the workhouse belonging to St Martin's-in-the-Fields, and later baptised Susannah Bird, after the watchhouse keeper, William Bird.[14]

There is also good evidence that watchmen frequently did everything in their power to avoid making an arrest. In 1774 Sarah Knight was working the streets of St Margaret's Westminster as a prostitute. Around midnight on one evening in September, John Barton, a watchman whose stand was by the door of the Red Lyon alehouse, saw Sarah having an argument with a man. He approached her and asked her to go about her business. Sarah answered, 'she would not go till she pleased'. Barton threatened her with a night in the watchhouse, and in reply she, 'called [him] many names and abused him'. Still, he did not arrest her, but came back half an hour later to find her alone in the same place. This time, Barton again 'desired her to go about her business or he would take her to the watchhouse', and she again answered, 'she would go when she pleased and would slap his face if he offered to touch her'. Barton meekly returned to his watch box. Sarah Knight was eventually arrested, but primarily because of her aggressive behaviour rather than as a consequence of her employment as a prostitute.[15]

If watchmen and watch boxes were part of the community of the street, watchhouses, where watchmen kept their great coats, lanterns and staffs, and where prisoners were held over night, acted almost as a community centre. Throughout the night, and during much of the day, you could be certain of finding someone at home. John Thomas Smith, a young artist living in London in the early 1780s, relied on the watchhouses for accommodation on cold nights when his fierce landlady refused him entrance after his twelve o'clock curfew:

> My finances at this period being sometimes too slender to afford an additional lodging for the night ... I fortunately hit upon the following expedient, which not only sheltered me form rain, but afforded me a seat by the fireside. I either used to go the watchhouse of St Paul, Covent Garden, or that of St Anne Soho ... having made myself free of both by agreeing with the watchhouse keeper to stand the expense of two pots of porter upon every nocturnal visit ...[16]

Beggars travelling with passes frequently stopped at the watchhouse for casual relief. In April 1782 Susannah McMullen and Sarah Forbes were travelling to Gosport with a pass. It was just a few degrees above freezing, on a clear night, when they called in at the watchhouse in Bishopsgate Ward Within.[17] They were arrested for vagrancy, but when two aldermen sitting as justices examined them the next day, the charges were immediately dismissed, as they 'had only taken the liberty about 11 in the evening of stopping at the parish watchhouse to solicit some small relief'. A shilling was given to each of the women as some small recompense for their maltreatment.[18]

Watchhouses were always noisy places, but could frequently be sociable. The neighbour of one Westminster watchhouse, Edward Kelk, claimed that he frequently heard noises from next door, and on one occasion, 'Orations, but whether they were rejoicing, or what it was [he] could not distinguish'.[19] Drink and food could be purchased throughout the night, while a fire and a ready conversation were always available. If you had just a few pence in your pocket an evening spent in a watchhouse could be quite pleasant; while if you had a few shillings the experience could be avoided altogether:

> Seek the constable's consid'rate ear;
> He will reverse the watchman's harsh decree,
> Mov'd by the rhet'rick of a silver fee.[20]

A night in the cells, usually located on the floor below the main drinking room, was less pleasant. In winter it was cold, and even in summer it was uncomfortable. But most people could expect to remain by the fire until four or five in the morning, drinking, chatting and sleeping, before being obliged to retire to the cells for the few hours left until morning took them to the justice's study.

According to the law, and innumerable decrees, watchmen, constables, marshals and beadles were obliged to arrest beggars. But they did not do so with any enthusiasm. During the course of the century there were some

24. Interior of Covent Garden Watchhouse, *c.* 1815. WAC, H137 Covent Garden Watch House (1). (*City of Westminster*)

25. Interior of the holding cell at St Marylebone watchhouse, built in 1729. WAC, T137 (2). (*City of Westminster*)

twenty-six new pieces of vagrancy legislation which theoretically made the legal response to begging ever more severe. Imprisonment at hard labour for seven days, whipping and removal were regularised, and by the 1790s were made mandatory punishments for male beggars. Rewards for apprehending beggars rose from the one shilling per arrest offered by the London Work- house at the beginning of the century, to two shillings each, paid by the City of London, to five shillings in 1744, with the proviso that ten shillings could be awarded in special circumstances.[21] Constables were particularly charged with rounding up beggars, and professional 'beggar-catchers' were employed by first the Governors of the Poor, and later the City of London. As early as 1705 six men were under contract to the London Workhouse charged with apprehending beggars, while later in the century reforming constables like William Payne, the 'little carpenter', earned a substantial proportion of their income from rewards for apprehending vagrants.[22] But even this level of remuneration could not overcome the distaste many constables felt for imprisoning the self-evidently poor. The emotional conundrum faced by watchmen and constables when confronted by a beggar is reflected in John Scott's sympathetic account:

> Can it then be justly thought a matter of surprise that the apprehension of vagrants is discouraged, rather than encouraged, by persons cautious of injur- ing their fellow-creatures? Avarice must have totally eradicated sensibility from the breast of him, who could deliver an unhappy human being to the whipping post, or house of correction, merely for asking charity.[23]

Beyond the dubious moral position of the constables and watchmen, it is also clear that any officer attempting to arrest a beggar was as likely to find himself the object of the unwanted attentions of the mob as he was to be the recipient of a 10s. reward. Philip Holdsworth, a senior City marshal complained bitterly about his officers' unwillingness to apprehend beggars in 1815:

> It is a duty that I have found the officers more unwilling to attend to than any other of their duties, for it is unpopular, and they always get abused when they lug these people to the prisons: After warning them, the people generally join with the mendicant, and the officers frequently are ill used; insomuch so, that one officer, the week before last, in taking up a sailor whose dog carries his hat, was seriously hurt.[24]

This does not mean that vagrants were not arrested. In the single year of 1739, 221 men and women were 'brought in the night-time by the constables to the Poultry Compter', a local holding prison, where debtors were held along side vagrants and felons awaiting transfer to Newgate. And hundreds, if not thousands, of vagrants were imprisoned and passed through the institutions of the capital each year. But it does reflect the extent to which it was relatively easy to avoid arrest. This contradiction lies at the heart of attitudes to beggars, and the ambiguous role of imprisonment in their lives.

Samuel Webb owned a horse and cart and sold greens about the City. He was confident enough in his social position to act as a character witness for a housemate, Thomas Holdsworth, when Holdsworth was accused of stealing four turkeys, two rabbits, one drake and two live fowl. In cross-examination, he was asked if he had been in custody during the last three months, and replied:

> No, nor within these two years. I'll tell you the truth; once I was a poor man; I went a begging, and was then taken up as a vagrant, but was never taken up upon any charge for any crime.[25]

The statute law of England would have flatly contradicted Webb's claim that vagrancy was not a crime. But few eighteenth-century paupers, or better off citizens, would have agreed with it. For many, arrest under the vagrancy laws was the only way to get home, or to get fed, or to get the medical attention they needed. Even arrest and imprisonment for more serious offences was frequently shrugged off as unimportant by the paupers of London, and was certainly not considered a matter for shame by many of them. Edward Courtney, a male prostitute, seemed entirely unconcerned when he was challenged in open court about the three occasions on which he was committed to Bridewell. He replied,

> 'Tis true ... I have been there three times, but was for no harm, and I'll tell ye how it happen'd. First I was servant at the Cardigan's Head at Charing Cross ... I abused my master's mother, for which I was sent to Bridewell ... Then I went to live at a Molly House, but my master broke, and in helping him to carry off his goods by night, a constable stopt me, and because I was saucy, and would not tell him where the rest of the goods were, I was carried before a justice and sent to Bridewell the second time. The third time was only for raising a disturbance about a Mollying Cull [cheating male prostitute] in Covent Garden.[26]

Ann Gowen was similarly blasé when, in 1735, she was confronted with her own long history of incarceration. When asked if she had ever been in Bridewell, she replied:

> Never but three times. I was an unfortunate woman and was drawn away by a man that I lived with for four years, and then I rioted him, and so I was sent to Bridewell the first time. Then I got a cut on my arm, and so I was sent the

second time: And the third time was when a gentleman said I had been vile with a man.[27]

Once arrested, a prisoner could be taken directly to gaol. The New Prison at Clerkenwell and the Clerkenwell Bridewell next door shared two rooms directly over the main gate for the reception of 'night charges'.[28] But most prisoners were held at the watchhouses until they could be examined by the justice. If found guilty, you were likely to be committed to a house of correction, and possibly to a whipping, followed by a journey to the county boundary in a cart, and eventual removal to your parish of settlement.

Houses of correction had originated with the establishment of Bridewell in London in the sixteenth century, located just by the Fleet River, and a stone's throw from Newgate and the Old Bailey. By the eighteenth century the City was also served by four compters or holding prisons, which combined roles as both a debtors' prison and primitive houses of correction. Outside the City, there were houses of correction at Clerkenwell and Tothill Fields, and south of the river there was the Borough Compter for debtors and vagrants arrested in Southwark. In Westminster there was the Gate House Prison, property of the Dean and Chapter of the Abbey. And beyond this, there were a series of more specialised prisons, such as the Marshalsea, King's Bench and the Fleet, which catered exclusively for debtors. There was the Savoy prison, specialising in correcting soldiers, while New Ludgate was formed out of the London Workhouse, and imprisoned clergymen and attorneys for debt. White Chapel prison incarcerated only those arrested for debt in the liberty and manor of Stepney, while Tower Hamlets Gaol in Well Close Square was kept by 'an honest Swede' in an alehouse.[29] Newgate, London's most notorious prison, was almost exclusively given over the incarceration of felons, although vagrants could occasionally be found among its inmates.[30]

Collectively these formed a rag-tag set of civic institutions whose roles were fluid, and whose administration was notoriously incompetent and venal. In the spring of 1776, John Howard visited each of these establishments, and:

> Summed up carefully the total number of prisoners in the sundry prisons [In] London and Westminster, together with three prisons in Southwark, viz. The King's Bench, Marshalsea and Borough Compter – debtors, 1274, felons etc. 228, petty offenders, 194. Total, 1696.[31]

Most of the 194 petty offenders Howard found were vagrants and the disorderly poor, and they would have been found primarily in the houses of correction. These were designed to set prisoners to work, and to discipline prostitutes and the disorderly, as well as beggars and vagrants. Debtors' prisons, where the majority of London's prisoners were incarcerated, housed men and women for years at a time, and were both less organised and less well funded than institutions like Bridewell and Newgate. In debtors' prisons no regular allowance for food was supplied, and the inmates were frequently forced to rely entirely on established charities and the good will of passers-by to supplement what little income they could generate through their own labour. The regime in debtors' prisons was also more relaxed than in houses of correction and gaols. John Howard claimed that: 'Gaming in various forms is very frequent: cards, dice, skittles, Mississippi and Porto-Bello tables, billiards, fives, tennis etc ...' [32]

Most vagrants, with wives, husbands and children in tow, found themselves in either the compters or one of the houses of correction, sharing wards with prostitutes, the disorderly and the lascivious. In one sample of people sent to the house of correction in Middlesex by justices acting on their own initiative or in petty sessions in 1721, 183 beggars were committed for vagrancy or as 'Loose, Idle and Disorderly' out of a total for the year of 1308 individuals. In comparison 501 were committed for prostitution, and 351 for theft.[33] And while some attempts were made to keep vagrants separate from other criminals, particularly towards the end of the century, most prisoners mixed freely during the day. In Francis Wheatley's 1787 portrait of John Howard, the remarkable thing is not the squalor of the prison scene but the presence of men and women, children and the elderly among the prisoners.

By the 1790s the process of transforming these prisons of the poor into reforming Benthamite fantasies had begun, but for most of the century they remained squalid and poorly organised:

> Vagrants and disorderly women of the very lowest and most wretched class of human beings, almost naked, with only a few filthy rags almost alive and in motion with vermin, their bodies rotting with the bad distemper, and covered with itch, scorbutic and venereal ulcers ... are drove in shoals to gaols, particularly to the two Clerkenwells and Tothill Fields; there thirty and sometimes near forty of these unhappy wretches are crowded or crammed together in one ward where, in the dark, they bruise and beat each other in a most shocking fashion.[34]

A beggar, arrested and committed to a house of correction, would have been taken by the constable from the justice's house, or from Bow Street, or from the Guildhall or Mansion House through the streets on foot to prison. Prisoners being escorted to the keeper's side of the house of correction at Clerkenwell frequently had to run a gauntlet of poor men and women: 'the alms people in Half Moon Alley are very disorderly and raise mobs and tumults when any prisoner is brought in'.[35] They were then delivered to the porter who was required to enter their name, and the details of their offence and punishment, into the prison register, before escorting them to the prison yard. Hundreds of men, women and children experienced the sense of uncertainty and fear Jacob Ilive, a printer convicted of libel, felt on the warm and cloudy July day 1756 when he was committed to the house of correction at Clerkenwell from Newgate Prison:[36]

> we walked immediately away through Smithfield to this dismall place, to which ... I was ... a stranger ... I arrived here between the hours of one and two at noon ...
>
> It was now I had the first opportunity to look about me ... and it being very fine weather, I observed a great number of dirty young wenches, intermixed with some men; some felons, who had fetters on, sitting on the ground against a wall, sunning and lousing themselves; others lying round asleep; some sleeping or lying with their faces in men's laps, and some men doing the same by the women ... The evening drawing on, I was alarmed by a loud and, as it were, menacing repetition of these words, All in, and all up. Which words were uttered by one who is here styled a locker; for he locks up about dark, all the year round, the prisoners in their several apartments. But such who have got money or their friends are there and treat them, such may go into the tap, call for what they like, eat, drink and then go to their beds, or lie on the boards. I soon understood the meaning of it, and the yard was quickly cleared of the prisoners.[37]

Ilive was reasonably well off, and was able to purchase a bed for the night, shared with a 'chum'. But even the best bed available was not particularly pleasant:

> The locker unlocked one of these cells or close wards as they call them, and holding the door in his hand, he asked me 'If I would lie in a bed'. I answered readily in the affirmative; and then he immediately subjoined, 'You must give me a shilling ...' I hesitated no longer, paid him [but], I slept little this night, which I conceived to be owing to the closeness of the cell, and the heat of the weather. I was forced several times to sit upright to fetch my breath. Another inconvenience was the piss-bowl, which now was half full of stale piss. In every one of these cells there is a large wooden bowl, which will hold a gallon, if not more, fixed in a corner near the head of the bed to piss in. This smelt so very offensively that it not only disturbed my rest, but made my head ache egregiously ... I also measured my cell and found it was in length about nine feet and about six side. I had almost forgot to tell the reader that the bed I lay on was a thin flock hard mattress, lying on a boarded bedstead. This

mattress also swarmed with lice, fleas, and bugs; insomuch that my body was greatly whaled.[38]

Most vagrants would have been hard pressed to provide the shilling required for a bed, or the money someone like Ilive would naturally expend every day to supplement the county ration of a penny loaf of bread. For them, night would have been spent with perhaps ten or twenty others, on straw, under a rug provided by the master. Ned Ward, in *The London Spy*, recounts a night spent on the Common Side at Poultry Street Compter:

I observed men lay piled in cabins one upon another, like coffins in a burying-vault, possessing only the same allowance above ground as the dead have under, their breadth and length, that's all. Other poor curs, that wanted the convenience of kennels (being supernumerary to the sleeping-huts), were lain upon benches, as if they had been bred up courtiers' footmen. Others coiled underneath like dogs and slept as sound as Low Country soldiers. Some lay round the fire, almost covered with ashes, like potatos roasting, with their noses in conjunction with one another's arses, like hogs upon a dunghill.[39]

There was also the difficult matter of the garnish money. Ned Ward was greeted with the cry of 'Garnish, garnish', and was to pay over two shillings to the other prisoners at the Poultry Street Compter.[40] At Bridewell, 'the prisoners demand one shilling garnish money of the new prisoners and if they have no money, compel them to pawn or sell their wearing apparel to raise it ...'.[41] As a result many prisoners were left not just penniless, but almost naked. When, at the end of the century, Francis Place visited a friend in Newgate Prison, he had to ask the gaoler to force the prisoners 'to tie up their rags so as to conceal their bodies which were most indecently exposed ...'. Of course, the offensive nakedness of the prisoners had the effect of forcing Place to collect '... all the halfpence I could and by throwing a few at a time over the heads of the felons set them scrambling, swearing, all but fighting, whilst [we] made [our] way as quickly as possible across the yard'. It is possible the prisoners's self-exposure was more instrumental than absolutely necessary.[42]

For some, commitment to the house of correction was literally a death sentence. John Arthur, for instance was imprisoned in Tothill Fields Bridewell in the spring of 1766, for an impostor, begging and pretending to be foolish. With other beggars, he slept on the straw in an open ward. Unfortunately, he was not an impostor and was mentally sub-normal. He could not speak more than a few words and could not control his own bowels. He was beaten by the master of the house, John Stevens, who was concerned that the noise John made and the smell of his urine soaked clothes would upset Steven's heavily pregnant wife. John was washed down every morning by the other prisoners at the pump in the prison yard, and allowed to sit out in the sun on warm days, almost naked. But even these precautions did not prevent John Stevens beating him severely with a large bunch of keys. An appeal was made to Sir John Fielding to allow him out, but to no avail. He ate his allowance and for weeks was able to maintain his health, until a mortification set in to his right leg and he died. Two surgeons were called, and the keeper was eventually tried for his murder, but acquitted.[43] What had killed him was not the harshness of the regime or the beating but his inability to keep body and soul together in the face of a new and challenging environment he was intellectually incapable of comprehending. Every death in a house of correction was followed by a mandatory coroners' inquest, but very few of these resulted in a prosecution. Ilive claims to have:

> seen five poor prisoners die for want of food since I have been here; on the death of one of whom I was myself empanelled as a juryman to enquire into the cause of her (for she was a woman) death. The jury found that she died for want, but then they also found that she did not die through any oppression or ill usage she had received from the keeper, or any one of his servants. And here the matter ended.[44]

For others imprisonment could include physical punishment, as well as the more commonly experienced short rations, hard labour and humiliation. There was always the likelihood of being whipped. The law directed that all vagrants should be whipped prior to being passed to their home parish. Sometimes this was done as an alternative to imprisonment, but it could also be in addition. Certainly, the Court of Aldermen in the City regularly reiterated its intention that, as well as being sent to the house of correction for seven days, 'vagrants and vagabonds as by law are to be whipped and sent to the place of their settlement'.[45] But, it is less clear how often the whipping actually took place, and how forcefully it was administered. In one detailed study of prisoners held at houses of correction in Westminster and Middlesex in the first decades of the eighteenth century, just over 50 percent were whipped on first arrival.[46] It is also uncertain how seriously this punishment was either administered by the prison authorities or perceived by the poor. Mary Saxby was taken up on a charge of vagrancy after singing ballads at Epping Market, and was committed to the house of correction for six weeks. Her experience is perhaps typical: 'As to being whipped, I know little but the shame of it; for he took care not to hurt me'.[47] And Ilive remarks that:

> Prisoners ... are often sentenced to be whipped privately. In this case their hands are fastened in a pair of stocks and their backs are stripped. And this

punishment many times is a mere ceremony, according to the disposition or temper the whipper is in.[48]

Whipping beggars and vagrants was also expensive. In 1792, after Parliament reiterated its demand that male vagrants should be whipped, the City of London was forced to spend five shillings per Bridewell prisoner having it done. In 1796 the City allocated £20 15s. 4d. to 'correcting' eighty-three Bridewell prisoners.[49] Justices were also notoriously unenthusiastic about having beggars whipped, perhaps, as John Scott observed in 1773, because there was, 'no distinction made between the vilest impostor and the most inoffensive accidentally distressed traveller'.[50]

Vagrants were also meant to perform hard labour while in the house, usually beating hemp, or grinding die woods, spinning or some other menial and laborious task. At the London Workhouse at Clerkenwell and at Bridewell in the City, prostitutes were 'made to work in the same dress they are brought in', making their labour doubly punitive.[51] For vagrants, labour was meant both to defray the charge of their incarceration and inculcate a new habit of industry. They occasionally received a few pence, the product of their hard work, by way of encouragement. Hogarth famously depicts Moll Hackabout labouring with her hemp mallet in the workroom at Bridewell, but perhaps more typical was the experience of her servant, standing by, adjusting her stockings, while a fellow prisoner sits quietly picking nits from her clothing on the far right-hand side of the image.

Regardless of the likelihood of being whipped, regardless of the real hardships of prison life, it is also clear that not every one found it an unsupportable experience. Henry Fielding, in a fictional representation of London prison life, claimed that 'the greater part of [the prisoners] instead of wailing and repining at their condition, were laughing, singing and diverting themselves with various kinds of sports and gambols'.[52] And Samuel Johnson compared it favourably with life on board ship, 'There is in a gaol better company, better conveniency of every kind; and a ship has the added disadvantage of being in danger'.[53] Through gritted and disapproving teeth, but with perhaps more direct experience of prison conditions, Jacob Ilive agreed:

they hourly, even while they are beating hemp, sing the most lewd songs men or devils have invented. They can scarce speak a word without swearing ... They take great delight in sitting in a ring, and telling stories of their own adventures; – how many men they had bilked, what sums they had robbed 'em of, and how many watches they had masoned. Tell who had their M[aiden-hea]ds; – how they were first debauched; ... As to their diversions, when they are not beating of hemp, they chiefly turn upon, Hunting the Slipper, Thread my Needle Nan and Prison and Bars. The men play at chuck-farthing, tossing up, Leap-Frog etc. They both take a particular delight in the Fairy Dance, called Rolly Powly, which is a very merry exercise, but abominably obscene. In rainy weather they will sit in the shed and sing in chorus, making a loud noise ... And thus they entertain and divert themselves. They are all both men and women great quidders and smokers of tobacco, and takers of snuff; and so habituated are they to both that they many times choose rather to buy tobacco and snuff than bread and beer.[54]

At night time men and women were separated off in to different wards, but during the day they were able to mix and socialise. Many commentators felt this inevitably led to sexual promiscuity and to prostitution, with poor female prisoners being particularly vulnerable. When David Thomas was released from the house of correction at Clerkenwell in 1705, he bragged to his alehouse cronies 'that he could have a whore every night'.[55] But it also meant that prison life was much more like life outside than it would later become. The presence of adolescents and small children with their mothers helped moderate the kinds of homosocial brutality that later single-sex prisons tended to breed.

In a similar way, although contemporaries complained bitterly about it, the existence of the taproom with its stream of visitors buying food and drink for friends, also helped to make prison life more bearable. Food could be purchased directly, or arrangements made to have it brought in from neighbouring alehouses. Salisbury Court was famous for its houses of prostitution, and gave its name to one of the century's most famous prostitutes, 'Sally Salisbury', but it also backed on to the Palace of Bridewell, just south of Fleet Street. The governors of Bridewell complained frequently of the 'communication of the women prisoners in the Matron's house with their companions in Salisbury Court', but this communication helped to support the women incarcerated there.[56] It was considered normal practice at the house of correction at Clerkenwell, for instance, for prostitutes to be sent broken victuals and a couple of pence a day by their bawd throughout the duration of their sentence.[57] And while commentators like Ilive certainly overstate both the pleasures and horrors of prison life, there must have been some people for whom the experience was at least supportable. He describes one woman as, 'sorry when her husband came, paid her fees, and took her out. She protested, she never lived better in her life, for she lay in bed ... she never was merrier, or ever met, as she said with civiler company ...'[58]

What must have made imprisonment for vagrancy more supportable as the century wore on was the growing level of charitable and medical care available. Despite the custodial nature of houses of correction, there continued

26. William Hogarth, 'A Harlot's Progress', plate iv, 'Scene in Bridewell' (1732).

to be at least a minimal level of relief available. At Wood Street and Poultry Compters food was always provided at levels well above the starvation rations of a penny loaf a day. In 1709, the steward of Wood Street Compter was ordered to:

> every day provide them [the prisoners] six sheeps' heads with the appurte-nances and that the same be boiled with oatmeal for broth for the sick and the flesh for those prisoners who are in health.

In the same year the steward of the Poultry Compter was ordered to:

> Provide sixty penny loaves each day to be equally distributed amongst the pris-oners now in the common wards ... over and above the allowance of bread they now have ...[59]

At Bridewell, around the same time, the diet included, a penny loaf, meal pottage, water gruel or pease pottage every day, with two meat meals a week, on Mondays and Thursdays.[60] In the 1770s John Fielding complained bitterly that there was no dietary provision at all at the Gate House prison. He observed that 'when a magistrate commits a man to that gaol ... he does not know that he commits him there to starve'.[61] And yet, a few years earlier, when James Smith died at the same prison, his continual receipt of a 'penny worth of bread every day' was brought in as evidence at the coroner's inquest.[62]

Nor was the provision of food the limit of relief available in the prisons. In 1781 Rebecca Burroughs was arrested for vagrancy and committed to Wood Street Compter. She was 'a poor naked woman [and] was ordered to be cloathed and maintained until she was able to go to her parish, the cloth-ing cost £1 1s. 0d.' The money was later reclaimed from her parish of settlement.[63] At Bridewell facilities for bathing prisoners and fumigating their clothes were created in the 1780s, and 'six suits of clothes for men and six suits for women prisoners' were purchased for those prisoners who needed them.[64] And at the beginning of the century in Clerkenwell, Susan Hall was given 'clothes to the value of 20s. and 5s. in her pocket to bear her charges', on her release.[65] By the 1790s at Bridewell, the provision of new clothes seems to have become almost commonplace.

> Finding Mary Edwards a person who was committed to this house ... almost destitute of cloathing and very much indisposed they directed the porter to apply to the Lord Mayor for proper cloathing and in case it should not be obtained they ordered him to purchase such cloathing as the matron should direct not exceeding 20 shillings.[66]

By the same period, the 1790s, financial rewards were being distributed for

27. Augustus Pugin and Thomas Rowlandson, 'The Passroom at Bridewell', from Rudolph Ackerman, *The Microcosm of London* (1808).

good behaviour. Mary Freemantle and Mary Guttrage were given three shillings and two shillings respectively to reward them for being 'extremely industrious' during their confinement; while Catherine Bryan, 'a basket woman at Fleet Market' was given a new basket, 'not exceeding 2s., she having behaved very well during her confinement'.[67]

Ironically, these formal sources of relief were substantially supplemented by begging. The very offence that had resulted in many prisoners being confined in the first instance became legitimate and even praiseworthy when practised on behalf of the capital's prisoners. Debtors and felons, as well as the petty criminals confined in the houses of correction, were all recipients of relief begged from grates in prison walls or by box men on the streets. The likelihood is that debtors formed the more compelling object of compassion, if only because no regular allowance was provided for them, but felons and vagrants could also make a good case for charity. And the profits of this sort of begging could be large. One keeper interviewed by John Howard even claimed that 'the liberality of the public is so great that we cannot keep the prisoners sober. Persons have even desired to be confined to have the liberty of begging at the grate'.[68]

On occasion the privilege led to disputes. In early December 1755 William Thornton and Thomas Gresham were both prisoners in Newgate. Thornton and at least one other man were begging at the prison grate, when Gresham approached him, calling him a 'ram's head, goat's head and buck's head'. Thornton pleaded with Gresham, 'let me alone ... let me alone to beg, beg for yourself'. And under the impression that Gresham was about to strike him with his one good arm, Thornton pushed him back. Thornton hit his head and died five days later.[69] You could not stroll past any of the many prisons of the capital without hearing the clatter of a begging box held out through the grate, or lowered on string from above, and the doleful plea:

Pity – the poor – and hungry – debtors – pray.[70]

Christopher Smart in his saccharine 1770 poem, 'Pray Remember the Poor', clearly thought the children of the well-to-do should be encouraged to give alms to prisoners:

I just came by the prison door,
I gave a penny to the poor;
Papa did this good act approve,
And poor Mamma cried out for love.[71]

'Box men' were also sent out to collect alms on the streets. In 1705 the box man employed by the King's Bench Prison, William Stevens, was actually arrested for vagrancy and committed to the house of correction at

Clerkenwell. He was later released, and a motion was passed incorporating a perhaps subtle distinction between begging for food and begging for money, reflecting the powerful ambiguity of the box man's role: 'Resolved that no boxman for prisoners be suffered to beg in the streets of this city, but basket men for prisoners may be suffered to come therein'.[72] Despite this ambiguity, box men retained their place on London's streets. Late in life Joseph Nollekens recalled a time in the 1730s when his mother took him to see St Paul's Cathedral:

> In going up that street, he observed a man running backwards and forwards shaking a box, into which many of the passengers put money ... for the poor prisoners in the Fleet ...[73]

And the figure of the box man was a normal part of most sets of London 'Cries' from the late seventeenth-century onwards.

Admittedly, box men were frequently complained of. In both 1760 and 1798 the Lord Mayor included all those 'going about as collectors for prisons, goals or hospitals' among his extensive list of occupations, the practitioners of which 'shall be deemed rogues and vagabonds', and for the apprehension of whom, a two shilling reward was offered.[74] At the same time the undoubted and well-understood suffering of prisoners ensured that box men were capable of presenting a good case for casual charity.

Indeed, prisons and prisoners were the objects of several charities that collectively brought a substantial amount of relief to prisoners confined for vagrancy. The Quaker sufferings of the latter half of the seventeenth century brought prison conditions to a wider dissenting audience, while prison visiting was made popular at the beginning of the eighteenth century by Thomas Bray, one of the founders of the Society for the Promotion of Christian Knowledge and a strong supporter of the Societies for the Reformation of Manners.[75] John Bellers took up the call in the 1710s and 1720s,[76] and by the 1740s the Methodists had made visiting and relieving prisoners a regular part of their weekly round, with Sunday afternoons, in particular, being given over to the care of the bodies and souls of poor prisoners. From the 1760s John Howard made prison visiting a near profession. All of which encouraged a widespread culture of charity directed towards prisoners. The money that was raised in this way was then carefully scrutinised and argued over by the inmates of London's institutions.

At Wood Street Compter, in 1709, the prisoners were given the opportunity to present their complaints to a committee of aldermen. At the top of their list was the misapplication of *their* charity money:

> Anthony Finney a prisonser ... says he has ... heard by the report of his fellow prisoners in the ... Compter that the charity money has been misapplied,

the drink in the cellar is purgative, [and] says Baskerville [the keeper] has beaten the prisoners for sending for drink.[77]

In the mid-1780s Josiah Dornford led a campaign for the relief of prisoners, and encouraged representatives from each of the capital's prisons to write to him, laying out their complaints. The substance of all the letters he received, was the prisoners' desire to take greater control over the charity money that flowed in to the prisons. The correspondent from the Poultry Compter wanted the £100 per annum, which had been granted by the Common Council in 1782 to four of the City's prisons in lieu of the right to collect meat and bread at Christmas time to be properly accounted for. The correspondent from Ludgate, writing on behalf of all the debtors confined there, praised some Lord Mayors and Sheriffs for sending in meat and coals on a regular basis, and for sending in fish confiscated at Billingsgate. But in the same breath he damned others for their lack of charity. He was particularly censorious of Sheriff Bates, who:

> In November 1784 killed an old cow (his own words) at Bacon's field and out of his abundant generosity sent to Ludgate 25lb. Weight for the prisoners to regale themselves with upon Lord Mayor's Day; but it was so very tough and dry they could scarcely masticate it.[78]

At the house of correction at Clerkenwell, even Jacob Ilive seems to have been impressed by the amount of charity flowing in to the institution. The Quakers, whose own workhouse shared a wall with the prison, regularly sent in cauldrons of broth and baskets of food for the prisoners, while the Methodists could be relied upon to help in a wide range of circumstances:

> There was not long ago, a poor woman with three children sent hither, till they could be passed. She was in a starving condition, without either money or friend, and both she and her children must inevitably have perished, had it not been for their kind and seasonable assistance. They gave seven shillings to Mrs Jones, and she bought meat for them, made them milk pottage etc. and gave them the dressing. This, with the county-bread supported them for seven days, when the order came for passing them away.[79]

Jacob Ilive himself was given two guineas to distribute to poor prisoners at Clerkenwell:

1. To Martha Knight and child, three pence a day for seven days, one and nine pence.

2. To Henrietta Church and child, one and nine pence.

3. To Anne Tongs, money, victuals and a pair of shoes, she was sick the latter part of her time, four shillings and a halfpenny.

Sold by H. Overton
without Newgate.

Remember the Poor Prisoners

Ayez Souvenance des Pauvres Prisonniers

Ricordateui di far carita a Poueri Carcerati

M. Lauron delin:

P. Tempest exc:

49

28. Marcellus Laroon, 'Remember the Poor Prisoners' from *Cryes of the City of London Drawn from Life* (1687).

4. To Andrew Ferguson, a poor man, sent hither by the Justices at Hick's hall, on Monday Feb. 21 for six months for begging, being passed. He had three pence a day (viz. seven shillings) for twenty-eight days ...

5. To Ann Middleton, one and nine pence.

6. To Mary Macgretter, fourteen pence.

7. To Minor Baskerville, fourteen pence.

And so on until the money ran out. He gave similar amounts to ten others, mainly vagrants and beggars waiting to be passed.[80]

If the county diet was more substantial than frequently represented, and if charity helped to make prison life more bearable, the real value of a period spent behind bars lay in the medical care inside prisons, and the possibility of transferring directly from the prison to the great hospitals, workhouses and civic charities of the capital.[81] A doctor inspected the prisoners at Bridewell several times a week, and throughout the eighteenth century the matron was given special responsibility for seeing that appropriate care was provided. Her detailed job description included this apparently onerous obligation:

To take care when the Doctor presents any medicines for the prisoners that they be rightly and duly administered according to his orders and prescriptions.

To make (when the doctor shall give orders for all the sick prisoners either men or women) proper sick diet and likewise attend upon them in all manner of distempers, which frequently happen to be distempers of the most infectious and nauseous nature, and consequently very irksome to the eye and offensive to the smell and there fore no small fatigue for the matron ...[82]

But it was not just in Bridewell, which Jacob Ilive considered a model of administration in this regard,[83] that medical care could be obtained. Despite John Fielding's concern for the lack of a standard diet, at the Gate House Prison an apothecary was always on hand. In the winter of 1763, Silas Barcotolf was committed to the Gate House and within a fortnight had become ill. The keeper immediately, 'sent for Mr Awister, an apothecary, who visited [him] and sent him medicines ...', but without effect.[84]

By the end of the century, at Tothill Fields house of correction a sick ward had been created.[85] It was no doubt on this ward that Ann Barker was placed when she was arrested as 'a rogue and vagabond' in 1798:

She was in a very bad state of health being full of sores and very offensive in consequence thereof, and was to have been passed to the parish of Poplar, but too ill to be removed ... Mr Hanvury, the parish apothecary, attended her every day and every assistance was rendered to her but without the desired effect ...[86]

Given the inevitable poor health and desperate circumstances, the relatively small number of deaths in prisons is striking. And although Newgate was particularly prone to outbreaks of 'gaol fever' or typhus, dramatically increasing mortality among both staff and prisoners, many prisons seem to have been remarkably healthy places. Despite Samuel Johnson's 1761 assessment that the Gate House Prison was so offensive that it ought to be demolished, it recorded only six deaths in the following five years, all determined to have been by natural causes.[87]

What was perhaps even more significant from a beggars' perspective is what happened after prison. If you were healthy, the completion of seven days' imprisonment for vagrancy resulted in removal to your parish of settlement, and either accommodation in a parochial workhouse, or out relief if no workhouse place was available. Having been punished, beggars were necessarily relieved. They became, at a stroke, the responsibility of the parish and the county. Indeed, having been removed at the cost of the county, and supported to the level of six pence a day during their journey, the parish of settlement had no choice but to accept beggars back. Even people without a settlement could use this process to gain access to parochial relief. In the spring of 1794 Mary Lovegrove and her infant child were repeatedly arrested and committed to Bridewell as vagrants. The apothecary examined her and decided that she was in fact insane and should be transferred from Bridewell to Bedlam. But in the process the prison subcommittee requested that the Lord Mayor:

> make her a casual pauper of the parish wherein she was last taken up, in order that she may be by them sent to Bethlem Hospital, and the infant taken care of ...[88]

Ironically, a beggar punished and removed, processed through the prison system and dealt with by the justices, had a more certain claim on parochial relief than did a more settled pauper applying to the overseer of the poor in response to illness or financial distress.

More significant still was the possibility of being referred directly to hospital or to one of the major London charities. The requirement that all prison deaths be subject to a coroner's inquest fed an ever-growing concern with the medical care provided to prisoners. The City of London in particular had an excellent and well-deserved reputation for the care it provided. In June 1705 Mary Collier must have been desperate. She had venereal disease and was begging on the street. The cost of curing the 'foul disease' could run to several pounds, and was certainly beyond her means.[89] The Court of Bridewell, however, ordered that she should be:

> Sent to the Hospital of St Thomas for cure of the foul disease and she being cured and brought before this court, it is ordered that she be sent to the churchwardens of Debtford in the county of Kent by them to be provided for, and that James Male one of the beadles ... do take care the same be performed ...[90]

Even impostors could access medical care in this way. Mary White was arrested in July 1747, a 'common impostor, falling down in the parish of St Nicholas Olave, London, and pretending to be in labour'. She was immediately transferred 'to St Barholomews to be cured of the foul disease'.[91] A cure did not necessarily spare patients the difficulties of a prison term, as many ill prisoners were forced to return to prison once their cure was complete. In October 1761 Ann Kettlewell and Jane Wicks were arrested for 'lodging in the open air', and committed to Bridewell:

> They are to be sent to St Bartholomew's Hospital, the one to be cured of a fever and ye other of the foul disease and when cured to be sent back.[92]

But time in hospital did ensure access to good food and clean linen, even if it entailed putting oneself in the not always clean hands of an eighteenth-century doctor.

A measure of the significance of this route in to the hospitals of London can be found in the massive 'cash books' kept by the City of London. Year by year, the amounts spent on capturing and processing vagrants was recorded. Money was spent to keep them alive during their prison sentences, and to pay for their whipping and their removal. But money was also paid to support them through illness. Gradually over the course of the second half of the eighteenth century, the City of London was forced to refer a higher and higher proportion of its vagrants to hospital for medical care. By the 1790s, the cost of these referrals had risen to an average of £756 14s. 1d. per year for vagrants clothed and supported in St Bartholomew's Hospital, and up to £1057 9s. 3d. for those referred to St Thomas's.[93] Almost £1800 per year was being spent giving vagrants and beggars the best hospital care available.[94] By the mid 1790s the magistrates were sending such 'great numbers of sick persons and infants utterly incapable of labour', that the prison committee responsible for Bridewell was forced to approach the Lord Mayor and aldermen, and to ask that they: 'confer with the governors of the two hospitals as to the necessity of adopting some measures for receiving immediately all such patients as the magistrates may think proper to send'.[95] And it was not just hospitals that could be accessed in this way. The Foundling Hospital and the Marine Society took children, and the Magdalen Hospital took women, from the prisons.

Mr Kirby was responsible for vagrants held at Wood Street Compter. In 1781 he submitted his annual bill for supporting 'poor vagrants until they were able to be passed to their respective parishes or admitted into the hospital [or] sent to the Marine Society'. For the single month of December 1779 he included the following people in his list:

> Susannha Wilkinson ... a poor sick woman when she died ... paid for her burial ...
>
> Sarah Davis, Elizabeth Infield} two poor women until they were taken in to the Hospital ...
>
> George Philips a poor boy for the Marine Society ... 10 days ...
>
> Charles Hill a poor boy for Marine Society ... 11 days ...
>
> Charity Nathan, Mary Hayward, Susannah Cooper} three poor women until they were passed ... 2 days lodging.
>
> Sarah Stacey, Mary Humphreys} two sick women ... until they were admitted into hospital. 2 days ...
>
> Eliz. Briggs, a poor woman until taken in the hospital ... 5 days ...
>
> Elizath Handley, a poor woman ... until she was passed ... 3 days ...
>
> Ann Stainsbury ... a poor woman ... hospital ... 5 days ...

In the calendar year of 1780 Mr Kirby relieved, supported and sent on to the hospital, the Marine Society, or their parish of settlement, 155 vagrants. His total bill came to over £109.[96]

For many, the apparent disaster of being arrested for vagrancy was in fact a boon. Uncertain and alone, perhaps unable to access parochial relief, the 'idle and disorderly', rogues, vagabonds and beggars, were reintegrated into the comprehensive system of parochial and private relief. In the process, the system itself was forced to respond to the real needs of the beggars and vagrants it housed, fed and occasionally cured. The ever-growing provision of medical care, in particular, is redolent of a system forced to provide new resources in response to the demands of individual men, women and children. That the system of prisons became better funded, and the conditions suffered by inmates more tightly regulated, was in part a response to the increasingly sophisticated manipulation of the system by the poor. Just as the criminal justice system, in all its wisdom, sought to manipulate and reform the poor, to force them to adopt new habits and new lifestyles, the poor themselves manipulated the system to their own ends.

8

The Begging Year

The beggarly poor were forced to make use of whatever resources came to hand. They knocked at kitchen doors and asked for food. They knocked at the doors of workhouses and watchhouses. They slept in barns and out-houses. They sold their bodies and their labour on the streets, and carefully crafted the image they presented to the world in order to encourage casual charity. They did these things, however, against a rough and varied back-drop; within the confines of a collection of assumptions and associations that changed with the seasons, with the days of the week, and the hours of the day.[1]

Looking back from the vantage point of 1826, Washington Irving lovingly catalogued the high days and holy days of Old London:

> The inhabitants most religiously eat pancakes on Shrove Tuesday, hot cross-buns on Good Friday, and roast goose at Michaelmas; they send love letters on Valentine's Day, burn the Pope on the fifth of November and kiss all the girls under the mistletoe at Christmas. Roast beef and plum-pudding are also held in superstitious veneration, and port and sherry maintain their grounds as the only true English wines ...[2]

If all the year was full of event, Christmas was nevertheless the highpoint of the beggars' annual round. As John Gay put it, as Christmas neared, Rosemary, Bay and Mistletoe:

> Are bawled, in frequent Cries, through all the town
>
> ...
>
> Now, Heav'n-born Charity, thy Blessings shed;
> Bid meagre Want uprear her sickly Head:
> Bid shiv'ring Limbs be warm; let Plenty's Bowle,
> In humble roofs, make glad the needy soul ...

At this time of year:

> Cloth'd are the Naked, and the Needy glad,
> While selfish Averice alone is sad.[3]

Christmas begging is still common. The dustman, the milkman, and the paper boy all expect a tip.[4] But in eighteenth-century London the culture of Christmas begging, and its corollaries throughout the rest of the festive year, was more widespread and more central to the lives of most Londoners than it has since become. Ritual begging as a part of communal celebrations was a facet of a shared culture of dependence in which the poor and the middling sort, servants and children all participated. The existence of this widespread culture of begging, and the participation of men, women and children from all classes helped create a context in which the very poor could ask for relief in safety and confidence. On high days and holidays, when householders and the well-to-do tolerated apprentices and servants begging through the streets and at their doors, it was difficult for them to then refuse the demands of ragged and hungry paupers. If parish relief and the extensive institutions of the capital formed two components of an economy of makeshift, the ability of every pauper to participate in an annual round of ritual begging, formed another.

One late seventeenth-century pamphlet juxtaposed Christmas against both fashion and pride, suggesting that a general hospitality at Christmas was the essence of good housekeeping and the *first* Christian duty.[5] During the Christmas of 1735, John Sherwin, a particularly devout and upright apprentice to John Low in St Bride's, partook fully of the most widespread begging custom – the Christmas box. In the weeks between Old and New Christmas Day, he eagerly counted up his takings, and, on a separate sheet of paper, listed who had given him how much, keeping careful track of the clinking coins in the tin box he hung by his place in the shop.[6] By the last day of Christmas he had accumulated around £3 in ready money – probably the single largest sum a London apprentice like Sherwin would see from one year to the next.[7] London apprentices had a traditional right to collect this money from all of their master's customers. Their tin or clay boxes, with a single slot at the top, formed an important symbol of Christmas, but, more importantly, when it was broken open, like a piggy bank, and shared among the apprentices, it gave meaning and substance to the season of good will, and embedded every apprentice in an almost universal culture of begging. Nor can we assume that simply because a boy or girl was an apprentice that they did not also beg on the streets. Charles Richmond was apprentice to a Mr Murray. At his trial for theft in 1791, he claimed his master, 'sent me out a begging' and on occasion had 'brought him eight shillings in one day'.[8]

Like apprentices, but without John Sherwin's tin box, servants could also make a considerable sum at Christmas. Household servants expected a gratuity from the tradesmen they dealt with in the day-to-day servicing of their families; while public servants – lamp-lighters, scavengers, delivery boys and the like – could ask for Christmas alms from the householders who collectively employed them.

A strong sense of right underpinned this annual financial boon, but one that spread unequally across divisions of class and gender. Most London apprentices were male, while most domestic servants were female. The use of a Christmas box by boys, and its absence in the pleas entered by women, reflects a different relationship to this sort of ritual begging – a different ability to claim the prerogatives of the season of goodwill depending on your gender. Boys, who were expected to be self-reliant, had a difficult time claiming the sympathy of almsgivers, outside the structured spaces provided by ritual.[9] Their begging behaviour was both extremely visible and frequently unacceptable. As a result they needed props to legitimise it. The girls and women who laboured as servants in the houses of middling-sort London did not need to reinforce their claim to charity in this way. Their begging was largely invisible, and certainly more frequently tolerated. For them beggary was always at their elbow – as close as a cross word with their mistress or the disappearance of a disregarded spoon. In many respects female servants were already 'objects of charity'. At the same time, and despite these differences, apprentices and servants, boys, girls, men and women used the authority of Christmas to help redistribute the wealth of London.

In 1746, Isabella Hannah, a household servant to William Montgomery, an insolvent debtor, lived in one of the raucous neighbourhoods adjacent to the river in the East End.[10] At Christmas she haunted the area around the Inn of the Highlander by Pelican Stairs in Shadwell, doing the rounds of all the neighbours and of her master's creditors, although she had only been working for him for a couple of months. When she came to William Smith, a lodger at Thomas Weymore's house some twenty yards away from Montgomery's, she asked for money for her Christmas box and was given half a crown. At first she went away, but came back a little while later complaining that it was not enough. In the spirit of the season, Smith gave her a further sixpence. When John Streeter went to one door and received only a shilling, he spat on the doorstep and walked off. The next year, when he came to the same door, he was given two shillings.[11]

Every London apprentice had a right to certain 'play days' each year. Even the least privileged apprentices could expect up to sixteen holidays every calendar year, including three and a half days for Christmas, and one and a half days for New Year. To all intents and purposes Christmas and New Year's formed a single long holiday, and was certainly the most important one. There was a well-structured and well-understood round to the begging associated with it. Between St Thomas' Day on 21 December – brought into the Christian calendar to replace the midwinter solstice – and old Christmas Day

on 6 January the poor had a growing number of opportunities to substantially increase their incomes. In churches up and down the country, queues
of the poor lined up to receive their pennies. In 1758 Thomas Turner
recorded how, 'This being St Thomas's Day, gave [thirty-three] people one
penny and a draught of beer for a Christmas gift ...'; while in 1773 Charles
Banbury gave out £2 10s. for 'the poor on St Thomas Day as usual'.[12] But the
real activity only began on Boxing Day – when the Christmas box was circulated. Every servant, apprentice and pauper, errand boy and street seller
was, for a few days, given the right to beg at the doors of neighbours and
shopkeepers, and to know that refusal would be a sign of bad fellowship.

In 1765, at Richard Birch's private workhouse in Rose Lane, Spitalfields –
a place described by Patrick Kearney as 'a slaughter house for poor human
bodies',[13] the poor of St Dionis Backchurch received 1s. each for their Christmas box (except for Thomas Gamuel, who was given only 6d.).[14] The
shilling piece personified as the eponymous hero of *The History of the Travels of a Shilling from Queen Elizabeth's Reign to King George II's*, an
advertising squib distributed throughout the 1730s and 1740s to popularise
the 'famous anodyne necklace', found its way into a Christmas box before
being exchanged for a subpoena and a warrant.[15]

César de Saussure, writing in the late 1720s, suggested that in the right
context a Christmas box could be very profitable indeed. He claimed that
Sir Robert Walpole's porter 'receive near on £80 as Christmas boxes'. He
remarked that although, 'this is a prodigious sum ... if you consider that his
master is first minister, it is not incredible, for some persons go to his house
so often and pay him so much court that they are obliged to give his porter
at least a guinea'.[16]

The amount you could collect was dependent on who you were and
whom you could depend on. John Gay pointed to this cruel irony in *Trivia*:

> Some boys are rich by birth beyond all wants,
> Belov'd by uncles, and kind good old aunts;
> When time comes round, a Christmas box they bear,
> And one day makes them rich for all the year.[17]

The parish of St Sepulchre's London Division made a series of fine distinctions when distributing its Christmas money to the men and women who
ran its workhouse. The master received a full £1 2s., while the man who set
the poor to work received 10s. The cook, washerwoman, school mistress
and spinning mistress received 2s. 6d. each; while their assistants were given
only 1s.[18]

According to the *Spectator*, the beadles and officers charged with preventing begging within confines of the Royal Exchange, having notably

failed in their duty, had 'impudence at Christmas to ask for the Christmas box, tho' they deserve[d]', according to Steele at least, to be beaten instead.[19] Jonathan Swift, in his *Journal to Stella*, even characterised the demands of the servants at his local coffeehouse as a 'tax':

> By the Lord Harry I shall be undone here with Christmas boxes. The rogues of the coffee house have raised their tax, every one giving a crown, and I gave mine for shame, besides a great many half crowns to great men's porters, etc.[20]

Jonas Hanway was deeply opposed to tipping of all kinds, and puts the following censorious words into the mouth of his plebeian ventriloquist's dummy, Thomas Trueman, 'I think it a most beggarly custom, to watch as it were, to pick the pockets of my Master's friends, after he has entertained them like a friend'.[21] Despite Hanway's reservations, the beadles of London's great hospitals eagerly accepted their Christmas boxes from the parishes of Westminster, which hoped to find their own paupers treated with greater leniency in consequence.[22] In St Martin's, in 1737, the insistent claims by nightwatchmen to be allowed the benefit of a Christmas box (possibly collected with unstated threats) led the parish to disallow the practice.[23] While in 1760 Samuel Lane, the Sheriff's Summoning Officer for the Liberty of Westminster, was convicted 'for having received contributions from sundry inhabitants, under the pretence of Christmas box, to excuse them (perhaps the most proper and fit persons) from serving on juries'.[24] When the early modern equivalent of the police assume that begging is a right, there can be little doubt of its centrality to eighteenth-century life

It is also clear that the annual boost to pauper incomes formed a central part of their calculations. In Henry Carey's 'Ballad of Sally in Our Alley' (1715), the Christmas box is the key to the narrator's future happiness. The eponymous Sally is the daughter of a cabbage-net maker, who:

> Through the streets does cry 'em
> Her mother she sells laces long
> To such as please to buy 'em;

The narrator is in love, and requires nothing so much as enough money to marry his darling Sally. His one hope lies with the turning of the year:

> When Christmas comes about again,
> O then I shall have money
> I'll hoard it up, and box and all
> I'll give it to my honey;
> And would it were ten thousand pounds,
> I'd give it all to Sally;

> She is the darling of my heart,
> And she lives in our alley.[25]

Of course not all apprentices were interested in marriage. In the three days after Boxing Day, James Sise, William Hayman, Richard Williams and Samuel Woodard managed to collect £4 16s. for their shared Christmas box, but rather than putting the money aside, they spent at least some of it on more immediate gratification. The apprentices accosted Mary Dodd as she walked home across St James' Park, and offered her 6d. from their hoard to have sex, on the grass, with William Hayman. She agreed, but thought better of the deal when the other three boys demanded sex as well, without further payment. She eventually managed to get away with £1 19s. 6d. from Hayman's inside pocket.[26]

Nor was it just the actual Christmas box that was important. The extended early modern Christmas was a period in which all kinds of begging became more legitimate. Christmas carols were a pan-European phenomenon from the fifteenth century onwards. In London they provided a regular, and predictable, opportunity for organised begging.[27] One group of 'Christmas Musicians' or waits were so angered at the promiscuous nature of carolling at Christmas that they determined to 'wear silver medals, with the impression of George and Dragon', and to advertise the fact in the press, in order to 'prevent impostors from obtaining money under false pretenses'.[28] The governors of Christ's Hospital were equally exercised. On 20 December 1727, the day before St Thomas's Day, when the round of Christmas celebrations began, they gave

> notice of an ill practice which prevails among the children of this house of going abroad to the houses of the governors and others in and about London especially at this season of year with a money box and the singing of carols in order to beg money ... To be stopped.[29]

In deepest Sussex, Thomas Turner recorded with some irritation the threepence he gave to a group of boys 'who came a-singing' on Boxing Day.[30] Similarly, Christmas provided a wide range of seasonal employments that bordered on begging. Rosemary, bay and mistletoe all needed to be hawked about the streets, providing employment to beggars with a casual connection to the countryside around London, and the health, energy and voice to cry their goods. Less obviously seasonal items, such as almanacs, also added variety to the wares sold about the streets. James Lackington, for instance, claimed that as a ten or eleven year old boy, he was employed 'to sell almanacks a few market days before and after Christmas ...', and that his success in this venture raised the envy and ire of 'the itinerant vendors

of Moore, Wing, Poor Robin, etc.'. One can only sympathise with the established hawkers, who, unlike Lackington, were dependent on selling their
stock of new almanacs for the new year.[31]

A carefully positioned beggar by the church door after a Christmas service could not be refused. Indeed, the extent to which casual charity, putting
'a penny in the old man's hat', forms perhaps the most important image in
British Christmas folklore reflects again how Christmas normalised begging.
Evidence of the extent to which the poor believed this is provided by the
number of vagrants picked up in the month of December. Early in the eighteenth century the Governors of the Corporation for the Poor of London
claimed that 'the streets and passages of this City are generally at this time
of year much annoyed with rogues, vagabonds and sturdy beggars'.[32] And in
one brief period for which we have a comprehensive list of vagrants for the
City of London, most months of the year saw an average of fewer than nine
examinations per month, while December saw over twenty.[33] This may reflect the authority's wish to draw a line between virtuous Christmas begging
and vagrancy, but it is clear that most other people could not. Thomas
D'Urfey certainly saw few distinctions when, in *Collin's Walk Through
London*, he had one of his protagonists claim:

> I came … of a good kind,
> So much to charity inclin'd,
> That even vagabonds and mumpers
> Have from my bounty had full bumpers,
> The blind and cripples in the street,
> I've oft reliev'd with broken meat;
> And many a Christmas Wassail Bowl,
> Has felt the largess of my soul.[34]

Food was another significant component of the round of Christmas begging. Broken food begged at a kitchen door during a period of feasting could
hardly be denied. It is clear that, whether the food was begged or not, the
poor genuinely looked forward to eating well at Christmas. The memory of
food at Christmas was so powerful that it could even insert itself in to the
driest of records. In 1746 Susan Browning, a young parish orphan from
Henfield in mid Sussex, couldn't resist telling the examining justice about
the shoulder of mutton, plum pudding, white cabbage and turnips she had
enjoyed with her allegedly brutal master the year before.[35] Of course, some
customs were upheld more fully in the country. Few Londoners could
expect the 'string of hogs-puddings with a pack of cards' Mr Spectator's
good friend, Sir Roger De Coverly, claimed to distribute each year to the
poor of his parish. But, like their country brethren, Londoners 'would suffer

very much from their poverty and cold, if they had not good cheer, warm fires and Christmas Gambols to support them'.[36]

The poor at the workhouse just off Chick Lane, belonging to St Sepulchres London Division, must have been in two minds about their Christmas feast. Located within a few yards of the rancid smell of the massive sheep pens next to Smithfield Market, the one hundred and fifty workhouse inmates living in the house at the time must have been disappointed to be find mutton instead of beef added to their usual diet on Christmas Day 1736.[37] While relatively well fed, they must have envied the inhabitants of the workhouse belonging to the united parishes of St Mary le Bow, St Pancras Soper Lane and All Hallows Honey Lane in 1733 who had roast beef, plum pudding and strong ale.[38]

The long holiday of Christmas only came to an end with Twelfth Day, or Old Christmas Day, on 6 January. In a final explosion of disorder, the apprentices of London took to the streets, assaulting their elders and betters. Francis Place (who claimed, as an apprentice, to have been given seventeen days off each year for Christmas and Whitsun) described his activities on Twelfth Day:

> On this day they used to divert themselves [by] nailing peoples cloaths to pastry cooks shops ... Each boy had a hammer and a quantity of short clout nails about three fourths of an inch long with broad flat head ... The noisy mirth these pranks occasioned was not confined to the boys who did the mischief, but was partaken of by grown persons, who ought to have known better; not by any means by the lowest of the people, but by those who were well dressed. These persons used to give the boys money to buy nails, and have been nailed themselves while in the act of giving the money.[39]

With this final levy on the purses of the better off, Christmas came to an end. Many hard-pressed shopkeepers must have been grateful to see the back of it.

Christmas was only the most important and universally observed period of legitimised public begging. Throughout the year different holidays had their own rituals and customs, and public begging of one sort or another was a common aspect of several of them. For alms givers each season had its own obligations; and, for beggars and the beggarly poor, each season its own opportunities. From 1718 the apprentices at Bridewell, there for training rather than punishment, and housed separately from the prisoners, could see the printed list of all their holidays posted on the wall of their workshops. Besides the five days they were given at Christmas and New Year, the apprentices at Bridewell could look forward to a half day off on

Shrove Tuesday, two and a half days at Easter, a half day for May Day, one full day for 'Restoration Day' on 30 May (awarded to encourage loyalty to the Protestant succession) and two and a half at Whitsun. The later part of the year had frequent, shorter holidays. Accession Day on 2 August, Election Day, Bartholomewtide, 2 September and 5 November for Guy Fawkes were all holidays of either a half or full day. Most people in London also took the eight hanging days a year as holidays, allowing them to witness the deaths of malefactors at Tyburn:

> a hanging day was to all intents and purposes a fair day. The streets from New-gate to Tyburn were thronged with people and all the windows of the houses were filled. The friends and acquaintance of those going to be hanged used to follow the carts in which the criminals were sealed, and if any one bore his fate with indifference or bravado he was occasionally applauded. People used to wait the coming of the carts in different places, some holding a pot of beer in their hands, others a measure of gin, to treat the criminals for which purpose the cart occasionally made a stop. Others threw oranges and apples to them. Pyemen and them with gingerbread nuts and other things bawl'd about [and] songs were sung and the ballads sold at the corners of the streets all along Holborn, St Giles's and Oxford Street.[40]

In relation to legitimate begging, the important holidays were May Day and Guy Fawkes; while lesser events such as the Lord Mayor's Procession provided additional moments of generosity.[41]   May Day was particularly important for milkmaids, chimney-sweeps, bunters and cinder sifters, and a popular subject for contemporary painters. Over the course of the eighteenth century, it gradually evolved to include props. And ever more emphasis was placed on the begging associated with the event. In 1817 J. T. Smith looked back to the eighteenth-century May Day in his *Vagabondiana*. He bemoaned the 'indecent conduct [of men who] hire old dresses and join the chimney sweepers, cinder-shifters or bunters' garland, or Jack in the Green, etc. and exhibit all sorts of grimace and ribaldry to extort money from their numerous admirers'.[42] In 1802 Robert Southey indulgently recorded how London chimney-sweeps made an attractive sight on May Day: 'Their table is spread under the maypole; their playmates beg with a plate ... and all dance round ... hand in hand.'[43]

For Pierre Jean Grosley, that most caustic of foreign visitors, May Day was just one more irritating activity, along with rioting and insolence, partaken of by the 'rabble'. He was particularly unimpressed by the chimney-sweeps, whom he described as 'ridiculous ... their faces are whitened with meal, their heads covered with high periwigs powdered as white as snow, and their clothes bedaubed with paper-lace'.[44] There is also some suggestion that the sweeps added a new character of menace to the day, using the threat of their own dirtiness to frighten middling-sort children and unwilling contributors.[45] Certainly, this notion that the sweeps would punish anyone who refused to give them money was common enough by the 1760s to form the butt of a political joke. In 1763 the *Whitehall Evening Post* suggested that on May Day a gang of noisy sweeps, with brushes and shovels, had danced a jig in front of the door of the recently resigned Prime Minister, Lord Bute, demanding money for their trouble. When they were refused, the paper claimed they retaliated by joining the Opposition.[46]

Misson described the scene at the end of the seventeenth century:

> On the first of May and the five or six days following, all the pretty young country girls that serve the town with milk, dress themselves up very neatly and borrow abundance of silver plate, whereof they make a pyramid, which they adorn with ribbands and flowers, and carry upon their head, instead of their common milkpails. In this equipaged, accompany'd by some of the fellow milk-maids, and a bagpipe, or fiddle, they go from door to door, dancing before the houses of the customers, in the midst of boys and girls that follow them in troops, and every body gives them something.[47]

And in 1776, one American visitor recorded:

> In Ave Mary Lane saw the milkmen and maids again with a garland so called; being a pyramid consisting of seven or eight stories in four angles of which stood a silver tankard ... the whole adorned with wreaths and festoons of flowers, gilt papers etc., carried on a beier and hand barrow, it being a custom amongst them to collect of the customers a yearly contribution.[48]

When John Collet produced his satirical group portrait of a May Day procession around 1760 he included a more varied crew. Besides a milkmaid with her headress of silver and copper pots, pans and tankards, there is a hurdy-gurdy man, a dwarf, a beggarly child with an infant in his arms, and a black man in livery to bring up the rear. Perhaps the most important figure, however, is that of a woman leaning out of a house window offering coins to the actors in this theatre of the streets.

The inclusion of chimney-sweeps in May Day processions from the third quarter of the eighteenth century if anything reinforced the financial aspects of the holiday and subtly changed its nature. Sweeps frequently cross-dressed as women, powdering their faces with flour, or took on the role of the milkmaid's sweetheart. By the early nineteenth century they had nearly stolen the show:

> The young chimney-sweepers, some of whom are fantastically dressed in girls' clothes, with a great profusion of brick-dust by way of paint, gilt-paper, etc.,

29. John Collet, 'May Morning' (*c.* 1760). (*Museum of London*)

making a noise with their shovels and brushes, are now the most striking objects in the celebration of May Day in the streets of London.[49]

From the 1770s a Jack-in-the-Green was frequently included:

a piece of pageantry consisting of a hollow frame of wood or wicker-work, made in the form of a sugarloaf, but open at the bottom, and sufficiently large and high to receive a man. The frame is covered with green leaves and bunches of flowers interwoven with each other, so that the man within may be competely concealed, who dances with his companions, and the populace are mightily pleased with the oddity of the moving pyramid.[50]

The element of disguise and cross-dressing occasionally created the opportunity to extort money rather than to simply beg for it. On May Day 1735 Frances MacDonal and her common law husband, Robert Landsman, in the company of two men cross dressed as women, assaulted William Mackenzy and robbed him of three guineas and five shillings, nine pence.[51]

For both sweeps and milkmaids the money raised, either through begging or more forceful persuasion, was an important part of their annual income. Milkmaids worked tremendously hard for a meagre livelihood and suffered from chronic economic insecurity. While they were frequently depicted as healthy and sexually attractive, the reality of their lives was degrading and difficult. Relatively typical of a milkmaid's experience is that of Anne Piper, the bastard child of an improvident mother. Born in 1734, she was passed between her mother, Elizabeth, and her widowed grandmother throughout her childhood. When she reached the age of eleven it became imperative that some provision be made for her future. She was placed in the workhouse belonging to St Luke's Chelsea in late February 1745 – effectively making the parish responsible for her apprenticeship.

She remained in the house for two months before being sent out on trial. Over the next two years she was sent out on no fewer than four apprenticeships, including a period spent with an embroiderer named Masque in Bond Street, whom even the parochial authorities recognised as a bad influence on a young child. It was only in May 1746 that she found a place that seemed to suit her. After having spent three and a half months 'on liking' with Mary Perry, a milkwoman in Charles Street, just south of St James's Park, Anne was finally, and formally, bound apprentice on 26 August.[52] The employment she eventually secured was neither healthy nor remunerative. Milk delivery can only be described as one of the pauper trades. Many milkmaids worked from insalubrious cellars or, if they were lucky, from the cowsheds that bordered the parks. Rising early, Anne was expected to either collect fresh milk from the farms around London, or else to milk Mary Perry's own cow probably housed in the sheds next to St James's Park and pastured in

Cavendish Square.

MILK BELOW!

30. William Marshal Craig, 'Milk Seller in Cavendish Square, Marylebone' (1804). (*Corporation of the City of London*)

the park itself. At the beginning of the century, one of Anne's sorority had a shock when she went to milk a cow in St James's. The cow, a red heifer, turning to face her, first suggested that the maid had come rather earlier than need be, and kicking over the bucket of milk, said:

> A long winter; a green spring;
> A fine summer; God bless the King.

Needless to say, the milkmaid in question went into a fit, although the cow's loyal sentiments were applauded by the town.[53]

After collecting the milk, Anne would have cried her wares on an established round, in the highest and shrillest pitch she could manage, 'in sounds so exceedingly shrill, that it often sets our teeth an edge';[54] before recording the bill for the milk as she passed: 'On doors the sallow milk-maid chalks her gains'.[55] By noon she would have been back at the cow-house for a second milking, before setting off on her afternoon rounds, finally finishing a long day around six in the evening.[56] The backbreaking nature of the work is captured in the stooped shoulders of the milkmaid in William Marshal Craig's 1804 image.

The milk that these maids delivered was not always the freshest or best. Tobias Smollett, in *Humphry Clinker*, described it and the maids who hawked it about the streets in stomach-churning terms:

> carried through the streets in open pails, exposed to foul rinsings, discharged from doors and windows, spittle, snot and tobacco-quids from foot passengers, overflowings from mud carts, spatterings from coach wheels, dirt and trash chucked into it by roguish boys for the joke's sake, the spewings of infants, who have slabbered in the tin-measure, which is thrown back in that condition among the milk, for the benefit of the next customer; and finally, the vermin that drops from the rags of the nasty drab that vends this precious mixture, under the respectable denomination of milkmaid.[57]

Dominated by Irish and Welsh women, consuming a constant supply of parish apprentices, the London milk trade did not produce large profits. A measure of the poverty associated with the trade can be found in the experience of Mary Allen. In 1727, her two gowns and her May Day hat were stolen by Elizabeth Evans. The total value placed on what were probably the only clothes she owned, beyond what she wore, came to just ten shillings.[58] The money collected at May Day was all the more important as a result. For someone like Anne Piper, dancing through the streets with a friend, followed by a band of chimney-sweeps and street children, May Day would have represented one of the few opportunities she was likely to have to accumulate a bit of money. How much she could have collected is difficult to determine, but given the status of the trade and the small sums earned by milkwomen, it need not have been more than a few shillings to make a substantial difference.

Like milkmaids, chimney-sweeps were at the bottom of the economic pile and would have looked forward to May Day with great anticipation. The sweep has always been a justifiable object of pity, and the object of one of the great social campaigns of the later eighteenth century.[59] A trade largely created by the redesign of chimneys after the Great Fire of London,[60] the pity evoking plight of the sweep was a constant strain in eighteenth-century verse. William Blake expressed the emotions associated with the sweep better than anyone else in his *Songs of Innocence* of 1789:

> When my mother died I was very young,
> And my father sold me while yet my tongue
> Could scarcely cry *'weep 'weep, 'weep 'weep*!
> So your chimneys I sweep, and in soot I sleep.
>
> There's little Tom Dacre, who cried when his head
> That curled like a lamb's back, was shaved: so I said,
> 'Hush Tom, never mind it, for when your head's bare,
> You know that the soot cannot spoil your white hair',
>
> And so he was quiet and that very night,
> As Tom was a-sleeping he had such a sight,
> That thousands of sweepers, Dick, Joe, Ned and Jack,
> Were all of them locked up in coffins in black;
>
> And by came an angel, who had a bright key,
> And he opened the coffins and set them all free;
> Then down a green plain leaping, laughing they run,
> And wash in a river and shine in the sun.
>
> Then naked and white, all their bags left behind,
> They rise upon clouds and sport in the wind.
> And the angel told Tom, if he'd be a good boy,
> He'd have God for his father and never want joy.
>
> And so Tom awoke, and we rose in the dark,
> And got with our bags and our brushes to work.
> Though the morning was cold, Tom was happy and warm;
> So if all do their duty, they need not fear harm.[61]

Blake was right to stress the youth, and precarious family background of most London sweeps. What he doesn't make explicit is the danger, physical suffering and economic precariousness that went with the trade. Mary

Alcock got closer to the physical side of sweeping in her 'Chimney-Sweeper's Complaint' of 1798:

> My legs you see are burnt and bruised,
> My feet are galled by stones,
> My flesh for lack of food is gone,
> I'm little else but bones.
>
> Yet still my master makes me work,
> Nor spares me day or night;
> His 'prentice boy he says I am,
> And he will have his right.[62]

Blake also overplayed his pathetic 'weep 'weep, 'weep 'weep!. Most recorded cries were rather more upbeat than this. One comic seventeenth-century version of a sweep's cry went:[63]

(Dering 170–177 in Brett 1967: 139–140)

There is no doubt, however, that London sweeps were on the edge of beggary, and frequently overstepped this boundary. David Porter, late in the century and as part of a campaign to reform working practices, claimed that masters took on as many as twenty-four apprentices – far more than they could actually employ – and that of around two hundred master chimney-sweeps in London, not more than twenty actually made a reasonable living. Porter recorded a world in which children were forced to rise at six in the morning, and were hired out at 6d. a day.[64] It was a trade to which they were bound as young as four, and in which frequently fatal diseases such as 'sooty warts' (a kind of skin cancer) were commonplace. It was also a world of social outcasts, made separate by the very filth of their profession. In a world in which clean clothes marked one off as a member of the

respectable poor, the chimney-sweep could never aspire to social accept-
ance.[65] Despite the otherwise democratic world of the street John Gay
depicts in his encyclopaedic *Trivia*, he excludes the sweep:

> The little chimney-sweeper skulks along,
> And marks with sooty stains the heedless throng.[66]

Even in prison chimney-sweeps were avoided by most people other than fellow sweeps. Jacob Ilive recorded a small piece of casual charity given to a
chimney-sweep incarcerated at the house of correction at Clerkenwell:

> To Robert Finch, one penny. This man, a chimney sweeper, came in drunk, as
> most of those who come in for quarrels do, had nothing but the county
> allowance, was as he said starving. No body came near him; but suddenly on
> the third day after he was brought in, some of the same fraternity came,
> brought his discharge, and paid his fees.[67]

When Jonas Hanway interviewed a group of young sweeps in the early
1770s he found, beneath the soot and filth, a real spirit of independence and
self-reliance.[68] And when, around 1730, the anonymous painter of 'The
Curds and Whey Seller, Cheapside' chose to depict a group of young sweeps
gathered around the neoclassical bulk of the Little Conduit, at the corner of
Blowbladder Street, he emphasised their cheeky self-assurance rather than
their rags.

Sweeps were also possessed of an unsavoury reputation. To 'sweep for the
soot' was a proverbial expression for theft on the docks of London.[69]

Despite the unenviable reputation of master chimney-sweeps, there is evidence that they could and frequently did care for their apprentices in
difficult circumstances. As David Porter suggested, master chimney sweeps
made a precarious living. Robert Campbell declined even to include the cost
of setting up as a master-sweep in his otherwise comprehensive table of London trades, dismissively (and incorrectly) assuring his readers that most
sweeps were disregarded parish children.[70] Luke Holder, for instance, a master-sweep in the 1750s, could afford to rent a house worth only £7 a year –
a sum that meant his widow later found herself removed from her home and
parish by the tender mercies of the settlement system.[71] And yet, despite
their poverty, some masters felt real concern for their apprentices. James
Duxon was a master chimney-sweep with just one apprentice, Thomas
Chidley. Together they set out late on a Monday afternoon, 25 March 1765,
to sweep the chimney belonging to a baker, Mr Smith, in Peter Street in
St James's Westminster. The baker assured Duxon several times that the
chimney was cool enough to climb, and so he sent young Thomas, dressed
in a leather jacket, up the flue. On the first two trips there was no problem,

and Thomas returned with a sack full of soot, but on the third occasion he became stuck. To the desperate calls of his master, Thomas struggled to free himself from the still hot and dirty chimney. Duxon called another master sweep and had his apprentice go up and try and help Thomas down – to no avail. Duxon eventually forced his outsized body up the chimney till he could grab and pull at Thomas' bare feet, wresting him from the deadly embrace of the brickwork. Thomas was rubbed and bled, but never regained consciousness. The anxiety, fear and sheer emotional power of Duxon's testimony when he appeared before a coroner's inquest the following Wednesday speaks powerfully to his sense of loss.[72]

Besides the sweeps and milkmaids, rag-pickers, or bunters, and cinder-sifters, also used May Day to supplement their incomes, either by tagging along with the sweeps and milkmaids, or with their own garlands and processions. The bunters, like the sweeps, were social outcasts. They rummaged at night for rags and bones in the dark streets and lay stalls of the capital. They were so disregarded that the very term 'bunter' came to be used as a term of contempt implying vulgarity. Bunters were frequently classed with professional beggars rather than with the legitimate trades of London.[73] Cinder-sifters were similarly at the margins of London's trades. The occupation was centred on Tottenham Court Road, and involved sifting the ashes from London's innumerable fires and preparing the resulting powder for use as fertiliser. It was a dirty and backbreaking job, frequently combined with the other pauper professions of the capital. In 1712 Elizabeth Price described how she 'had follow'd sometimes the business of picking up rags and cinders, and at other times of selling fruit and oysters, crying hot-pudding and gray-peas in the streets and the like'.[74] We can be certain that she never made a substantial livelihood from any of these jobs. Indeed, the poet Soame Jenyns inadvertently classed the cinder-sifter as the absolute bottom of London's social hierarchy, when he depicts his 'modern fine lady' envy her when forced to quit the town for the country:

> She bids adieu to all the well-known streets.
> And envies ev'ry cinder-wench she meets.[75]

For the sweeps of London, for the bunters and cinder wenches, as for the milkmaids, May Day provided an opportunity to procure, through a legitimate form of begging, a substantial addition to an otherwise meagre income. For the sweeps, it was also an opportunity to use the dirt and filth ground into their very flesh, the sign of their exclusion, to their advantage. It was also a moment when they could participate in a broader social custom that allowed these social outcasts to dance and flirt down the streets of the capital.

31. 'The Curds and Whey Seller, Cheapside' (*c.* 1730).
(*Museum of London*)

Other holidays brought less structured opportunities to cadge a meal or some cash. On the outskirts of London, in rural Middlesex, Shrove Tuesday was characterised by cock-throwing, wrestling matches and football, with any resulting money being put to the use of the poor. Easter was characterised by both feasting and the distribution of special parish doles. The workhouse inmates at St Sepulchres London Division, who might have been disappointed by their feast of mutton at Christmas, could not have complained when, at Easter 1736, the vestry ordered that they have 'a calf of 13 or 14 stone ... provided for dinner on Easter Sunday next, and plum pudding and to have hasty pudding on Saturday next'.[76] For parish pensioners as well, and almost certainly for a wider proportion of the population than this, Easter represented one of those moments in the ritual year when their demands required special attention. After their 'procession to the Spittal at Easter', led by the schoolmaster of Bridewell, the apprentices had feasts on both Easter Monday and Tuesday.[77] Hocktide, the ancient thanksgiving held on the Monday or Tuesday two weeks after Easter, provided another opportunity for organised begging.[78]

Interspersed with these traditional Christian celebrations were new national ones. Grosley, writing just after the middle of the eighteenth century records how:

> On the 26th of April the butchers' boys celebrated the anniversary of the duke of Cumberland's birthday. Being about fifty in number, they, in uniforms, that is to say, in caps and white aprons, paraded the streets of London by break of day, having each a great marrow-bone in his hand, with which they beat time upon a large cleaver: this produced a sort of music as sharp as dissonant. The air of those who played in this manner, being as savage as their music, made them appear like a company of hangmen marching in ceremony to some great execution.[79]

As at all such informal processions, the street-side audience would have been expected to contribute to post-procession celebrations with the clinking coins of loyalty.

Rogation, which overlapped with the celebrations associated with May Day, was also a profitable moment for at least the younger poor of the parish. Schoolboys and children were always expected to participate in 'beating the bounds' of the parish with willow wands at this time of year, and they in turn expected bread and beer in recompense, while parish officers used the occasion to distribute doles to the poor before retiring for their own more substantial feasts.[80] Just a couple of weeks later, Whitsun came along, with its ales and feasting:

> While the epicure alderman's cramming his belly,
> And feasting on pheasants, on ven'son and jelly;
> While turtles and turbots his tables bespread,
> A poor family dines on a morsel of bread.[81]

Whitsun was followed by Midsummer Day and a host of lesser holidays including Bartholomewtide and Accession Day.

Christmas and May Day certainly provided the most substantial opportunities for legitimised begging, but the Autumn saw the approach of both the Lord Mayors' Procession and Guy Fawkes Night on 5 November, when nationalism and religion seemed to combine forces to give new legitimacy to the demands of the poor. In London, the Lord Mayor's Procession on 29 October, in the first half of the century and on 9 November in the second half, was at heart a carnivalesque opportunity to turn the world upside down. Even after the decline of the pageants that had formed so important a gift from the lord mayor and his guild to the populace of London in earlier centuries, the procession continued to be seen as one of the moments when the powerful needed to pay attention to the powerless.[82] Its at least symbolic role in the ritual begging so important to the lives of the poor is reflected in the £2 13s. 4d. recorded in the City Cash Accounts each year throughout the early eighteenth century. This amount was given as a 'customary gift' to the poor of St Margaret's Westminster, to 'keep the poor from following the Lord Mayor and Aldermen on the said day ...'[83]

Guy Fawkes' Night was if anything even more carnivalesque, and more important as an opportunity to raise some cash. Looking back from the early nineteenth century, Francis Place recalled with unalloyed joy his youthful experiences on Guy Fawkes Night. For him it was a moment when apprentices were allowed 'to play the blackguard', and to form themselves into roving gangs. In the evening effigies were hanged upon a gibbet and bonfires were lit at strategic locations around the capital. Place particularly recalls the gangs of butcher boys from Clare Market, and the glassblowers from White Fryers, each of whom had their own bonfires and Guys. His own gang had a bonfire in 'Norfolk Street in the Strand, where it is crossed by Howard Street'.

For months before the 5th, Place and his fellows collected wood and squirreled it away in cellars and outhouses, but the important figure was always the Guy. Made of old clothes stuffed with straw, and with an old barber's block, with a mask for a face, the Guy was:

> seated in an old chair through which two poles were passed ... and was carried ... by two boys. A number of boys went in front, another party behind and two or three on each side, they were all armed with bludgeons. The strongest or

most valiant of the boys carried the begging box in the front and led the way. The box hung from his neck and was also fastened round his body to prevent its being smugged – (stolen), as the boys passed along they begged money.

Accompanied by martial and nationalistic verses, sung at the top of the boys' voices, only the very strong-minded could refuse the request for a 'penny for the Guy'. At the end of the day, the money collected was divided equally. While Place claims that it was all spent on fireworks for the night's revelry, poorer children no doubt kept part of their share for food. The lack of anxiety around this kind of ritualised begging is also noteworthy. Place remarks, 'Very few tradesmen seem to have considered it any disgrace to them or their sons that they should go with a Guy and beg money'.[84]

What is perhaps most noteworthy about accounts of the revelry on Guy Fawkes Night in the eighteenth century is the threat of violence and disorder it contained. The symbolism of burning a man to death is disconcerting enough, but most accounts also include large numbers of young men armed with staves and collecting money with threats when it was not given freely.

A memorable, and carefully described, Guy Fawkes Night occurred in 1718, when the apprentice boys from Bridewell went on the rampage. As early as 1702 the Court of Governors of Bridewell complained that

> the apprentices of this hospital had in an insolent manner demanded money
> of some gentlemen and particularly of the governors of this hospital ... on the
> occasion of the solemnity on Gunpowder Treason Day to the dishonour of this
> house.

In response, the gates of the hospital were padlocked on festival days and the apprentices denied the run of the streets enjoyed by other young men.[85] A few years later, during a period when the political importance and symbolism of celebrations like Guy Fawkes' Night had if anything grown in importance, and with the connivance of at least a couple of the masters and mistresses, the boys decided to break out. Between eight and nine at night the wife of one of the apprentice masters approached a couple of the boys and said 'she would pay for the padlock' if they wanted to blow up the gate, but 'bid them make no noise about' it:

> three half penny worth of gun powder was taken in at the side of the little gate
> of this hospital (where there is room for a man's hand) and was put into the
> padlock and fired by James Rainsford and did not split the lock ... Afterwards
> three half penny worth more of powder was taken in the same way, which
> William Sly put into the lock and propped it up that the powder might not
> scatter. And he having a candle in his hand, [Jonathan] Trevisa lighted a
> piece of paper by it, and set fire to the powder but that not blowing the lock

32. F. P. Stephanoff, 'Children Collecting Pennies for the Guy' (1816). (*Corporation of the City of London*)

asunder Rainsford forc'd it open with a piece of iron. The boys immediately ran out together.

The picture that emerges from the examinations recorded at the Court of Aldermen a week later emphasises the violence and sense of threat that could accompany Guy Fawkes' Night.

A group of them, dressed in their distinct blue uniforms, headed north to the Fleet Bridge, collecting 'staves and clubs' and ' knocking against the windows' as they went. In the alehouses along the route, people warned the clientele that the 'Bridewell boys were a coming'. Up Ludgate Hill and down Great Old Bailey to Newgate Street, until they reached Newgate Prison, 'a mob of near 200 ... headed by the blue coat boys ... beat against the doors and windows ... they went into public houses ... particularly went into the Three Tuns on Snow Hill, [and] had money given them at several places ...' From here some headed north to 'a fire in Holborn' where 'some people gave them money'. Others headed east to a bonfire in Bow Street, near Cheapside, crying the politically disastrous Jacobite slogan, 'Ormond and High Church'. All along the way the apprentices waved their sticks and demanded alms with menaces from everyone they encountered, frequently being given ale and beer instead.

Drunk, but well supplied with all the small change they could wring out of a frightened populace, the boys eventually went home to sleep it off. In due course they would reap a painful reward of whippings and expulsions for their night of action, but their sense of power and authority on the street is nevertheless palpable.[86]

The precise contribution ritualised begging at holidays contributed to the economies of makeshift employed by the poor of London is impossible to determine. It is nonetheless clear that at least most children and young people below the elite felt entirely at ease with the notion of begging. They took it in their stride and made what profit they could from it. Perhaps like 'trick or treat' at Halloween, this kind of ritualised begging was seen as a simple reflection of neighbourliness. There seems to have been a clear and well-understood boundary between boys roaming the streets with their collection boxes and the spectre of vagrancy and mendicity that civic leaders were so exercised about. At the same time there were a range of other events and customs that effectively tied holiday begging into more prosaic forms. Perhaps the most important of these was the pleas for money that came with every wedding. Early modern and eighteenth-century weddings were commonly held on public feast and holy days. In one sample of 286 couples married in the year 1667 at St James's, Duke Place (a popular venue for marriages from all classes), St Thomas's Day witnessed over twenty weddings, while New Year's Day saw a further seventeen. Easter and Whitsun were also very popular dates for tying the knot. When it is remembered that Sunday was the preferred day of the week for weddings, the extent to which wedding days were begging days is clear.[87]

Eighteenth-century couples were nervous about getting married. They shunned publicity and large gatherings. While there was still a tradition of the 'large' or 'great' wedding, it was rapidly being replaced by a desire for a more private ceremony. Part of the reason for this transition was the very public custom of playing rough music – pans and pots, bones and kettles beaten and banged together – below the windows of newly-wed couples.[88] The cacophony would continue until the musicians were paid off with a few pence or shillings each. One London tradition suggested that the butchers' boys had monopolised this particular opportunity to beg. In one early eighteenth-century broadside a schedule of charges is even published for 'His Majesty's Royal Peel of Marrowbones and Cleavers'. For the most part, however, the custom seems both more universal and less organised. Certainly there is no suggestion in Henri Misson's remarks to suggest one group or another had a monopoly on marital begging: 'If the drums and fiddlers have notice of it, they will sure to be with them by day-break, making a horrible racket till they have got the pence'.[89]

Newly-weds did not appreciate the attentions they received. In September of 1714 John Cannon, an improvident but verbose excise officer from Somerset, came to London in order to marry Susannah Deane:

Taking a glass of wine, went directly to the church of St Catharine Coleman, where met us my intended bride, attended with her uncle and her sister Sarah and kinswoman housekeeper ... where we were solemnly married and paying the fees, viz 10s. to the minister, 5s. to the clerke and 2s. 6d. to the sexton ... The ceremony over [we] returned to our Uncle William Keen's house where we were with our small yet grateful company decently entertained and bedded there. [The next morning] the City music smelled out our wedding and came early in the morning and played under our window. But our aunt prevented them to save our pockets, as well knowing their ways that if they were never so gratefully rewarded they disguising themselves would ingratefully return and send another company being confederates in rooking. So she told them the bride lodged not there [and] they passed off.[90]

John Cannon escaped without being forced to reward the musicians on his wedding morning, but most people considered it an act of hospitality and good cheer rather than an unreasonable duty.

Francis Goodchild, William Hogarth's smug and self-satisfied 'virtuous apprentice', hero to the Thomas Idle's anti-hero, in 'Industry and Idleness', happily gives money on his wedding morning to the City Music. Hogarth's print of this scene powerfully reflects the legitimacy of several kinds of begging. The City Music, a smartly dressed group of butcher boys with their bones and cleavers, alongside drummers and cello players, all struggle for attention, while one of their number happily begs from the already bourgeois future Lord Mayor. The drummer doffs his hat and performs a half bow, in recognition of Goodchild's superiority, while receiving alms from his smiling benefactor. There is none of John Cannon's aunt's irritation in the exchange. But the extent to which this particular form of begging provides a bridge to other kinds of relationships is best illustrated by two begging figures Hogarth places apart from the musicians. The first of these is 'Philip in the Tub', a well-known crippled beggar familiar to Londoners in the 1740s. He holds up a new song, 'Jesse: or The Happy Pair', and has clearly dragged his broken body to the Goodchilds' door in the certain expectation that a man on his wedding morning would not refuse to supply his needs. Equally powerful is the figure of a woman, a child strapped to her back, kneeling at the doorstep, while receiving broken food from a servant. Together, these two figures reflect the extent to which begging, door to door and even with the flimsy pretext provided by Philip's ballad, was legitimate, even admirable in the right context.[91]

In a similar way, funerals and Sundays offered opportunities for ritual begging. Sunday, of course, with its range of traditional associations with notions of Christian charity and neighbourliness, made refusal to provide alms for beggars stationed at the church door particularly difficult. Several commentators suggested that professional beggars paid bribes to parish beadles in order to gain access to this coveted position.[92] While the children at Christ's Hospital, predominantly the sons of London Freemen, went 'begging in the cloysters on Sunday evenings', much to the irritation of the school's governors.[93]

Seventeenth-century funerals had traditionally featured the distribution of alms.[94] There are examples of huge crowds of the poor gathering at the churchyard in order to collect their money. But by the eighteenth century this tradition had largely disappeared, at least in London. Nevertheless, it was still possible to turn a profit while interring the dead. Rings, mourning attire, strong drink and substantial food were the order of the day. On 30 September 1716 thousands of Londoners turned out for the funeral of Thomas Bean, who had recently been hanged for his role in the anti-Hanoverian Mug-House Riots. Many were issued with 'White Hoods and Favours' which could be easily converted to cash after the event.[95] And in 1754, when Sarah Twigg was discovered with 'one pair of

The INDUSTRIOUS PRENTICE out of his Time, & Married to his Master's Daughter.

Goodchild & West.

Proverbs Ch:XII. Ver:4.
The Virtuous Woman is a
Crown to her Husband.

33. William Hogarth, 'Industry and Idleness', plate vi, 'The Industrious 'Prentice out of his Time and Married to his Master's Daughter' (1747).

women's leather gloves, and three yards of black silk lace', the property of her employer Barnard Townsend, her first instinct was to claim 'she had them at a funeral'.[96] After a death in the Jewish community the beadle of the synagogue went form house to house, with a great copper money box, demanding alms from each.[97]

Life as an apprentice or a child, a journeyman or a servant in eighteenth-century London was dominated by the season and the calendar, by the passing of the weeks and of the months. Embedded in that rhythm were moments when normal order was turned on its head. Some of these occasions, like St Bartholomew's Fair, Shrove Tuesday or the Lord Mayor's Procession, were predominantly about disorder; they were opportunities for young people to turn the world upside down. At these points in the calendar they could express their solidarity with their fellows, have fights and riots, see plays, flirt and court, see and be seen, taste new foods and meet new people. But a proportion of these holy days, these 'play days', were also given over to collecting money, to begging. It was a kind of begging that would not lead to the House of Correction, and would not result in a whipping, but it was begging nonetheless. This begging was a central part of the economics of adolescence for eighteenth-century Londoners. You simply could not expect to live comfortably for the rest of the year without the capital accumulated in your Christmas box, or collected at May Day or for Guy Fawkes Night. These small sums of money made the difference between being able to plan and project, and sinking in to an ever more abject state of dependency on friends and masters. The clinking coins that fell from the broken shards of a Christmas box, or were prised from the collecting tin, represented a kind of freedom. The profits of ritual begging provided the real substance to the world turned up side down. Bartholomew Fair, for instance, was certainly a transgression against good order, but it was the money beggars accumulated over Christmas and May Day that gave them an element of real freedom.

This kind of ritual begging raises one further point. There were many times when it was impossible to say no. What ritual begging did was to make use of the rhetoric of Christianity, hospitality and nationalism to prise open the closed hands of the financially secure. It also ensured that while they might cavil at the begging knock at their front door, or the pathetic plea at the street corner, the self-satisfied and powerful could not entirely condemn begging in all its forms. How to turn away 'Philip in the Tub' on your wedding morning, after having just given generously to the City Music, was a problem eighteenth-century people struggled unsuccessfully to resolve.

9

A Beggar's Mask

On Sunday 12 December 1708 two men were found begging and vagrant in Bridge Ward in the City. One of them was dressed in women's clothing and, when the beadle attempted to arrest him, managed to escape with the help of the crowd. The second man, John Davis alias Fox, was taken in to custody. He 'pretended dumbness, shewing a certificate printed which set forth that he lost the use of his speech by sleeping in a field ...' Davis was taken before the Lord Mayor, examined and then sent to the workhouse before being forcibly enlisted in the army. In the process, he also 'offered to discover several other cheats as himself'.[1] An account of John Davis's deceptions, and those of his cross-dressing companion, were recorded at length in the manuscript records of the City of London. From here they eventually found their way in to John Strype's monumental 1720 edition of the *Survey of the Cities of London and Westminster*. As a result of this, and a hundred similar instances, a particular type of beggar was given undue prominence in the broader perception of poverty.

The identity of beggars was always a matter of clear prejudice and preconception for the authorities. All statistical and legal records confirm that most beggars of London were adult women with children in tow.[2] Even the few adult, male beggars on the streets were for the most part either elderly or disabled. More than this, the women, children and men who begged in London, did so among their neighbours, from door to door, for broken food and cast off clothing; often offering work in exchange for charity. Very few would have named themselves as 'beggars'. More frequently, they described themselves as ballad sellers or charwomen, porters or errand boys, who used charity as a part of a complex economy of makeshifts. And yet the image created in the art and literature of the eighteenth century is of a lonely male beggar, pursuing a well-defined profession – a healthy adult, avoiding hard work through artifice, and seeking hard cash from strangers. There were people in this mould: there were just enough healthy, adult, male beggars on the street to provide fuel to this bonfire of stereotypes. And some people did, no doubt, use make-up and disguise, cross-dressed and lied to present a particular image. But, if the stereotype owed little to the reality of begging it nevertheless had a profound impact on the poor themselves. It was this distorting image, created by writers and artists, law-makers, petty bureaucrats and the designers of social policy, that beggars needed to respond to each time they sought charity. Every time a beggar stretched out her hand, or approached a workhouse, watchhouse or kitchen door, she would be measured against John Davis and his fellows. In a period before social statistics, social policy was largely driven by preconception. It was precisely the stereotypes presented in literature and art that fuelled the decisions of workhouse designers and justices sitting in petty sessions. As a result, even the poorest charwoman, distanced from eighteenth-century images of beggars by both gender and her laborious occupation, was forced to respond, second hand, to high culture.

The origins of this stereotype, and broader elite assumptions about begging, can be found in a series of clear and distinct sources. Rogue literature, and a still strong sixteenth- and seventeenth-century tradition that saw disorder and threat in the unknown face of every beggar, continued to impact on English attitudes even as the genre fell into disuse. Dutch, and more particularly Spanish, art also had an impact – giving a range of alternative ways of viewing the beggarly poor. And perhaps most importantly, Cervantes, with his picaresque vision of the poor, seen through the mad eyes of Don Quixote, powerfully impacted on the ways in which writers in English depicted beggars and the poor in general.

The sixteenth and early-seventeenth centuries witnessed the rise of a whole genre of rogue literature in which the canting language and the despicable tricks of beggars were supposedly laid out for a wary, if amused, audience. This literature posited the existence of an organised underworld of vagrants and beggars, set up in opposition to the social order, and peopled with clever 'tricksters' bent on cheating honest citizens. In part, it was a response to the economic, social and religious disruptions of the sixteenth century, with its high levels of long-distance migration and periodic famines and plagues. It reached its apogee in the crisis-ridden decade of the 1590s, and its height coincided with the passage of the Old Poor Laws (1598–1601).[3] In the works of Thomas Awdeley, Thomas Harman, Robert Greene, Thomas Dekker and Samuel Rid, the literary stereotype of the essentially dishonest and lazy rogue and vagrant was created. It was this stereotype that formed the foundation for many eighteenth-century depictions.[4]

The truest inheritor of the traditions of rogue literature was Ned Ward. He included a 'beggars club' in his 1709 *History of London Clubs*. His description goes as follows:

This society of old bearded hypocrites, wooden legg'd implorers of charity, strolling clapperdugeons, limping dissembers, sham-disabled seamen, blind gun powder blasted mummers and old broken limb'd labourers, hold their weekly meeting at a famous boozing ken in the midst of old street ... they sing this song, which is call'd the beggars new ballad.

> Tho' Begging is an honest trade
> That wealthy knaves despise.
> Yet rich men may be beggars made
> And we that beg may rise.
> The greatest king may be betray'd
> And lose his sovereign power,
> But we that stoops to ask our bread
> Can never fall much lower.
>
> ...
>
> What tho' we make the world believe
> That we are sick and lame,
> Tis now a virtue to deceive,
> The Righteous do the same.
> In trade dissembling is no crime
> And we shall live to see
> That begging in a little time,
> A common trade will be.[5]

In this piece, the organisational and professional aspects of literary begging are highlighted, and the underworld posited by Elizabethan rogue literature given a new form suitable for a world newly obsessed with sociability.

Ward was not alone in lifting aspects of this older stereotype. Perhaps the most famous English literary beggar is John Gay's narrator in the *Beggar's Opera*. He may not figure in the story, and he may serve as a metaphorical critique of elite behaviour, but at the same time he represents beggars in general, and his life and attributes powerfully reflect the rogue literature tradition. Gay's beggar lives in the same crowded back alleys of St Giles in which Ned Ward located his beggars' club, and makes money by writing ballads, but perhaps more striking is the character's claim that he attends 'weekly festivals' of beggars, in the 'great room' of an alehouse.[6]

Others placed the emphasis squarely on the deceit practised by beggars upon the unwary citizens of London. In the *Spectator*, for instance, Richard Steele is clearly appealing to a rogue literature stereotype of the beggar as a thief and 'trickster' when he allows one correspondent to complain how he

looked out of my window the other morning earlier than ordinary, and saw a blind beggar, an hour before the passage he stands in is frequented, with a needle and thread, thriftily mending his stockings. My astonishment was still greater, when I beheld a lame fellow, whose legs were too big to walk within an hour after, bring him a pot of ale.[7]

Of course, there were beggars who both saw themselves in the light of the narrator of the *Beggar's Opera*, and who no doubt had read the works of Ned Ward, John Gay and Richard Steele. Nor should we assume that all beggars were either illiterate or cut off from a broader print culture. Simon Edy, who begged with his dog by the gate to St Giles's Churchyard throughout the 1770s and early 1780s, always carried with him:

> cuttings of curious events from old newspapers: scraps from *Fox's Book of Martyrs* and three or four dog-eared and greasy thumbed numbers of the *Gentleman's Magazine*. From these and such like products he gained a great part of the information with which he sometimes entertained those persons who stopped to look at him.[8]

Samuel Bethell was a casual stable hand when he stole his copy of the *Spectator* in early December 1784.[9] And at least one London street beggar had seen the first couple of acts of the *Beggar's Opera*. Paul Patrick Kearney may have been a fraud and beggar, but in 1728 he was also in the audience of an early production of the *Beggars' Opera* at Tunbridge Wells. He was arrested for his involvement in a complex fraud case as he sat watching the play.[10]

Even in the year of its first production, the *Beggar's Opera* seems to have been recognised as an important touchstone for popular attitudes towards crime and begging. It is one of the few play titles that is actually mentioned in court records, suggesting that even the court reporter at the Old Bailey found the commission of a crime in the vicinity of a production of the opera worth noting. The subtle implications of this association are reflected in the experience of Mary Fox and Mary Lewin, alias Archer, who were arrested for picking the pocket of Ann Pearson as she was 'going to the *Beggar's Opera*, in the Passage going into the New Playhouse'. Mary Lewin was sentenced to transportation, but Mary Fox was let off with a lame joke: 'the cunning Fox was acquitted'.[11]

Many were convinced that the opera had a detrimental effect on the poor. In 1772 Sir John Fielding wrote to David Garrick complaining about the *Opera*, and followed this up the next year with a request from the full Middlesex Bench, that, 'Mr Garrick ... desist from performing that opera' on the grounds that it 'never was represented on the stage without creating an additional number of thieves'.[12] There is also some evidence that the individual criminals modelled their behaviour on the characters in the *Beggar's Opera*. When Paul Lewis, a convicted highwayman, was incarcerated in Newgate Prison awaiting execution, he came to divine service 'strutting and rattling his irons as if proud of the cause in which he wore them ... He affected a real McHeath [and] boasted to a visitor that he could, like that hero, buy off the Old Bailey, and merrily sang, 'if gold from law can take out the sting, etc.', as in the *Beggar's Opera*.[13]

An instance of a man whom contemporaries would have seen in the light of a rogue literature stereotype is Samuel Badham. There is no evidence that he was familiar with literary depictions of beggars, but he both fitted the contemporary image, and lived within a culture that bore some resemblance to the separate world of begging depicted in rogue literature and in the work of writers such as Ned Ward. Born in Southwark in 1692, he lived most of his life in St Olaves Street, just south east of London Bridge. He was apprenticed to a shoemaker, and for many years kept a stall in Tooley Street just a few yards from his home. He married, had five children and enjoyed a regular income of between fifteen and twenty shillings a week. In 1729, however, his wife died and his business decayed. He tried to earn a living for a while 'coney-wool cutting' (preparing rabbit fur for hatters), but he was not very successful.[14] In 1732, he was forced to go out begging when, at the age of forty, 'an illness ... seized him ... the consequence of which was that he could never wear any shoes, but always walked with a thick bundle of rags tied under the soles of his feet, and with a stick in each hand'. As a shoemaker Badham was not dependent on his ability to walk in order to make a living, and therefore his decision to beg instead, and to do so in a peripatetic manner, set him apart as an idle beggar. Although barely literate, he was gifted with a remarkable memory for biblical quotations, which he used in his begging. In his own words: 'I went out and being lame I asked charity, and in my way of begging, I always used a great many scripture words with good success'. For the next eight years Badham lived an unsettled life, spending days on end wandering the streets of London, 'asking charity'. He 'went different ways, because it is not convenient to be always about one place, and at what part soever of the town I happened to be at night, there I used to seek out for a cheap lodging house'.

The sort of place Badham stayed was described by Saunders Welch a few years later. It forms a depressing model for the 'beggars' club' so joyously described by Ward:

There have within a few years arisen in the outskirts of this town a kind of traffic in old ruinous houses which the occupiers fill up with straw and flock beds, which they nightly let out for twopence for a single person or threepence for a couple ... Four or five beds are often in one room, and what with the nastiness of these wretches and their numbers such an inconceivable stench has arose from them that I have been hardly able to bear it the little time that my duty required my stay. Spirituous liquors afford means of intoxication ... and the houses are open all night to entertain rogues and receive plunder.[15]

Samuel Badham himself was well known in the low lodging houses of London. Certainly he was referred to familiarly as 'Sam' by Elizabeth Adger, who had a dram with him at William Ray's shop at the corner of Lincoln's Inn Fields on Tuesday 29 April 1734. Just as Welch describes, straw was laid on the floor of the house for sleeping, while William Ray stood at a counter serving gin. Mary Ray, William's wife, kept shop. She and her husband were themselves profoundly poor, 'poverty was upon them both', and she was positively skeletal: 'wasted to a 'notomize'.[16] This was just the sort of place Badham stayed the night, although it is less clear he got much sleep. He complained of a similar house in Rosemary Lane that, 'the bed was so nasty and so full of vermin, that [he] could get no rest'.

The low lodging house where Badham was perhaps best known, however, was the Crooked Billet, in Hog Lane, St Giles. John Strype described the area as 'very meanly built, and as ordinarily inhabited, the greatest part by ... the poorer sort'.[17] This was just the area Saunders Welch believed played host to 'near twenty of these places', and where both John Gay and Ned Ward located their confraternities of beggars. Indeed the name, 'Crooked Billet', was shared by at least five low alehouses in London, and was almost certainly an explicit reference to the accommodation the house offered to beggars and the criminal poor. In the eighteenth century 'crooked' could mean either crippled or dishonest. Neither of these lodging houses was home to an organised subculture of beggars, but writers like Ned Ward would have had no trouble jabbing a finger in the direction of the Crooked Billet, if asked to point to the model for their literary creations.

It was at the Crooked Billet that Badham met his common law wife, Susannah Hart, some time in 1738. She had been abandoned by her husband, Simon Hart, and 'she used to sweep the French gentle folks' doors in Rathbone Place and scour the brass knockers and go on errands for the servants; and as she could talk French very fluently, upon that account the people used to be very kind to her'. Badham moved into the room she rented up two pairs of stairs in Farmer's Court in St Giles, but continued to go out on his begging expeditions until 20 May 1740. That day he came home tired after a fretful night at a low lodging house in the East End, and fell asleep on the bed in their single room. Susannah came home drunk at 11 a.m. and the two fell in to an argument. In the end, Samuel strangled Susannah with his single right hand, leaving bruises that matched his thumb and four fingers round her neck. On 9 July 1740 he was tried for murder and convicted. He hanged at Tyburn later that summer.[18]

Badham was a recognisable figure. He fitted the stereotype of the essentially healthy (despite his feet), adult male beggar, who used his intelligence, his ability to weave the right words in to a subtle plea, in order to wrest a meagre income from well-to-do Londoners. His rag-bound feet and use of crutches would have been seen as 'tricks'. His habit of staying in low lodging houses, his rags, and his strength and anger all tie him to literary stereotypes of the sort promulgated by Ward, Gay, Addison and Steele. And although it is doubtful that Badham was familiar with either Elizabethan rogue literature or its eighteenth-century counterparts, when he came to dictate his autobiography to the Ordinary of Newgate, prior to his execution, it was constructed in such a way as to meld seamlessly with that broader literary tradition.

Even the most up-to-date and experimental of eighteenth-century literature deployed facets of this same stereotype. The blind beggar in Francis Coventry's *Pompey the Little* (1751) is a case in point. Coventry includes a beggar among the masters served by his hero, a small lapdog. The blind beggar Pompey briefly serves is a hardened professional, a charlatan and father of two of the most rapscallion characters literary Bath has ever seen. And although the readers of *Pompey the Little* no doubt struggled to empathise with the vain and self-serving Pompey, they would have readily recognised the healthy, if blind, male beggar who temporarily becomes his owner.[19]

The stereotype deployed here is of the beggar as 'trickster' and thief. It is largely restricted to male beggars; with only the occasional woman being given the credit for the guile needed to play this role.[20] What is remarkable, however, is the extent to which this image exists both in elite commentary about begging and in the rarer accounts by beggars themselves.[21] Criminal records contain numerous examples of beggars pretending to be blind or deaf and dumb in order to elicit the sympathy of their contributors. On a cold and cloudy Tuesday, 18 December 1750 Michael Lince was taken up in the parish of Allhallows Lombard Street in the City of London, 'with his leg tied up, pretending to be lame and afterwards running away from the constable'. On the very same day William Maxwell was arrested in St Bride's parish, 'with a false, forged and counterfeit pass pretending to be deaf and dumb'.[22]

Rogue literature, however, forms only one facet of a complex amalgam of influences. Equally significant for most writers and artists was the work of Miguel de Cervantes, and more broadly, the Spanish picaresque literary tradition. *Don Quixote*, written in the first decades of the seventeenth century and rapidly translated in to English, provided the model for almost all eighteenth-century vagrant lives. Its influence can be seen in the works of

Defoe and Swift, Richardson, Fielding and Smollett. It is from Cervantes that the eighteenth-century novel gains its sense of humour, and its licence to depict the poor.[23] At the very heart of the Spanish tradition is the juxta-position of high and low characters; with beggars frequently performing in the lowly role. The theme of a journey, from madness to sanity and through the countryside, is also central to this tradition, and tied *Don Quixote* in to a broader Christian tradition of pilgrimage. It is in part from this source that the eighteenth-century English novel inherited its geo-graphical mobility. To satisfy the demands of a quixotic narrative, the characters who peopled English fiction found themselves on the road, engaging with both the rich and the beggarly poor. As a result every pica-resque novel needed its vagrant characters. While Francis Coventry, for instance, may have drawn his stereotype of a blind beggar from Elizabethan rogue literature, it was from Cervantes that he stole the form of his novel, and in the process the imperative to include a beggar in the first instance. *Pompey the Little* is constructed as one half of Cervantes' *Diverting Dialogue between Scipio and Berganza*, an account of the stories told by two dogs as they amused each other over a long evening spent in a barn.[24] It was Coven-try's desire to imitate Cervantes' work that ensured he included a 'beggar' character among his cast list. That he then turned to a domestic literary tra-dition, Elizabethan rogue literature, for the precise character of his beggar is understandable.

Cervantes, however, added more to eighteenth-century prejudice than a simple literary imperative to set its characters upon the road, and to include beggars and the poor in every novel. His works helped to romanticise the freedom and independence of the beggar. Daniel Defoe, an avid reader of Cervantes, viewed *Don Quixote* within a Christian tradition that bracketed it with other, more explicitly religious journey narratives such as the *Pilgrims Progress*. Defoe thanked one critic of *Robinson Crusoe* for pointing up his 'quixotism'.[25] But, more striking is Defoe's use of several distinctly quixotic characters in his *Compleat Mendicant: or Unhappy Beggar* (1699). In this work, Defoe depicts a free and easy world of the road in which every house is an opportunity, every community open to the blandishments of a well-schooled beggar with a ready pen. Defoe's hero is educated in the art of begging as he journeys over much of the south of England by a knowing old reprobate. The hero is eventually saved from the house of correction by a sympathetic, if perhaps gullible, magistrate, but it is clear that Defoe is depicting a life possessed of many charms. As is usual with Defoe, humour based on crime and immorality is joined to a moral pilgrimage in which redemption is achieved only after a long journey in the wilderness. And while Defoe is careful to draw out the moral lesson in the end, the attractions of disorder, of the vagrant life, are fully chronicled.[26] The relationship between Defoe's two characters is reminiscent of that between Don Quixote and Sancho; while the good cheer and professional competence of the Defoe's mendicants seems to speak of the encounter between Sancho and Ricote.[27] In a similar way, Jane Barker ambiguously celebrates the vagrant life in her *The Lining of the Patchwork Screen* (1726). In the 'Lady Gipsy', the heroine found 'constraint and home breeding ... to be very tiresome', and longed to leave her parents' country estate for the joys of London. Able to bear her provincial life no longer:

> she saw some Gypsies enter the gates, who presently approaching, addressed her with the gibble-gabble cant after their accustomed manner; but she took one of them aside, as if to hear her fortune; and ask'd her, if they would receive a distressed person into their clan; to which they readily accorded. She then asked them which way they were strolling? They said, towards London, to gather up some rents for some nurse-children they had taken. Their going towards London pleased our Lady extreamly, it being the place she longed to see ...[28]

Here, as with Defoe's 'unhappy beggar', the seductive freedom of a begging life lures a character in to trouble.

What can be seen both in the behaviour of some early eighteenth-century beggars and in the literary productions of the first half of the century is what amounts to a shared, or at the least overlapping, image, and certainly a complex dialogue between beggars and the middling-sort writers who depicted them in print. The confusion between the real lives of the poor and the literary traditions of rogue literature and the Spanish picaresque is best captured in *The Life and Adventures of Bampfylde-Moore Carew* (1745), and its partially fictionalised successor, *An Apology for the Life of Bampfylde-Moore Carew ... King of the Beggars* (1749). The first version of Carew's life was written as the legitimate autobiography of a real individual. It gives a detailed account of his birth, travels, marriage and acquaintances – almost all of which can be verified from other sources. He also gives specific descriptions of a whole series of tricks and cunning plans designed to encourage the generosity of the rich. On page after page of *The Life and Adventures* Carew describes his *modus operandi*. Cross-dressing (with the occasional borrowed infant for verisimilitude), pretending to be a ship-wrecked sailor, feigning withered limbs and a broken body, were all tricks Carew played and described in his own words. Throughout the *Life and Adventures* these tricks are used to reinforce the image of Carew as a famous and wonderfully clever man. In the process Carew self-consciously deploys the assumptions of rogue literature. And although he is careful to eliminate the notion of a beggarly underworld, or parallel society, he is happy to see himself in the character of a 'trickster'.

Carew's autobiography was a tremendous success, but was not quite close enough to the fictional stereotype to satisfy an eighteenth-century publisher. In 1741 Robert Goadby published a translation of Cervantes's *Two Humorous Novels*, containing a number of begging characters.[29] In 1749 he decided to use Carew's autobiography as the basis for an expanded edition, and in Charles Lamb's phrase, could not 'relish a beggar-man, or a gipsy, for thinking of the suitable improvement'.[30] Goadby added a lengthy attack on *Tom Jones*, as an inadequate imitation of Cervantes, and spiced up Carew's story with liberal drafts of traditional rogue literature. From an essentially believable and generally accurate account of one man's life, Goadby's edition became a complex mix of the real, of the picaresque, and of rogue literature. By the third edition, Carew was depicted falling in with a group of Gypsies, rising through their ranks and eventually achieving the sobriquet of 'King of the Beggars', a concept derived directly from the wilder shores of Elizabethan writing. Carew's travels are chopped and edited to emphasise their pilgrimage-like characteristics; and the people he meets upon the road are made ever more humorous. What had been a working-class autobiography, was amended to include all the characteristics beggars had been ascribed in Elizabethan rogue literature, and then shoe-horned in to the form of a Quixotic journey of a gentleman through a world of rich and poor.[31] In its long afterlife of regular editions, Carew's text became increasingly amphibious, partaking both of the solid, if wet and slippery nature of fact, and the life giving air of fiction. A real beggar was turned in to a picaresque hero, and then damned with all the imagined failings of his fellows.

The developments described above reached a high point in the 1750s and 1760s, with the work of Fielding and Smollett, but as this literary story was unfolding, an equally complex set of developments influenced the evolution of visual representations of the poor. Some influences were shared between the visual and the literary. Cervantes, for example was supremely important to the development of both. But in the case of art, Dutch genre painting and the work of the seventeenth-century Spanish artist, Bartolomé Esteban Murillo, were also significant.

Dutch genre painting had always provided a privileged space for the poor. Its domestic interiors and rarer street scenes were frequently filled with working people and beggars. Jacob Ochtervelt, for instance, included two street musicians begging at the door of a wealthy house in one of his compositions. More than anyone else, the person responsible for importing this tradition, both its realism and its licence, into Britain was Marcellus Laroon.

Born in the Hague, son of an émigré French artist, he was briefly apprenticed to a Dutch history painter before accompanying his father to London
in 1660.[32] Throughout his career Laroon the younger retained both a commitment to the realism of Dutch painting and a fascination for images of
the poor. In 1687 he published his Cryes of the City of London Drawne after
Life, and in the process melded the Dutch tradition with a much more naïve
domestic one. He also established the standard visual rhetoric used to the
depict poor Londoners for the next two centuries.

Published 'Cries' relating to most major European cities can be found
from the fifteenth or sixteenth centuries onwards. By the seventeenth century in London, sets of cries were being published cheaply for a wide
audience every few decades. But, the resulting images were frequently car-
toonish and unbelievable; and, while they established the variety of trades
that could be depicted, they did relatively little to individualise the people
involved. Even where early cries were 'drawn after life', they rapidly lost
whatever purchase they had on the street culture of the capital, as one artist
copied another in a depressing cycle of plagiarism. Laroon broke this pattern, and transformed the Cries from small scale, almost symbolic
depictions of economic functions, in to large portraits of individual Londoners. Despite his occasional romanticisation, and eye for a well-turned
ankle, Laroon added a strong commitment to depicting what and whom he
saw. Laroon himself provides names for eight of his subjects in the legends
to his prints, while others were happy to add further names to the list.
Samuel Pepys identified eighteen of his contemporaries among Laroon's
Cries, while James Granger added four more.[33] One needs look no further
than to the Cries themselves, however, for confirmation of their realism.
Every aspect of Laroon's mackerel seller, from her blind eye to her extremely
long arms, oversized hands and stolid pose, suggests a well-known and
recognisable individual.[34]

The influence of Laroon's Cries was profound. They were reprinted and
pirated throughout the eighteenth century, and attracted many imitators.
They went through six editions prior to 1709, and were reprinted four times
between 1711 and 1733.[35] They were adapted and revised again and again in
the latter half of the century. They were also imitated. The Dutch painter,
Jacob Amigoni, published a set of four Cries in 1739, which both reproduced
Laroon's characters and provided a new layer of realism to the genre with
the addition of a recognisable urban backdrop.[36] This quartet of images was
in turn followed by a similar set drawn by J. S. Müller, published around
1740. Several versions of the Cries of London, more or less derived from
Laroon, were published as educational tools, with titles such as, Edward
Ryland's, *The Cries of London: or Child's Moral Instructor for the Use of*

Four for Six pence Mackrell
Maquereux quatre pour Six Sols
Quatre Sgombriß sei Soldi

Mauron delin:

P Tempest exc:
Cum Privilegie

34. Marcellus Laroon, 'Four for Six Pence Mackrell', from *Cryes of the City of London Drawn from Life* (1687).

35. Paul Sandby, 'Old Chairs to Mend' (*c.* 1759). (*Museum of London*)

Schools, Private Families, Governessess, Tutors etc. And, in a twist which reflects the moral ambiguity of the Cries, John Kirk used them to decorate a set of playing cards.[37] At the end of the century Francis Wheatley published a version, as did Thomas Rowlandson. And in 1804 William Marshal Craig published a new set with detailed commentary on each of the trades depicted.

The undoubted high point of the tradition begun by Laroon, and the moment in which the Cries became a point of artistic and social contention, was 1759. In that year L. P. Boitard, a French artist notorious for pirating William Hogarth's *The Rake's Progress,* set his hand to Laroon's designs, and with the help of François Boucher modified the original plates, adding a touch of sex, fashion and several new characters. Boitard's efforts were not artistically successful, but their commercial success encouraged Paul Sandby to try his hand at the genre. Sandby filled a sketchbook with images of around a hundred hawkers and criers, and in the next year published his *Twelve London Cries Drawn from Life.* His cries were not as financially rewarding as he had hoped, but they represent eighteenth-century figure painting at its best, and comprise our most compelling image of London's poor.[38] Sandby's 'Old Chair's to Mend', *c.* 1759, is full of a profound physicality, that confirms Israel Potter's comments on working the streets of London three decades later:

> I possessed strong lungs, which I found very necessary in an employment the success of which depended, in a great measure, in being enabled to drown the voices of others ... by my own. "Old Chairs to Mend", became now my constant cry through the streets of London, from morning to night ...[39]

The Cries were certainly not unalloyed representations of eighteenth-century reality. They are careful selections of images and individuals, and suppress as much as they reveal. They almost inevitably divorce the London poor from their domestic context, forcing the viewer to see them in the light of their economic roles, much more than their personal ones. But, they were the image of the London poor most familiar to both travellers and Londoners. In sheer numbers they swamped other types of depictions, and were sold as single sheets for just a few pence. Paul Sandby's powerful images could be purchased for just 2*d.* each. Many travellers bought a set as a momento. In 1710, Count von Uffenbach took home a set of Laroon's Cries: 'bought the "Cryes of London" in seventy four sheets for half a guinea'.[40]

For the poor, the Cries both guided and reinforced their behaviour and self-presentation. Street traders internalised these images and then reproduced them in their day to day lives. Israel Potter remarks: 'When I first entered the city of London, I was almost stunned, while my curiosity was not a little excited by what is termed the "Cries of London" …'[41] The remarkable thing is Potter's designation of the general run of street traders calling their wares as representatives of a clear generic group drawn from art. In decades spent as a street seller, Potter came to positively identify himself with the Cries. As a result, just as the Cries were themselves drawn from life, life on the streets of London was drawn from the Cries.

The depiction of the eighteenth-century London poor, however, did not stop with the Cries. Indeed, their very popularity and generic stability undermined their impact. Instead, the image of the poor that most fundamentally effected politics and social policy, while taking the Cries as one starting point, added a new moral narrative to the mix. If the Cries were the images most easily assimilated by the poor, William Hogarth's more complex stories were much more to the taste of the rich. Like his literary contemporaries, Hogarth was committed to the picaresque, and drew much of his inspiration from Cervantes. He designed and executed a series of illustrations for *Don Quixote* in 1726, which, with one exception, were only published after his death. In the same year he also produced a series of large-scale illustrations for Samuel Butler's poetic interpretation of *Don Quixote*, *Hudibras*.[42] This latter series effectively crystallised Hogarth's comic style, his ability to combine the serious with the burlesque, and his habit of juxtaposing the rich and the poor. In the process, Hogarth turned figures drawn from the Cries tradition into moral actors whose presence was justified, not by their usefulness or hard work, but by their ability to represent one sin or another. Where many of the Cries had striven for Dutch realism, Hogarth achieved caricature. Each of the street sellers in Hogarth's 'The Enraged Musician' is a recognisable figure from the Cries, but are drawn to mock their failings, rather than celebrate their usefulness.[43]

Hogarth did more than any one else to bring together art and social policy. His patronage of the Foundling Hospital set a pattern for later artists and his numerous prints gave a visual dimension to a range of social policy initiatives. His diptych, 'Beer Street and Gin Lane' (February 1750/1) for instance, was produced as part of a successful political campaign that resulted in the passage of the Gin Act the following summer. If the Cries tradition provided a positive image of the poor, which could be adopted by Londoners as representative of their own behaviour, Hogarth made the poor in to a series of social problems in need of a solution. For Hogarth, a clear and distinct social distance existed between him, his audience, and the poor subjects of his painting. It was this distance between reality and caricature that would provide the overriding characteristic of both artistic and literary depictions of the poor in the last few decades of the eighteenth century.[44]

36. William Hogarth, 'The Enraged Musician' (November 1741).

37. Sir William Beechey, 'The Children of Sir Francis Ford Giving Coin to a Beggar Boy' (1793).

In both art and literature the generations after mid century added something new and distinct to the ways in which the poor could be depicted. The Cries continued as a vibrant tradition in to the nineteenth century, and the picaresque novel survived early romanticism, but from the 1770s onwards a new tone of sentimentality can be discerned. In art, this new style in the depiction of the poor came to be associated with a style of painting called 'Fancy Pictures'. Johan Zoffany, Francis Wheatley, Thomas Gainsborough, Joshua Reynolds, William Beechey and J. M. W. Turner all produced 'Fancy Pictures' in which beggars and the poor became increasingly romanticised. Zoffany's 'Beggars on the Road to Stanmore' (1771), for instance, combines both an overtly religious theme, of a mother and child, with a rosy and unrealistic depiction of poverty that seems to invite contempt at the same time as it seeks to evoke pity. The highly conventional religious framing of the family group allows the viewer to retain an intellectual distance from their plight, just as the figure of the small boy on the left uses every trick of what would later become a nineteenth-century chocolate-box style to engender pity. Joshua Reynolds' link-boys and chimney-sweeps are healthy cherubs, whose laborious lives have been painted out. William Beechey's, 'The Children of Sir Francis Ford Giving Coin to a Beggar Boy', epitomises both the pity Romantic painters sought to evoke, and the extent to which they denied their subjects any real humanity, beyond the shared possibility of physical pain. Beechey's beggar boy is simply pathetic, and his encounter with the children of the rich plantation owner, Sir Francis Ford, more a study in social distance and manners (the manners of rich children) than it is an observation of a pauper.[45]

One newly important influence in these depictions of the poor was the work of the seventeenth-century Spanish painter Bartolomé Esteban Murillo. Just as earlier literary constructs of the poor had drawn on Cervantes, later artists drew on Murillo – whose images of the poor were themselves influenced by the Spanish picaresque tradition. By the third quarter of the eighteenth century, Murillo's works had achieved an important place in the broader European artistic canon, and were known to artists like Reynolds and Gainsborough, having been displayed in the auction houses of London. The uncanny similiarity between Murillo's 'Young Beggar', c. 1650, and Gainsborough's 'Beggar Boy', c. 1780–85, suggests the substantial influence of one on the other.[46]

'Fancy Pictures' certainly gave a new space for images of poverty. But they did not provide working Londoners with a model of self-presentation. Instead, they took the distance Hogarth had so effectively created, between rich and poor, between a fallible elite, and the socially disastrous poor, and added a saccharine wall of pity. By creating a new means of evoking

38. Thomas Gainsborough, 'Beggar Boy' (*c.* 1780–85). (*Ashmolean Museum*)

emotion, even empathy, late eighteenth-century artists effectively objectified their models.

This same and growing distance can also be seen in literature. At first sight, under the influence of early Romanticism, beggars seem to take on a more rounded and personal air. The barefoot beggar encountered by Harley, the hero of Henry McKenzie's *Man of Feeling* (1771), for instance, is anything but a cardboard villain of the sort described by Francis Coventry two decades earlier. The beggar in this literary ragout is a healthy man brought down by illness, and forced to beg for a living in difficult circumstances, only to find that the tricks and props of the professional, a trained dog and ragged clothes, were necessary to the role.[47] McKenzie's character still prac- tises the deceit and trickery of earlier literary figures, but is also possessed of intelligible motivations. He, along with most beggars of the Romantic period becomes simply a victim, to be pitied rather than feared.

In the works of Oliver Goldsmith, George Crabbe, Robert Southey and, most importantly, William Wordsworth, the literary beggar was recast in the last decades of the eighteenth century as an increasingly pathetic sufferer. Even writers from poor backgrounds, like William Blake, who should have known better from their own experience of poverty, increas- ingly cast the poor as the irredeemably downtrodden.[48] In the process beggars were transformed from the picaresque into the pathetic. Their emo- tions and beliefs, their suffering and experience became somehow more meaningful for their very poverty. At the same time the reader is encour- aged to objectify and distance themselves from the beggar. As a result, while Romantic beggars are more attractive than their roguish predecessors, they are denied any effective agency. Instead of being clever rapscallions like Bamphylde Carew, with their own agenda and intent, beggars become the objects of upper-class compassion, to be patronised. Wordsworth, in 'The Female Vagrant' and 'The Cumberland Beggar', uses tales of suffering sup- posedly told by a beggar to engender sympathy. Robert Southey's 'The Widow' exemplifies this occasionally mawkish emotional manipulation:

> Cold was the night wind, drifting fast the snows fell,
> Wide were the downs and shelterless and naked,
> When a poor wanderer struggled on her journey
> weary and way sore.
>
> . . .
>
> 'Once I had friends, – but they have all forsook me!
> Once I had parents, – they are now in heaven!
> I had a home once – I had once a husband –
> Pity me, strangers!

I had a home once – I had once a husband –
I am a widow poor and broken-hearted!'
Loud blew the winde, unheard was her complaining,
    On drove the chariot.[49]

Some paupers did see themselves in this light. Ann Candler, for instance, the 'Workhouse Poet', adopted much the same tone as Southey and Wordsworth in 1802 when describing her own experience as an inmate of the Tattingstone House of Industry:

How many years are past and gone,
How alter'd I appear,
How many strange events have known,
Since first I enter'd here!

Within these dreary walls confin'd
A lone recluse, I live,
    ...
No sympathising friend I find,
Unknown is friendship here;
No one to soothe, or calm the mind,
When overwhelm'd with care ...

Candler's greatest ambition was to occupy a picturesque pauper's cottage, of the sort she had read about in books, but her life was nevertheless one of real poverty and homelessness.[50] A similar literary conceit can also be detected in the superficially religious autobiography of Mary Saxby published as the *Memoirs of a Female Vagrant* (1803), the title of which echoes Wordsworth's poem, *The Female Vagrant* published five years earlier.[51] But for the working poor, for women and men who begged and worked on the streets of London, this was not a set of images with which they would happily choose to become associated.

Eventually, in the early decades of the nineteenth century, this essentially Romantic tradition was itself transformed in to the picturesque. And while rural hedgerows and cottages were the primary focus of the picturesque imagination, London's beggars were also important.[52] Looking back to the eighteenth century from the vantage-point of 1822, Charles Lamb could see London's beggars in just this picturesque light:

The mendicants of this great city were so many of her sights, her lions ... No corner of the street is complete without them. They are as indispensible as the Ballad Singer; and in their picturesque attire as ornamental as the Signs of old London. They were the standing morals, emblems, mementos, dial-mottos, the spital sermons, the books for children, the salutary checks and pauses to the high and rushing tide of greasy citizenry.[53]

Perhaps the highpoint of this picturesque literary tradition, however, and the one that most thoroughly confuses literary and artistic creation on the one hand, and pauper biography on the other, is *Vagabondiana* by John Thomas Smith. Published in 1817, just after the completion of the early nineteenth-century Mendicity Reports, *Vagabondiana* strove to memorialise well-known London beggars and to provide a ragged history of beggars in art and literature. Smith, the keeper of prints at the British Museum, includes drawings, with pen portraits of individuals:

> The following plate of a walking beggar, attended by a boy was taken from a drawing made in West Smithfield. The object of it is well known about Finsbury Square and Bunhill House. His cant is, 'Do, my worthy tender hearted Christians remember the blind – pray pity the stone dark blind'. The tricks of the boy that attended this man when the drawing was made brought to mind the sportive Lazarillo De Tormes when he was the guide of a beggar ...[54]

The sense of humanity that infuses Smith's work, and in particular his drawings, certainly sets it apart from most Romantic literary and artistic depictions. His characters are real, and the words he records and images he reproduces are as close to the experience of begging as a financially secure member of the middling sort could hope to have. Yet Smith, along with the whole Romantic and picturesque tradition of literary beggars, still flatters to deceive. Much more than a beggar pretending to be dumb ever could, these literary and artistic depictions of begging lie about who begged on the streets and why. Even when, as with Smith's *Vagabondiana*, the characters described were real men (he depicts only one woman), whose actions and appearance were recorded with care, there was a broad and unbridgeable gulf between the stereotype and the reality.

The vast majority of the beggarly poor did not fit any of these essentially literary or artistic images. It was not that men and women who conformed to these stereotypes were absent from the streets. They were there – a familiar, irritating and constantly changing set of individuals. Instead, the significant issue is that literary and artistic depictions of beggars uniformly over-emphasised a relatively narrow set of characteristics, taking a tiny minority as the norm. The evidence of the real lives of the generality of London's street beggars suggests that the literary and artistic images represent only a small fragment of a much larger whole. At the same time these elite stereotypes were important for the poor. Whether crying goods about the streets, or begging money at kitchen doors, it was the images and assumptions

39. 'Remember the blind', from John T. Smith, *Vagabondiana* (1817).

embedded in literature and art, that determined your reception. Male beggars frequently cross-dressed to distance themselves from the stereotype; while the physically whole faked wounds and illness for the same purpose. If you were lucky, you would be seen in the light of the useful characters of the Cries of London. If you were not, you were likely to repeat the soul-destroying experience of John James Bezer, when, in the early nineteenth century, on his final day as a beggar on the streets of London, he approached the Mendicity Society in Red Lyon Square, having heard they would provide him with clothes, food and work. Having secured the necessary ticket from a gentleman, he hurried along, and after hours of frustrated waiting was ushered before the committee. He was asked:

> 'Are you a beggar?', 'Yes, sir'. 'How long?' 'Eight days.' 'Only eight days, – are you sure of that?' ... 'Yes, sir, that is all'. 'Are you married?', 'Yes, sir.' 'Ah, I thought so. How many children have you got?' 'One sir.' 'O, I wonder you didn't say a dozen – most beggars say a dozen.' 'How do you beg?', 'I sing hymns, sir.' 'O, one of the pious chanters.'[55]

Having been neatly labelled with a canting phrase drawn from the three hundred year tradition of rogue literature, and having been defined as just another beggar in a literary mould, Bezer could not take the humiliation. Having thoroughly berated the committee, and broken the society's rules by insisting on taking the bread and cheese they gave him back to his wife, Bezer rushed from the offices of the Mendicity Society and never went out begging again. He eventually found a new sense of pride and purpose through radical politics.

10

The History of the Poor

After just a few hours in an eighteenth-century archive hands are dark with the accumulated grime of two centuries. The fine dust of the nineteenth-century lies heavily on the carefully folded letters and huge parchment rolls that provide the evidence for this book. Many documents, coroner's inquests for instance, form complex bundles of paper wrapped in robust parchment, some of which remained unopened, unread, until I came across them. The outside surface of these bundles is frequently black, unreadable and discoloured, marked by their location in a random pile of material disregarded for centuries. Gently untying the string that holds these bundles together, and prising open the stiff parchment wrapper, gradually reveals the clean, cream-coloured paper inside. Sometimes the sand used to blot the ink slides off the paper, making the floor beneath slippery and dangerous. These kinds of documents record words spoken in the front room of an eighteenth-century alehouse, just hours after an event, often a death. From an eighteenth-century mind, to eighteenth-century lips, to an eighteenth-century pen, to our eyes, these kinds of documents create a profound connection between us and people long dead.

Sitting in the archive, the physical product of dead hands spread in front of you, the connection with eighteenth-century minds is palpable. No aids are needed to feel the humanity we share with those dead Londoners. But to create that connection outside the archive, in the mind's eye of a reader who will never have the opportunity to hold the original manuscript, requires artifice. As a result this book has necessarily taken the form of an experiment that requires an explanation. It has incorporated a variety of literary techniques and historical arguments, none of which have been explicitly pointed out to the reader. It is an experiment in the use of sources. It combines poetry and painting with pauper letters and criminal records in a way that will make some historians uncomfortable. It is also a literary experiment that self-consciously plays with history as a genre. It deploys forms of narrative more commonly found in fiction. And perhaps most important of all, it is an attempt to create a new kind of 'history from below', a new intellectual and political explanation for the importance of the actions and lives of working people in constructing a shared history. All these practices and arguments are embedded in the text without comment. As a result, they sit beneath the surface, and in the footnotes. But they also require an explicit explanation.

For the last thirty years the nature of historical texts and historical truth has been continually and ever more vigorously contested. Historians, who once claimed access to a true and knowable past, were forced to admit that the sources upon which their judgements were based are all more or less fictions. We have been forced to acknowledge that account books are as contrived as poetry, and that petitions are constructed with as much artifice as a novel. Structuralism, post-structuralism, post-modernism, discourse theory and the linguistic turn, have each chipped away at our certainties with powerful and revealing arguments, and left us ever more uncertain in the face of forms of knowledge that seem ever more complex. This book is a response to the underlying conundrum created by acknowledging this powerful complexity. It recognises that all forms of text share distinctive structures and fictions; that there is no clear and knowable truth that can be discerned beyond the self-referential and essentially fictional world of text itself. This does not imply an abandonment of the attempt to accurately depict what we can know about the past, but it does recognise that each depiction is partial and distorted.

In recognising the power of literary critiques of historical methodology and the depth of the problem for historians created in the process, this book attempts to recast the conundrum of fictionality as part of the solution. If all our sources are more or less fictional then we are newly liberated to use a wider variety of sources. We need to be ever more sensitive to the conditions which contributed to the creation of any given text, and to the internal structures that embed new meanings, but the recognition of the profound complexity of all texts allows us to juxtapose poetry with accounting, petitions with novels. The process of constantly contextualising each individual piece of evidence, of asking why it was created, and for what purpose, makes all the different forms of text newly usable. By recognising the specific grammar of each variety of source we are liberated to translate their content, and to add their evidence to a single whole. This book assumes that prose and numbers, poetry and bald description can, with care, be used to create an admittedly constructed, but convincing, vision of the past.

In using a pauper letter, for instance, one needs to know the letter's intended audience, its purpose, and the literary models upon which it is based. We need to understand the legal requirements of settlement, and the obligations of the overseers of the poor. The letter's language needs to be read with an ear for the cultural significance of every word. We need to know, for instance, that words like 'unfortunate', placed in the mouth of an eighteenth-century women implied prostitution. But the letter itself still represents a single act initiated at a particular moment. In other words, a pauper letter provides compelling evidence for the behaviour of a single author; and even evidence for that individual's relationship to a broader system.[1]

Sources such as poetry, perhaps the most carefully constructed text after legal statutes and financial contracts, can and should also be read as evidence. Poetry gives us access to the vocabulary of description available to its author; and, in many of its forms, to what it was possible for eighteenth-century people to describe. When John Gay, in his 'Trivia', a poem used extensively in this book, warns of the dangers posed to a walker's clothes by the dirt of a chimney sweep this can be read as evidence first of an opinion Gay himself could and did hold, and likewise one that he hoped his readers would recognise as reasonable. It is not good evidence of the personal hygiene of chimney-sweeps, but it does say something important about how they were perceived by men of Gay's elevated social class – a perception which in turn sheds light on the environment inhabited by chimney sweeps.

The worth and complexity of different types of text, and the assumptions made in this book when they are used, is perhaps best reflected in the relationship between criminal records and fiction. The published accounts of the trials held at the Old Bailey, for instance, certainly contain a complex attempt to describe real behaviour. But most of the statements published in the *Proceedings* had been rehearsed in depositions, or told over and over again in alehouses, till the relationship between words and actions at a particular moment is at least suspect. The words spoken in court were also mis-transcribed prior to being shoe-horned into a form a broader reading public would find palatable. Accents and nuance were censored; colloquialisms eliminated or replaced. Even an honest attempt to describe a particular event has come down to us as a constructed narrative – the outcome of a process of winnowing and revision. And yet, within the limits imposed by the ability of eighteenth-century men and women self-consciously to lie in court, these records do contain a deliberate attempt to represent specific behaviour. To do anything other than to take them seriously as evidence would be to patronise both its eighteenth-century authors and eighteenth-century readers.[2] At the same time, precisely the kinds of narrative found in court records were being used as the very stuff of literary fiction. Daniel Defoe, Henry Fielding and Charles Dickens all borrowed liberally from the *Old Bailey Proceedings* in the creation of their novels.[3] As a result, both the novels and the *Proceedings* take on an amphibious character, seeming both true and fiction. The authority of the novels in part derives from their use of language familiar from the courtroom; while the power of courtroom evidence rests in part on its ability to fit a constructed novel-like narrative. Both were accepted as reflecting a real experience by eighteenth-century readers. Neither are true, but both are remarkably convincing, and it is the things about both these types of text that make them convincing, the incidental detail and descriptive passages, that have been used most extensively as evidence in this book.

Coroners' inquests, pamphlet literature, newspaper accounts, settlement examinations, workhouse reports and legal contracts, the records of petty sessions and hospitals, have all been used in precisely this way. Each, however fictional, however complex and constructed, contains a fragment of truth. The attempt here has been to use each of these sources to form one lens in an insect-like compound eye. The image drawn from poetry is myopic. The scene revealed in novels, full of cataracts. Account books, subject to astigmatism, and court records as distorted as the rest. But together, balanced one against the other, they bring a single image in to a sharper focus; made just a little clearer with the addition of each new source. The images brought together in this way are each distorted, and the single view created by their combination contains all the flaws of each of its components. But it is more 'true' than any single vision can be. It is not 'true' in a positivist sense. There is no claim here that the past is fundamentally 'knowable'. But there is a claim to the power of the juxtaposition of a wide variety of sources to create a compelling image that is perhaps as close to 'truth' as one can reasonably hope for.

The methodological constraints placed on historians in their use of sources forms only one side of a heavy coin of criticism. On the obverse face is the recognition that historians have traditionally used many of the tricks of narrative presentation common in fiction. Despite claiming access to a knowable past, historical writing has been exposed as contrived and manipulative. Thirty years ago Haydon White pointed out the essentially generic form of historical writing – that history convinced its readers of its truth through subtle literary tricks rather than through the transparent presentation of evidence.[4] By analysing the power of narrative, and the visual impact of graphs, by exposing the frequently empty authority of footnotes, we have been left with an image of history that seems more akin to fiction than truth. Again, this book has been an attempt to recast the question in search of an answer.

If, as post-modernists claim, meaning is created and recreated with each rereading, then as writers we need to deploy the forms of literary representation in ways that encourage each new reader to come to a particular conclusion. At the same time, as readers we need to be sensitive to the authorial intent embedded in every text. Beyond simply creating an argument, authors need to deploy images and ideas in such a way as to preclude readings and rereadings that are at odds with an authorial intent. If only out of respect for the intention behind a particular text, readers need to be self-conscious about their own encodings and decodings. In other words, this book has attempted to make use of some of the forms of fiction in order to more fully convince the reader of the admittedly partial truths it seeks to convey.

The use of individual lives in a narrative form, for instance, helps to suggest a level of detailed knowledge, which is not in fact there. Once a piece of evidence – an arrest, a vagrancy charge, or single statement – is expressed as a moment in a longer biographical narrative, however schematic that narrative is, the reader is given permission to supply a range of further details from their own imagination. A single moment becomes a journey from birth and childhood, to maturity and death. A first kiss, an aching back, a disappointed lover, are supplied without the footnote required in a more analytical historical form.

In a similar way the use of minor detail, the weather, a smell or sound, gives an impression of complete knowledge, when that knowledge does not exist. Presented with just a couple of words about the weather on a particular day, the reader naturally fills in the details. The single detail certainly exists, and extensive footnotes have been provided for each one. But their inclusion changes a single event acted out on an empty stage, into a part of a weather story; with rain and sunshine punctuating is various acts. Many of the sources used for this book are bald and uninformative. They list names, dates and offences, localities and punishments. In the past they have been used to construct tables and charts that create new information; at the same time they distance us from the humanity of the people being studied. By mixing these administrative records with details drawn from other sources, a sense of completeness is created that exists in the assumptions of the reader, rather than in the evidence itself.

Mixing traditional sources of social history with prose fiction and poetry is a similar literary device. Novels derive their power and impact from their ability to convey a reader into the mind of a character; while poetry is almost always written from a self-consciously revealing and personal perspective. Almost no non-fiction source shares these qualities. Using extended quotes from novels, for instance, next to descriptions of behaviour drawn from more parochial sources is intended to allow the reader to apply their imagination to the sources of social history. Novel reading is about entering in to a process of imaginative reconstruction. The intention here is to create a text that encourages the reader along that reconstructive path.

There is artifice here, but it is sleight of hand in the service of a knowledge as close to 'truth' as we can achieve without an Enlightenment form of positivism. It is also a sleight of hand based in the full recognition of the reader's ability to decode its artifice. By using these techniques, this book inevitably moves history in the direction of rhetoric, but rhetoric with all the subtlety and power associated with the essentially medieval authority of that discipline.

The form and sources for this book are fundamental to its basic intent. At the same time, and within this thin shell of practice and presentation, it is also an attempt to write a specific type of history: 'history from below'. In the 1980s the social history of the poor, and of the political struggles of the working class, gradually evolved from what had been perhaps the most humane and internationally important facet of British history into an increasingly disregarded fragment of historical studies. In a perhaps vain attempt to provide social scientific proof of contested economic models, and using the tools of early computing, historians of working people began to write increasingly unreadable books that challenged the commitment of the most ardent enthusiast for history from below. At the same time, the growing sophistication and technical complexity of literary criticism discouraged many historians from engaging with the emotional content of historical documents. It is a profound irony that the single most inclusive history of England, Tony Wrigley and Roger Schofield's *Population History of England, 1541–1871: A Reconstruction*, is also the most unreadable.[5] And while a few stalwarts continued to produce accessible working-class history for a wider audience, the academy largely turned its back on the poor in a new-found interest in the middling sort.

Inspired by post-modernism, and post-structuralism, by the discourse theory of Michel Foucault and the competing neo-liberalism of Jürgen Habermas, it came to seem to many that the language of the past was our only legitimate object of study. And that only the middling sort and then the middle classes could use it effectively. In the process, the poor, the women and men who left few words between leather bindings, lost their appeal for many historians. For the followers of Michel Foucault the individual (of whatever class) almost disappeared. By locating authority in 'discourse', in the linguistic conventions of a particular genre or subject, Foucault and his many imitators, allowed historians to ignore the experience of the individual in favour of an analysis of that peculiar miasma of words that fill the archives and libraries of our imagination. By suggesting that we are all prisoners of the language we use, Foucault robbed the individual of any substantial agency.[6]

Similarly, in political history, after the false triumphalism of historians such as Jonathan Clark, the 1980s heard the siren call of Jürgen Habermas, with his 'authentic public sphere' and coffee house politics.[7] The 1989 publication in translation of his neo-liberal *Structural Transformation of the Public Sphere* provided a powerful justification for an increasing concentration on the writings and thinkings, musings and actions of the middling sort and elite. In the work of John Brewer, Paul Langford, Dror Wahrman and Kathleen Wilson, the significance of what middling sort and rich people did became ever more central to the political history of Britain.[8]

In field after field, this process of refocusing away from the experience of the poor and onto the words of the middling sort can be found. Even in fields like economic history (traditionally so concerned with the behaviour of the 'masses') consumption came to take pride of place – effectively excluding the poor by virtue of their limited ability to buy.[9] In women's history, and despite the efforts of several excellent historians, the gentry and the aristocracy, the flashy and the well-heeled, took up more and more space, leaving their servants and drudges the smallest of walk-on parts.[10]

In other words, for much of the last twenty to twenty-five years academic history seems to have largely abandoned the poor in favour of the glittering lives of the better off. One excuse for this gradual decline in academic interest in the lives of the poor has been the perennial complaint that the poor are difficult. That while we all have sympathy for the benighted and poverty struck, they just did not leave the kinds of scripts that the modern historian, influenced by literature, post-modernism and psychology, needed in order to practise their craft. This book has been an attempt to demonstrate that there is no lack of sources for the lives of the poor, and that their most personal and internal worlds can be recovered. In the process of recovering those lives, it has also been an attempt to lay a foundation for a new narrative that will reinsert the poor into the broad story of Western development.

The historical literature of the 1980s and 1990s about early modern and nineteenth-century England and Britain has at its root concerned itself with one overarching issue and development: the emergence of 'modernity'. This has been a modernity refracted in the psychology of the individual, their sexual, racial and national identities, and in the creation of a new kind of nation state that responded to these newly 'modern' individuals. It has been a modernity found in the bright lights of a new shopping experience, and in the emotional affect felt on reading a good novel. It has also been a modernity found primarily between the ears of the middling sort. What this volume has attempted to provide is an alternative.[11] It does not rewrite the history of modernity, but, by recreating a specific place, eighteenth-century London, and viewing it from the perspective of the poor, it is an attempt to encourage modern readers to see the poor in a new light. It is an attempt to demonstrate that the archives of eighteenth-century Britain do allow us to write a history *from* below that speaks powerfully to the lives of individual paupers, and that at least hints at a very different 'meta-narrative' to the inherently elitist script found in histories of consumption and middling sort political discourse. Peter Mandler has recently pointed out that the poor need to understand how social policy and the niceties of social interaction work much more thoroughly than do their richer neighbours. For the poor knowledge of these systems was a necessary key to survival.[12] In eighteenth-century London paupers knew how the system worked, and by viewing this incomparably rich environment, this fulcrum of modernity, through their eyes and actions, we gain access to a better informed and more subtle image of the past. In other words, to see the evolution of the modern world more clearly, we need to reinsert the actions and agency of the poor, of working people.

Notes

Notes to Introduction

1. James Dawson Burn, *The Autobiography of a Beggar Boy*, ed. David Vincent (1978), pp. 41–42, 54.

Notes to Chapter 1: The Streets of London

1. Henry Fielding, *An Enquiry into the Causes of the Late Increase of Robbers* (1751), pp. 46–47; quoted in Deborah Valenze, 'Charity, Custom, and Humanity: Changing Attitudes towards the Poor in Eighteenth-Century England', in Jane Garnett and Colin Matthews, eds, *Revival and Religion since 1700: Essays for John Walsh* (1993).
2. William Hutton, *A Journey from Birmingham to London* (Birmingham, 1785), p. 30.
3. *Spectator*, no. 269.
4. Ibid., no. 613.
5. WAM, Records of the Coroner's Court for Westminster, 19 May 1770, 'William Matthews'.
6. [Erasmus Jones], *Man of Manners: or Plebeian Polish'd Being Plain and Familiar Rules for a Modest and Genteel Behaviour on Most of the Ordinary Occasions of Life* (1737), p. 2.
7. Mary Saxby, *Memoirs of a Female Vagrant: Written by Herself with Illustrations* (1806), p. 6.
8. George Parker, *A View of Society and Manners in High and Low Life; Being the Adventures in Engalnd, Ireland, Scotland, Wales, France &c. of Mr G. Parker, in Which is Comprised a History of the Stage Itinerant* (1781), i, pp. 117–18; for a modern analysis of the pleasures of alms giving in eighteenth-century culture see Carolyn D. Williams, '"The Luxury of Doing Good": Benevolence, Sensibility, and the Royal Humane Society', in Roy Porter and Mary Mulvey Roberts, eds, *Pleasure in the Eighteenth Century* (Basingstoke, 1996).
9. Matthew Martin, *An Appeal to Public Benevolence for the Relief of Beggars: With a View to a Plan for the Suppression of Beggary* (1812), p. 14.

10. Matthew Martin, *Letter to the Right Hon. Lord Pelham on the State of Mendicity in the Metropolis* (London, 1803), p. 6.

11. *Report from Committee on the State of Mendicity in the Metropolis* (1817), appendix 4, p. 90.

12. Ibid., p. 92; for a general account of the interaction between the rise of quantification and the evolution of social policy see Sandra Sherman, *Imagining Poverty: Quantification and the Decline of Paternalism* (Columbus, Ohio, 2001). Surprisingly, this book does not deal directly with the work of Matthew Martin.

13. Ibid., p. 91.

14. *OBP*, 16 April 1760, Margaret, wife of John King, Mary, wife of Francis Granvile, t17600416–17.

15. John T. Smith, *Vagabondiana* (1817). The figure of forty-seven includes two boys leading blind beggars, but excludes people depicted as a part of the audience for beggarly entertainers.

16. Adam Smith, *An Inquiry into the Nature and Causes of the Wealth of Nations* (1776; Everyman edn, 1910), i, p. 128.

17. For recent work on the history of the laws of settlement and their impact see James Stephen Taylor, 'The Impact of Pauper Settlement, 1691–1834', *Past and Present*, 73 (1976), pp. 42–74; K. D. M. Snell, 'Pauper Settlement and the Right to Poor Relief in England and Wales', *Continuity and Change*, 6 (1991), pp. 375–415; Nicholas Rogers, 'Policing the Poor in Eighteenth-Century London: The Vagrancy Laws and Their Administration', *Histoire Sociale/Social History*, 24 (1991), pp. 127–47; Nicholas Rogers, 'Vagrancy, Impressment and the Regulation of Labour in Eighteenth-Century Britain', *Slavery and Abolition*, 15 (1994), pp. 102–13; Tim Hitchcock and John Black, eds, *Chelsea Settlement and Bastardy Examinations, 1733–1766* (London Record Society, 33, 1999). For a more pessimistic analysis of the role of the settlement see David Feldman, 'Migrants, Immigrants and Welfare from the Old Poor Law to the Welfare State', *Transactions of the Royal Historical Society*, sixth series, 13, pp. 79–104. For a recent general account of the Old Poor Law see Lynn Hollen Lees, *The Solidarities of Strangers: The English Poor Laws and the People, 1700–1948* (Cambridge, 1998).

18. The weather in London on 9 January 1779 was recorded by Samuel Curwen in *The Journal of Samuel Curwen, Loyalist*, ed., Andrew Oliver (Cambridge Massachusetts, 1972), ii, p. 518.

19. GL, 'St Botolph without Aldgate, Pauper Examinations Relating to the East Smithfield part of the Parish, 1777–1779', MS 2676/12, p. 108.

20. John Brown, *A Memoir of Robert Blincoe, an Orphan Boy; Sent from the Workhouse of St Pancras, London, at Seven Years of Age, to Endure the Horrors of a Cotton-Mill* (Manchester, 1832, 1977 edn), pp. 7–8.

21. For Martin's figures see Martin, *Letter to the Right Hon. Lord Pelham on the State of Mendicity in the Metropolis, passim.*

22. The gender breakdown Martin identifies has been supported by recent work on vagrancy examinations, both in relation to the predominance of women and married and widowed women in particular. Of a sample of 648 women vagrants examined in Middlesex between 1757 and 1799, some 23 per cent were described as widows, and 23.5 per cent as married. See Rogers, 'Policing the Poor in Eighteenth-Century London', pp. 133, 134 and table I.

23. See CLRO, 'Courts of the President and Governors of the Poor of London, 1702–5', MS New 377c/1/22, fols 246–47.

24. There is now a substantial literature on migration. See for example Peter Clark and David Souden, eds, *Migration and Society in Early Modern England* (1987); Malcolm Kitch, 'Capital and Kingdom: Migration to Later Stuart London', in A. L. Beier and R. Finlay, eds, *London, 1500–1700: The Making of the Metropolis* (London, 1986), pp. 224–51; John Wareing, 'Changes in the Geographical Distribution of the Recruitment of Apprentices to the London Companies, 1486–1750', *Journal of Historical Geography*, 6 (1980), pp. 241–49; and most recently David Souden and Peter Clark, *Migration and the Early Modern English Town* (TLTP CDRom, ver. A 1.4, Glasgow, 1998).

25. More accurately, this author has not been able to locate them.

26. For the use of this same variety of sources in modelling the role of desertion in the lives of female Londoners see A. D. Kent, '"Gone for a Soldier": Family Breakdown and the Demography of Desertion in a London Parish, 1750–1791', *Local Population Studies*, 45 (1990), pp. 27–42.

27. Hitchcock and Black, eds, *Chelsea Settlement and Bastardy Examinations*, item 322.

28. *The Ordinary of Newgate, His Account*, 6 August 1740, appendix, 'Samuel Badham's Account of Himself'.

29. The workhouse at Chelsea was largely typical of other London houses. It was distinguished from the eighty-five other workhouses that existed in London and Middlesex by 1776 only by the quality of the records it kept, and by the large number of military paupers brought to the workhouse door by its proximity to the Royal Military Hospital at Chelsea. See Hitchcock and Black, eds, *Chelsea Examinations*, and Tim Hitchcock, '"Unlawfully Begotten on Her Body": Illegitimacy and the Parish Poor in St Luke Chelsea', in Tim Hitchcock, Peter King and Pamela Sharpe, eds, *Chronicling Poverty: The Voices and Strategies of the English Poor, 1640–1840* (Basingstoke, 1997).

30. Of all types of pauperism, casual poverty and the casual relief that accompanies it is the least studied. Indeed, the only literature which addresses the problem of the casual poor is that on sixteenth-century vagrancy. See, for example, A. L. Beier, *Masterless Men: The Vagrancy Problem in England,*

1560–1640 (1985); Paul Slack, 'Vagrants and Vagrancy in England, 1598–1664', *Economic History Review*, second series, 27 (1974).

31. Jonas Hanway, *Letters on the Importance of the Rising Generation* (1768), ii, pp. 80–81.

32. Hitchcock and Black, eds, *Chelsea Settlement and Bastardy Examinations, 1733–1766*, item 319. See also LMA, St Luke's Chelsea Workhouse Register, Microfilm X/15/37, entries for, 'Elizabeth Bullock, aged 25, 1 February 1757'; 'Elizabeth Bullock, aged 4, 1 February 1757'; 'Elizabeth Bullock, aged 5, 3 March 1758' and 'William Bullock, age 2, 1 February 1757'.

33. On desertion see A. D. Kent, '"Gone for a Soldier"'.

34. There seems to be no more specific definition of 'infirm' than the *Oxford English Dictionary*'s 'Of persons, with reference to physical condition: not strong and healthy; physically weak or feeble, esp. through age …'

35. Alexander Pope, 'The Alley; An Imitation of Spencer' (written by 1709, published 1727), reproduced in Lonsdale, ed., *Eighteenth-Century Verse*, pp. 87–88.

36. James Dawson Burn, *The Autobiography of a Beggar Boy*, ed. David Vincent, (1978), p. 56–57.

37. *Report from Committee on the State of Mendicity in the Metropolis* (1815), appendix, 'The Population of the Irish Poor Resident in the Metropolis', p. 95.

38. *OBP*, 21 February 1787, William Droyre, t17870221–29.

39. David R. Green, *People of the Rookery: A Pauper Community in Victorian London*, occasional paper 26, University of London, King's College, Department of Geography (1986).

40. Quoted in Peter Earle, *A City Full of People: Men and Women of London, 1650–1750* (1994), p. 232.

41. *A Trip Through Town: Containing Observations on the Humours and Manners of the Age* (4th edn, 1735), p. 11; Thomas Brown, *The Works of Thomas Brown: Serious and Comical, in Prose and Verse in Four Volumes* (2nd edn, 1720), i, p. 171; *Spectator*, no. 6; John Gay, 'Trivia: or The Art of Walking the Streets of London' (1716), in Vinton A. Dearing, ed., *John Gay: Poetry and Prose*, (1974), p. 164, book iii, lines 133–38; *Spectator*, no. 509. For beggars apprehended by Sharp on London Bridge see for example the examinations of Thomas Ossier, 3 May 1738, Abraham Cartwright, 31 March 1738 and 3 May 1738, and Mary Johnson, 19 September 1738. CLRO, 'Vagrant Books, Together with Five Loose Pages and a Bill of Mortality, 1738–42', Misc. MS 322.5; *Low-Life: or One Half of the World, Knows Not How the Other Half Live* (2nd edn, 1749), p. 97; [Isaac Bickerstaff] *The Life, Strange Voyages and Uncommon Adventures of Ambrose Gwinett: Formerly Known to the Public as the Lame Beggar; Who for a Long Time Swept the Way at the Mew's Gate, Charing Cross* (4th edn, c. 1770); *Spectator*, no. 454; *Pastorals, Choice Fables and Tales, with Other Occasional Poems … To Which is Added the Adventures of a Farthing, or The Humours of Low-Life*

(1785), p. 61; Ned Ward, *The London Spy* (1709; Folio Society edn; Chatham, 1955), pp. 231–32; *Spectator*, no. 269; Abraham Mondius, 'A Frost Fair on the Thames at Temple Stairs', *c.* 1684, reproduced in Mireille Galinou and John Hayes, *London in Paint: Oil Paintings in the Collection at the Museum of London* (1996), pp. 58–59; An early eighteenth-century image of Westminster Hall with a beggar in the foreground is reproduced without attribution in Ned Ward, *The London Spy* (1709, Folio Society edn), between pp. 152 and 153.

42. *Proposal for Relief and Punishment of Vagrants, Particularly Such as Frequent the Streets and Publick Places of Resort Within this Kingdom* (1748), p. 2.

43. Historians have fully reproduced this bifurcated vision of London. For the essentially dystopian view see the still authoritative M. Dorothy George, *London Life in the Eighteenth Century* (2nd edn, 1966) and Randolph Trumbach, *Sex and the Gender Revolution, i, Heterosexuality and the Third Gender in Enlightenment London* (Chicago Michigan, 1998). For a more optimistic vision achieved by actively excluding the poor see Peter Thorold, *The London Rich: The Creation of a Great City from 1666 to the Present* (1999). For a recent attempt to assess the changing reputation of London in the seventeenth century, see Paul Slack, 'Perceptions of the Metropolis in Seventeenth-Century England', in Peter Burke, Brian Harrison and Paul Slack, eds, *Civil Histories: Essays Presented to Sir Keith Thomas* (Oxford, 2000), pp. 161–80.

44. BL, Add. MS 27828, 'Place Papers, vol. xl, Manners and Morals', iv, fol. 7.

45. Francis Place, *The Autobiography of Francis Place, 1771–1854*, ed. Mary Thale (Cambridge, 1972), p. 229.

46. Quoted in Peter Jackson, *George Scharf's London: Sketches and Watercolours of a Changing City, 1820–50* (1987), p. 20.

47. *Low-Life: or One Half of the World Knows Not How the Other Half Live* (2nd edn, 1749), pp. 80–81,

48. Gay, 'Trivia', book ii, line 214.

49. Canaletto's relative inability to depict rapid movement is exemplified in works such as his 'London: Westminster Bridge from the North on Lord Mayor's Day' (1746), in which a confusion of boats on the Thames speaks more of an imminent naval catastrophe than a procession. For a brief discussion of Canaletto's use of a camera obscura see Christopher Baker, *Canaletto* (1994), pp. 15–16.

50. For an account of Thomas De Veil's career see Tim Hitchcock, '"You Bitches … Die and Be Damned": Gender, Authority and the Mob in St Martin's Round-House Disaster of 1742', in Tim Hitchcock and Heather Shore, eds, *The Streets of London from the Great Fire to the Great Stink* (2003).

51. For an excellent treatment of Hogarth's 'Times of the Day' series see Sean Shesgreen, *Hogarth and the Times-of-the-Day Tradition* (Ithaca, New York, 1983).

52. BL. Add. MS 27826, 'Place Papers, xxxviii: Manners and Morals', ii, fols 173–5.

53. For a readily accessible version of this image see Sean Shesgreen, *Images of the Outcast: The Urban Poor in the Cries of London* (Manchester, 2002), plate 8.

54. For a discussion of Paul Sandby's career and relationship to both Hogarth and Canaletto, see Sheila O'Connell, *London 1753* (2003), pp. 125–26. For a more detailed discussion of Sandby's early attack on William Hogarth's 'Analysis of Beauty', see David Bindman, *Hogarth and His Times* (1997), pp. 174–80.

55. The figure in one of Paul Sandby's most powerful Cries, 'Old Chairs to Mend', *c.* 1759 appears as a tiny figure in an image attributed to Thomas Sandby, Paul's brother, entitled, 'View of Beaufort Buildings Looking Towards the Strand', *c.* 1765. For the Cry, see Shesgreen, *Images of the Outcast*, plate 1; for Thomas Sandby's picture using the same figure see Sheila O'Connell, *London 1753* (2003), plate 10, 3.70, p. 174; the chair mender is visible on the north side of the road walking towards the viewer.

Notes to Chapter 2: Sleeping Rough

1. *The Journal of John Harrower, an Indentured Servant in the Colony of Virginia, 1773–1776*, ed. Edward Miles Riley (Williamsburg, Virginia, 1963), pp. 3–17.

2. For the still authoritative account of the role of migration in the construction of the population of London see E. A. Wrigley, 'A Simple Model of London's Importance in Changing English Society and Economy, 1650–1750', *Past and Present*, 37 (1967), pp. 44–70; see also Jeremy Boulton, 'London, 1540–1700' in Peter Clark, ed., *The Cambridge Urban History of Britain*, ii, *1540–1840* (Cambridge, 2000); Roger A. P. Finlay and Beatrice Shearer, 'Population Growth and Suburban Expansion' in A. L. Beier and Roger Finlay, eds, *London, 1500–1700: The Making of the Metropolis* (1986); John Lander, *Death and the Metropolis: Studies in the Demographic History of London, 1670–1830* (Cambridge, 1993); Craig Spence, *London in the 1690s: A Social Atlas* (2000); John Wareing, 'Migration to London and Transatlantic Emigration of Indentured Servants, 1683–1775', *Journal of Historical Geography*, 7 (1981), pp. 356–78; Adrian Wilson, 'Illegitimacy and Its Implications in Mid Eighteenth-Century London: The Evidence of the Foundling Hospital', *Continuity and Change*, 4 (1989), 103–64. There is also an extensive literature on the migratory patterns of specific communities.

3. For a wonderful account of the difficulties of finding one's way around London see Cynthia Wall, '"At *Shakespear's-Head*, Over-Against *Catharine-Street* in the *Strand*": Forms of Address in London Streets', in Tim Hitchcock and Heather Shore, eds, *The Streets of London from the Great Fire to the Great Stink* (2003).

4. Ann Candler, *Poetical Attempts by Ann Candler, a Suffolk Cottager with a Short Narrative of her Life* (Ipswich, 1803), p. 10.

5. John Bancks, 'A Description of London' (1738), reproduced in Roger Lonsdale, ed., *Eighteenth-Century Verse* (Oxford, 1984), p. 275.

6. Malcom Falkes, 'Lighting in the Dark Ages of English Economic History: Town Streets before the Industrial Revolution', in D. C. Coleman and A. H. John, eds, *Trade Government and Economy in Pre-Industrial England* (London, 1976); for a general discussion of the development of street furniture and domestic architecture see Dan Cruickshank and Neil Burton, *Life in the Georgian City* (1990), part 1.

7. César de Saussure, *A Foreign View of England in 1725–1729: The Letters of Monsieur César de Saussure to his Family*, translated and edited by Madame Van Muyden (1995), p. 47.

8. This figure is based on the index to Rocques map in *Find Your Way Round Mid-Georgian London* (Motco Enterprises Ltd, CD Rom, 2003).

9. The classic account of the architectural history of eighteenth-century London is John Summerson, *Georgian London*, (1978); see also Peter Borsay, *The English Urban Renaissance: Culture and Society in the Provincial Town, 1660–1770* (Oxford, 1989); Mary Hobhouse and Ann L. Saunders, eds, *Good and Proper Materials: The Fabric of London Since the Great Fire: Papers Given at a Conference Organised by the Survey of London*, London Topographical Society Publications, 140 (1989); T. F. Reddaway, *The Rebuilding of London After the Great Fire* (1940); and Cruickshank and Burton, *Life in the Georgian City*, part 3.

10. Saussure, *A Foreign View of England in 1725–1729*, p. 103.

11. CLRO, London Sessions Papers, December 1782, '31 Examinations of Supposed Vagrants, Many Charged by the City Marshal', see the examination of William Jones; for details of the weather on 11 December 1782 see *The Journal of Samuel Curwen, Loyalist*, ed. Andrew Oliver (Cambridge Massachusetts, 1972), ii, 10 and 11 December 1782, p. 878.

12. William Blizard, *Desultory Reflections on Police: With an Essay on the Means of Preventing Crimes and Amending Criminals* (1785), quoted in BL, Add MS 27826, 'Place Papers, xxxviii, Manners and Morals', ii, fos 159–60.

13. CLRO, 'Guildhall Justice Room Minute Book, 1785, 20 January to 14 February', GJR/M30, 27 January 1785.

14. The use of hay as a general cleaning, packing and insulation material is one aspect of early modern life that historians have largely neglected. There is no literature on its use.

15. The barometric pressure that day was low, but a wide range of astronomical observations could still be made at Greenwich. The temperature was recorded as 52 degrees Fahrenheit. James Bradley, *Astronomical Observations Made at the Royal Observatory at Greenwich from the Year MDCCL to the Year MDCCLXII*, part 2 (1805), pp. 211, 302.

16. See for example, OBP, 4 December 1745, Joseph Payne, t17451204–33.

17. CLRO, 'Guildhall Justice Room, Minutes, 1761, 14 October to 27 November', GJR/M2, 16 Oct 1761.

18. WAM, Westminster Coroner's Inquests, 10 March 1763, 'William Border'.

19. OBP, 22 February 1786, John Peazy, t17860222–126.

20. CLRO, Coroner's Inquest, 6 January 1792, 'Thomas Shaw'.

21. For a detailed account of the evolution of a large London Inn see Caroline Dalton, 'Mountjoy's Inn, Fenchurch Street', London Topographical Record, xxvii, no. 149 (1995), pp. 69–90. For a more general account of the evolution of London inns, see A. E. Richardson and H. Donaldson Eberlein, The English Inn: Past and Present: A Review of Its History and Social Life (1925), ch. 4.

22. OBP, 22 February 1786, John Peazy, t17860222–126. At Greenwich, most of the preceding week had been lost to bad weather, and the temperature had remained between 36 and 34 degrees Fahrenheit. Two days later it fell to 23 degrees. See Nevil Maskelyne, Astronomical Observations Made at the Royal Observatory at Greenwich in the Years 1765, 1766, 1767, 1768 and 1769 (1774), part 2, p. 121.

23. BL, Add. MS 27825, 'Place Papers, xxxvii, Manners and Morals' i, fol. 158.

24. James Lackington, Memoirs of the First Forty-Five Years of the Life of James Lackingon (1791), p. 24.

25. OBP, 13 October 1736, Grace Powell, t17361013–33.

26. The barometer at Greenwich was low throughout the week and fell sharply towards its end. Astronomical observations could only be made on 20, 24 and 26 February, the other nights being too cloudy. The Astronomer Royal described 20 February as 'very hazy'. On 15 February the recorded temperature at Greenwich was 29 degrees; on 24 February it was 42 degrees, and on 26 February, 43 degrees. See James Bradley, Astronomical Observations Made at the Royal Observatory at Greenwich from the Year MDCCL to the Year MDCCLXII, ii (1805), pp. 215, 303, 391, 412.

27. For a trial that reflects the social character of New Bedford Court, and in particular the nature of the lodging houses there, see OBP, 30 April 1783, Robert Edwards, Ann Witney, Sarah Taylor, t17830430–30.

28. WAM, Westminster Coroner's Inquest, 28 February 1765, 'Jane Austin'.

29. Low-Life: or One Half of the World, Knows Not How the Other Half Live (1749), p. 5.

30. OBP, 10 April 1782, Job Wilkinson, Joseph Clark, t17820410–53.

31. John Thomas Smith, A Book for a Rainy Day: or Recollections of the Events of the Last Sixty Years (1845), p. 74.

32. John Strype, A Survey of the Cities of London and Westminster (1720), book iii, p. 63.

33. M. Dorothy George, London Life in the Eighteenth Century (1966 edn),

pp. 173–74; for a recent account of this incident which helps to unpack the motivations of the women involved see Sarah Lloyd, ' "Agents in the Own Concerns?" Charity and the Economy of Makeshifts in Eighteenth-Century Britain' in Steven King and Alannah Tomkins, eds, *The Poor in England, 1700–1850: An Economy of Makeshifts* (Manchester, 2003), pp. 118–19.

34. John Strype, *A Survey of the Cities of London and Westminster* (1720), book iv, p. 118.

35. No astronomical observations were possible that night, and the temperature was recorded as 74 degrees Fahrenheit the evening before. See Nevil Maskelyne, *Astronomical Observations Made at the Royal Observatory at Greenwich from MDCCLXXXVII to MDCCXCVIII* (1799), part 1, p. 357, part 2, p. 109.

36. WAM, Westminster Coroner's Inquest, 27 June 1796, 'Information of the seven persons within mentioned accidental by falling down of two houses each a deodand of £10'.

37. Francis Place, *The Autobiography of Francis Place, 1771–1854*, ed. Mary Thale (Cambridge, 1972), p. 104.

38. Ibid., p. 107.

39. That evening the barometer was low, and only lunar observations could be made at Greenwich. The temperature was recorded as 58 degrees Fahrenheit. James Bradley, *Astronomical Observations Made at the Royal Observatory at Greenwich from the Year MDCCL to the Year MDCCLXII*, ii (1805), pp. 218, 305.

40. WAM, Westminster Coroner's Inquest, 20 April 1762, 'Jeremiah Flarty'.

41. CLRO, London Sessions Papers, 25 and 27 February 1734, 'Presentation of the Grand Jury to the Court Concerning the Number of Vagrants and Beggars in the Streets in London, 27 Feby 1733'.

42. *The Shipmates: Being a Supplement to the Tract Entitled 'Conversation in a Boat', by the Same Author, Formerly a Lieutenant in the Royal Navy*, Religious Tract Society, 135 (n. d.), p. 5.

43. Mary Saxby, *Memoirs of a Female Vagrant, Written by Herself* (1806), pp. 5–6

44. Claire Walsh, 'Shop Design and the Display of Goods in Eighteenth-Century London', *Journal of Design History*, 8 (1995), pp. 157–76; see also Peter W. M. Blayney, 'John Day and the Bookshop that Never Was' in Lena Cowen Orlin, ed., *Material London, ca. 1600* (Philadelphia, Pennsylvania, 2000) and Hoh-Cheung Mui and Lorna H. Mui, *Shops and Shopkeeping in Eighteenth-Century England* (1989).

45. The barometric pressure had been falling for over a week, and no astronomical observations had been possible for several days. We have temperature measurements for two days during this week. The Astronomer Royal recorded 63 degrees Fahrenheit on 11 June and 60 degrees on 14 June. See Nevil Maskelyne, *Astronomical Observations Made at the Royal Observatory at Greenwich from MDCCLXXXVII to MDCCXCVIII* (1799), part 1, p. 210, part 2, p. 70.

46. CLRO, Guildhall Justice Room Minute Book, GJR/M50, Wednesday 13 June 1792.

47. John Smith, 'A Solitary Canto to Chloris the Disdainful' (1713), line 14, reproduced in Roger Lonsdale, ed., *Eighteenth-Century Verse* (Oxford, 1984), pp. 104–6.

48. John Gay, 'Trivia', *Poetry and Prose*, ed. Vinton A. Dearing, (Oxford, 1974), ii, lines 135–40.

49. *Low-Life: or One Half of the World Knows Not How the Other Half Live* (1749), p. 20.

50. Guildhall Library, 'Court of Governors, Bridewell and Bethlem: Minutes, 16 May 1701 to 19 June 1713', MS 33011/18, 10 October 1701, p. 37.

51. GL, 'Court of Governors, Bridewell and Bethlem: Minutes, 26 October 1722 to 15 December 1737', MS 33011/20, 13 November 1735, p. 363.

52. GL, 'Court of Governors, Bridewell and Bethlem: Minutes 1 January 1737/8 to 4 April 1751', MS 33011/2, 1 October 1742, p. 158.

53. *OBP*, 8 December 1742, Susanna Jones, t17421208–29.

54. For two works that treat more than one market see Betty R. Masters, *The Public Markets of the City of London Surveyed by William Leybourn in 1677*, London Topographical Society Publication, 17 (1974); and Colin Stephen Smith, 'The Market and the Market's place in London, c. 1660–1840' (University of London Ph.D. thesis, 1999).

55. 'Bartholomew Fair' (n.d., n.p.), a collection of unattributed published ephemera, BL, c. 70. h. 6. (2).

56. George Parker, *A View of Society and Manners in High and Low Life* (1781), ii, p. 58.

57. GL, 'Court of Governors, Bridewell and Bethlem: Minutes, 22 May 1751 to 1 December 1761', MS 33011/22, 7 February 1757, p. 242; 4 June 1761, p. 362. On the day Ann Glassborough was arrested, the Astronomer Royal, James Bradley, noted 'Clouds' that evening and recorded the temperature at 42 degrees Fahrenheit. On 5 May 1761, when Kettlewell and Willis were arrested, it was too cloudy to make any observations, but the next temperature reading, taken on 7 May, was recorded at 67 degrees Fahrenheit. See James Bradley, *Astronomical Observations Made at the Royal Observatory at Greenwich from the Year MDCCL to the Year MDCCLXII*, part 2 (1805), pp. 69, 202, 242, 298.

58. The barometer was falling fast all that week and no astronomical observations could be made. The temperatures recorded at Greenwich hovered between 39 degrees Fahrenheit and 44 degrees. See Bradley, *Astronomical Observations Made ... MDCCL to the Year MDCCLXII*, ii, pp. 215, 303.

59. GL, 'Court of Governors, Bridewell and Bethlem: Minutes, 7 January 1762 to 15 March 1781', MS 33011/23, 7 January 1762, p. 1; 11 May 1763, p. 50. No

observations were possible at Greenwich that week, while the temperature was recorded as 53 degrees Fahrenheit on both 5 and 15 May. See Bradley, *Astronomical Observations Made ... MDCCL to the Year MDCCLXII*, ii, p. 400.

60. CLRO, Guildhall Justice Room, Minute Books, Wednesday, 12 January 1785, GJR/MB.

61. *OBP*, 14 October 1741, John Woolford, t17411014–24.

62. CLRO, Coroner's Inquest, 21 December 1799, 'A Woman Unknown'.

63. See Betty R. Masters, *The Public Markets of the City of London Surveyed by William Leybourn in 1677*, London Topographical Society, 117 (1974), pp. 20–31.

64. Saussure, *A Foreign View of England in 1725–1729*, pp. 106–7.

65. GL, 'Court of Governors, Bridewell and Bethlem: Minutes 26 June 1713 to 2 August 1722', MS 33011/19, 20 April 1722, p. 508.

66. Ibid., 9 February 1721/2, p. 502.

67. Ibid., 20 April 1722, p. 508.

68. GL, 'Court of Governors, Bridewell and Bethlem: Minutes, 7 January 1762 to 15 March 1781', MS 33011/23, 30 November 1769, p. 274. Several astronomical observations were made that night, 29 November 1769, at the Greenwich observatory, and the temperature was recorded as 43 degrees Fahrenheit. The comet remained visible between the end of August and the end of November. See Nevil Maskelyne, *Astronomical Observations Made at the Royal Observatory at Greenwich in the 1765, 1766, 1767, 1768 and 1769* (1774), part 1, p. 173, part 2, p. 58, 71.

69. For an account of the 'soundscape' of the area just north of Smithfield, see Bruce R. Smith, *The Acoustic World of Early-Modern England: Attending to the O-Factor* (Chicago, 1999), pp. 56–60. Smith is uncharacteristically silent on the sounds of the market.

70. GL, 'Court of Governors, Bridewell and Bethlem: Minutes, 26 June 1713 to 2 August 1722', MS 33011/19, 25 July 1718, p. 353.

71. GL, 'Court of Governors, Bridewell and Bethlem: Minutes, 23 August 1695 to 2 May 1702', MS 33011/17, 21 August 1696, p. 55.

72. For the histories of Covent Garden and Billingsgate see Robert Thorne, *Covent Garden Market: Its History and Restoration* (1980); James Bird, 'Billingsgate: A Central Metropolitan Market'. *Geographical Journal*, 124 (1958), 464–75; and Colin Mantin and John Edwards, *Bygone Billingsgate* (Chichester, 1989).

73. *OBP*, 6 December 1732, Richard Albridge alias Alder, t17321206–5.

74. CLRO, Hoard Book, 1730–54, MS 033C/9/25, 21 August 1730.

75. WAM, Westminster Coroner's Inquest, 2 January 1767, 'Edward Allen'.

76. WAM, Westminster Coroner's Inquest, 22 December 1777, 'A Man Unknown'; the details of the weather are taken from, *Journal of Samuel Curwen*, i, 19 December 1777, p. 421.

77. *Autobiography of Francis Place, 1771–1854*, pp. 48–49.

78. Daniel Defoe, *Some Considerations upon Street-Walkers* (1726); quoted in Sean Shesgreen, *Images of the Outcast: The Urban Poor in the Cries of London* (Manchester, 2002), pp. 114–15.

79. Ned Ward, *The London Spy* (Folio Society edn, 1955), pp. 27–28

80. Daniel Defoe, *The History and Remarkable Life of the Truly Honourable Col. Jacque, Commonly Call'd Col. Jack, Edited with an Introduction by Samuel Holt Monk* (1722; Oxford, 1970), p. 7.

81. Ibid., p. 8.

82. Ibid., p. 9.

83. Ibid., p. 16.

84. Ibid., p. 37.

85. GL, 'Court of Governors, Bridewell and Bethlem: Minutes, 12 January 1737/8 to 4 April 1751', MS 33011/21, 14 January 1747/8, p. 346.

86. Common Council Proclamation, Barnard Mayor, Tuesday 1 January 1737.

87. Ben Weinreb and Christopher Hibbert, eds, *The London Encyclopaedia* (1983), 'Rag Fair', p. 635.

88. BL, Add. MS 27828, 'Place Papers, xl, Manners and Morals', iv, fol. 118.

89. BL, Add. MS, 27828, 'Place Papers, xl, Manners and Morals', iv, fol. 119.

90. *OBP*, 6 September 1716, Mary Pewterer alias Finch, t17160906–24.

91. CLRO, London Sessions Papers, LSP/1731/1.

92. *OBP*, 4 July 1730, Robert Wheeler, John Collins, t17300704–44.

93. CLRO, London Sessions Papers, LSP/1731/1.

94. *OBP*, 8 December 1731, Joseph Paterson alias Paternoster, Joseph Darvan, t17311208–26.

95. *OBP*, 24 February 1731, Andrew Noland, John Allwright, t17310224–19.

96. *OBP*, 2 June 1731, Edward Perkins, t17310602–9; 10 July 1734, John Fossey, t17340710–38.

97. *OBP*, 19 April 1732, Henry Whitesides, George Scott, t17320419–22.

98. *OBP*, 2 June 1731, Edward Perkins, t17310602–9.

99. *OBP*, 14 July 1731, Edward Perkins, t17310714–14.

100. *OBP*, 8 December 1731, Joseph Paterson alias Paternoster, Joseph Darvan, t17311208–26.

101. See *OBP*, 8 December 1731, Joseph Paterson alias Paternoster, Joseph Darvan, t17311208–26; *OBP*, 8 December 1731, Joseph Paterson alias Peterson alias Paternoster, Joseph Darvan, t17311208–27; *OBP*, 8 December 1731, Joseph Paterson alias Peterson alias Paternoster, Joseph Darvan, t17311208–74.

102. *OBP*, 25 May 1732, John Crotch, alias Yarmouth, t17320525–22.

103. *OBP*, 15 January 1731, Thomas Coleman alias John Haynes, t17310115–59; *OBP*, 2 May 1739, Thomas Coleman, t17390502–42.

104. At Greenwich that evening observations could be made only of the moon and one particularly bright star. The temperature recorded the day before was

68.5 degrees Fahrenheit, and the day after 60.5 degrees. See Bradley, *Astro-nomical Obsevations ... MDCCL to the Year MDCCLXII*, ii, pp. 163, 283.

105. *OBP*, 12 September 1759, Nicholas Randall, t17590912-22.

Notes to Chapter 3: Pauper Professions

1. Tobias Smollett, *The Expedition of Humphry Clinker* (1777; Harmondsworth 1967), p. 153.

2. Israel R. Potter, *The Life and Remarkable Adventures of Israel R. Potter* (1824; New York, 1962), pp. 68–69. For an excellent body of work treating in particular the art historical tradition of the 'Cries of London' see Sean Shesgreen, *The Criers and Hawkers of London: Engravings and Drawings by Marcellus Laroon* (Aldershot, 1990); and Sean Shesgreen, *Images of the Outcast: The Urban Poor in the Cries of London* (Manchester, 2002).

3. BL, Add. MS 27828, 'Place Papers, xl,: Manners and Morals', fos 7–8.

4. Tom Brown, *Amusements Serious and Comical Calculated for the Meridian of London* (1700), pp. 20–21; quoted in Shesgreen, *Images of the* Outcast, p. 110. A 'maid' in this context is a fish, usually a skate.

5. Jonathan Swift, *Journal to Stella*, ed. Harold Williams, (Oxford, 1948), ii, p. 581.

6. The most comprehensive account of the regulation of porters and porterage is still Walter M. Stern, *The Porters of London* (1960).

7. See Mark Jenner, 'Circulation and Disorder: London Streets and Hackney Coaches, *c.* 1640 – *c.* 1740', in Tim Hitchcock and Heather Shore, eds, *The Streets of London from the Great Fire to the Great Stink* (2003).

8. Potter, *The Life and Remarkable Adventures of Israel R. Potter*, p. 94.

9. William Marshall Craig, 'Mansion House. Matches' (1804); reproduced in Shesgreen, *Images of the Outcast*, p. 158.

10. John Brown, *A Memoir of Robert Blincoe, an Orphan Boy; Sent from the Work-house of St Pancras, London at Seven Years of Age, to Endure the Horrors of a Cotton-Mill* (Manchester, 1832, 1977 edn), p. 13.

11. *OBP*, 26 February 1783, Mary Shepherd, t17830226-62.

12. John Gay, *Poetry and Prose*, 'Trivia', ed., Vinton A. Dearing (Oxford, 1974), ii, lines 425–39.

13. *Low-Life: or One Half of the World Knows Not How the Other Half Live* (2nd edn, 1749), p. 16.

14. Potter, *The Life and Remarkable Adventures of Israel R. Potter*, p. 78.

15. Francis Place, *The Autobiography of Francis Place, 1771–1854*, ed. Mary Thale (Cambridge, 1972), p. 47.

16. WAM, Westminster Coroner's Inquests, 4 November 1766, 'John Hoser'. Information of Elizabeth Collman.

17. WAM, Westminster Coroner's Inquests, 3 July 1766, 'James Jeffreys'. Information of John Edwards. A good set of observations were made at Greenwich on this day, 1 July 1766, and the temperature was recorded at 69 degrees Fahrenheit. See Nevil Maskelyne, *Astronomical Observations Made at the Royal Observatory at Greenwich in the Years 1765, 1766, 1767, 1768 and 1769* (1774), part 1, p. 52, part 2, p. 19.

18. On 17 March 1796 a temperature of 46 degrees Fahrenheit was recorded at Greenwich. See Nevil Maskelyne, *Astronomical Observations Made at the Royal Observatory at Greenwich from MDCCLXXXVII to MDCCXCVIII* (1799), part 2, p. 106.

19. CLRO, 'Guildhall Justice Room Minute Book 1796, February 15 – March 25' MS GJR/M55, 'Friday 18 March 1796'. The earliest recorded reference to a 'mudlark' is from 1785 (*Oxford English Dictionary*), but it is clear that collecting coals from the foreshore of the Thames was a much older occupation than this suggests. The author of the 1749 *Low-Life*, p. 89, records: 'A great number of people looking for coals at low-water mark, on the sand-bank near Cuper's Stairs on the shore'.

20. BL, Add. MS 27826, 'Place Papers, xxxviii, Manners and Morals', ii, fol. 174.

21. I would like to thank John Styles and Giorgio Riello of the Victoria and Albert Museum for providing information on the early history of pre-prepared shoe polish.

22. Carl Phillip Moritz, *Travels of Carl Philipp Moritz in England in 1782* (1795; 1926), p. 34.

23. For an elderly, pauper shoeblack see Guildhall Library, 'St Martin Ludgate, Examinations of Paupers, 1774–1786', MS 1331/1, p. 35; for Paul Sandby's powerful image, see Shesgreen, *Images of the Outcast*, plate 3, p. 134.

24. Gay, 'Trivia', ii, lines. 141–44, 213–16.

25. LMA, Middlesex Sessions Papers, 1720/27.

26. GL, 'Court of Governors, Bridewell and Bethlem: Minutes 26 October 1722 to 15 December 1737', MS 33011/20, 27 March 1724, p. 26.

27. Daniel Defoe, *The History and Remarkable Life of the Truly Honourable Col. Jacque, Commonly Call'd Col. Jack*, edited with an introduction by Samuel Holt Monk (1722; Oxford, 1970), p. 7.

28. Gay, 'Trivia', ii, lines 91–94.

29. William Whitehead, 'The Sweepers' (1754), reproduced in Roger Lonsdale, ed., *Eighteenth-Century Verse* (Oxford, 1984), pp. 29–30.

30. Ned Ward, *The London Spy*, ed. Paul Hyland (4th edn, 1709; East Lansing Michigan, 1993),

31. *Low-Life*, p. 30.

32. [Isaac Bickerstaff], *The Life, Strange Voyages and Uncommon Adventures of Ambrose Gwinett Formerly Known to the Public as the Lame Beggar; Who for a*

Long Time Swept the Way at the Mew's Gate, Charing Cross (4th edn, 1770), p. 35.

33. *OBP*, 25 Februrary 1736, Stephen otherwise John Turner, t17360225–33.

34. Gay, 'Trivia', ii, lines 456–60.

35. CLRO, Courts of the President and Governors for the Poor of London, 1702–5, MS New 377c/1/22, fol. 29.

36. For an account of paving in London see Sally Jeffery, 'Pebbles, Posts and Purbeck Paving: A Study of Early Eighteenth-Century Street Paving in London. With a Gazetteer by Robert Crayford', *Transactions of the Association for Studies in the Conservation of Historic Buildings*, 13 (1988), pp. 29–36; and Louis W. G. Malcolm, 'Early History of the Streets and Paving of London', *Transactions of the Newcomen Society*, 14 (1934), pp. 83–94.

37. *Monthly Review* (1760), quoted in Charlotte Charke, *A Narrative of the Life of Mrs Charlotte Charke*, ed. Robert Rehder (1999), p. xlviii.

38. Moritz, *Travels*, p. 35.

39. Malcom Falkus, 'Lighting the Dark Ages of English Economic History: Town Streets before the Industrial Revolution', in D. C. Coleman and A. H. John, eds, *Trade, Government and Economy in Pre-Industrial England* (1976), p. 248.

40. *Low-Life*, p. 97.

41. See for example Edward Howard's *The Six Days Adventure* (1671); *OBP*, 11 July 1726, Margaret Clap, t17260711–54.

42. Quoted in, Sheila O'Connell, *London 1753* (2003), p. 147.

43. Charke, *Narrative of the Life of Mrs Charlotte Charke*, p. 39.

44. Ibid, p. 39.

45. *The Midnight Rambler: or New Nocturnal Spy for the Present Year. Containing a Complete Description of the Modern Transactions of London and Westminster from the Hours of Nine in the Evening till Six in the Morning* (c. 1770; another edn, 1766), p. 91.

46. *OBP*, 8 December 1736, Joseph Anthill, Thomas Waters, Daniel Maccartey, Philip Brown, t17361208–74.

47. For an account of the development of British depictions of street children see Martin Postle, *Angels and Urchins: The Fancy Picture in Eighteenth-Century British Art* (1998); CLRO, 'Guildhall Justice Room Minute Book, 1791, 14 January to 17 February', MS GJR/M46, Saturday, 15 January 1791.

48. *OBP*, 16 Arpil 1740, Mary North, t17400416–15.

49. *OBP*, 28 February 1759, Ruth Child, t17590228–14. At Greenwich no observations could be made that whole week, while the temperature recorded ranged between 42 and 46 degrees Fahrenheit. See James Bradley, *Astronomical Observations Made at the Royal Observatory at Greenwich from the Year MDCCL to the Year MDCCLXII*, ii (1805), pp. 150, 277.

50. Ned Ward, *The London Spy Compleat: in Eighteen Parts* (c. 1700), ii, part 2,

p. 10; quoted in Sarah Pennell, '"Great Quantities of Gooseberry Pye and Baked Clod of Beef": Victualling and Eating Out in Early Modern London', in Paul Griffiths and Mark Jenner, eds, *Londinopolis: Essays in the Cultural and Social History of Early Modern London* (Manchester, 2000), p. 242.

51. For a general treatment of the evolution of the 'area' and the servicing of eighteenth-century townhouses see Dan Cruickshank and Neil Burton, *Life in the Georgian City* (1990), part 2.

52. WAC, F2004, fol. 198, 17 October 1677, quoted in Jeremy Boulton, 'Going on the Parish: The Parish Pension and Its Meaning in the London Suburbs, 1640–1724', in Tim Hitchcock, Peter King and Pamela Sharpe, eds, *Chronicling Poverty: The Voices and Strategies of the English Poor, 1640–1840* (Basingstoke, 1997), p. 33.

53. E. A. Haywood, *A New Present for a Servant-Maid: Containing Rules for her Moral Conduct both with Respect to Herself and her Superiors: The Whole Art of Cookery, Pickling, Preserving* (1771), p. 11.

54. In larger households the provision of charity at the kitchen door was more regularised. Susanna Whatman, for instance, directed that 'all broken victuals are to be at the disposal only of the housekeeper, and no liberty is allowed of any other servant giving anything away that is left after the housekeeper has seen to the poor people's broth etc., which generally takes up all the remains of bits of bread etc.' *The Housekeeping Book of Susanna Whatman, 1776–1800* (1987), p. 46.

55. Peter Earle, *A City Full of People: Men and Women of London, 1650–1750* (1994), see table A4, p. 270.

56. *OBP*, 6 June 1717, Katharine Field, Jane Chalk, t17170606–2.

57. Public Record Office, PROB 24/54, fol. 93; quoted in Earle, *A City Full of People*, p. 240.

58. *OBP*, 6 July 1748, Rebecca Portore, t17480706–2.

59. *OBP*, 10 October 1722, Sarah Churchill, t17221010–22; *OBP*, 4 April 1744, Elizabeth Edwards, otherwise Lareman, t17440404–23.

60. CLRO, Coroners' Inquest, 4 August 1794, 'A Man Unknown'.

61. *The Ordinary of Newgate's Account*, 6 August 1740.

62. For the history of domestic service in London see Bridget Hill, *Servants: English Domestics in the Eighteenth Century* (Oxford, 1996); Tim Meldrum, *Domestic Service and Gender, 1660–1750: Life and Work in the London Household* (Harlow, 2000); and A. D. Kent, 'Ubiquitous but Invisible: Female Domestic Servants in Mid Eighteenth-Century London', *History Workshop Journal*, 28 (1989), pp. 111–28; for the insecurity of employment among domestic servants, see Tim Hitchcock and John Black, eds, *Chelsea Settlement and Bastardy Examinations, 1733–1766*, (London Record Society, 33, 1999), passim.

63. A good range of observations were made at Greenwich that evening, 8 Decem-

ber 1768, the temperature was recorded at 36 degrees Fahrenheit. See Maskelyne, *Astronomical Observations Made ... Years 1765, 1766, 1767, 1768 and 1769*, part 1, p. 140, part 2, p. 47.

64. WAM, Westminster Coroner's Inquest, 16 December 1768, 'Ann Dyson'.
65. WAM, Westminster Coroner's Inquest, 27 December 1771, 'William Urin'.
66. George Parker, *A View of Society and Manners in High and Low Life*, (1781), p. 58.
67. BL, Add. MS 27825, 'Place Papers, xxxvii, Manners and Morals', i, fol. 144.
68. *Spectator*, no. 454.
69. *OBP*, 7 September 1722, John Dyer, t17220907–49.
70. *The Journal of Samuel Curwen, Loyalist*, ed. Andrew Oliver (Cambridge Massachusetts, 1972), i, pp. 51–52.
71. Haywood, *A New Present for a Servant-Maid*, p. 3.
72. BL, Add. MS 27825, 'Place Papers, xxxvii, Manners and Morals', i, B. Grossness, Songs', fol. 147.
73. Ibid., fol. 151.
74. Ibid., fol. 167.
75. Ned Ward, *The London Spy*, p. 82. St Paul's Churchyard was a traditional space for ballad singing and political speechifying, and had been a flash point for political demonstrations in the lead up to the Civil War. But with the rebuilding of the cathedral after the Great Fire, most of the open space was enclosed within a high cast-iron paling which effectively excluded most beggars and political activists. The cost of this 'passive policing' was over £11,000, reflecting how important this aspect of control had become. See Dan Cruickshank and Peter Wyld, *Georgian Townhouses and their Details* (London, 1975), p. 211.
76. CLRO, 'Courts of the President and Governors for the Poor of London, 1702–5', MS New 377c/1/22, fol. 246.
77. See Paula McDowell, *The Women of Grub Street: Press, Politics and Gender in the London Literary Marketplace, 1678–1730* (Oxford, 1998), pp. 74–82.
78. GL, 'Court of Governors, Bridewell and Bethlem: Minutes, 1 January 1762 to 15 March 1781', MS 3011/23, pp. 249, 256.
79. John James Bezer, 'The Autobiography of One of the Chartist Rebels of 1848', in D. M. Vincent, ed., *Testaments of Radicalism* (London, 1977), p. 179.
80. *Journal of Samuel Curwen*, ii, p. 586.
81. High and low temperatures were recorded for 19 and 25 March 1796. On 19 March the high temperature was 49 degrees and the low, 41 degrees. On 25 March these figures were 41 and 39 degrees Fahrenheit. See Maskelyne, *Astronomical Observations ... MDCCLXXXVII to MDCCXCVIII*, part 2, p. 106.
82. CLRO, Coroner's Inquest, 23 March 1796, 'A Man Unknown'.
83. *OBP*, 24 April 1745, Mary Cut and Come-Again, t17450424–31.
84. Mary Saxby, *Memoirs of a Female Vagrant Written by Herself* (1806), pp. 8, 9.

85. *OBP*, 10 May 1744, Sarah Lowther, late of London, spinster, otherwise Sarah the wife of Robert Rochead, t17440510–29.

86. *OBP*, 24 April 1745, Margaret Mears, otherwise Kirby, Jane Smerk , otherwise Singing Jenny, Catharme Bowyer, t17450424–32.

87. See John T. Smith, *Vagabondiana* (1817), p. 37. There is also a suggestion that this image is based on a figure from Pieter Breugel's *Justice*. See Sheila O'Connell, *London, 1753* (2003), p. 56.

88. See McDowell, *The Women of Grub Street*, pp. 59, 60.

89. Public Record Office, State Papers (Domestic), 35/67/60, fol. 121; quoted in Paula McDowell, *The Women of Grub Street*, p. 58.

90. *OBP*, 24 April 1745, Mary Cut and Come-Again, t17450424–31.

91. Jonathan Swift, *Journal to Stella*, ii, p. 570.

Notes to Chapter 4: Menaces and Promises

1. *OBP*, 16 April 1740, John Collet, t17400416–19.

2. Henry Fielding, *An Enquiry into the Causes of the Late Encrease of Robbers and Related Writings*, ed. M. R. Zirker (Oxford, 1988), pp. 139–49.

3. John Gay, *Poetry and Prose*, 'Trivia', ed., Vinton A Dearing (Oxford, 1974), iii, line 136.

4. Daniel Defoe, *The History and Remarkable Life of the Truly Honourable Col. Jacque, Commonly Call'd Col. Jack*, edited with an introduction by Samuel Holt Monk (1722; Oxford, 1970), pp. 8–9.

5. John Gay, *Poetry and Prose*, 'Trivia', iii, lines 133–38.

6. *Proposal for Relief and Punishment of Vagrants, Particularly such as Frequent the Streets and Publick Places of Resort Within this Kingdom* (1748), p. 3.

7. Charles P. Moritz, *Travels, Chiefly on Foot, Through Several Parts of England in 1782. Described in Letters to a Friend* (1795), pp. 141–42.

8. Quoted without attribution in Christopher Hibbert, *King Mob: The Story of Lord George Gordon and the Riots of 1780* (1959), p. 107.

9. BL, Add. MS 27825, 'Place Papers, xxxvii, Manners and Morals', i, fol. 146v.

10. Quoted without attribution in Hibbert, *King Mob*, p. 122.

11. *OBP*, 28 June 1780, Thomas Taplin, t17800628–18.

12. At Greenwich Nevil Maskelyne recorded a daytime temperature of 74 degrees Fahrenheit. See Nevil Maskelyne, *Astronomical Observations Made at the Royal Observatory at Greenwich from the Year MDCCLXXV to the Year MDCCLXXXII inclusive* (1783), part 1, p. 179, part 2, p. 56.

13. *OBP*, 28 June 1780, George Banton, t17800628–45.

14. *OBP*, 18 May 1768, Daniel Saxton, t17680518–23. For examples of the extensive literature on 'mob' violence in the eighteenth-century see Robert Shoemaker, *The London Mob: Violence and Disorder in Eighteenth-Century England* (2004);

Nicholas Rogers, *Crowds, Culture and Politics in Georgian Britain* (Oxford, 1998); and Kathleen Wilson, 'Empire, Trade and Popular Politics in Mid-Hanoverian Britain: The Case of Admiral Vernon', *Past and Present*, 121, November 1988, pp. 74–109.

15. *OBP*, 19 October 1785, James Rook, James Jordan, t17851019–34.

16. For an account of Garrow's career see Alyson N. May, *The Bar and the Old Bailey, 1750 to 1850* (Charleston, North Carolina, 2003), ch. 3.

17. GL, 'Court of Governors, Bridewell and Bethlem: Minutes, 12 January 1737/8 to 4 April 1751', MS 33011/21, p. 234.

18. GL, 'Court of Governors, Bridewell and Bethlem: Minutes, 26 June 1713 to 2 August 1722', MS 33011/19, p. 392.

19. Defoe, *Col. Jacque*, pp. 203–4.

20. Mary Saxby, *Memoirs of a Female Vagrant Written by Herself* (1806), p. 7.

21. In 1772 Pierre Jean Grosley commented on the apparent contradiction between contemporary perceptions of crime and the general honesty of Londoners: 'However the inhabitants of London may think themselves surrounded with thieves, they do not act in consequence with regard to pewter pots, in which the publicans distribute strong beer to the houses in their neighbourhood. As soon as these pots are emptied, that the boys belonging to the alehouses may gather them with the greater ease, they are thrown into the entries of open houses, and often into the street at the foot of the door, which is shut. I saw pots thus lying in the streets at every turn; and thus sight encouraged me not to be afraid of thieves'. Pierre Jean Grosley, *A Tour to London: or, New Observations on England, And its Inhabitants, Translated from the French by T. Nugent* (London, 1772), p. 50.

22. *OBP*, 23 Feb 1715, Ann Hammond, t17150223–43.

23. *OBP*, 6 June 1717, Ann Brown alias Hammond, t17170606–19.

24. *OBP*, 17 July 1717, Mary Richardson, alias Ann Hammond, t17170717–1.

25. *Covent Garden Journal*, no. 28, 7 April 1752; quoted in Heather Shore, 'Crime, Criminal Networks and the Survival Strategies of the Poor in Early Eighteenth-Century London', in Steven King and Alannah Tomkins, eds, *The Poor in England, 1700–1850: An Economy of Makeshift* (Manchester, 2003), p. 137.

26. *OBP*, 15 May 1755, Margaret Davis, t17550515–13. The weather that day allowed a full range of astronomical observations to be made at Greenwich, while the recorded temperature there stood at 68 degrees Fahrenheit. See James Bradley, *Astronomical Observations Made at the Royal Observatory at Greenwich from the year MDCCL to the Year MDCCLXII*, i (1798), part 1, pp. 25–26 and part 2, p. 12.

27. This list simply reproduces in order all the items stolen by people tried at the Court of Bridewell in May 1744. GL, 'Court of Governors, Bridewell and Bethlem: Minutes, 12 January 1737/8 to 4 April 1751', MS 33011/21, pp. 180–83.

28. *A Trip from St James's to the Royal Exchange* (1744), p. 24.

29. Gay, 'Trivia', iii, lines 247–53, 285–89.

30. GL, 'Court of Governors, Bridewell and Bethlem: Minutes, 26 October 1722 to 15 December 1737', MS 3011/20, p. 76.

31. [John Badcock], *The London Guide* (1818), pp. 81–82; reproduced in John Marriott, ed., *Unknown London: Early Modernist Visions of the Metropolis, 1815–45* (2000), vol. 1.

32. *OBP*, 2 July 1735, John Boswell, t17350702–15.

33. *OBP*, 11 July 1750, William Wilson, t17500711–53.

34. [Erasmus Jones], *The Man of Manners: or, Plebeian Polish'd. Being Plain and Familiar Rules for a Modest and Genteel Behaviour, on most of the Ordinary Occasions of Life* (1737), pp. 59–60. For a useful account of the sixteenth-century to gambling and the 'tricks of the town', see Gāmini Salgādo, *The Elizabethan Underworld* (Stroud, Gloucestershire, 1992).

35. Several observations were made that night at Greenwich, and the temperature was recorded at 36 degrees Fahrenheit. See Nevil Maskelyne, *Astronomical Observations Made at the Royal Observatory at Greenwich in the Years 1765, 1766, 1767, 1768 and 1769* (1774), part 1, p. 107, part 2, p. 34.

36. WAM, Westminster Coroner's Records, 22 February 1768, 'Abraham Javelleaue'.

37. GL, 'Court of Governors, Bridewell and Bethlem: Minutes, 12 January 1737/8 to 4 April 1751', MS 33011/21, pp. 279, 280.

38. Curtis, Mayor, Tuesday *the 2d day of February 1796, and in 36 George III.*

39. LMA, 'A Copy of an Order of Sessions against Wheelbarrows, 1707', Acc/268/uncat.

40. It is not entirely certain that the Sarah Bland arrested in 1743 is the same Sarah Bland whose name appeared in the Court of Bridewell records for 1751, but there were only four female children of that name born between 1700 and 1730 in the greater London area. The evidence for Sarah Bland and Mary Maurice working as prostitutes is circumstantial. In part, the fact that they were picked up together and that Sarah Bland in her evidence to the Old Bailey presented them as a couple suggests as much. More than this, the loud silence of the trial records in relation to their occupation is indicative. No one is described as a prostitute, yet much significance is given to the occupations of women, when they are identified. *OBP*, September 1742, William Bird, t17420909–37. For a modern account of the 'Roundhouse Disaster' see Tim Hitchcock, '"You Bitches ... Die and Be Damned": Gender, Authority and the Mob in St Martin's Round-House disaster of 1742', in Tim Hitchcock and Heather Shore, eds, *The Streets of London from the Great Fire to the Great Stink* (2003).

41. GL, 'Court of Governors, Bridewell and Bethlem: Minutes, 26 June 1713 to 2 August 1722', MS 33011/19, p. 103.

42. CLRO, Mansion House Justice Room, Charge Book, 1728–33, New 392C. The 'Pot Act', 11 and 12 William III, c. 15 is briefly discussed in Sidney and Beatrice Webb, *The Manor and the Borough*, pt 2 (1908; 1963), p. 676.

43. GL, 'Court of Governors, Bridewell and Bethlem: Minutes, 12 January 1737/8 to 4 April 1751', MS 33011/21, p. 92.

44. Gay, 'Trivia', iii, lines 267–73.

45. *OBP*, 4 June 1747, Sarah Lar, t17470604–8.

46. *OBP*, 25 April 1781, Sarah Robinson, Elizabeth Clarke, t17810425–37. The crime took place on 23 April, which Samuel Curwen describes as 'Brisk and mildish air, wind S.W.', Samuel Curwen, *The Journal of Samuel Curwen, Loyalist*, ed. Andrew Oliver (Salem, Massachusetts, 1972), ii, p. 747. At Greenwich they recorded a temperature of 60 degrees Fahrenheit, but were unable to make any astronomical observations. See Maskelyne, *Astronomical Observations ... 1765, 1766, 1767, 1768 and 1769*, part 1, p. 205, part 2, p. 63.

47. *OBP*, 14 September 1785, Sarah Cooper, t17850914–95.

48. *OBP*, 11 January 1717, Mary Long, t17170111–18.

49. BL, Add. MS. 27826, 'Place Papers, xxxviii, Manners and Morals', iv, fol. 119.

50. *OBP*, 11 October 1738, Margery Stanton, t17381011–15; *OBP*, 15 October 1740, Margaret Stanton , otherwise Ruggetty Madge, t17401015–60. See also BL. Add. MS. 27826, 'Place Papers, xxxviii, Manners and Morals', ii, fol. 33.

51. The Astronomer Royal noted, 'air clear and Jupiter's belts distinct', and recorded a daytime temperature of 58 degrees Fahrenheit. See Maskelyne, *Astronomical Observations ... 1765, 1766, 1767, 1768 and 1769*, part 1, p. 326, part 2, p. 124.

52. WAM, Westminster Coroner's Inquest, 12 September 1774, 'Sarah Knight'.

53. CLRO, Courts of the President and Governors for the Poor of London, 1702–5, MS New 377c/1/22, fol. 193.

54. James Gillray, 'The Whore's Last Shift' (1779) reproduced in J. A. Sharpe, *Crime and the Law in English Satirical Prints, 1600–1832* (Cambridge, 1986), p. 165.

55. *OBP*, 7 December 1757, Martha Tilman, t17571207–34.

56. GL, St Dionis Backchurch, Papers Relating to a Poor Law Appeal from Paul Patrick Kearney, 1771', MS 11280C, letter 3, 13 March 1771.

57. GL, St Dionis Backchurch, Workhouse Inquests Minute Book (Rough), 1762–79, MS. 4219/2, Hoxton, 4 March 1777.

58. CLRO, Guildhall Justice Room, Minute Book, 1762, 19 April to 14 May, MS. GJR/M3, Tuesday 27 April 1762.

59. Royal College of Surgeons, Board Minutes, 1763–65, 26 April 1764, pp. 140–42. My thanks to Kevin Siena for this reference.

60. Quoted in Faramerz Dabhoiwala, 'The Pattern of Sexual Immorality in Seventeenth- and Eighteenth-Century London', in Paul Griffiths and Mark

S. R. Jenner, eds, *Londinopolis: Essays in the Cultural and Social History of Early Modern London* (Manchester, 2000), p. 95.

61. GL, 'Minutes of the Brewers Company', MS 5520, vol. 27, 10 December 1731. My thanks to Dianne Payne for this reference.

62. William Hutton, *A Journey From Birmingham to London* (Birmingham, 1785), pp. 74–75.

63. On the structure and organisation of prostitution in eighteenth-century London see Tony Henderson, *Disorderly Women in Eighteenth-Century London: Prostitution and Control in the Metropolis, 1730–1830* (1999); Randolph Trumbach, *Sex and the Gender Revolution, i, Heterosexuality and the Third Gender in Enlightenment London* (Chicago, Illinois, 1998); Faramerz Dabhoiwala, 'Sex, Social Relations and the Law in Seventeenth- and Eighteenth-Century London', in Michael J. Braddick and John Walter, eds, *Negotiating Power in Early Modern Society: Order, Hierarchy and Subordination in Britain and Ireland* (Cambridge, 2001); Faramerz Dabhoiwala, 'The Pattern of Sexual Immorality in Seventeenth- and Eighteenth-Century London', in Paul Griffiths and Mark Jenner, eds, *Londinopolis: Essays in the Cultural and Social History of Early Modern London* (Manchester, 2000); Sarah Lloyd, '"Pleasure's Golden Bait": Prostitution, Poverty and the Magdalen Hospital in Eighteenth-Century London', *History Workshop Journal*, 41 (1996), 50–70.

64. For a classic discussion of misogyny in late seventeenth-century English culture see Felicity Nussbaum, *The Brink of All We Hate* (Lexington Kentucky, 1984).

65. For a discussion of sexual assault in the context of domestic service, see Tim Meldrum, 'London Domestic Servants from Depositional Evidence, 1660–1750: Servant-Employer Sexuality in the Patriarchal Household', in Tim Hitchcock, Peter King and Pamela Sharpe, eds, *Chronicling Poverty: The Voices and Strategies of the English Poor, 1640–1840* (Basingstoke, 1997). For a more general history of rape in this period see Anna Clark, *Women's Silence, Men's Violence: Sexual Assault in England, 1770–1845* (1987); Antony Simpson, 'Masculinity and Control: The Prosecution of Sex Offences in Eighteenth-Century London' (New York University Ph.D. thesis, 1984); Antony Simpson, 'Vulnerability and the Age of Female Consent: Legal Innovation and its Effect on Prosecution for Rape in Eighteenth-Century London', in George S. Rousseau and Roy Porter, eds, *Sexual Underworlds of the Enlightenment* (Manchester, 1987). For a well argued response to Clark's perspective see Roy Porter, 'Rape: Does it have a Historical Meaning?', in S. Tomaselli and Roy Porter, eds, *Rape: An Historical and Cultural Enquiry* (Oxford, 1986); and for a sophisticated analysis of evidence presented in court at rape trials see Miranda Chaytor, 'Husband(ry): Narratives of Rape in the Seventeenth Century', *Gender and History*, 7 (1995) 378–407.

66. *Constables Hue and Cry after Whores and Bawds etc. With a Pleasant Description of the Habits, Complections, Nature* ... (*c.* 1700), p. 8.

67. William King, 'The Beggar Woman' (1709), reproduced in Lonsdale, *Eighteenth-Century Verse*, pp. 79–80.

68. At Greenwich the barometer was steady all that week, and the temperatures recorded ranged between 52 degrees and 60 degrees Fahrenheit. See James Bradley, *Astronomical Observations Made at the Royal Observatory at Greenwich from the year MDCCL to the Year MDCCLXII*, ii (1805), pp. 180, 289.

69. *OBP*, 16 April 1760, Margaret King, t17600416–17.

70. William Woty, 'A Mock Invocation to Genius' (1770), reproduced in Roger Lonsdale, *Eighteenth-Century Verse* (Oxford, 1984), pp. 491–92.

71. *OBP*, 15 October 1740, William Duell, t17401015–53.

72. *OBP*, 8 September 1736, Elizabeth Burroughs, Bryan Carney, t17360908–59.

Notes to Chapter 5: The Rhetoric of Rags

1. César de Saussure, *A Foreign View of England in 1725–1729: The Letters of Monsieur César de Saussure to his Family*, translated and edited by Madame Van Muyden (1995), pp. 117–18.

2. Jonathan Andrews, 'Begging the Question of Idiocy: The Definition and Socio-Cultural Meaning of Idiocy in Early Modern Britain: Part 2', *History of Psychiatry*, 9 (1998), pp, 184, 185.

3. Reports of beggars who dressed in rags and ate broken meat became a staple of the *Annual Register*. Almost every year the *Register* reported the large amounts left in the wills of beggars. In 1765 it recorded that 'In Kent-street, Southwark, John Cornwall, aged 91 ... though a common beggar for more than 60 years last past, left ... upwards of 400 guineas in gold'. *Annual Register for 1765*, p. 127.

4. *Tatler*, no. 68.

5. 'The Beggar', lines 5–8, published in the *Annual Register for 1770*, p. 222.

6. For a history of non-elite clothing and the used clothing trade see Beverly Lemire, *Dress, Culture and Commerce: The English Clothing Trade before the Factory, 1660–1800* (Basingstoke, 1997). Phillis Cunnington and Catharine Lucas, *Occupational Costume in England: From the Eleventh Century to 1914* (1967); E. Ewing, *Everyday Dress, 1650–1900* (1984). For the clothing of the very poor see John Styles, 'Clothing the North: The Supply of Non-Elite Clothing in the Eighteenth-Century North of England' *Textile History*, 25 (1994), pp. 139–66; John Styles, 'Involuntary Consumers? Servants and Their Clothes in Eighteenth-Century England', *Textile History*, 33 (2002), pp. 9–21; Sam Smiles, 'Defying Comprehension: Resistance to Uniform Appearance in Depicting the Poor, 1770s to 1830s, *Textile History*, 33, 1 (2002), pp. 22–36.

7. There is no substantial literature that deals specifically with 'body linen', but see Georges Vigarello, *Concepts of Cleanliness: Changing Attitudes in France since the Middle Ages* (1988); A. Corbin, *The Foul and the Fragrant: Odour and the French Social Imagination* (1986); and Claudia and Richard Bushman, 'The Early History of Cleanliness in America', *Journal of American History*, 74 (March 1988), pp. 1213–38.

8. BL, Add. MS. 27827, fos 50–51; quoted in *The Autobiography of Francis Place, 1771–1854* ed. Mary Thale (Cambridge, 1972), p. 51n.

9. See, for example, *Autobiography of Francis Place*, p. 118.

10. *OBP*, 5 October 1740, John Loppenburg, t17401015-66.

11. At Greenwich the Astronomer Royal described his observations as 'faint', and the weather as 'very hazy'. He recorded a temperature of 64 degrees Fahrenheit. See James Bradley, *Astronomical Observations made at the Royal Observatory at Greenwich from the Year MDCCL to the Year MDCCCLXII*, ii (1805), pp. 218, 306.

12. WAM, Westminster Coroner's Records, 1 May 1762, 'Elizabeth Beck'.

13. *OBP*, 14 January 1789, Mary Wade, Jane Whiting, t17890114-58.

14. George Parker, *A View of Society and Manners in High and Low Life: Being the Adventures ... of the Stage Itinerant* (1781), p. 225.

15. For a recent account of the moneys spent on clothing the poor by parishes see Steven King, 'Reclothing the English Poor, 1750–1840', *Textile History*, 33 (2002), pp. 37–47.

16. *OBP*, 14 July 1762, Sarah Metyard, Sarah Morgan Metyard, t17620714-30.

17. GL, 'St Olave Hart Street, London, Viscount Sudbury Charity, Hospital and Almshous Committee Minutes 1739–69', MS. 869A, fos 1, 2.

18. *The Journal of John Harrower, an Indentured Servant in the Colony of Virginia, 1773–1776*, ed. Edward Miles Riley (Williamsburg, Virginia, 1963), p. 14.

19. John Thomas Smith, *A Book for a Rainy Day: or Recollections of the Events of the Last Sixty Years* (1845), p. 73.

20. See Bradley, *Astronomical Observations ... MDCCL to the Year MDCCCLXII*, ii, pp. 221, 307.

21. WAM, Westminster Coroner's Inquests, 6 July 1762, 'John Webb'.

22. For a brief discussion of the role of 'rags' in the self-presentation of vagrants and the very poor, see Steven King and Christiana Payne, 'Introduction: The Dress of the Poor', *Textile History*, 33 (2002), pp. 6–7.

23. *OBP*, 6 July 1748, Mary Ann Lawless, t17480706-38.

24. GL, 'Petititons for Relief to St Helen's within Bishopsgate, 1741–5', MS. 6888.

25. Joseph Barker, *The History and Confessions of a Man as Put Forth by Himself* (1846), p. 74.

26. GL, 'Court of Governors, Bridewell and Bethlem: Minutes, 12 January 1737/8 to 4 April 1751', MS 33011/21, pp. 263, 274.

27. CLRO, 'Journal of Common Council', for. 56, fos 382–83.

28. Israel R. Potter, *The Life and Remarkable Adventures of Israel R. Potter* (1824; New York, 1962), p. 28.

29. Daniel Defoe, *The History and Remarkable Life of the Truly Honourable Col. Jacque, Commonly Call'd Col. Jack*, edited with an introduction by Samuel Holt Monk (1722; Oxford, 1970), pp. 9, 26–27.

30. James Lackington, *Memoirs of the First Forty-Five Years of the Life of James Lackington* (1791), pp. 126, 127–28.

31. On the depiction of rags by artists see Christiana Payne, '"Murillo-Like Rages or Clean Pinafores": Artistic and Social Preferences in the Representation of the Dress of the Rural Poor', *Textile History*, 33 (2002), 48–62.

32. CLRO, Coroner's Inquest, 27 April 1793, 'Woman Unknown'.

33. CLRO, Coroner's Inquest, 21 December 1799, 'Woman Unknown'.

34. See Nevil Maskelyne, *Astronomical Observations Made at the Royal Observatory at Greenwich from MDCCLXXXVII to MDCCXCVIII* (1799), part 2, p. 72.

35. CLRO, Coroner's Inquest, 27 December 1792, 'Man Unknown'.

36. Jonathan Swift, *A Proposal for Giving Badges to the Beggars in all the Parishes of Dublin* (1737), reproduced in Jonathan Swift, *The Prose Works*, ed., Herbert Davis (1937–74), xiii, p. 140.

37. *Spectator*, no. 232.

38. See Maskelyne, *Astronomical Observations ... MDCCLXXXVII to MDCCXCVIII*, part 2, p. 80.

39. CLRO, Coroner's Inquest, 8 November 1793, 'Man Unknown'.

40. For a discussion of the role of vermin, including larger animals such as foxes, see Mary Fissell, 'Imagining Vermin in Early Modern England' *History Workshop Journal*, 47 (1999), pp. 1–29.

41. James Dawson Burn, *The Autobiography of a Beggar Boy*, ed., David Vincent (1978), p. 73.

42. See *The Workhouse Cruelty: Being a Full and True Account of one Mrs Whistle* (c. 1731); for a prose account of the same incident see *The Workhouse Cruelty, Workhouses Turn'd Gaols and Gaolers Executioners* (c. 1731); for the associated autopsy see BL, MS 4078, fol. 159.

43. *Richard Hutton's Complaints Book: The Notebook of the Steward of the Quaker Workhouse at Clerkenwell, 1711–1737*, ed. Tim Hitchcock, London Record Society, 24 (1987), item 139.

44. [Edward Ward], *The History of the London Clubs: or the Citizens Pastime, Particularly The Lying Club, The Beggars Club, The Yorkshire Club ... The Thieves Club, The Basket Women's Club. With a Sermon Preach'd to a Gang of Highway-men*, part 1 (1709), p. 7.

45. Jonathan Swift, *Gulliver's Travels*, ed., Harold Williams, (Oxford, 1965), pp. 112–13.

46. *Fascimile of the Cries of London First Published, c. 1754*, (Lympne Castle, Kent, 1978).

47. BL. Add. MS 27828, 'Place Papers, xl, Manners and Morals', iv, fol. 122; also quoted in *Autobiography of Francis Place*, p. 52.

48. *Autobiography of Francis Place*, p. 87.

49. There is a growing literature on the history of disability much of which relates specifically to pre-modern societies. See, for example, Anne Borsay, 'Returning Patients to the Community: Disability, Medicine and Economic Rationality before the Industrial Revolution', *Disability and Society*, 13 (1998), pp. 645–63; David Wright and Anne Digby, eds, *From Idiocy to Mental Deficiency: Historical Perspectives on People with Learning Disabilities* (1996); Margaret Pelling, 'Old Age, Poverty, and Disability in Early Modern Norwich: Work, Remarriage, and Other Expedients', in Margaret Pelling and R. M. Smith, eds, *Life, Death and the Elderly: Historical Perspectives*, (1991); Margaret Pelling, 'Healing the Sick Poor: Social Policy and Disability in Norwich 1550–1640', *Medical History*, 29 (1985), pp. 115–37.

50. Anon., 'The Lame Crew', c. 1660; original held at GL, item no. 26614.

51. John T. Smith, *Vagabondiana* (1817), p. 37.

52. For statistics on one London workhouse population see Tim Hitchcock, 'The English Workhouse: A Study in Institutional Poor Relief in Selected Counties, 1696–1750' (Oxford University D.Phil. thesis, 1985), pp. 194–210.

53. Joshua Gee, *Trade and Navigation of Great-Britain Considered* (1729); quoted in C. J. Ribton-Turner, *A History of Vagrants and Vagrancy and Beggars and Begging* (1887), p. 187.

54. [Ward], *The History of the London Clubs*, p. 7.

55. GL, 'Court of Governors, Bridewell and Bethlem: Minutes, 12 January 1737/8 to 4 April 1751', MS 33011/21, p. 143.

56. CLRO, Vagrant Books (4), together with 5 loose pages and a bill of mortality, 1738–42, Misc. MS 322.5, examination dated 20 March 1741.

57. Quoted in Ribton-Turner, *A History of Vagrants and Vagrancy and Beggars and Begging*, pp. 178–79.

58. For an excellent treatment of eighteenth-century attitudes towards idiocy see Jonathan Andrews, 'Begging the Question of Idiocy: The Definition and Socio-Cultural Meaning of Idiocy in Early Modern Britain', *History of Psychiatry*, 9 (1998), parts 1 and 2.

59. *A View of London and Westminster: or The Town Spy, etc.* (1728), part 1, pp. 42–43.

60. *A Trip from St James's to the Royal Exchange: The Manners, Customs and Amusements of the Inhabitants of London and Westminster* (1744), p. 12–13.

61. Early modern 'Body History' has become a well established sub-discipline in the last two decades. For an excellent treatment of women's bodies see Laura

Gowing, *Common Bodies: Women, Touch and Power in Seventeenth-Century England* (New Haven Connecticut, 2003). For a general guide to some of this literature, see Tim Hitchcock, *English Sexualities, 1700–1800* (Basingstoke, 1997), ch. 4.

62. *The Ordinary of Newgate's Account*, 6 August 1740; *OBP*, 9 July 1740, Samuel Badham, t174000709–2

63. *London Journal*, 13 February 1731/2.

64. Joshua Gee, *The Trade and Navigation of Great-Britain Considered* (1729); quoted in Ribton-Turner, *A History of Vagrants and Vagrancy and Beggars and Begging*, p. 188–89.

65. George Galloway, 'To the Memory of Gavin Wilson (Boot, Leg and Arm Maker)' (1795), reproduced in Roger Lonsdale, ed., *Eighteenth-Century Verse* (Oxford, 1984), pp. 805–6.

66. CLRO, London Sessions Papers, December 1782, '31 Examinations of Supposed Vagrants', see the examination of Thomas Dargaval, 16 November 1782.

67. At least five versions of this ballad and one act play were published during the eighteenth century. See for example, Robert Dodsley, *The Blind Beggar of Bethnal Green* (1741).

68. For a brief discussion of the Foundling Hospital's policy see Ruth McClure, *Coram's Children: The London Foundling Hospital in the Eighteenth Century* (New Haven, 1981), p. 229. For a much more detailed treatment of attitudes towards blindness in the eighteenth century see William R. Paulson, *Enlightenment, Romanticism and the Blind in France* (Princeton, New Jersey, 1987).

69. *OBP*, 15 May 1755, Thomas Cooper, t17550515–21.

70. *Annual Register for 1761*, p. 96.

71. CLRO, 'Court of the President and Governors for the Poor of London, 1702–5', MS New 377C/1/22, fol. 200.

72. CLRO, 'Mansion House Justice Room, Charge Book, 1728–1733', MS New 392C, 27 May 1730.

73. GL, 'Court of Governors, Bridewell and Bethlem: Minutes, 16 October 1722 to 15 December 1737', MS 3011.20, p. 81.

74. *OBP*, 16 April 1740, Elizabeth Evans, t17400416–24.

75. GL, 'Court of Governors, Bridewell and Bethlem: Minutes, 22 May 1751 to 1 December 1761', MS 3011/22, p. 349.

76. *A Trip From St James's to the Royal-Exchange: With Remarks Serious and Diverting on the Manners, Customs and Amusements of the Inhabitants of London and Westminster* (1744), pp. 25–26.

77. John Gay, 'Trivia', book i, line 144.

78. *Spectator*, no. 232.

79. Parker, *A View of Society and Manners in High and Low Life* (1781), pp. 117–18.

80. *Trip Through Town*, pp. 11–12.

81. For Samuel Badham see *The Ordinary of Newgate's Account*, 6 August 1740; *OBP*, 9 July 1740, Samuel Badham, t17400709-2.

82. Burn, *Autobiography of a Beggar Boy*, pp. 54–55.

83. *Spectator*, no. 454.

84. John Thomas Smith, *Vagabondiana* (1817), p. 25.

85. *A Trip From St James's to the Royal-Exchange*, pp. 24–25.

86. For a detailed analysis of this image see Sean Shesgreen, 'William Hogarth's Enraged Musician and the Cries of London', in David Bindman, Frederic Ogee and Peter Wagner, eds, *Hogarth: Representing Nature's Machines* (Manchester, 2001).

87. See Tim Hitchcock, 'Demography and the Culture of Sex in the Long Eighteenth Century', in Jeremy Black, ed., *Culture and Society in Britain, 1660–1800* (Manchester, 1997); R. B. Outhwaite, '"Objects of Charity": Petitions to the London Foundling Hospital, 1768–72', *Eighteenth-Century Studies*, 32 (1999), 497–510; and Anna Clark, 'Whores and Gossips: Sexual Reputation in London, 1770–1825', in A. Angerman, G. Binnema, A. Keunen, V. Poels, J. Zirkzee, eds, *Current Issues in Women's History* (1989). See also Tony Henderson, *Disorderly Women in Eighteenth-Century London: Prostitution and Control in the Metropolis, 1730–1830* (1999).

88. Burn, *Autobiography of a Beggar Boy*, pp. 56–57.

89. John Fielding, *A Brief Description of the Cities of London and Westminster, the Public Buildings, Palaces, Gardens, Squares, etc.* (1776), p. xv.

90. Henri Misson, *Memoirs and Observations in his Travels over England*, translated by Mr Ozell (1719), p. 221.

91. *Tatler*, no. 105.

92. Estimates of Britain's Black population in the eighteenth century range from between four and thirty thousand individuals. See Stephen J. Braidwood, *Black Poor and White Philanthropists: London's Blacks and the Foundation of the Sierra Leone Settlement, 1786–1791* (Liverpool, 1994), pp. 22–23. For more general literature of the history of the black communities of Britain and attitudes towards race see David Dabydeen, *Hogarth's Blacks: Images of Blacks in Eighteenth-Century English Art* (Mandelstrup and Kingston-upon-Thames, 1985); Ghazala Faizi, *A History of the Black Presence in London* (1986); Nigel File and Chris Power, *Black Settlers in Britain 1555–1958* (1984); Peter Fryer, *Staying Power, The History of Black People in Britain* (1984); Gretchen Gerzina, *Black London: Life Before Emancipation* (New Jersey, 1995); Clare Midgeley, *Women Against Slavery: The British Campaigns, 1780–1870* (1992); Norma Myers, *Reconstructing the Black Past: Blacks in Britain, 1780–1830* (1996); James Walvin, *Black and White: The Negro and English Society, 1555–1945* (1973); James Walvin, *Black Ivory: A History of British Slavery* (1992) and James Walvin, *England, Slaves and Freedom, 1776–1838* (Basingstoke and London, 1986).

93. NA, AO 13/79, fol. 746; quoted in Braidwood, *Black Poor and White Philan-thropists*, p. 30.

94. E. Robinson, ed., *John Clare's Autobiographical Writings* (Oxford, 1986), pp. 140–41. I would like to thank Peter King for drawing my attention to this quote.

95. John T. Smith, *Vagabondiana* (1817), pp. 33–34.

96. Burn, *Autobiography of a Beggar Boy*, p. 73.

Notes to Chapter 6: Begging from the Parish

1. No observations could be made at Greenwich on this day, and the barometric pressure was falling rapidly. The temperature on the preceding day was recorded as 64.5 degrees Fahrenheit. See Nevil Maskelyne, *Astronomical Obser-vations Made at the Royal Observatory at Greenwich in the Years 1765, 1766, 1767, 1768 and 1769* (1774), part 2, p. 18.

2. GL, 'St Dionis Backchurch, vouchers, 1766–72', MS 11280 box 6, no. 11.

3. GL, 'St Dionis Backchurch, papers relating to a poor law appeal from Paul Patrick Kearney, 1771', MS 11280C.

4. *OBP*, Paul Kerney, 4 December 1728, t17281204–54; see also the punishment summary for the same sessions, s17281204–402. The connection between 'Paul Kerney' and Paul Patrick Kearney is not absolute, but the case involved Ker-ney pretending to be a 'Spanish Merchant', which is precisely how Paul Kearney is described in a later case in Chancery. Michael Doyne, in an affidavit sworn in August 1767, claimed Paul Patrick Kearney was living in the parish of St Mary at Hill throughout 1726, 1727 and 1728, and dates Kearney's financial problems from the latter year, demonstrating at the least that Paul Kearney was in London in 1728. No one of a similar name appears in the records of the Old Bailey at any other time during the whole of the eighteenth century. See GL, MS 11280C, no. 7.

5. See NA, McCarty v. Kearney, Geo. I and II, C11/1329/41; NA, Ma'Carty v. Kearny, C11/2473/28.

6. GL, MS 11280C, no. 1.

7. NA, 'Paul Kearney to W[illiam]m Sharpe', 17 June 1748, SP 54/39/45B; NA, 'Lt Gen Bland to John Potter', 19 July 1748, SP 54/39/47A.

8. GL, MS 11280C, no. 4.

9. Kearney consistently refers to all the parish officers as 'churchwardens', and this usage has been followed here. It is clear, however, that some of the men mentioned were acting in the legal capacity of 'overseer of the poor', and would have been appointed as such.

10. GL, MS 11280C, no. 1.

11. For a discussion of the role of the Lord Mayor as magistrate see J. M. Beattie,

Policing and Punishment in London, 1660–1750 (Oxford, 2001), ch. 2. Numerous instances the Lord Mayor intervening in poor law cases can be found in 'Mansion House Justice Room Minute Books' held at the CLRO. See for example MJR/M5. For Middlesex justices acting in this same way see Ruth Paley, ed., *Justice in Eighteenth-Century Hackney: The Justicing Notebook of Henry Norris and the Hackney Petty Sessions Book,* London Record Society, 28 (1991).

12. *OBP,* William Kippax appears on the jury list at the front of the Session held on 13 January 1764, s17640113–526; see also *OBP,* John Franklin, 22 February 1764, t17640222–44.

13. GL, MS 11280C, no. 1.

14. For the contract dated 1761, see GL, 'St Dionis Backchurch, Miscellaneous Parish Papers, 1606–1818', MS 11280A/4. For a general and partial account of the rise of contract workhouses see Elaine Murphy, 'The Metropolitan Pauper Farms, 1722–1834', *London Journal,* 27 (2002), pp. 1–18.

15. GL, MS 11280C, no. 1.

16. GL, MS11280A/4, memorandum dated 23 August 1765.

17. GL, 'St Dionis Backchurch, Workhouse Inquest Minute Book, 1761–1788', MS 4219/1, 11 June 1761, 6 January 1762, 2 June 1762, 3 August 1762.

18. GL, MS 11280C, no. 1.

19. The precise date was 26 May 1769, and the weather at Greenwich was clear enough to allow astronomical observations to be made. The temperature was an unseasonable 47 degrees Fahrenheit. See Maskelyne, *Astronomical Observations ... 1765, 1766, 1767, 1768 and 1769,* part 1, p. 49, part 2, p. 18.

20. GL, MS 11280 box 6; see also GL, MS 11280C, no. 1.

21. GL, MS 11280 box 6, see two letters from William Robinson dated 13 November and 12 December 1766.

22. GL, MS 11280C, no. 1.

23. GL, MS 11280/Box 6, No. 14.

24. GL, MS. 11280C, no. 1.

25. See GL, 'St Dionis Backchurch, Workhouse Inquests Minute Book (Rough), 1762–1779', MS 4219/2, 6 July 1767. For a more general account of pauper farms in Hoxton see Murphy, 'The Metropolitan Pauper Farms, 1722–1834', p. 5.

26. The temperature recorded at Greenwich was 37 degrees Fahrenheit, and no observations of stars could be made. See Maskelyne, *Astronomical Observations ... 1765, 1766, 1767, 1768 and 1769,* part 1, p. 210, part 2, p. 88.

27. GL, MS 11280C, no. 1.

28. GL, MS 11280C, no. 6.

29. GL, MS 11280C, no. 3; for a general history of private madhouses in this period see William Parry-Jones, *The Trade in Lunacy: A Study of Private Madhouses in England in the Eighteenth and Nineteenth Centuries* (1972).

30. GL, MS 11280C, no. 2.

31. GL, MS 11280C, no. 3.

32. GL, 'St Dionis Backchurch, Pauper Letters, 1738–1759', MS 19233, items 2, 3, 5 and 6.

33. GL, MS 4219/1, 2 June 1772.

34. For recent work on the history of the Old Poor Law and parochial relief see Lynn Hollen Lees, *The Solidarities of Strangers: The English Poor Laws and the People, 1700–1948* (Cambridge: Cambridge University Press, 1998), and Steven King, *Poverty and Welfare in England 1700–1850: A Regional Perspective* (Manchester, 2000). For recent attempts to place parish relief within the context of an 'economy of makeshift' and pauper narratives see Steven King and Alannah Tomkins, eds, *The Poor in England, 1700–1850* (Manchester, 2003), passim; and Tim Hitchcock, Peter King and Pamela Sharpe, eds, *Chronicling Poverty: The Voices and Strategies of the English Poor, 1640–1840* (Basingstoke, 1997). For recent work on the Old Poor Law in London see Jeremy Boulton, 'The Poor Among the Rich: Paupers and the Parish, in the West End, 1600–1724', in J. R. Maddicott and David M. Palliser, eds, *The Medieval State: Essays Presented to James Campbell* (London and Rio Grande Ohio, 2000).

35. The literature on eighteenth-century workhouses is remarkably patchy. See Paul Slack, 'Hospitals, Workhouses and the Relief of the Poor in Early Modern London' in Ole Peter Grell and Andrew Cunningham, eds, *Health Care and Poor Relief in Protestant Europe, 1500–1700* (1997); Lynn MacKay, 'A Culture of Poverty?: The St. Martin-in-the-Fields Workhouse, 1817', *Journal of Interdisciplinary History*, 26 (1995), pp. 209–31; Tim Hitchcock, 'Paupers and Preachers: The SPCK and the Parochial Workhouse Movement', in Lee Davison, Tim Hitchcock, Tim Keirn and R. B. Shoemaker, eds, *Stilling the Grumbling Hive: The Response to Social and Economic Problems in England, 1689–1750* (Stroud, 1992); M. E. Fissell, *Patients, Power and the Poor in Eighteenth-Century Bristol* (Cambridge, 1991); Kathryn Morrison, *The Workhouse: A Study of Poor-Law Buildings in England* (Swindon, 1999).

36. House of Lords Records Office, 'Poor Rate Returns, 1777', Parchment Collection, box 162.

37. Matthew Martin, *Letter to the Right Hon. Lord Pelham on the State of Mendicity in the Metropolis* (1803), p. 17.

38. Quoted on the title page of William Young, *Considerations on the Subject of Poor-Houses and Workhouses, their Pernicious Tendency, and the Obstructions to the Proposed Plan for Amendment of the Poor Laws; in a Letter to the Rt Hon. W. Pitt* (1796).

39. OBP, 17 January 1759, Jane, wife of William Dutton, t17590117–17.

40. GL, 'Moneys Recd from the Boys', MS 3251.

41. See for instance, GL, MS 3137/3, p. 115; GL, MS 3149/5, p. 39; WAC, E573 Shelf 30, 'St Margarets Westminster, Workhouse Rules, Orders and Correspondence,

1746–1766', rule 2; GL, MS 8690, 4 August 1738; Hackney Library Services, Rose Lipman Library, P/M/1, 'St Marys, Stoke Newington, Vestry Minutes, 1681–1743', p. 384.

42. John Brown, *A Memoir of Robert Blincoe, an Orphan Boy; Sent from the Work-house of St Pancras, London at Seven Years of Age, to Endure the Horrors of a Cotton-Mill* (Manchester, 1832, 1977 edn), pp. 12, 17.

43. Ibid., p. 15.

44. This apparently benign excursion to the fair also resulted in what Mary would later describe as her rape at the hands of her father. *OBP*, 13 January 1779, Philip Sherwin, t17790113–36. Samuel Curwen was in Sidmouth that day, and described it as a 'Pleasant morn, Clouds thin', see *Samuel Curwen*, i, p. 478.

45. *Report from Committee on the State of Mendicity in the Metropolis* (1815), 'Min-utes of Evidence', p. 38.

46. The Greenwich Observatory recorded the day as 'Cloudy', but was nonetheless able to record several observations. The court case describing these events claims 3 July 1755 was a Sunday, although this date actually falls on a Thurs-day. See James Bradley, *Astronomical Obsevations Made at the Royal Observatory at Greenwich from the Year MDCCL to the Year MDCCLXII*, i (1798), part 1, pp. 262–63.

47. *Ordinary of Newgate's Account … 12th of November 1755* (1755), pp. 5–6; *OBP*, 10 September 1755, Mabell Hughes, t17550910–41.

48. *The Workhouse Cruelty* [1731].

49. *The Workhouse Cruelty, Workhouses Turn'd Goals and Gaolers Executioners* [1731].

50. BL, 'A Report on the Autopsy of Margaret Whistle, 10 September 1731', Sloane MS. 4078, fol. 159.

51. *Workhouse Cruelty, Workhouses Turn'd Goals and Gaolers Executioners* [1731].

52. See Tim Hitchcock, 'The English Workhouse: A Study in Institutional Poor Relief in Selected Counties, 1696–1750' (Oxford University D.Phil. thesis, 1985), pp. 193–210.

53. GL, 'St Sepulchre's London Division, Workhouse Committee Book, 1727–29', MS 3137, i, p. 29.

54. GL, 'St Ann Blackfryars, London, Workhouse Committee Book, 1734–1767', MS 8690, 22 May 1735.

55. For background on the workings and impact of the system of settlement see Tim Hitchcock and John Black, eds, *Chelsea Settlement and Bastardy Exami-nation, 1733–1766*, London Record Society, 33 (1999), Introduction; Norma Landau, 'Who Was Subjected to the Laws of Settlement? Procedure Under the Settlement Laws in Eighteenth-Century England', *Agricultural History Review*, 43 (1995), pp. 139–59; K. D. M. Snell, 'Settlement, Poor Law and the Rural

Historian: New Approaches and Opportunities', *Rural History*, 3 (1992), pp. 145–72; and J. S. Taylor, 'The Impact of Pauper Settlement 1691–1834', *Past and Present*, 73 (1976), pp. 42–74.

56. No observations could be made on 9 January 1786, and the temperature during that week was recorded as lying between 41.5 and 44.5 degrees Fahrenheit. See See Nevil Maskelyne, *Astronomical Observations Made at the Royal Observatory at Greenwich in the Years 1765, 1766, 1767, 1768 and 1769* (1774), part 2, p. 121.

57. WAC, 'St Clement's Settlement and Bastardy Examinations Book', MS B1187, fos 147–50. I am grateful to Dr John Black for this reference.

58. *Hints and Cautions for the Information of the Churchwardens and Overseers of the Poor of the Parish of St Giles in the Fields and St George, Bloomsbury, in the County of Middlesex, and Rules, Orders and Regulations for the Maintaining, Governing, Employing and Regulating the Said Poor* (1781, page references refer to the 1797 edition), p. 12.

59. *Hints and Cautions*, p. 7.

60. *Hints and Cautions*, p. 4.

61. *Hints and Cautions*, p. 6.

62. WAM, Coroner's Inquests, 4 December 1797, 'Joseph Bowring'.

63. GL, 'St Giles Cripplegate, Workhouse Committee Minute Book', MS 6051/1, p. 135. The temperature recorded at Greenwich that day was 39 degrees Fahrenheit, and Nevil Maskelyne noted, 'air very clear', in his account of a lunar eclipse later that evening. See Nevil Maskelyne, *Astronomical Observations Made at the Royal Observatory at Greenwich from MDCCLXXXVII to MDCCXCVIII* (1799), part 1, p. 402, part 2, p. 122.

64. GL, 'St Helens in Bishopsgate, Settlement Examinations, 1738–1796', MS. 6886, 'Memorandums for the Examination of Eliz. Gray. 28 June 1780'. Samuel Curwen was in Bristol that day, but describes the weather as 'Air moist, wind fresh S.', *Samuel Curwen*, ii, p. 643.

65. For two recent articles on the workings of the vagrancy laws and removal see Nicholas Rogers, 'Vagrancy, Impressment and the Regulation of Labour in Eighteenth-Century Britain', *Slavery and Abolition*, 15 (1994), pp. 102–13, and Nicholas Rogers, 'Policing the Poor in Eighteenth-Century London: The Vagrancy Laws and their Administration', *Social History [London]*, 24 (1991), pp. 127–48.

66. John Howard, *The State of the Prisons in England and Wales with Preliminary Observations, and an Account of Some Foreign Prisons* (1777), p. 260.

67. The most authoritative history of houses of correction in this period is Joanna Innes, 'Prisons for the Poor: English Bridewells, 1555–1800', in Francis Snyder and Douglas Hay, eds, *Labour, Law and Crime: An Historical Perspective* (1987).

68. Joanna Innes, 'English Houses of Correction and "Labour Discipline", c. 1690–1780: A Critical Exmaination' (July 1983, unpublished typescript), pp. 11–13.

69. Howard, *The State of the Prisons*, p. 261.

70. House of Lords Records Office, 'Poor Rate Returns, 1777', Parchment Collection, Box 162.

71. GL, 'St Helens in Bishopsgate, Settlement Examinations, 1738–1796', MS 6886, 'Ann Yeates, May 1778'. The route Ann took was also followed by John and Susannah Simmons or Seamans and their two children when they were removed to St Helens from Norwich in January of 1779.

72. Information on the weather is taken from *Samuel Curwen*, i, p. 451. Curwen was living in Devon in May 1778, but would have experienced the same large-scale weather patterns as Ann Yeats.

73. GL, 'Court of Governors, Bridewell and Bethlem: Minutes, 26 October 1722 to 15 December 1737', MS 3011/20, p. 300.

74. For an account of the increasing role the British state in the lives of soldiers, seamen and their families, see Patricia Lin, 'Extending Her Arms: Military Families and the Transformation of the British State, 1793–1815' (University of California at Berkeley, Ph.D. thesis, 1999).

75. GL, 'St Peter Cornhill, Pauper and Vagrant Passes, 1757–1808', MS. 4198, 'Ann Brown, 6 June 1772'.

76. See GL, 'Saint Sepulchre's Middlesex Division, Pauper Examinations, 1792–1795', MS 9095/4, fol. 63.

77. *A New Plot Newly Discovered by the Help of the London Bell-Man: or Wicked and Hellish Conspiracies against the Peace of this Kingdom* (1680), pp. 6–7.

78. CLRO, 'Guildhall Justice Room, Minute Book, 1784, June 10 to June 28', GJR/M26, 19 June. According to Samuel Curwen the day was 'Mild air, sky cloudy, wind Wly.', *Sanuel Curwen*, ii, p. 1001.

79. CLRO, 'Repertories of the Court of Aldermen', Rep. 149, 2 April 1745, pp. 213–14.

80. James Dawson Burn, *The Autobiography of a Beggar Boy*, ed. David Vincent (1978), p. 58.

81. Israel R. Potter, *The Life and Remarkable Adventures of Israel R. Potter* (1824; New York, 1962 edn), pp. 86–87; for a recent account of the importance of Potter's memoir for Herman Melville and American literature see, Newton Arvin, *Herman Melville* (New York, 2002), pp. 244–47.

Notes to Chapter 7: Chartiy in Stone

1. The sky was relatively overcast, allowing observations to be made of the moon only. The barometric pressure was low, at 29.91 inches, and the next few days saw a severe cold snap, with the temperature dropping to 17 degrees Fahrenheit on 5 January. See Nevil Maskelyne, *Astronomical Observations Made at the Royal Observatory at Greenwich from MDCCLXXXVII to MDCCXCVIII*, (1799), part 1, p. 85 and part 2, p. 33.

2. WAM, Westminster Coroner's Inquests, 5 January 1789, 'Thomas Perkins'.

3. For a discussion of the historiography of the watch, and its later reputation see Ruth Paley, '"An Imperfect, Inadequate and Wretched System"? Policing London before Peel', *Criminal Justice History*, 10 (1989), pp. 95–130. For its evolu- tion see J. M. Beattie, *Policing and Punishment in London, 1660–1750* (Oxford, 2001), ch. 4, and Elaine A. Reynolds, *Before the Bobbies: The Night Watch and Police Reform in Metropolitan London, 1720–1830* (Basingstoke, 1998).

4. For a detailed account of the organisation of the watchhouse belonging to St Martin's-in-the-Fields see Tim Hitchcock, '"You Bitches … Die and Be Damned": Gender, Authority and the Mob in St Martin's Round-House Disaster of 1742', in Tim Hitchcock and Heather Shore, eds, *The Streets of London from the Great Fire to the Great Stink* (2003).

5. CLRO, 'Guildhall Justice Room Minute Book, 1782 July 31 – August 26', MS GJR/M17, 16 August 1782. For a detailed account of the career of William Payne see Joanna Innes, 'William Payne of Bell Yard, Carpenter *c.* 1718–1782: The Life and Times of a London Informing Constable' (unpublished MS). For details of the weather on 16 August 1782 see *Samuel Curwen*, ii, p. 849.

6. *Covent Garden Journal*, 49, 20 June 1752, p. 444; quoted in Heather Shore, 'Crime, Criminal Networks and the Survival Strategies of the Poor in Early Eighteenth-Century London', in Steven King and Alannah Tomkins, eds, *The Poor in England, 1700–1850: An Economy of Makeshift* (Manchester, 2003), p. 141.

7. There were 672 watchmen employed in the City in 1737. See Beattie, *Policing and Punishment in London, 1660–1750*, p. 195.

8. César de Saussure, *A Foreign View of England in 1725–1729: The Letters of Monsieur César de Saussure to his Family* trans and ed. by Madame Van Muyden (1995), p. 42.

9. *Fascimile of the Cries of London First Published, c. 1754* (Lympne Castle, Kent, 1978).

10. Henry Fielding, *The History of Amelia*, (1752; 1926), i, ch. 2, p. 12.

11. GL, 'St Giles Cripplegate, Workhouse Committee Minute Book', MS 6051/1, 11 April 1745, p. 180.

12. See Ruth Paley, '"An Imperfect, Inadequate and Wretched System"? Policing London before Peel', *Criminal Justice History*, 10 (1989), pp. 95–130.

13. John Gay, *Poetry and Prose*, 'Trivia', ed., Vinton A Dearing (Oxford, 1974), *Trivia*, book ii, lines 307–10.

14. WAC, 'St Martin-in-the-Fields, Parish Records, Workhouse Day Book, 1737–42', MS F4003, p. 438.

15. WAM, Westminster Coroner's Inquest, 12 September 1774, 'Sarah Knight'.

16. John Thomas Smith, *A Book for a Rainy Day: or Recollections of the Events of the Last Sixty Years* (1845), pp. 107–8.

17. The temperature recorded at Greenwich that evening was 36 degrees Fahrenheit, and a full set of observations was made. See Nevil Maskelyne, *Astronomical Observations Made at the Royal Observatory at Greenwich in the Years 1765, 1766, 1767, 1768 and 1769* (1774), part 1, p. 236, part 2, p. 72.

18. CLRO, 'Guildhall Justice Room Minute Books, 1782, March 5 to April 5', MS GJR/M16, 'Wednesday 3 April 1782'.

19. *OBP*, 9 September 1742, William Bird, t17420909-37.

20. Gay, 'Trivia', book ii, lines 316–20.

21. Rogers, Nicholas, 'Policing the Poor in Eighteenth-Century London: The Vagrancy Laws and Their Administration', *Histoire Sociale-Social History*, 24 (May 1991), pp. 128–31.

22. CLRO, 'Courts of the President and Governors for the Poor of London, 1702–5', MS New 377c/1/22, fol. 244; Payne was awarded twenty guineas in 1776 for his role in apprehending beggars and prostitutes. See CLRO, 'Journal of Common Council', For. 66, fos 294–95, 298.

23. [John Scott], *Observations on the Present State of the Parochial and Vagrant Poor* (1773), p. 4.

24. *Minutes of Evidence taken before Committee on the State of Mendicity in the Metropolis* (1815), p. 21.

25. *OBP*, 12 September 1787, Joseph Herbert, Thomas Holdsworth, t17870912-5.

26. *OBP*, 20 April 1726, George Whytle, t17260420-68.

27. *OBP*, 11 September 1735, Edward Birch, t17350911-75.

28. John Howard, *The State of the Prisons in England and Wales with Preliminary Observations and an Account of Some Foreign Prisons* (1776), pp. 181, 185. For an account of the rebuilding of many of London's prisons in the 1770s see Christopher Chalklin, 'The Reconstruction of London's Prisons, 1770–9: An Aspect of the Growth of Georgian London', *London Journal*, 9 (1983), pp. 21–34.

29. The best guide to these prisons and their facilities is Howard, *The State of the Prisons in England and Wales*. For London's prisons see pp. 165–208. The Compters have been particularly under researched, but see Bruce Watson, 'The Compter Prisons of London', *London Archaeologist*, 7 (1993), pp. 115–21. For King's Bench see Joanna Innes, 'The King's Bench Prison in the Later

Eighteenth Century: Law, Authority and Order in a London Debtors' Prison', in John Brewer and John Styles, eds, *An Ungovernable People? The English and their Law in the Seventeenth and Eighteenth Centuries* (1980), pp. 250–98. The broader development of the prison system has generated a large and sophisticated historiography. For a still excellent account of the development of this literature and the related literature on crime see Joanna Innes and John Styles, 'The Crime Wave: Recent Writing on Crime and Criminal Justice in Eighteenth-Century England', in Adrian Wilson, ed., *Rethinking Social History: English Society, 1570–1920 and its Interpretation* (Manchester, 1993), pp. 201–65.

30. W. J. Sheehan, 'Finding Solace in Eighteenth-Century Newgate', J. S. Cockburn, ed., *Crime in England, 1550–1800* (1977). See also R. B. Pugh, 'Newgate Between Two Fires', *Guildhall Studies in London History*, iii, 3, October 1978, pp. 137–63 and iii, 4, April 1979, pp. 199–222.

31. Howard, *State of the Prisons*, p. 35.

32. Ibid., p. 26.

33. Robert B. Shoemaker, *Prosecution and Punishment: Petty Crime and the Law in London and Rural Middlesex, c. 1660–1725* (Cambridge, 1991), table 3.5, p. 58.

34. William Smith, *State of the Gaols in London, Westminster and Borough of Southwark* (1776), pp. 9–10; quoted in Sidney and Beatrice Webb, *Engish Prisons under Local Government* (1922), p. 19.

35. CLRO, 'Courts of the President and Governors for the Poor of London, 1702–5', MS New 377c/1/22, fol. 43.

36. The weather allowed only the briefest of observations to be made at Greenwich that day although some stars were observed, while the temperature was recorded as 64 degrees Fahrenheit. See James Bradley, *Astronomical Obsevations Made at the Royal Observatory at Greenwich from the Year MDCCL to the Year MDCCLXII*, ii (1805), pp. 28, 233.

37. [J. Ilive], *Reasons Offered for the Reformation of the House of Correction in Clerkenwell* (1757), pp. 11–12.

38. Ibid, pp. 12–13.

39. Ned Ward, *The London Spy*, ed. Paul Hyland (1709; East Lansing Michigan, 1993), p. 71.

40. Ibid., p. 68.

41. GL, 'Court of Governors, Bridewell and Bethlem: Minutes, 26 June 1713 to 2 August 1722', MS 33011/19, p. 77.

42. BL, Add. MS 27826, 'Place Papers, xxxviii, Manners and Morals', ii, fol. 186.

43. *OBP*, 9 April 1766, John Stevens, t17660409-67; see also WAM, Westminster Coroner's Inquest, 1 April 1766, 'John Arthur'.

44. [Ilive], *Reasons* (1757), p. 4.

45. CLRO, 'Repertories of the Court of Aldermen', Rep. 142, p. 178.

46. Shoemaker, *Prosecution and Punishment*, p. 188.

47. Mary Saxby, *Memoirs of a Felame Vagrant Written by Herself* (1806), p. 14.

48. [Ilive], *Reasons* (1757), p. 38.

49. CLRO, 'City Cash Accounts, 1796', MS 2/65, pp. 365–68.

50. [Scott], *Observations* (1773), p. 4; quoted in Webb, *English Local Government: The Old Poor Law* (1927), p. 381.

51. CLRO, 'Courts of the President and Governors for the Poor of London, 1702–5', MS New 377c/1/22, fol. 193.

52. Fielding, *Amelia* (1752; 1926), i, ch. 3, p. 18.

53. Quoted in Liza Picard, *Dr Johnson's London: Life in London, 1740–1770* (2000), p. 145.

54. [Ilive], *Reasons* (1757), pp. 22–24.

55. CLRO, 'Courts of the President and Governors for the Poor of London, 1702–5', MS New 377c/1/22, fol. 258.

56. GL, 'Court of Governors, Bridewell and Bethlem: Minutes, 16 May 1701 to 19 June 1713', MS 33011/18, p. 18.

57. [Ilive], *Reasons* (1757), p. 25.

58. Ibid, p. 16.

59. CLRO, 'A Book of the Proceedings of Committees of the Court of Aldermen and Common Council begun the 22nd of March 1708', Misc. MS 210.7, pp. 2, 16.

60. *Middlesex County Records, 1689–1709*, p. 244; cited in Sean Shesgreen, *The Criers and Hawkers of London* (Aldershot, 1990), p. 172.

61. Quoted in Michael Ignatieff, *A Just Measure of Pain: The Penitentiary in the Industrial Revolution, 1750–1850* (1978), p. 33.

62. WAM, Westminster Coroner's Inquest, 24 March 1767, 'James Smith'.

63. CLRO, 'Mr Kirby's bill for subsistance money etc for poor vagrants etc. sent to Wood Street compter by the Lord Mayr and Aldermen, £109 2s. 7d.' Misc MS 288/8.

64. GL, 'Bridewell Minute Book of the Prison Committee, beginning 11 October 1775', MS 33131/1, n. p., 23 December 1782.

65. CLRO, 'Courts of the President and Governors for the Poor of London, 1702–5', MS 377c/1/22, fol. 232.

66. GL, 'Bridewell, Prison Subcommittee, 1792 to 1802', MS 33,132/1, 24 January 1793.

67. GL, 'Bridewell, Prison Subcommittee, 1792 to 1802', MS 33,132/1, 20 June 1793, 23 July 1795.

68. Quoted in Ignatieff, *A Just Measure of Pain*, p. 34.

69. *OBP*, 15 January 1756, William Thornton, t17560115–29.

70. John Byrom, 'Tom the Porter' (1746), reproduced in Roger Lonsdale, ed., *Eighteenth-Century Verse* (Oxford, 1984), pp. 209–10.

71. Christopher Smart, 'Pray Remember the Poor' (1770), reproduced in Lonsdale, *Eighteenth-Century Verse*, p. 449.

72. CLRO, 'Courts of the President and Governors for the Poor of London, 1702–5', MS 377c/1/22, fol. 194.

73. Quoted in Sean Shesgreen, ed., *The Criers and Hawkers of London* (Aldershot, 1990), p. 172.

74. Blakiston, Mayor, *The First Court Held on Tuesday the Twenty-Fifth Day of November 1760* (1760). See also the equivalent document for 11 December 1798.

75. H. P. Thompson, *Thomas Bray* (1954), p. 41.

76. See in particular John Bellers, *An Epistle to Friends of the Yearly, Quarterly and Monthly Meetings: Concerning the Prisoners and Sick in the Prisons, and Hospitals of Great Britain* (1724); reproduced in George Clarke, ed., *John Bellers: His Life, Times and Writings* (1987), pp. 272–55.

77. CLRO, 'A Book of the Proceedings of Committees of the Court of Aldermen and Common Council begun the 22nd of March 1708 to 1716', Misc. MS 210.7, p. 6–7.

78. Josiah Dornford, *An Address to the Livery and Citizens of London, on the Proceedings of the Court of Common Council on Friday the 24th of February 1786 Respecting Mr Alderman Clarke and Mr Dornford* (1786), pp. 6, 12–13, 30. See also Josiah Dornford, *Nine Letters to the Right Honorable the Lord Mayor and Aldermen of the City of London on the State of the Prisons and Prisoners* (1786).

79. [Ilive], *Reasons*, pp. 28–29.

80. Ibid., pp. 29–30n.

81. For a recent, positive analysis of medical care in a group of provincial gaols see P. M. Higgings, 'Medical Care in Three Gloucestershire Prisons in the Early Nineteenth Century', *Transactions of the Bristol and Gloucestershire Archaeological Society*, 120 (2002), pp. 213–28.

82. GL, 'Court of Governors, Bridewell and Bethlem: Minutes, 26 October 1722 to 15 December 1737', MS 3011/20, p. 390.

83. [Ilive], *Reasons*, p. 43.

84. WAM, Westminster Coroner's Inquest, 9 February 1763, 'Silas Barcotolf'.

85. The existence of a 'sick ward' is mentioned in WAM, Westminster Coroner's Inquest, 2 April 1799, 'Mary Welch'.

86. WAM, Westminster Coroner's Inquest, 29 January 1798, 'Ann Barker'.

87. See Ben Weinreb and Christopher Hibbert, *The London Encyclopaedia* (1983), p. 305, and Maria L. White, 'Westminster Inquests' (Doctor of Medicine thesis, Yale School of Medicine, 1980), p. 61.

88. GL, 'Bridewell, Prison Subcommittee, 1792 to 1802', MS 33,132/1, n.p., 8 May 1794.

89. For an excellent account of the treatment of venereal disease in eighteenth-century London, see Kevin P. Siena, *Venereal Disease, Hosptials and the Urban Poor, London's "Foul Wards", 1600–1800* (Rochester New York, 2004).

90. GL, 'Court of Governors, Bridewell and Bethlem: Minutes, 16 May 1701 to 19 June 1713', MS 33011/18, p. 255.

91. GL, 'Court of Governors, Bridewell and Bethlem: Minutes, 12 January 1737/8 to 4 April 1751', MS 33011/21, p. 329.

92. GL, 'Court of Governors, Bridewell and Bethlem: Minutes 22 May 1751 to 1 Decmeber 1761', MS 33011/22, p. 385.

93. From 1773 St Bartholomew's insisted that the City not only pay for medical care and washing, but also for clothing prisoners sent to the hospital. St Bartholomew's Hospital Archives, 'St Bartholomew's Governors' Minutes, 1770–86', Journal HA 1/14, p. 206. My thanks to Kevin Siena for this reference.

94. CLRO, 'City's Cash Accounts', 1791–99, MS 2/61, fos. 130–31, 294–95; MS 2/62, pp. 303–5, 358–61; MS 2/64, pp. 353–56; MS 2/65, pp. 365–68; MS 2/66, pp. 344–47; MS 3/67, pp. 352–55; MS 3/68, pp. 263–66.

95. CLRO, 'Repertories of the Court of Alderman', Rep. 158, p. 116–17.

96. CLRO, 'Mr Kirby's Bill for Subsistence Money etc. for Poor Vagrants etc., sent to Wood Street Compter by the Lord Mayor and Aldermen, £109 2s. 7d., received 15 May 1781', Misc. MS 288/8. It is not certain that children sent to the Marine Society ever arrived. The vast majority of the names listed on this receipt do not appear in the society's records. It is entirely possible that the promise of going to the Marine Society was enough to secure release. My thanks to Dianne Payne for this information.

Notes to Chapter 8: The Begging Year

1. For two good, recent guides to the ritual year see David Cressy, *Bonfires and Bells: National Memory and the Protestant Calendar in Elizabethan and Stuart England* (1989) and Ronald Hutton, *Stations of the Sun: A History of the Ritual Year in Britain* (Oxford, 1996).

2. Washington Irving, *The Sketchbook of Geoffrey Crayon, Gent.* (1826), 'Little Britain'.

3. John Gay, *Poetry and Prose*, 'Trivia', ed. Vinton A Dearing, (Oxford, 1974), book ii, lines 438, 443–46, 449–50.

4. The still irritating and beggarly aspect of Christmas tipping is reflected in the recent contract imposed on dustmen in Wandsworth, which explicitly forbids them from accepting tips of this kind. I would like to thank Pene Corfield for this information.

5. See *Poor Robin's Hue and Cry after Good House-Keeping: or A Dialogue betwixt Good House-Keeping, Christmas and Pride* (1687).

6. The *Oxford English Dictionary* describes a Christmas box as, 'a box having a cleft on the lid, or in the side, for money to enter it; used ... by butlers and prentices'.

7. *OBP*, 25 February 1736, Elizabeth Davis, t17360225–3.

8. *OBP*, 7 December 1791, Charles Richmond, t17911207–21.

9. For a brief discussion of the intersection between eighteenth-century masculinity and Christmas boxes see Margot Finn, 'Men's Things: Masculine Possession in the Consumer Revolution', *Social History* , 25 (May 2000), pp. 149–50.

10. *OBP*, 25 October 1752, William Montegomery, t17521026–45.

11. *The Diary of Thomas Turner, 1754–1765* ed. David Vaisey (Oxford, 1984), pp. 169, 171, 196, 338.

12. *Diary of Thomas Turner*, p. 169; for Charles Banbury see David N. Durant, *Where Queen Elizabeth Slept and What the Butler Saw: Historical Terms from the Sixteenth Century to the Present* (Pontypool, 1998), p. 64.

13. GL, 'St Dyonis Backchurch, papers relating to a poor law appeal from Paul Patrick Kearney, 1771', MS 11280C.

14. GL, 'St Dyonis Backchurch, Workhouse Inquests Minute Book, 1761–1788', MS 4219/1, 8 January 1765.

15. *The English Man's Two Wishes: One, That Hanover was Farther. The Other, That − − − etc* (1728?), p. 5.

16. César de Saussure, *A Foreign View of England in 1725–1729: The Letters of Monsieur César de Saussure to his Family*, translated and edited by Madame Van Muyden (1995), p. 121.

17. Gay, 'Trivia', book i, lines 184–87.

18. GL, 'St Sepulchre's London Division, Workhouse Committee Book, 1730–1734', MS 3137 v. 3, p. 49.

19. *Spectator*, no. 509.

20. Jonathan Swift, *Journal to Stella*, ed., Harold Williams, (Oxford, 1948), i, p. 140.

21. [Jonas Hanway], *The Sentiments and Advice of Thomas Trueman, a Virtuous and Understanding Footman: In a letter to his Brother Jonathan* (1760), p. 7.

22. Kevin Patrick Siena, 'Poverty and the Pox: Venereal Disease in London Hospitals, 1600–1800' (University of Toronto Ph.D. thesis, 2001), p. 108.

23. WAC, 'St Martin in the Fields, Parish Records, Vestry Draft Minutes, 1736–54', MS F2028, p. 48.

24. *London Chronicle*, 23–26 June 1760; quoted in James Oldham, 'Law Reporting in the London Newspapers, 1756–1786', *American Journal of Legal History*, 31 (1987), p. 195.

25. Henry Carey, 'The Ballad of Sally in our Alley' (1715?), reproduced in Roger Lonsdale, ed., *Eighteenth-Century Verse* (Oxford, 1984), pp. 138–39.

26. *OBP*, 15 January 1756, Mary Dodd, t17560115–3.

27. Joel F. Harrington, '"Singing for his Supper": The Reinvention of Juvenile Streetsinging in Early Modern Nuremberg', *Social History*, 22, 1 (1997), p. 29.

28. See the advertisement reproduced over the label, 'London Waits in the

Eighteenth Century', in Percy A. Scholes, *The Oxford Companion to Music*, ed. John Owen Ward (10th edn, Oxford, 1970), plate 166, p. 993.

29. GL, 'Christ's Hospital Almoners' and Rentors' Minutes', MS 12811/9, 20 December 1727. I would like to thank Dianne Payne for very kindly providing this reference.

30. *Diary of Thomas Turner*, p. 128.

31. James Lackington, *Memoirs of the First Forty-Five Years of the Life of James Lackington* (1791), p. 35.

32. CLRO, 'Courts of the President and Governors for the Poor of London, 1702–1705', i, MS 32B, fos. 172–73.

33. CLRO, 'Vagrant Books, Together with Five Loose Pages and a Bill of Mortality, 1738–1742', Misc. MS 322.5.

34. [Thomas D'Urfey], *Colin's Walk through London and Westminster: A Poem in Burlesque Written by T. D. Gent* (1690), p. 27.

35. Norma Pilbeam and Ian Nelson, eds, *Mid-Sussex Poor Law Records, 1601–1835*, Lewes, Sussex Record Society, 83 (1999), p. 226.

36. *Spectator*, no. 269.

37. For the numbers in the house see GL, 'St Sepulchres London Division, Workhouse Maintenance Committee Book, 1728–1746', MS 3227, passim. For the meal served that day see GL, 'St Sepulchres London Division, Workhouse Committee Book, 1729–1730', MS 3137 v. 2, p. 127.

38. GL, 'The United Parishes of St Mary le Bow, St Pancras Soper Lane and All Hallows Honey Lane, Workhouse Minute Book, 1732–1765', MS 5048, 21 December 1733.

39. *The Autobiography of Francis Place, 1771–1854*, ed. Mary Thale (Cambridge, 1972), p. 64.

40. BL, Add. MS 27826, 'Place Papers, xxxviii, Manners and Morals', ii, fol. 97.

41. Jeremy Boulton, 'Economy of Time? Wedding Days and the Working Week in the Past', *Local Population Studies*, 43, Autumn 1989, pp. 40–41.

42. John Thomas Smith, *Vagabondiana* (1817), p. 41.

43. Robert Southey, *Letters from England*, ed., Jack Simmons (Stroud, Gloucestershire, 1951), p. 80.

44. Quoted in Rick Allen, *The Moving Pageant: A Literary Sourcebook on London Street-Life, 1700–1914* (1998), pp. 68–69.

45. Charles Phythian-Adams, 'Milk and Soot: The Changing Vocabulary of a Popular Ritual in Stuart and Hanoverian London', in D. Fraser and Anthony Sutcliffe, eds, *The Pursuit of Urban History* (London, 1983), p. 100.

46. *Whitehall Evening Post*, 26 May 1763; quoted in Sean Shesgreen, *Images of the Outcast: The Urban Poor in the Cries of London* (Manchester, 2002), p. 110.

47. Quoted in Roy Judge, *The Jack-in-the-Green: A May Day Custom* (Cambridge, 1979), pp. 4–5.

48. Quoted in Phythian-Adams, 'Milk and Soot', p. 96. Reference given as from G. L. Phillips, 'The Chimney Sweepers' Assimiliaton of the Milkmaids' Garland', *Folklore*, 62 (1951), p. 384.

49. Quoted in Judge, *The Jack-in-the-Green*, p. 11.

50. J. Strutt, *Sports and Pastimes of the People of England* (1876), p. 461; quoted in Judge, *The Jack-in-the-Green*, p. xi.

51. *OBP*, 22 May 1735, Robert Landsman, t17350522–24.

52. Anne remained for only a year, at the end of which Perry died. She eventually ended up back in the workhouse, before being passed to St Margaret's Westminster in 1751. LMA, 'St Luke's Chelsea, Workhouse Register, 1743–66', Microfilm X/15/ 37, Ann Piper, 25 February 1745, 10 April 1745, 2 April 1746, 12 November 1751, Elizabeth Clark, 21 May 1743, 21 May 1744, 12 February 1748, 5 February 1755, Elizabeth Piper, 12 November 1751, 29 November 1757; LMA, 'St Luke's Chelsea, Workhouse Committee Minutes, 1735–50', Microfilm, P74/Luk/X26/1, Ann Piper, 2 May 1746, 25 Sept. 1750, 9 October 1750, 16 October 1750, 23 October 1750, 30 October 1750, 6 November 1750; LMA, 'St Luke's Chelsea, Workhouse Committee Minutes, 1750–55', Microfilm, P74/Luk/X26/1, Ann Piper, 13 November 1750, 20 November 1750, 27 November 1750, 4 December 1750, 11 December 1750, 18 December 1750, 26 December 1750, 1 January 1751, 8 January 1751, 12 November 1751, Elizabeth Piper, 1 October 1751, 8 October 1751, 22 October 1751, 29 October 1751, 12 November 1751, 23 January 1753, 30 January 1753, 6 February 1753, 13 February 1753, 20 Feb. 1753, 20 March 1753, 10 September 1753, 14 January 1754, 21 January 1754, 7 April 1755; Tim Hitchcock and John Black, eds, *Chelsea Settlement and Bastardy Examinations, 1733–1766*, London Record Society, 33 (1999), no. 242.

53. *The Red Cow's Speech, to a Milk-Woman, In St J_s's P_k*, (n.d.), a single sheet, BL, 816. m. 19. (36.). In this instance the cow was apparently a monarchist, but there was also a radical tradition of bovine prophecy. The Cumberland Cow, for instance, prophesied: 'Two hard winters, a wet spring; a bloody summer and no king'. Quoted in E. P. Thompson, 'The Crime of Anonymity', in Douglas Hay, Peter Linebaugh, John G. Rule, E. P. Thompson and Cal Winslow, *Albion's Fatal Tree: Crime and Society in Eighteenth-Century England* (1975), p. 303.

54. *Spectator*, no. 251.

55. Gay, 'Trivia', book ii, line 11.

56. Shesgreen, *Images of the Outcast*, p. 120.

57. Tobias Smollett, *The Expedition of Humphry Clinker* (1771; Penguin edn, 1967), p. 154.

58. *OBP*, 6 December 1727, Elizabeth Evans, t17271206–34.

59. See M. Dorothy George, *London Life in the Eighteenth Century* (1966), pp. 239–42.

60. Shesgreen, *Images of the Outcast*, p. 114.
61. William Blake, 'The Chimney Sweep' (1789), reproduced in Lonsdale, *Eighteenth-Century Verse*, p. 691.
62. Mary Alcock, 'The Chimney-Sweeper's Complaint' (written by 1798; published 1799), reproduced in Lonsdale, *Eighteenth-Century Verse*, pp. 830–31.
63. Bruce R. Smith, *The Acoustic World of Early Modern England: Attending to the O-Factor* (Chicago, Illinois, 1999), p. 66.
64. *Spectator*, no. 454.
65. George, *London Life*, pp. 239–41.
66. Gay, 'Trivia', book ii, lines 33–34.
67. [J. Ilive], *Reasons Offered for the Reformation of the House of Correction in Clerkenwell* (1757), pp. 29–30n.
68. George, *London Life*, p. 240.
69. *OBP*, 11 September 1745, James Leppard, t17450911–11.
70. R. Campbell, *The London Tradesman* (1747; New York, fascimile edn, 1969), pp. 328, 333.
71. Hitchcock and Black, *Chelsea Settlement and Bastardy Examinations*, no. 301.
72. WAM, Westminster Coroner's Inquest, 27 March 1765, 'Thomas Chidley'.
73. Penelope Corfield, 'Walking the City Streets', *Journal of Urban History*, 16 (1990), p. 145; Judge, *The Jack-in-the-Green*, p. 8; George, *London Life*, p. 161.
74. *Ordinary's Account*, 31 October 1712; quoted in J. M. Beattie, *Policing and Punishment in London, 1660–1750: Urban Crime and the Limits of Terror* (Oxford, 2001), p. 70.
75. Soame Jenyns, 'The Modern Fine Lady' (1751), reproduced in Lonsdale, *Eighteenth-Century Verse*, pp. 458–60.
76. GL, 'St Sepulchres London Division, Workhouse Committee Book, 1734–1737', MS 3137 v. 4, 22 April 1736, p. 237.
77. GL, 'Court of Governors, Bridewell and Bethlem: Minutes 7 January 1762 to 15 March 1781', MS 3011/23, 22 June 1775, p. 482 and 17 October 1777, p. 601.
78. Cressy, *Bonfires and Bells* (1989), pp. 19–20.
79. Quoted in Rick Allen, *The Moving Pageant: A Literary Sourcebook on London Street-Life, 1700–1914* (1998), p. 68. For a more general account of the development of patriotic celebrations in this period see Nicholas Rogers, 'Crowds and Political Festival in Georgian England' in Tim Harris, ed., *The Politics of the Excluded, c. 1500–1850* (Basingstoke, 2001), pp. 233–64.
80. Cressy, *Bonfires and Bells*, p. 24.
81. 'A Song' (1769), reproduced in Lonsdale, *Eighteenth-Century Verse*, pp. 556–7.
82. Benjamin Klein, '"Between the Bums and Bellies of the Multitude": Civic Pageantry and the Problem of Audience in Late Stuart London', *London Journal*, 17 (1992), pp. 18–26; César de Saussure, *A Foreign View of England in 1725–1729*, pp. 68–69.

83. See for example CLRO, 'City's Cash Accounts, 1699–1701', MS 1/23, fol. 200.

84. *Autobiography of Francis Place*, pp. 66–67.

85. GL, 'Court of Governors, Bridewell and Bethlem: Minutes 16 May 1701 to 19 June 1713', MS 33011/18, 6 November 1702, p. 120.

86. CLRO, 'Committee of inquiry into the behaviour of children in Bridewell, 1710–1718', Misc. MS 58.35; J. L. Fitts, 'Newcastle's Mob', *Albion*, 5 (1973), pp. 41–49.

87. Boulton, 'Economy of Time? Wedding Days and the Working Week in the Past', p. 40.

88. On the roles of 'rough music' in popular culture see E. P. Thompson, *Customs in Common* (London, 1991), pp. 467–531. For its role in marriage ceremonies see, in particular, p. 470 n. 3.

89. For the early broadside see *His Majesty's Royal Peel of Marrowbones and Cleavers*, GL, Noble Collection C22/85; Henri Misson, *Memoirs and Observations in his Travels over England* (1697) (1719), p. 352; see also John R. Gillis, *For Better, For Worse: British Marriages, 1600 to the Present* (Oxford, 1985), pp. 68, 138.

90. John Cannon, 'Memoirs of the Birth, Education, Life and Death of Mr John Cannon: Sometime Officer of the Excise and Writing Master at Mere Glastenbury and West Lydford in the County of Somerset' (1743), Somerset Record Office MS DD/SAS C/1193/4, pp. 115–19.

91. Joseph Burke and Colin Caldwell, *Hogarth: The Complete Engravings* (London, n.d.), plate 208.

92. See for example, *Low-Life: or One Half of the World Knows Not How the Other Half Live* (1749), p. 54.

93. GL, 'Christ's Hospital Almoners' and Rentors' Minutes', MS 12811/9, 31 May 1720. My thanks to Dianne Payne for providing this reference.

94. See for example, *Lancashire and Cheshire Wills*, ii (Chetham Society, second series, 28), p. 35; for a more general account of seventeenth-century life-cycle ritual see David Cressy, *Birth, Marriage and Death: Ritual, Religion, and the Life-Cycle in Tudor and Stuart England* (Oxford, 1997).

95. *OBP*, 10 October 1716, James Beaver, William Eldridge, Hester Stibbs, Eleanor Hornsby, Anne Lane, t17161010-2.

96. *OBP*, 27 February 1754, Sarah Twigg, t17540227–1.

97. Cecil Roth, *History of the Great Synagogue* (1950), ch. 8.

Notes to Chapter 9: A Beggers Mask

1. John Strype, *A Survey of the Cities of London and Westminster ... By John Stow ... Now Lately Corrected* (1720), i, p. 197. An account of two pretended lame men, and one falsely blind woman found their way in to the published record via an even more circuitous route. In 1703 the mayor of Northampton wrote to

the Governors of the London Corporation of the Poor bragging of his detection of these three frauds. The Governors ordered that the full text of the letter be published, at the Corporation's expence, in the *Postman*. CLRO, 'Courts of the President and Governors for the Poor of London, 1702–1705', i, MS 32B, fol. 9.

2. See above Chapter 1.

3. For an excellent recent account of the complex reactions to the crisis of the 1590s see Steve Hindle, 'Dearth, Fasting and Alms: The Campaign for General Hospitality in Late Elizabethan England', *Past and Present*, 172 (2001), pp. 44–86.

4. For discussions of the history of 'rogue literature' and in particular its veracity and generic qualities see Jodi Mikalachki, 'Women's Networks and the Female Vagrant: A Hard Case', in Susan Frye and Karen Robertson, eds, *Maids and Mistresses, Cousins and Queens: Women's Alliances in Early Modern England* (Oxford, 1999); A. L. Beier, *The Problem of the Poor in Tudor and Early Stuart England* (London, 1983); Gámini Salgado, *The Elizabethan Underworld* (Stroud, 1992); Alfred F. Kinney, ed., *Rogues, Vagabonds and Sturdy Beggars: A New Gallery of Tudor and Early Stuart Rogue Literature* (Boston, Massachusetts, 1990); Linda Woodbridge, 'Impostors, Monsters, and Spies: What Rogue Literature Can Tell us about Early Modern Subjectivity', *Early Modern Literary Studies*, special issue, 9 (January 2002); William S. Carol, *Fat King, Lean Beggar: Representations of Poverty in the Age of Shakespeare* (Ithaca, New York, 1996).

5. Ned Ward, *The History of London Clubs: or The Citizens Pastime, Particularly The Lying Club, The Beggars Club* (1709), p. 7.

6. The only information on the beggar/narrator provided by Gay can be found in the 'Introduction'. See John Gay, *The Beggar's Opera* (1728).

7. *Spectator*, no. 430.

8. John Thomas Smith, *A Book for a Rainy Day: or Recollections of the Events of the Last Sixty Years* (1845), p. 74.

9. *OBP*, 12 January 1785, Samuel Bethell, t17850112-78.

10. See GL, 'St Dionys Backchurch, Papers Relating to a Poor Law Appeal from Paul Patrick Kearney, 1771', MS 11280C; *OBP*, 4 December 1728, Paul Kerney, t17281204-54. It is not entirely certain that the Paul Kerney who was arrested at the Beggar's Opera was the same Paul Kearney who formed the subject of the poor law appeal, but the nature of the 1728 crime (fraud), and his identification as a 'Spanish Merchant', are both very much in line with the behaviour and personal characteristics and earlier employment of the pauper, Paul Kearney. It should also be noted that, regardless of variations in spelling, only one Paul Kerney appears as either a witness, defendant or juror at the Old Bailey throughout the eighteenth century.

11. See for example OBP, 1 May 1728, Mary Fox , Mary Lewin , alias Archer, t17280501-41. One hundred and forty years earlier Thomas Harman had

characterised a vagrant as a 'wily fox'. Quoted in A. L. Beier, *Masterless Men: The Vagrancy Problem in England, 1560–1640* (1985), p. 7.

12. *Annual Register for 1773*, September, p. 132.

13. *Ordinary of Newgate Account, His Account*, May 1763, pp. 32, 35. For Lewis's trial see *OBP*, April 1763, Paul Lewis, t17630413–19. Lewis, of course, misrepresents the plot as McHeath did not bribe the court, but received a later government pardon. I would like to thank Robert Shoemaker for this reference.

14. *Ordinary of Newgate, His Account*, 6 August 1740. Quoted in Peter Earle, *A City Full of People: Men and Women of London, 1650–1750* (1994), p. 191–92.

15. Saunders Welch, *A Proposal to Render Effective a Plan to Remove . . . Prostitutes* (1758), pp. 52–53, quoted in M. Dorothy George, *London Life in the Eighteenth Century* (1965), p. 97.

16. *OBP*, 30 June 1734, William Ray, t17340630–15.

17. John Strype, *A Survey of the Cities of London and Westminster* (1720), iv, p. 77.

18. The full range of materials associated with Badham includes *OBP*, 30 June 1734, William Ray, t17340630–15; *OBP*, 9 July 1740, Samuel Badham, t17400709–2; *The Ordinary of Newgate, His Account*, 6 August 1740; and Earle, *A City Full of People*, pp. 191–92.

19. Francis Coventy, *The History of Pompey the Little: or The Life and Adventures of a Lap-Dog*, ed. Robert Adams Day (Oxford, 1974) chs 15–20, pp. 76–105.

20. This is a largely separate phenomenon from the notion of the 'Tricks of the Town' discussed in Chapter 4.

21. The idea of a 'trickster' persona is familiar from the histories of slave and black culture in North America and the Caribbean, and there is a well-developed literature that relates this phenomenon to African folklore and the conditions of relative powerlessness associated with enslavement and racial abuse. See John Roberts, 'Brer' Rabbit and John: Trickster Heroes in Slavery', in *Trickster to Badman: The Black Folk Hero in Slavery and Freedom* (Philadelphia, 1989); Lawrence Levene, *Black Culture and Black Consciousness* (Oxford, 1977); H. Tiffin, 'The Metaphor of Anancy in Caribbean Literature', in R. Sellick, ed. *Myth and Metaphor* (Adelaide, 1984). It is also a fragment of a larger body of behaviour associated with resistance to over powerful and dominant authorities by the least powerful – it is a cultural extension of what James C. Scott has characterised for peasant societies as the 'weapons of the weak'. See James C. Scott, *Weapons of the Weak: Everyday Forms of Peasant Resistance* (New Haven, Connecticut, 1985).

22. GL, 'Court of Governors, Bridewell and Bethlem: Minutes, 12 January 1737/8 to 4 April 1751', MS 33011/21, p. 470. The weather prevented any observations being made on that day at Greenwich, while the temperature recorded two days earlier, on 16 December was 37.5 degrees Fahrenheit. The next recorded temperature was taken on 22 December and was 48 degrees Fahrenheit. See James Bradley,

Astronomical Observations Made at the Royal Observatory at Greenwich from the Year MDCCL to the Year MDCCLXII, i (1798), part 1, p. 14 and part 2, p. 8.

23. For an authoritative account of Cervantes's influence on eighteenth-century literature see Ronald Paulson, *Don Quixote in England: The Aesthetics of Laughter* (Baltimore Maryland, 1998).

24. For Cervantes's influence on Coventry see Coventy, *Pompey the Little*, 'Introduction', p. xviii.

25. Paulson, *Don Quixote in England*, pp. 158–60.

26. Daniel Defoe, *The Compleat Mendicant: or Unhappy Beggar* (1699).

27. *Don Quixote*, chapter 44.

28. Jane Barker, *The Lining of the Patch Work Screen: Design'd for the Farther Entertainment of Ladies* (1726) see, in particular, 'The History of the Lady Gypsie', in *The Galesia Trilogy and Selected Manuscript Poems of Jane Barker*, ed., Carol Shiner Wilson (Oxford, 1997), pp. 227, 228. The character of eighteenth-century English Gypsy communities is a subject of some debate. For the earliest creditable, first-hand account of a Gypsy life see Mary Saxby, *Memoirs of a Female Vagrant Written by Herself* (1806). For a more general modern account see Thomas Acton, ed., *Gypsy Politics and Traveller Identity* (Hatfield, 1997), and Thomas Acton and Gary Mundy, eds, *Romani Culture and Gypsy Identity* (Hatfield, 1997).

29. *Two Humorous Novels, viz. I. A Diverting Dialogue between Scipio and Bergansa ... II. The Comical History of Rinconete and Cortadillo. Both Written by the Celebrated Author of Don Quixote, Translated by Robert Goadby* (1741). *Rinconete and Cortadillo*, in particular, recounts the story of two ragged, teenage boys living on the cusp between begging and theft. Coventy, *The History of Pompey the Little*, ed. Day, 'Introduction', p. xviii.

30. Quoted in the introduction of *The King of the Beggars: Bampfylde-Moore Carew*, ed. C. H. Wilkinson (Oxford, 1931), p. xvi.

31. The authoritative edition of Carew is *The King of the Beggars: Bampfylde-Moore Carew*, ed., C. H. Wilkinson (Oxford, 1931). For the publishing history of the volume and the role of Robert Goadby see the Introduction by Wilkinson.

32. For a brief but authoritative biography of Marcellus Laroon see Sean Shesgreen, *The Criers and Hawkers of London: Engravings and Drawings by Marcellus Laroon* (Aldershot, 1990), pp. 61–62.

33. The most authoritative account of the history of the 'Cries' is Sean Shesgreen, *Images of the Outcast: The Urban Poor in the Cries of London* (Manchester, 2002). For a discussion of Laroon's use of named individuals see p. 88.

34. For a detailed commentary on this image see Shesgreen, *Criers and Hawkers of London*, p. 158.

35. Shesgreen, *Images of the Outcast*, p. 119.

36. Shesgreen, *Images of the Outcast*, pp. 79–87.

37. Ibid., pp. 151–54.

38. Ibid., pp. 124–31.

39. Israel R. Potter, *The Life and Remarkable Adventures of Israel R. Potter* (1824; New York, 1962), p. 69.

40. *London in 1710, from the Travels of Zacharia Conrad von Uffenbach*, translated and edited by W. H. Quarrell and Margaret Mare (1934), p. 164.

41. Potter, *Life and Remarkable Adventures*, p. 68.

42. Paulson, *Don Quixote in England*, pp. 45–47.

43. For a discussion of the interrelationship between the 'Enraged Musician' and the Cries tradition, see Shesgreen, *Images of the Outcast*, pp. 102–4.

44. For a discussion of contemporary reactions to this painting see Postle, *Angels and Urchins*, pp. 93–94.

45. For a sophisticated discussion of the depiction of the labouring poor in eighteenth- and early nineteenth-century painting see John Barrell, *The Dark Side of the Landscape: The Rural Poor in English Painting, 1730–1840* (Cambridge, 1980).

46. For a brief discussion of Murillo's influence on Gainsborough, see Michael Rosenthal and Martin Myrone, eds, *Gainsborough* (2002), p. 228.

47. Henry McKenzie, *The Man of Feeling* (1771), ed. Brian Vickers (Oxford, 2001), ch. 14, pp. 15–18.

48. For a general discussion of vagrancy and romanticism see Toby R. Benis, *Romanticism on the Road: The Marginal Gains of Wordsworth's Homeless* (New York, 2000).

49. Robert Southey, 'The Widow' (1797), reproduced in Roger Lonsdale, ed., *Eighteenth-Century Verse* (Oxford, 1984), pp. 823–24.

50. Candler, who was born in 1740, married an alcoholic whose financial improvidence led her in to real poverty, including a brief period spent in London in 1780. See Ann Candler, *Poetical Attempts by Ann Canlder, a Suffolk Cottager. With a Short Narrative of her Life* (Ipswich, 1803).

51. Mary Saxby, *Memoirs of a Female Vagrant Written by Herself With Illustrations* (1806).

52. Sarah Lloyd, 'Cottage Conversations: Poverty and Manly Independence in Eighteenth-Century England', *Past and Present*, (forthcoming, 2004).

53. Charles Lamb, 'A Complaint of the Decay of Beggars in the Metropolis', *Essays of Elia* (June 1822).

54. John Thomas Smith, *Vagabondiana; or Anecdotes of Mendicant Wanderers Through the Streets of London. With Portraits of the Most Remarkable, Drawn from Life* (1817), p. 28.

55. John James Bezer, 'The Autobiography of One of the Chartist Rebels of 1848', in D. M. Vincent, ed., *Testaments of Radicalism* (1977), p. 185.

Notes to Chapter 10: The History of the Poor

1. For an excellent study of the conditions under which pauper letters were written, and the complexities of reading them, see Thomas Sokoll, *Essex Pauper Letters, 1731–1837* (Oxford, 2001), pp. 3–80.

2. For information on the publishing history of the *Proceedings* see Simon Devereaux, 'The City and the Sessions Paper: "Public Justice" in London, 1770–1801, *Journal of British Studies*, 35 (1996), pp. 466–503; Simon Devereaux, 'The Fall of the Sessions Paper: Criminal Trial and the Popular Press in Late Eighteenth-Century London', *Criminal Justice History*, 18 (2002); Michael Harris, 'Trials and Criminal Biographies: A Case Study in Distribution', in R. Myers and M. Harris, eds, *Sale and Distribution of Books from 1700* (Oxford, 1982); Andrea McKenzie, 'Making Crime Pay: Motives, Marketing Strategies, and the Printed Literature of Crime in England, 1670–1770', in G. T. Smith et al., eds, *Criminal Justice in the Old World and the New: Essays in Honour of J. M. Beattie* (Toronto, 1998).

3. For a recent analysis of the interrelationship between trial reports and fiction see Hal Gladfelder, *Criminality and Narrative in Eighteenth-Century England: Beyond the Law* (Baltimore, 2001).

4. See in particular Hayden White, *Metahistory: The Historical Imagination* (Johns Hopkins, 1973); for a recent discussion of responses to the problems raised by White's work see Ewa Damanska, 'Hayden White: Beyond Irony', *History and Theory*, 37, (1998), pp. 173–81.

5. Ironically, it is also very well written. It is unreadable simply because of the complex technical descriptions required to present complex historical demography. Tony Wrigley and Roger Schofield, *Population History of England, 1541–1871: A Reconstruction* (1981).

6. For some recent literature on Michel Foucault and his work see Mitchell Dean, *Critical and Effective Histories: Foucault's Methods and Historical Sociology* (Routledge, 1994) and Michael Kelly, ed., *Critique and Power: Recasting the Foucault/Habermas Debate* (Boston, Massachusetts, 1994).

7. See in particular Jonathan Clark, *English Society 1688–1832: Ideology, Social Structure and Political Practice During the Ancien Regime* (Cambridge, 1985) and Jonathan Clark, *Revolution and Rebellion: State and Society in England in the Seventeenth and Eighteenth Centuries* (Cambridge, 1986). For an attempt to critically contextualise Clark's work see Joanna Innes, 'Jonathan Clark, Social History and England's "Ancien Regime"' *Past and Present*, 115 (1987), pp. 165–200.

8. Jürgen Habermas, *Structural Transformation of the Public Sphere* trans. Thomas Burger with Frederick Lawrence (Boston, Massachusetts, 1989). For recent work on the middling sort see John Brewer, *The Pleasures of the Imagination:*

English Culture in the Eighteenth Century (1997); Paul Langford, *A Polite and Commercial People: England, 1727–1783* (Oxford, 1989); Dror Wahrman, *Imagining the Middle Class: The Political Representation of Class in Britain, c. 1780–1840* (Cambrdige, 1995), and Kathleen Wilson, *The Sense of the People: Politics, Culture and Imperialism in England, 1715–1785* (Cambridge, 1995).

9. The history of consumption gained its first major statement with Neil McKendrick, John Brewer, and Sir John Harold Plumb, *The Birth of a Consumer Society: The Commercialization of Eighteenth-Century England* (Bloomington, Indiana, 1982); a recent series of collections of essays and an authored volume by John Brewer reflect this historical literature in its maturity. John Brewer and Roy Porter, eds, *Consumption and the World of Goods in the Seventeengh and Eighteenth Centuries* (1993); John Brewer and Susan Staves, eds, *Early Modern Conceptions of Property* (1995); Ann Bermingham and John Brewer, eds, *The Consumption of Culture: Word, Image, and Object in the Seventeenth and Eighteenth Centuries* (1995); and Brewer, *The Pleasures of the Imagination.*

10. See for instance Amanda Vickery, *The Gentleman's Daughter: Women's Lives in Georgian England* (New Haven, Connecticut, 1998). For an excellent counter-example see Bridget Hill, *English Domestic Servants in the Eighteenth CenturyEnglish Domestic Servants in the Eighteenth Century* (Oxford, 1996).

11. There is a growing literature in the same vein. See for example Robert Shoemaker, *The London Mob: Violence and Disorder in Eighteenth-Century England* (2004); Peter King, *Crime, Justice, and Discretion in England, 1740–1820* (Oxford, 2000); Anna Davin, 'Waif Stories in Late Nineteenth-Century England', *History Workshop Journal*, 52 (2001), pp. 67–98; Laura Gowing, *Common Bodies: Women, Touch and Power in Seventeenth-Century England* (New Haven, Connecticut, 2003); Keith Wrightson, *Earthly Necessities: Economic Lives in Early Modern Britain* (New Haven, Connecticut, 2000); Steve Hindle, 'Exhortation and Entitlement: Negotiating Inequality in English Rural Communities, 1550–1650', in Michael Braddick and John Walter, eds, *Negotiating Power in Early Modern Society: Order, Hierarchy and Subordination in Britain and Ireland* (Cambridge, 2001); Paul Griffiths, 'Overlapping Circles: Imagining Criminal Communities in London, 1545–1645', in Alexandra Shepard and Phil Withington, eds, *Communities in Early Modern England: Networks, Place, Rhetoric* (Manchester, 2000); Pamela Sharpe, *Adapting to Capitalism: Working Women in the English Economy, 1700–1850* (2000); Robert B. Shoemaker, 'Male Honour and the Decline of Public Violence in Eighteenth-Century London', *Social History*, 26 (2001), pp. 190–208; Heather Shore, *Artful Dodgers: Youth and Crime in Early Nineteenth-Century London* (Oxford, 1999); John Marriott, ed., *Unknown London: Early Modernist Visions of the Metropolis, 1815–45* (2000) and Catherina Lis and Hugo Soly, *Disordered Lives: Eighteenth-Century Families and their Unruly Relatives* (Cambridge, 1996).

12. Peter Mandler, ed., *The Uses of Charity: The Poor on Relief in the Nineteenth-Century Metropolis* (Philadelphia, 1990), pp. 1, 15–16.

Bibliography

Place of publication is London, unless otherwise stated.

MANUSCRIPT SOURCES

British Library, Manuscript Collection

Place Papers, vol. xl: Manners and Morals, parts 1–4. Add MS 27825; Add. MS 27826; Add. MS 27827; Add. MS 27828.

Sloane MS 4078, fol. 159, 'Report on the Autopsy of Margaret Whistle, 10 September 1731'.

Camden Public Libraries, Swiss Cottage Library, Archives Department

St Giles in the Fields, Vestry Minutes, 1673–1771.

St Andrew Holborn and St George the Martyr, Overseers of the Poor, Minutes of Various Meetings, 1731–35, MS 1A1.

Corporation of London Record Office

'An Account of Money Received to Reward such Constables who Shall be Assissting in Apprehending Petty Chapmen, ... 1748–63'. Misc. MS 210.6.

'Account of the Children in the Corporation Workhouse, 1710', Misc. MS. 22/44.

'An Account of the Expences of Conveying Vagrants Onwards to their Legall Settlements ... 1748–50', Misc. MS 241.6.

'Account of the Vagrant Passess that was Past from Southward of the Thames to St Magnus London Bridge ... 1748–49', Misc. MS 241/5.

'A Book of the Proceedings of Committees of the Court of Aldermen and Common Council begun the 22nd of March 1708', Misc. MS 210.7

'The Case of the Citizens and Shopkeepers of London with Respect to the Pedlars within this City ...', Misc. MS 85.22.

'Children in the Grey Coat Hospital on the Parish Account' , Misc. MS 11.15.

'City's Cash Accounts, 1699, onwards', MS 1/23–68.

'Committee of Aldermen ... State of the Prisoners, 1784–5', Misc. MS 184/4.

'Committee of Inquiry into the Behaviour of Children in Bridewell, 1710–18', Misc. MS 58.35.

'Committee Papers re London Workhouse, 1743, 1747–48; Various Accounts, 1744–47; Anonymous Letter to the London Workhouse Committee, 1747', Small MS, box 13, no. 5.

'Committee Report on Moving Prisoners form Ludgate to the Corporation Work-house, 1761', Misc. MS 183/1.

'Committee Report on the London Workhouse, 1708', MS Alchin, box B35.

'Committee to Consider the Distresses of the Poor at this Severe and Inclement Sea-son, 1776', Misc. MS 4/24.

'Committee to Enquire in to the Present State of the London Workhouse, 1790, Misc. MS 230/21.

'Coroner's Inquests'.

'Courts of the President and Governors for the Poor of London, 1702–5', MS New 377c/1/22.

'Duplicate Vagrant Passes, June to September 1792' , MS box 1 (temp 334A) 221F.

'The Grand Jury's Presentment, 7 January 1739', Misc MS 18.40.

'Guildhall Justice Room, Minute Books, 1753 onwards', MS GJR/M1–55.

'Hoard Book, 1696–1754', MS 033C/9/25.

'Journals of the Common Council of the Corporation of London', For. 51–65.

London Session Papers, 1751, 'Settlement and Vagrant Papers'.

London Sessions Papers, 'Confession of Thomas Coleman', MS LS/P1731/1.

London Sessions Papers, 1734 'Presentment re Beggars'.

London Sessions Papers, 1749, 'Grand Jury Presentment, October 1749'.

London Sessions Papers, 1753–54, 'Petition', box 30.

London Sessions Papers, 'List of Fees to be Taken by Justices' Clerks, 24 July 1753'.

'London Workhouse Accounts, 1709', Misc. MS 66.10.

'Mansion House Justice Room, Charge Book, 1699–1705', MS New 392c.

'Mansion House Justice Room, Charge Book, 1728–33', MS New 392c.

'Mansion House Justice Room, Minute Book, 1784', MS MJR/M1–14.

'Mansion House Justice Room, Miscellaneous Books: Summonses, 1798', MS MJR/Misc. 6.

'Mr Kirby's Bill for Subsistence Money &c for Poor Vagrants &c Sent to Wood Street Compter by the Lord Mayor and Aldermen, recd 15 May 1781', Misc. MS 288/8.

'Orders of Quarter Sessions and Orders on Appeal, 1743–50', 209A, MS SMO 1B.

'Printed Orders of Common Council', MS Par Book 1, ex: 29B 1/22, 376B.

'The Repertories of the Court of Aldermen of the Corporation of London, 1697–1800', Rep. 102–203.

'Report on the Conditions and Management of the Corporation of the Poor', Misc. MS no. 35, Alchin, box B.

'Two Warrants for Confining Individuals to the London Workhouse, 1725', Misc. MS 331/6.

'Vagrant Accounts, Miscellaneous', Misc. MS 158/34

'Vagrant Books (4), Together with Five Loose Pages and a Bill of Mortality, 1738–42', Misc. MS 322.5.

Guildhall Library

'Alhallows Lombard Street. Two letters from Paupers', MS 18982.

'Bridewell, Prison Committee, Orders of Admission, 1691–95', MS 33137/1.

'Bridewell, Prison Subcommittee, 1792–1802' , MS 33132/1.

'Court of Governors, Bridewell and Bethlem', MS 3011/17–25.

'Petitions for Relief of St Helen's within Bishopsgate, 1741–45', MS 6888.

'St Andrew by the Wardrobe with St Ann Blackfriars, Poor Law Papers, Passes, Orders, Petitions', MS 7596.

'St Andrew Holborn, Book of Examinations, 1782–89', MS 9630.

'St Ann Blackfriars, Statements Made by Paupers when Claiming Relief, 1776–78', MS 1075/1.

'St Ann Blackfriars, Statements Made by Paupers when Claiming Relief, 1779–85', MS 1075/2.

'St Botolph Aldgate, Pauper Examinations for the East Smithfield part of the Parish, 1742–1800', MS 2676/1–22.

'St Dionis Backchurch, Miscellaneous Parish Papers, 1606–1818', MS 11280A/4.

'St Dionis Backchurch, Papers Relating to a Poor Law Appeal from Paul Patrick Kearney, 1771', MS 11280C.

'St Dionis Backchurch, Pauper Letters, 1738–59', MS 19233.

'St Dionis Backchurch, Vouchers, 1766–72', MS 11280/box 6.

'St Dionis Backchurch, Workhouse Inquests Minute Book, 1761–88', MS 4219/1.

'St Giles Cripplegate, Workhouse Committee Minute Book', MS 6051/1.

'St Helens in Bishopsgate, Settlement Examinations, 1738–96', MS 6886.

'St Martin Ludgate, Examinations of Paupers, 1774–86', MS 1331/1.

'St Nicholas Acons, List of Inhabitants, 1756–1806', MS 4295.

'St Peter Cornhill, Pauper and Vagrant Passes, 1757–1808', MS 4198.

'St Sepulchre, Middlesex Division, Pauper Examinations, 1765–73', MS 9095/1.

'St Sepulchre, Middlesex Division, Bastardy Book, 1793–1805', MS 9096.

House of Lords Record Office
House of Lords Records Office, Poor Rate Returns, 1776, parchment collection, box 162.

London Metropolitan Archives
'Consistory Court of London, Deposition Book, January 1720 to 1 December 1721', Holloway con Guildford, Microfilm, reel 304 DL/C. 634. X19/157.

Middlesex Sessions Papers, 'Gaol Delivery Roll, 9 September 1742', MJ/SR 2783.

'Middlesex Quarter Sessions Books', MJ/SBB/370-1070.

'Middlesex Sessions, Orders of Court', MJ /OC/1.

'Middlesex Sessions, Order of Court for Westminster', WJ/OC/1.

'Middlesex Sessions, Orders of Court', MJ/OC/4.

'St Luke's Chelsea, Sidney Street Chelsea Workhouse Committee Book', P74/Luk/3.

'St Luke Chelsea, Workhouse Admissions and Discharges', Microfilm, X/1S/37.

'St Giles in the Fields, Holborn, Admissions Register', Microfilm, X/20/S4.

'St John at Hackney, Vestry Minutes', P79/JN1/139.

'St John at Hackney, Workhouse Committee Minutes', P79/JN1/160.

'St John at Hackney, Churchwardens' Accounts', P79/JN1/219.

'St John at Hackney, Minutes of the Petty Sessions', P79/JN1/214.

'St Mary at Lambeth, Workhouse Order Book', P8S/MRY1/288.

'St Mary at Lambeth, Workhouse Expenses', P8S/MRY1/289.

National Archives
Chancery, '*McCarty* v. *Kearney*, George I & II', MS C11/1329/41.

Chancery, '*Ma'Carty* v. *Kearney*, 1742', MS C11/2473/28.

State Papers, 'Paul Kearney to W[illia]m Sharpe', 17 June 1748', SP54/39/45B.

State Papers, 'Lieutenant General Bland to John Potter', MS SP54/39/47A.

Westminster Archives Centre
'Precinct of the Savoy, Westminster, Workhouse Committee Minutes, 1737–44', K324.

'St Anne's, Westminster, Vestry Minutes, 1701–42', A2202a.

'St Clement Dane, Settlement and Bastardy Examinations Book', B1187.

'St George Hanover Square, Westminster, Vestry Minutes, 1725–35, Fair Copy', C766a–1.

'St George Hanover Square, Westminster, Vestry Minutes, 1725–52', C766–8.

'St George Hanover Square, Westminster, Workhouse Committee Minutes, 1726–46', C869–78.

'St James, Westminster, Vestry Minutes, 1694–1750', D1757–60.

'St Margaret's, Westminster, Vestry Minutes and Orders, 1674–93', E2416, shelf 38.

'St Margaret's, Westminster, Vestry Minutes and Orders, 1724–38', E2419–20, shelf 38.

'St Margaret's, Westminster, Workhouse Committee Minutes, 1726–49', E2632–8, shelf 28.

'St Margaret's, Westminster, Workhouse Rules, Orders and Correspondence, 1746–66', E573, shelf 30.

'St Martin in the Fields, Examination Books, 1731–33', F5025.

'St Martin in the Fields, Examination Books, 1739–66', F5032.

'St Martin in the Fields, List of Names of the Poor, 1725–29', F4002.

'St Martin in the Fields, Lists of Paupers, 1727–41', F4073.

'St Martin in the Fields, Parish Records, Watch Rates, Collector's Book, 1735–57', F2676.

'St Martin in the Fields, Vestry Clerks Bills, 1736–72', F2339.

'St Martin in the Fields, Vestry Draft Minutes (Scavengers), 1750–71', F2030.

'St Martin in the Fields, Vestry Draft Minutes Relating to the Watch, 1736–54', F2028.

'St Martin in the Fields, Vestry Draft Minutes, 1736–54', F2028.

'St Martin in the Fields, Westminster, Vestry Minutes, 1666–1778', F2004–7.

'St Martin in the Fields, Workhouse Day Book, 1737–42', F4003.

'St Martin in the Fields, Workhouse Day Book, 1742–46', F4004.

'St Martin in the Fields, Workhouse Register', F4074'.

Westminster Abbey Muniment Room

'Brief for the Dean and Chapter of Westmr against the Bill for Regulating the Nightly Watch, 1719', MS 65923.

'The Humble Peiticon of the Inhabitants of ... Westminster ... 1719', MS 65923.

'List of Almspeople's Rents, 1779', MS 66002.

'Names of the Poor People that are Partakers of the Bread, Meat and Belonging to Westminster Abby, 1758', MS 65984.

'Petition of George Watts to Mr Emery Hills Almshouses', MS 34391.

'Petition re Payments to Almspeople', MS 66035*.

'Petititon of William Davis, 1705', MS 65906.

'Records of the Coroner's Court for Westminster, 1762–1800'.

'Statement Relating to Compensation for Tearing Down the Little Almonry in Dean's Court, 1779', MS 660000.

PUBLISHED PRIMARY SOURCES, 1500–1870
(including modern editions of manuscript sources)

Account of a Great and Famous Scolding-Match Between Four Remarkable Scolding Fish-Women of Rosemary-lane, and the Like Number of Basket-Women of Golden-lane, near Cripplegate (1699).

Account of Several Workhouses for Employing and Maintaining the Poor (1725, 1732).

Account of the Institutions and Proceedings of the Asylum or House of Refuge … for the Reception of Orphan Girls (1763).

Annals for Europe for the Year 1741 (1742).

Annals of Europe for the Year 1742 (1743).

Authentic Memoirs of the Celebrated Mis Nancy D*ws*n (c. 1765).

Authentic Narrative of the Most Remarkable Adventures and Curious Intriques Exhibited in the Life of Miss Fanny Davies (1786).

Autobiography of Joseph Mayett of Quainton, 1783–1839, ed. Ann Kussmaul, Buckinghamshire Record Society, no. 23 (1986).

[Barbon, Nicolas], An Apology for the Builder: or A Discourse Shewing the Cause and Effects of the Increase of Building (1685).

Barker, Jane, The Galesia Trilogy and Selected Manuscript Poems of Jane Barker, ed. Carol Shiner Wilson (Oxford, 1997).

Barker, Joseph, The History and Confessions of a Man (1846).

[Bevan, Timothy], An Account of the Rise, Progress and Present State of the School and Work-house Maintain'd by the People Called Quakers, at Clerkenwell London (1746).

Bickerstaff, Isaac, The Life, Strand Voyages and Uncommon Adventures of Ambrose Gwinett (1770).

Blake, William, The Complete Poems, ed. Alicia Ostriker (1977).

Bogg-Witticisms: or Dear Joy's Common-Places (1690s?).

Boswell, James, The Life of Samuel Johnson (1799 edn).

Bowen, Thomas, Extracts from the Records and Court Books of Bridewell Hospital (1798).

Bradley, James, Astronomical Observations Made at the Royal Observatory at Greenwich from the Year MDCCL to the Year MDCCLXII, two volumes (1798, 1805).

Brown, Thomas, The Works of Thomas Brown, Serious and Comical (1715).

Burn, James Dawson, *The Autobiography of a Beggar Boy*, edited with an introduction by David Vincent (1978).

Byrd, William, *William Byrd of Virginia: The London Diary (1717–21) and Other Writings*, Louis B. Wright and Marion Tinling, eds (New York, 1958).

Campbell, R., *The London Tradesman* (1747).

Candler, Ann, *Poetical Attempts, by Ann Candler, Suffolk Cottager; with a Short Narrative of her Life* (Ipswich, 1803).

Case of the Dean and Chapter of Westminster (1720).

Case of the Parish of St Giles in the Fields as to their Poor and a Work-House Designed to be Built for Employing Them (n.d., 1725?).

Cassini, *Prognostication Concerning the Frost by Monsieur Cassini* (1697).

Character of a Coffee-House, with the Symptons of a Town-Wit (1673).

Characters of Gentlemen That Have Put in to the Ladies Invention (n.d.).

Charke, Charlotte, *A Narrative of the Life of Mrs Charlotte Charke*, ed. Robert Rehder (1755, Pickering & Chatto edn, 1999).

Chelsea Pensioner: A Comic Opera in Two Acts (1779).

Clarke, George, ed., *John Bellers: His Life, Times and Writings* (1987).

Constables Hue and Cry after Whores & Bawds (1700).

Copy of Verses Humbly Presented ... by the Careful Society of Lamp-Lighters (Norwich, 1765).

Coquhoun, Patrick, *The State of Indigence and the Situation of the Casual Poor in the Metropolis* (1799).

Country-Man's Fare-well to London: or A Broadside Against Pride (n.d.).

Coventry, Francis, *The History of Pompey the Little: or The Life and Adventurs of a Lap-Dog*, ed. Robert Adams Day (1751, Oxford University Press edn, 1974).

Cupid's Revenge: or An Account of a King, who Slighted All Women, and at Length was Forced to Marry a Beggar (n.d.).

Curwen, Samuel, *The Journal of Samuel Curwen, Loyalist*, ed. Andrew Oliver (Salem, Massachusetts, 1972).

[D'Urfey, T.], *Collin's Walk Through London and Westminster: A Poem in Burlesque* (1690).

De Saussure, César, *A Foreign View of England in 1725–1729: The Letters of Monsieur César de Saussure to his Family*, translated and edited by Madame van Muyden (London, 1995).

De Veil, Sir Thomas, *Observations on the Practise of a Justice of the Peace* (1747).

Defoe, Daniel, *Giving Alms no Charity and Employing the Poor a Greivance to the Nation* (1704).

Defoe, Daniel, *The Compleat Mendicant* (1699).

Defoe, Daniel, *The History and Remarkable Life of the Truly Honourable Col. Jacque, Commonly Call'd Col. Jack*, ed. Samuel Holt Monk (1722; OUP edn, 1965).

Defoe, Daniel, *The Life, Adventures and Piracies of the Famous Captain Singleton* ed. H. Halliday Sparling (1719, 1887 edn).

[Defoe, Daniel], *The Compleat Mendicant: or Unhappy Beggar* (1699).

Defoe, Daniel, *A Tour Through the Whole Island of Great Britain* (1724–26; Penguin edn, 1971).

Dickens, Charles, *Sketches by Boz* (1835, Ware, Hertfordshire, 1999).

Discovery of the Thieves, Thief Takers and Locks alia Receivers of Stolen Goods ... An Account of the Flash Words ... by a Prisoner in Newgate (n.d.).

Dodsley, R., *The Blind Beggar of Bethnal Green* (1741).

Dornford, Josiah, *An Address to the Livery and Citizens of London on the Proceedings of the Court of Common Council on Friday the 24th of February 1786 Respecting Mr Alderman Clarke and Mr Dornford* (1786).

Dornford, Josiah, *Nine Letters to the Right Honourable the Lord Mayor and Aldermen of the City of London on the State of the Prisons and Prisoners* (1786).

Dunton, John, *The Night-Walker* [1696].

Effigies, Parentage, Education, Life, Merry-Pranks and Covnersaton of the Celebrated Mrs Sally Salisbury (1722–23).

Eight Letters to His Grace Duke of _____, On the Custom of Vails-Giving in England (1760).

English Man's Two Wishes: One, That Hanover was Farther Away (1728?).

Extracts for the Reports of the English Society for Bettering the Condition of the Poor (Dublin 1799).

Faithfull Narrative of the Wonderful and Surprising Appearance of Councellor Morgan's Ghost (1746?).

Famous and Notable Sayings of an Eminent Holder-Forth near Covent Garden (1691).

Faulkner, Thomas, *An Historical and Topographical Description of Chelsea* (1829).

Fielding, Henry, *The Covent-Garden Journal and a Plan of the Universal Register-Office*, ed. Bertrand Goldgar (1988).

Fielding, Henry, *The History of Amelia* (1752; 1832 edn).

Flos Ingenii vel Evacuatio Discriptionis: Being an Exact Description of Epsam and Epsam Wells (1674).

Gay, John, *An Argument Proving from History, Reason, and Scripture, That the Present Mohocks and Hawkubites are the Gog and Magog Mention'd in the Revelations* (1712).

Gay, John, *Poetry and Prose*, ed. Vinton A. Dearing ed. (Oxford, 1974).

Gay, John, *The Beggar's Opera* (1728).

Gentleman's Magazine.

Gibbon, Edward, *Memoirs of My Life*, ed. Betty Radice (1991).

Gilbert, Thomas, *Observations upon the Orders and Resolutions of the House of Commons with Respect to the Poor, Vagrants and Houses of Correction* (1775).

Goldsmith, Oliver, *The Collected Works of Oliver Goldsmith*, ed. Arthur Friedman, 5 vols (Oxford, 1966).

Grant, Roger, *A Full and True Account of a Miaculous Cure of a Young Man in Newington that was Born Blind, and was in Five Minutes Brought to Prfect Sight* (1709).

Green, William, *The Art of Living in London: A Poem in Two Cantos* (1768).

Greenwood, James, *The Seven Curses of London* (1869; Oxford 1981 edn).

Gronniosaw, James Albert Ukansaw, *A Narrative of the Most Remarkable Particulars in the Life of James Albert Ukawsaw Gronniosaw, an African Prince, Written by Himself* (Bath, 1774).

Grose, Franicis, *Classical Dictionary of the Vulgar Tongue* (1785).

Grose, Francis, *The Grumbler: Containing Sixteen Essays* 1791).

Grub Street Journal (1736).

Guide to Young Communicants: or The Whole Duty of the Sacrament ... A Dialogue between Divine and a Beggar (n.d.).

Hadgi, Ali Mohammed, *A Brief and Merry History of Great Britain* (1730).

Hanway, Jonas, *Observations on the Causes of Dissoluteness* (1772).

Hanway, Jonas, *A Sentimental History of Chimney Sweepers in London and Westminster* (1785).

[Hanway, Jonas], *The Sentiments and Advice of Thomas Trueman, a Virtuous and Understanding Footman* (1760).

Hart, Nicholas, *The Sleepy Man Awak'd* (1710).

Haywood, E. A., *A New Present for a Servant Maid* (1771).

Hell upon Earth (1729).

Heywood, Eliza, *The History of Miss Betsy Thoughtless*, ed. Beth Fowkes Tobin (1751; Oxford edn, 1997).

High Life Below Stairs: A Farce of Two Acts (1768).

Hill, William, *A Full Account of the Life and Visions of Nicholas Hart* (1711).

Hints and Cautions for the Information of the Churchwardens and Overseers ... of St Giles in the Fields (1781).

History of Jonathan Griffin and William Peterson; Pointing Out an Asylum to the Destitute (Cheap Repository Tract, c. 1800).

Hitchcock, Tim and Black, John, *Chelsea Settlement and Bastardy Examinationas, 1733–1766*, London Record Society, 33 (1999).

Hitchcock, Tim, ed., *Richard Hutton's Complaints Book: The Notebook of the Steward of the Quaker Workhouse at Clerkenwell, 1711–1737* , London Record Society, 24 (1987).

Hone, William, *The Year Book of Daily Recreations and Information, Concerning Remarkable Men and Manners, Times and Seasons, Solemnities and Merry-Makings, Antiquities and Novelties* (1832).

Housekeeping Book of Susanna Whatman, 1776–1800 (1987).

Howard, John, *That State of the Prisons in England and Wales with Preliminary Observations and an Account of Some Foreign Prisons* (1777).

Hoyland, John, *A Historical Survey ... of the Gypsies* (1816).

Hue and Cry after Edward Kerby (1700).

Hue and Cry After Good House-Keeping: or A Dialogue betwixt Good House-Keeping, Christmas and Pride (1687).

Hutton, William, *A Journey from Birmingham to London* (Birmingham, 1785).

[Ilive, J.], *Reasons Offered for the Reformation of the House of Correction in Clerkenwell* (1757).

Irving, Washington, *Sketch Book of Geoffrey Crayon* (1819–1820).

Israel R. Potter, *The Life and Remarkable Adventures of Israel R. Potter*, with an Introduction by Leonard Kriegel (1st edn Providence, Rhode Island, 1824; New York, 1962).

Jacob, Giles, *The Complete Parish Officer* (1723).

Johnson, Christopher, *The History of the Life and Intrigues of ... Posture-Mistress, Eliz. Mann* (1724).

Johnson, Samuel, *London: A Poem. In Imitation of the Third Satire of Juvenal* (1738).

Jones, Erasmus, *The Man of Manners: or Plebeian Polish'd* (1737).

[Jones, Erasmus], *Luxury, Pride and Vanity, the Bane of the British Nation* (1736?).

Journal of John Harrower: An Indentured Servant in the Colony of Virginia, 1773–1776, ed. Edward Miles Riley (Williamsburg, Virginia, 1963).

King of the Beggars: Bampfylde-Moore Carew, ed. C. H. Wilkinson (Oxford, 1931).

Lackington, James, *Memoirs of the Life of James Lackington* (1791).

Lady of Pleasure and Fashion (1820).

Lamb, Charles, 'A Complaint of the Decay of Beggars in the Metropolis', *Essays of Elia* (June 1822).

Laws of Arrests in both Civil and Criminal Cases. By an Attorney at Law (1742).

Laws Relating to the Highways (1720).

Lewis, W. S., ed., *Horace Walpole's Correspondence* (Oxford, 1955).

Life of Tho. Neaves, the Noted Stret-Robber Executed at Tyburn on Friday the Seventh of February, 1728–9 (1729).

London, What it is, Not What it Was: To Which is Added a Remonstrance Against the Great Number of Shops (1725).

Low-Life: or One Half of the World Knows Not How the Other Half Live (1749).

Lysons, Daniel, *Collectanea: or A Collection of Advertisements and Paragraphs from the Newspapers* (1st edn, 1818; 2nd edn, 1840).

Lysons, Daniel, *The Environs of London: Being an Historical Account of the Towns, Villages and Hamlets within Twelve Miles of the Capital* (1795).

M. Misson's Memoirs and Observations in his Travels over England, trans. by Mr Ozell (1719).

Mackenzie, Henry, *The Man of Feeling*, ed. Hamish Miles (1771; Scholartis Press edn, 1928).

Malcom, James Pellor, *Anecdotes of the Manners and Customs of London during the Eighteenth Century* (1808).

Mandeville, Bernard, *The Grumbling Hive: or Knaves Turn'd Honest* (1705).

Martin, Matthew, *An Appeal to Public Benevolence for the Relief of Beggars: With a View to a Plan for Suppression of Beggary* (1812).

Martin, Matthew, esq., *Letter to the Right Hon. Lord Pelham on the State of Mendicity in the Metropolis* (1803).

Maskelyne, Nevil, *Astronomical Observations Made at the Royal Observatory at Greenwich from MDCCLXXXVII to MDCCXCVII* (1798).

Maskelyne, Nevil, *Astronomical Observations Made at the Royal Observatory at Greenwich in the Years 1765, 1766, 1767, 1768 and 1769* (1774).

Memoirs of the Life and Times of Sir Thomas Deveil, Knight (1748).

Memorial Concerning the Erecting in the City of London or the Suburbs thereof an Orphanatropy (1728).

Midnight Rambler: or New Nocturnal Spy (c. 1770).

Modern Practise of the London Hospitals (1764).

Moraley, William, *The Infortunate: The Voyage and Adventures of William Moraley, an Indentured Servant*, ed. Susan E Klepp and Billy G. Smith, (Pennsylvania, 1992).

Murray, Thomas Archibald, *Remarks on the Situation of the Poor in the Metropolis* (1801).

Narrative of the Most Cruel and Barbarous Treatment of Miss Sarah Molloy (1762).

Neglected Tar (1791).

New Plot Newly Discovered, by the Help of the London Bell-Man ... Cunning Gypsies (1680).

New Plot Newly Discovered ... Discovery of Several Cunning Gyspies (1680).

Newgate Calendar.

Nocturnal Revels: or A General History of Dreams (1707).

Nocturnal Revels: or A Universal Dream-Book (1706).

Observations upon the Vagrant Laws: Providing that the Statutes in Queen Elizabeth's Time are the Most Proper (1742).

Old Bailey Proceedings, 1714–1799. Consulted at, and all quotes taken from, 'The Old Bailey Online' at http://www.oldbaileyonline.org (1 February 2004).

Paley, Ruth, ed., *Justice in Eighteenth-Century Hackney: The Justicing Notebook of Henry Norris and the Hackney Petty Sessions Book*, London Record Society, 28, 1991).

Parker, George, *A View of Society and Manners in High and Low Life: Being the Adventures ... of the Stage Iternant* (1781).

Parliamentary Papers, *First Report from the Committee on the State of the Police in the Metropolis* (1817).

Parliamentary Papers, *Report on the State of Mendicity in the Metropolis* (1815).

Parliamentary Papers, *Third Report from the Committee on the State of the Police Mendicity in the Metropolis* (1818).

Pilbeam, Norma and Nelson, Ian, eds, *Poor Law Records of Mid Sussex 1601–1835*, Sussex Record Society, 83 (2001).

Place, Francis, *The Autobiography of Francis Place, 1771–1854*, ed. Mary Thale (Cambridge, 1972).

Poor Joseph: An Authentic Narrative. Religious Tract Society no. 143 (n.d.).

Poor Robins Intelligence: or News for City and Country on Fryday, July 17th (1691).

Pottle, Frederick A., ed., *Boswell's London Journal, 1762–1763* (New York, 1950).

Proclamation Inhibiting All Persons after the Four and Twentieth Day of June Next to Use the Trade of a Pedlar or Petty Chapman unless they be Licensed (1686).

Ramsay, Allan, *The Caledonian Miscellany ... The Adventurs of a Farthing* (1785).

Red Cow's Speech, to a Milk-woman in St J—s's P—k (n.d.).

Report of the Committee to whom the Petition of the Principal Inhabitants of the Several Parishes of St Martin in the Fields (1742).

Report of the Select Committee Appointed by a General Court of Governors of ... Bridewell and Bethlem (1792).

Reports from Select Committees, Respecting the Arts-Masters ... of Bridewell (1799).

Representation of Some Mis-Managements by Parish-Officers in the Method at Present Followed for Maintaining the Poor (1726).

Reverie: or A Flight to the Paradise of Fools (Dublin, 1762).

Robinson, Eric, ed., *John Clare's Autobiographical Writings* (Oxford, 1983).

Royal Merchant: or Beggars-Bush. A Comedy Acted at the Theatre Royal (1705/6).

Rules ... in the Parish School of Industry in ... St James's (1792).

Rules and Orders for the Government of the Work-House Erected for the Use of the Poor of the Several Parishes of St Andrews, Holborn (above the bars) and St George the Martyr (1733).

Rules and Orders to be Observed by the Officers and Servants in St Giles's Workhouse and by the Poor Therein (n.d.).

Rules and Regulations for the Government of the Workhouse Belonging to the Parish of St Andrew Holborn (1791).

Rules ... for the Government of the Workhouse Belonging to the Parish of St Andrew Holborn (1791).

Satan's Harvest Home: or The Present State of Whorecraft (1749).

Saxby, Mary, *Memoirs of a Female Vagrant Written by Herself* (1806).

School of Politicks: or The Humours of a Coffee-House. A Poem (1691).

Scott, John, *Observations on the Present State of the Parochial and Vagrant Poor* (1773).

Scott, Thomas, *Hints for the Consideration of Patients in Hospitals* (1797).

Screw-Plot Discovered: or St Paul's Presevered (1710).

Select Trials for Murder, Robbery, Burglar (1744).

Shipmates: Being a Supplement to the Tract Entitled 'Conversation in a Boat' (Religious Tract Society, n.d.).

Short View of the Frauds, Abuses and Impositions of Parish Officers with Some Considerations on the Laws Relating to the Poor (1744).

Smith, Adam, *An Enquiry into the Nature and Causes of the Wealth of Nations* (1776; Everyman edn, 1910).

Smith, John Thomas, *A Book for a Rainy Day: or Recollections of the Events of the Last Sixty Years* (1845).

Smith, John Thomas, *Etchings of Remarkable Beggars* (1815).

Smith, John Thomas, *Nollekins and His Times* (1828; Century Hutchinson edn, 1986).

Smith, John Thomas, *Vagabondiana* (1817).

Smollett, Tobias, *Humphrey Clinker*, ed. Angus Ross (1771; Penguin edn, 1967).

Smollett, Tobias, *The Adventures of Peregrine Pickle*, ed. James L. Clifford (1751; Penguin edn, 1983).

Sokoll, Thomas, ed., *Essex Pauper Letters, 1731–1837* (Oxford, 2001).

Southey, Robert, *Letters from England* (1807; Stroud, Gloucestershire, 1984).

Spittlefields and Shorditch in an Uproar: or The Devil to Pay with the English and Irish (1736).

St Paul's Church: or The Protestant Ambulators. A Burlesque Poem (1716).

Standing Rules [for] the Royal Hospitals of Bridewell and Bethlem (1792).

Steele, Richard and Addison, Joseph, *Spectator, 1711–14*, ed. D. F. Bond, 5 vols (Oxford, 1965).

Steele, Richard *The Tatler* (1709).

Strype, John, *A Survey of the Cities of London and Westminster* (1720).

Swift, Jonathan, *A Proposal for Giving Badges to the Beggars in All the Parishes of Dublin* (1737).

Swift, Jonathan, *A Tale of a Tub and other Satires*, ed. Kathleen Williams (1975).

Swift, Jonathan, *Causes of the Wretched Condition of Ireland* (1721).

Swift, Jonathan, *Directions to Servants* (1925).

Swift, Jonathan, *Gulliver's Travels* (1726).

Swift, Jonathan, *Journal to Stella*, ed. Harold Williams (Oxford, 1948).

T— B—'s Last Letter to his Witty Friends and Companions (1718).

Tocqueville, Alexis de, *Memoir on Pauperism*, trans. Seymour Drescher (Chicago, 1997 edn).

Town Rakes: or The Frolicks of the Mohocks or Hawkubites (1712).

Townend, Joseph, *The Autobiography of the Rev. Joseph Townend* (1869).

Travels of Carl Philip Moritz in England in 1782: A Reprint of the English Translation of 1795 (1926).

[Trenchard, John], *The Natural History of Superstition* (1709).

Tricks of the Town Laid Open: or A Companion for Country Gentlemen (1747).

Trimmer, Sarah, *The Oeconomy of Charity: or An Address to Ladies Concerning Sunday Schools* (Dublin, 1783).

Trip from St James's to the Royal Exchange: The Manners, Customs and Amusements of the Inhabitants of London and Westminster (1744).

Trip Through London (1728).

Trip Through Town: Containing Observations on the Humours and Manners of the Age (4th edn, 1735).

True State of the Case of Bosavern Penlez, who Suffered on Account of the Late Riot in the Strand (1749).

Turnor, Edward and Turnor, Arthur, *The True Case of Mrs Clerke: Set Forth by her Brothers* (1718?).

Uffenbach, Zacharias Conrad von, *London in 1710: From the Travels of* (1934).

Upon Rebuilding the City (1669).

Vaisey, David, ed., *The Diary of Thomas Turner, 1754–1765* (Oxford, 1984).

View of London and Westminster (1728).

View of Society and Manners in High and Low Life (1781).

[Ward, Ned], *The History of the London Club: or The Citizens' Pastime* (1709).

Ward, Ned, *The London Spy*, ed. Paul Hyland (1709; East Lansing, 1993).

[Ward, Ned], *The Poet's Ramble after Riches: or A Night's Transactions upon the Road Burlesqu'd* (1691).

[Ward, Ned], *The Rambling Rakes: or London Libertines* (1700).

[Ward, Ned], *Second Part of the History of London Clubs* (n.d.).

[Ward, Ned], *Sot's Paradise: or The Humours of a Derby-Ale-House* (1698).

[Ward, Ned], *A Step to Stir-Bitch-Fair: With Remarks upon the University of Cambridge* (1700).

[Ward, Ned], *A Walk to Islington with a Description of New Tunbridge-Wells and Salder's Musick-House* (1699).

Warren, Thomas Alston, *Beneficence: or Verses Addressed to the Patrons of the Society for Bettering the Poor* (1803).

Weekly Remembrancer: Shewing the Best Way to Thrive and to Provide for the Poor (1702).

Whipping Post: At a New Session of Oyer and Terminer (1705).

Williams, Marjorie, ed., *The Letters of William Shenstone* (1939).

Wordsworth, William, *Complete Poetical Works* (1888).

Young, William, *Considerations on the Subject of Poor-Houses and Workhouses* (1796).

Theses and Typescripts

Borsay, Ann, 'Patrons and Governors: Aspects of the Social History of the Bath Infirmary, c. 1739–1830' (Lampeter University, PhD thesis, 1999).

Evans, Tanya, 'Unmarried Motherhood in Eighteenth-Century London' (London University, PhD thesis, 2001).

Hitchcock, Tim, 'The English Workhouse: A Study in Institutional Poor Relief in Selected Counties, 1696–1750' (Oxford University, DPhil thesis, 1985).

Levene, Alysa Shoshana, 'Health and Survival Chances at the London Foundling Hospital and the Spedale Degli Innocenti of Florence, 1741–99' (Cambridge University, DPhil thesis, 2002).

Siena, Kevin Patrick, 'Poverty and the Pox: Venereal Disease in London Hospitals, 1600–1800' (Toronto University, PhD thesis, 2001).

Simpson, Antony Eric, 'Masculinity and Control: The Prosecution of Sex Offenses in Eighteenth-Century London' (New York University, PhD thesis, 1984).

Smith, Colin Stephen, 'The Market and the Market's Place in London, c. 1660–1840' (London University, PhD thesis, 1999).

White, Maria L., 'Westminster Inquests' (Yale University, School of Medicine, Doctor of Medicine thesis, 1980).

SECONDARY SOURCES, 1871 TO PRESENT

Ackroyd, Peter, *London: The Biography* (2000).

Allen, Rick, *The Moving Pageant: A Literary Sourcebook on London Street-Life, 1700–1914* (1998).

Amelang, James S., *The Flight of Icarus: Artisan Autobiography in Early Modern Europe* (Stanford, California, 1998).

Andrew, Donna T., *London Debating Societies, 1776–1799*, London Record Society, 30 (1994).

Andrew, Donna T., *Philanthropy and Police: London Charity in the Eighteenth Century* (Princeton, New Jersey, 1989).

Andrews, Jonathan, 'Begging the Question of Idiocy: The Definition and Socio-Cultural Meaning of Idiocy in Early-Modern Britain: Part 1' *History of Psychiatry*, 9 (1998); 'Part 2', 9 (1998).

Archer, Ian, 'The Charity of Early Modern Londoners', *Transactions of the Royal Historical Society*, sixth series, 12 (2002), pp. 223–44.

Baker, Christopher, *Canaletto* (1994).

Barker, Theo and Gerhold, Dorian, *The Rise and Rise of Road Transport, 1700–1990* (Cambridge, 1993).

Barnett, David, *London, Hub of the Industrial Revolution: A Revisionary History, 1775–1825* (1998).

Barr, John, *Britain Portrayed: A Regency Album, 1780–1830* (1989).

Barrrell, John, *The Dark Side of the Landscape: The Rural Poor in English Painting, 1730–1840* (Cambridge, 1980).

Barry, Jonathan and Brooks, Christopher, eds, *The Middling Sort of People: Culture, Society and Politics in England, 1550–1800* (Basingstoke, 1994).

Barry, Jonathan and Jones, Colin, eds, *Medicine and Charity Before the Welfare State* (1991).

Barry, Jonathan and Morgan, Kenneth, eds, *Reformation and Revival in Eighteenth-Century Bristol*, Bristol Record Society, 45 (1994).

Barty-King, Hugh, *The Worst Poverty: A History of Debt and Debtors* (Stroud, Gloucestershire, 1991).

Beattie, J. M., 'The Criminality of Women in Eighteenth-Century England', *Journal of Social History*, 8 (Summer, 1975), pp. 80–116.

Beattie, John, *Policing and Punishment in London, 1660–1750: Urban Crime and the Limits of Terror* (Oxofrd, 2001).

Beier, A. L., *Masterless Men: The Vagrancy Problem in England, 1560–1640* (1985).

Beier, Lee, 'Anti-Language or Jargon? Canting in the English Underworld in the Sixteenth and Seventeenth Centuries', in Peter Burke and Roy Porter, eds, *Languages and Jargons: Contributions to a Social History of Language* (Cambridge, 1995).

Ben-Amos, Ilana Krausman, *Adolescence and Youth in Early Modern England* (New Haven, Connecticut, 1994).

Benis, Toby R., *Romanticism on the Road: The Marginal Gains of Wordsworth's Homeless* (New York, 2000).

Bennett, Judith M., 'Conviviality and Charity in Medieval and Early Modern England', *Past and Present*, 134, February 1992, pp. 19–41.

Berry, Helen, 'Rethinking Politeness in Eighteenth-Century England: Moll King's Coffee House and the Significance of "Flash Talk"', *Transactions of the Royal Historical Society*, sixth series, ii (2001), pp. 65–82.

Bindman, David, *Hogarth and His Times* (1997).

Bolam, David W., *Unbroken Community: The Story of the Friends' School at Saffron Walden, 1702–1952* (Cambridge, 1952).

Borsay, Peter, 'The Rise of the Promenade: The Social and Cultural Use of Space in the English Provincial Town, c. 1660–1800', *British Journal for Eighteenth-Century Studies*, 9 (1986) pp. 125–40.

Boulton, Jeremy, '"It is Extreme Necessity That Makes Me do This": Some "Survival Strategies" of Pauper Households in London's West End During the Early Eighteenth Century', *International Review of Social History*, 45 (2000), pp. 47–69.

Boulton, Jeremy, 'Economy of Time? Wedding Days and the Working Week in the Past', *Local Population Studies*, 43, Autumn 1989, pp. 28–46.

Boulton, Jeremy, 'London 1540–1700', in Peter Clark, ed., *The Cambridge Urban History of Britain*, ii, *1540–1840* (Cambridge, 2000).

Boulton, Jeremy, 'London Widowhood Revisited: The Decline of Female Remarriage in the Seventeenth and Early Eighteenth Centuries', *Continuity and Change*, 5 (1990), pp. 323–55.

Boulton, Jeremy, *Neighbourhood and Society: A London Suburb in the Seventeenth Century* (Cambridge, 1987).

Boulton, Jeremy, 'The Most Visible Poor in England? Constructing Pauper Biographies in Early Modern Westminster', *Westminster History Review*, 1 (1997), pp. 13–18.

Braidwood, Stephen J., *Black Poor and White Philanthropists: London's Blacks and the Foundation of the Sierra Leone Settlement, 1786–1791* (Liverpool, 1994).

Brewer, John and Staves, Susan, eds, *Early Modern Conceptions of Property* (1996).

Brewer, John and Styles, John, eds, *An Ungovernable People: The English and their Law in the Seventeenth and Eighteenth Centuries* (1980).

Brewer, John, *The Common People and Politics, 1750–1790s* (Cambridge, 1986).

Brewer, John, *The Pleasures of the Imagination: English Culture in the Eighteenth Century* (New York, 1997).

Brimblecome, P., *The Big Smoke: A History of Air Pollution in London since Medieval Times* (1987).

Broad, John, 'Housing the Rural Poor in Southern England, 1650–1850', *Agricultural History Review*, 48 (2000), pp. 151–70.

Broad, John, 'Parish Economies of Welfare, 1650–1834', *Historical Journal*, 42 (1999), pp. 985–1006.

Brown, David, '"Persons of Infamous Character" or "an Honest Industrious and Useful Description of People"? The Textile Pedlars of Alstonfield and the Role of Peddling in Industrialization', *Textile History*, 31 (2000), pp. 1–26.

Brown, Frank E., 'Continuity and Change in the Urban House: Developments in Domestic Space Organisation in Seventeenth-Century London', *Comparative Studies in Society and History: An International Quarterly*, 28 (1986), pp. 558–90.

Brown, Roger Lee, 'The Rise and Fall of the Fleet Marriage', in R. B. Outhwaite, ed., *Marriage and Society: Studies in the Social History of Marriage* (1981).

Brown, Roger Lee, *A History of the Fleet Prison, London: The Anatomy of the Fleet*, Studies in British History, 42 (Lampeter, 1996).

Burke, Joseph and Caldwell, Colin, *Hogarth: The Complete Engravings* (n.d., c. 1990).

Burnett, John, *Useful Toil: Autobiographies of Working People from the 1820s to the 1920s* (1974).

Butt, John and Carnall, Geoffrey, *The Age of Johnson, 1740–1789* (Oxford, 1979).

Bynum, W. F. and Porter, Roy, eds, *Medicine and the Five Senses* (Cambrdige, 1993).

Cage, R. A., *The Scottish Poor Law, 1745–1845* (Edinburgh, 1981).

Capp, Bernard, 'The Poet and the Bawdy Court: Michael Drayton and the Lodging-House World in Early Stuart London', *The Seventeenth Century*, 10, 1, Spring 1995.

Chisick, Harvey, 'The Wealth of Nations and the Poverty of the People in the Thought of Adam Smith', *Canadian Journal of History/Annales Canadiennes d'Histoire*, 35, December 1990.

Clark, Anna, *The Struggle for the Breeches: Gender and the Making of the British Working Class* (Berkeley, California, 1995).

Clark, Anna, *Women's Silence, Men's Violence: Sexual Assault in England, 1770–1845* (1987).

Clark, J. C. D., *English Society, 1688–1832* (Cambridge, 1985).

Clark, Peter, *The English Alehouse: A Social History, 1200–1830* (Harlow, 1983).

Clayton, Antony, '"A Writer of Comedy with a Pencil": William Hogarth in Westminster', *Westminster History Review*, 1 (1997), pp. 2–9.

Clifford, James, 'Some Aspects of London Life in the Mid-Eighteenth Century', in Paul Fritz and David Williams, eds, *City and Society in the Eighteenth Century* (Toronto, 1973), pp. 19–38.

Cody, Lisa Foreman, '"No Cure, No Money", or the Invisible Hand of Quackery: The Language of Commerce, Credit and Cash in Eighteenth-century British Medical Advertisements', *Studies in Eighteenth-Century Culture*, 28 (1999), pp. 103–30.

Coldham, Peter Wilson, *Emigrants in Chains: A Social History of Forced Migration to the Americas of Felons, Destitute Children, Political and Religious Non-Conformists, Vagabonds, Beggars and other Undesirables, 1607–1776* (Baltimore Maryland, 1992).

Corbin, Alain, *The Foul and the Fragrant: Odor in the French Social Imagination* (Leamington Spa, 1986).

Corfield, Penelope J., 'The Age of Vauxhall', *London Topographical Society Newsletter*, 33, November 1991.

Corfield, Penelope J., 'Walking the City Streets: The Urban Odyssey in Eighteenth-Century England', *Journal of Urban History*, 16, February 1990, pp. 132–74.

Corfield, Penelope J., *Power and the Professions in Britain, 1700–1850* (1995).

Cowan, Brian. 'What Was Masculine about the Public Sphere? Gender and the Coffeehouse Milieu in Post-Restoration England', *History Workshop Journal*, 51 (2001), pp. 127–57.

Cox, Pamela and Shore, Heather, eds, *Becoming Delinquent: British and European Youth, 1650–1950* (Aldershot, 2002).

Cresswell, Tim, *The Tramp in America* (2001).

Cressy, David, *Birth, Marriage and Death: Ritual, Religion and the Life-Cycle in Tudor and Stuart England* (Oxford, 1997).

Cressy, David, *Bonfires and Bells: National Memory and the Protestant Calendar in Elizabethan and Stuart England* (1989).

Critchley, T. A., *A History of Police in England and Wales* (London, 1978).

Croxson, Bronwyn, 'The Foundation and Evolution of the Middlesex Hospital's Lying-In Service, 1745–86', *Social History of Medicine*, 14 (2001), pp. 27–57.

Croxson, Bronwyn, 'The Public and Private Faces of Eighteenth-Century London Dispensary Charity', *Medical History*, 41 (1997) pp. 127–49.

Cruickshank, Dan and Burton, Neil, *Life in the Georgian City* (1990).

Cunningham, Hugh and Innes, Joanna, eds, *Charity, Philanthropy and Reform from the 1690s to 1850* (Basingstoke, 1998).

Cunningham, Hugh, 'The Employment and Unemployment of Children in England, *c.* 1680–1851', *Past and Present*, 126, February 1990, pp. 115–50.

Cunningham, Peter, *London Past and Present* (1891).

Dalton, Caroline, 'Mountjoy's Inn, Fenchurch Street', *London Topographical Record*, 27 (1995), pp. 69–90.

Davey, B. J., *Rural Crime in the Eighteenth Century: North Lincolnshire, 1740–80* (Hull, 1994).

Davies, Owen, *Cunning-Folk: Popular Magic in English History* (2003).

Davin, Anna, 'Waif Stories in Late Nineteenth-Century England', *History Workshop Journal*, 52, Autumn 2001, pp. 67–98.

De Beer, E. S., 'The Early History of London Street-Lighting', *History*, new series, 25, June 1940-March 1941.

De Beer, E. S., 'The London Hospitals in the Seventeenth Century', *Notes and Queries*, 18 November 1939.

De Certeau, Michel, *The Practice of Everyday Life*, trans. Steven Rendall (Berkeley, California, 1984).

Desbrisay, Gordon, 'City Limits: Female Philanthropy and Wet Nurses in Seventeenth-Century Scottish Towns', *Journal of the Canadian Historical Association*, new series, 8 (1997), pp. 39–60.

Dobrée, Bonamy, *The Early Eighteenth Century, 1700–1740: Swift, Defoe and Pope* (Oxford, 1959).

Doherty, Francis, *A Study in Eighteenth-Century Advertising Methods: The Anodyne Necklace* (Lewiston, New York, 1992).

Dowdell, E. G., *A Hundred Years of Quarter Sessions: The Government of Middlesex, 1660 to 1760*, (Cambridge, 1932).

D'Sena, Peter, 'Perquisites and Casual Labour on the London Wharfside in the Eighteenth Century', *London Journal*, 14 (1989), pp. 130–47.

Dugaw, Dianne, *Warrior Women and Popular Balladry, 1650–1850* (Chicago, Illinois, 1989).

Dyos, H. J. and Wolff, Michael, ed, *The Victorian City: Images and Realities*, 2 vols (1973).

Earle, Peter, *A City Full of People: Men and Women of London, 1650–1750* (1994).

Earle, Peter, *Sailors: English Merchant Seamen, 1650–1775* (1998).

Egmond, Florike, *Underworlds: Organized Crime in The Netherlands, 1650–1800* (Cambridge, 1993).

Emmison, F. G., 'Relief of the Poor at Eaton Socon, 1706–1834', *Bedfordshire Historical Record Society Publications*, 14–16 (1931–34).

Emsley, Clive, *The English Police: A Political and Social History* (1991).

Fabian, Ann, *The Unvarnished Truth: Personal Narratives in Nineteenth-Century America* (Berkeley, California, 2000).

Falkus, Malcom, 'Lighting the Dark Ages of English Economic History: Town Streets before the Industrial Revolution', in D. C. Coleman and A. H. John, eds, *Trade, Government and Economy in Pre-Industrial England* (1976).

Farge, Arlette, *Fragile Lives: Violence, Power and Solidarity in Eighteenth-Century Paris* (Cambridge, 1993).

Feldman, David, 'Migrants, Immigrants and Welfare from the Old Poor Law to the Welfare State', *Transactions of the Royal Historical Society*, sixth series, 13 (2003), pp. 79–104.

Fildes, Valierie, 'Maternal Feelings Re-assessed: Child Abandonment and Neglect in London and Westminster, 1550–1800', in Valerie Fildes, ed., *Women as Mothers in Pre-Industrial England* (1990).

Fissell, Mary E., *Patients, Power, and the Poor in Eighteenth-Century Bristol* (Cambridge, 1991).

Fissell, Mary, 'Imagining Vermin in Early Modern England', *History Workshop Journal*, 47, 1999, pp. 1–29.

Fontaine, Laurence, *History of Pedlars in Europe* (Cambridge, 1996).

Forbes, Thomas R., 'Coroners' Inquests in the County of Middlesex, England, 1819–42', *Journal of the History of Medicine and Allied Sciences*, 32, October 1977.

Foucault, Michel, *Discipline and Punish: The Birth of the Prison*, trans. Alan Sheridan (Harmondsworth, 1977).

Fox, Celina, ed., *London: World City, 1800–1840* (New Haven, Connecticut, 1992).

Fox, Celina, *Londoners* (1987).

Foyster, Elizabeth, 'A Laughing Mattter? Marital Discord and Gender Control in Seventeenth-Century England', *Rural History*, 4 (1993), pp. 5–21.

Frank, Judith, *Common Ground: Eighteenth-Century English Satiric Fiction and the Poor* (Palo Alto, California, 1997).

Frye, Susan and Robertson, Karen, ed., *Maids and Mistresses, Cousins and Queens: Women's Alliances in Early Modern England* (Oxford, 1999).

Fuller, Ronald, *The Beggars' Brotherhood* (1936). 8865

Galinou, Mireille and Hayes, John, *London in Paint: Oil Paintings in the Collection at the Museum of London* (1996).

Gammon, Vic, 'Song, Sex, and Society in England, 1600–1850', *Folk Music Journal*, 4 (1982), pp. 208–45.

Garrioch, David, 'House Names, Shop Signs and Social Organisation in Western European Cities, 1500–1900', *Urban History*, 21 (April 1994), pp. 20–48.

Gater, Sir George, and Godfry, Walter H., *Survey of London* (1940).

Gatrell, V. A. C., *The Hanging Tree: Execution and the English People, 1770–1868* (Oxford, 1994).

George, M. Dorothy, 'The Early History of Registry Offices', *Economic History: A Supplement to the Economic Journal*, 1 (1926–29), pp. 570–90.

George, M. Dorothy, *London Life in the Eighteenth Century* (2nd edn, 1966).

Gerzina, Gretchen, *Black London: Life before Emancipation* (New Brunswick, New Jersey, 1995).

Gilbert, Arthur N., 'Buggery and the British Navy, 1700–1861', *Journal of Social History*, 10 (1976), pp. 72–98.

Gillis, John R., *For Better, For Worse: British Marriages, 1600 to the Present* (Oxford, 1985).

Gillis, John, 'Making Time for Family: The Invention of Family Time(s) and the Re-invention of Family History', *Journal of Family History*, 21, January 1996, pp. 4–21.

Gladfelder, Hal, *Criminality and Narrative in Eighteenth-Century England: Beyond the Law* (Baltimore, Maryland, 2001).

Glasser, Irene and Bridgman, Rae, *Braving the Street: The Anthropology of Home-lessness* (New York, New York, 1999).

Goldberg, Rita, 'Charity Sermons and the Poor: A Rhetoric of Compassion', in Paul J. Korshin, ed., *The Age of Johnson*, 4 (1991).

Goldsmith, Netta Murray, *The Worst of Crimes: Homosexuality and the Law in Eighteenth-Century London* (Aldershot, 1998).

Gorsky, Martin, *Patterns of Philanthropy: Charity and Society in Nineteenth-Century Bristol* (Woodbridge, 1999).

Gowing, Laura, 'Gender and the Language of Insult in Early Modern London', *History Workshop Journal*, 35 (1993), pp. 1–21.

Gowing, Laura, 'Language, Power and the Law: Women's Slander Litigation in Early Modern London', in Jenny Kermode and Garthine Walker, eds, *Women, Crime and the Courts in Early Modern England* (1994).

Gowing, Laura, *Common Bodies: Women, Touch and Power in Seventeenth-Century England* (New Haven, Connecticut, 2003).

Gowing, Laura, *Domestic Dangers: Women, Words and Sex in Early Modern London* (Oxford, 1996).

Gowing, Laura, 'Secret Births and Infanticide in Seventeenth-Century England', *Past and Present*, 156, August 1997, pp. 87–115.

Grant, Joan, 'William Brown and Other Women: Black Women in London, c. 1740–1840', in Joan Grant, ed., *Women, Migration and Empire* (1996).

Green, David R., *People of the Rookery: A Pauper Community in Victorian London*, Occasional Paper 26, University of London, King's College, Department of Geography (1986).

Griffiths, Paul and Jenner, Mark S. R., ed., *Londinopolis: Essays in the Cultural and Social History of Early Modern London* (Manchester, 2000).

Griffiths, Paul, 'Meanings of Nightwalking in Early Modern England', *The Seventeenth Century*, 13 (1998), pp. 212–38.

Griffiths, Paul, 'Secrecy and Authority in Late Sixteenth and Seventeenth Century London', *Historical Journal*, 40 (1997), pp. 925–51.

Griffiths, Paul, Fox, Adam Fox and Hindle, Steve, eds, *The Experience of Authority in Early Modern England*, (1996).

Grifftiths, Paul, 'The Structure of Prostitution in Elizabethan London', *Continuity and Change*, 8 (1993), pp. 39–63.

Grundy, Isobel, *Lady Mary Wortley Montagu* (Oxford, 1999).

Guillery, Peter, 'The Further Adventures of Mary Lacy: "Seaman", Shipwright, Builder', *History Workshop Journal*, 49 (2000), pp. 212–20.

Habermas, Jürgen, *The Structural Transformation of the Public Sphere*, trans. Thomas Burger (Cambridge, 1989).

Hallett, Mark, *The Spectacle of Difference: Graphic Satire in the Age of Hogarth* (New Haven, Connecticut, 1999).

Hammond, J. L. and Hammond, Barbara, *The Skilled Labourer, 1760–1832* (1919; 1995 edn).

Hammond, J. L. and Hammond, Barbara, *The Town Labourer, 1760–1832: The New Civilisation* (1917; 1995 edn).

Hammond, J. L. and Hammond, Barbara, *The Villiage Labourer, 1760–1832: A Study of the Government of England before the Reform Bill* (Stroud, Gloucestershire, 1987).

Harris, Tim, 'The Bawdy House Riots of 1688', *Historical Journal*, 29 (1986) pp. 537–56.

Harris, Tim, ed., *Popular Culture in England, c. 1500–1850* (Basingstoke, 1995).

Harris, Tim, ed., *The Politics of the Excluded, c. 1500–1850* (Basingstoke, 2001).

Harrison, Joel, F., 'Escape from the Great Confinement: the Genealogy of a German Workhouse', *Journal of Modern History*, 71 (June 1999), pp. 308–345.

Harrison, Joel F., '"Singing for his Supper": The Reinvention of Juvenile Streetsinging in Early Modern Nuremburg', *Social History*, 22, January 1997, pp. 27–45.

Haskell, Thomas, 'Capitalism and the Origins of the Humanitarian Sensibility', *American Historical Review*, 90 (1985), pp. 339–361 and part 2, 90 (1985), pp. 547–566.

Hay, Douglas, Linebaugh, Peter, Rule, John G., Thompson, E. P. and Winslow, Cal, *Albion's Fatal Tree: Crime and Society in Eighteenth-Century England* (1975).

Heal, Ambrose, *The Signboards of Old London Shops* (London, 1957).

Heal, Felicity, *Hospitality in Early Modern England* (Oxford, 1990).

Henderson, Tony, *Disorderly Women in Eighteenth-Century London: Prostitution and Control in the Metropolis, 1730–1830* (1999).

Herber, Mark, *Criminal London: A Pictorial History from the Medieval Times to 1939* (Chichester, 2002).

Herber, Mark, *Legal London: A Pictorial History* (Chichester, 1999).

Herlan, Ronald W., 'Social Articulation and the Configuration of Parochial Poverty in London on the Eve of the Restoration', *Guildhall Studies in London History*, 2, April 1976, pp. 43–53.

Herndon, Ruth Wallis, *Unwelcome Americans: Living on the Margin in Early New England* (Philadelphia Pennsylvania, 2001).

Hibbert, Christopher, *King Mob: The Story of Lord George Gordon and the Riots of 1780* (1959).

Hill, Bridget, *Women, Work and Sexual Politics in Eighteenth-Century England* (1994).

Hindle, Steve, 'The Shaming of Margaret Knowsley: Gossip, Gender and the Experience of Authority in Early Modern England', *Continuity and Change*, 9 (1994), pp. 391–419.

Hindle, Steve, 'Dear, Fasting and Alms: The Campaign for General Hospitality in Late Elizabethan England', *Past and Present*, 172, August 2001, pp. 44–86.

Hindle, Steve, *The Birthpangs of Welfare: Poor Relief and Parish Governance in Seventeenth-Century Warwickshire*, Dugdale Society Occasional Papers, 40 (2000).

Hindle, Steve, 'Exclusion Crises: Poverty, Migration and Parochial Responsibility in English Rural Communities, c. 1560–1660', *Rural History*, 7 (1996).

Hindle, Steve, 'The Problem of Pauper Marriage in Seventeenth-Century England', *Transactions of the Royal Historical Society*, sixth series, 8 (1998), pp. 71–90.

Hitchcock, Tim and Shore, Heather, eds, *The Streets of London from the Great Fire to the Great Stink* (2003).

Hitchcock, Tim, *English Sexualities, 1700–1800* (Basingstoke, 1997).

Hitchcock, Tim, Sharpe, Pamela and King, Peter, eds, *Chronicling Poverty: The Voices and Strategies of the English Poor, 1640–1840* (Basingstoke, 1907).

Hobsbawm, E. J., *Labouring Men: Studies in the History of Labour* (1964).

Hole, Christina, *English Custom and Usage* (3rd edn, 1950).

Hoppit, Julian, *A Land of Liberty? England, 1689–1727* (Oxford, 2000).

Hoppit, Julian, 'The Myths of the South Sea Bubble', *Transactions of the Royal Historical Society*, sixth series, 12 (2002) pp. 141–65.

Howson, Gerard, *Thief-Taker General: The Rise and Fall of Jonathan Wild* (1970).

Huchon, René, *George Crabbe and his Times, 1754–1832* (1968).

Humble, J. G. and Hansell, Peter, *Westminster Hospital, 1716–1974* (2nd edn, 1974).

Humphreys, Robert, *No Fixed Abode: A History of Responses to the Roofless and Rootless in Britain* (Basingstoke, 1999).

Hunt, Alan, *Governing Morals: A Social History of Moral Regulation* (Cambridge, 1999).

Hunt, Margaret, 'Hawkers, Bawlers and Mercuries: Women and the London Press in the Early Enlightenment', *Women and History*, 9 (1984), pp. 41–68.

Hunt, Margaret, *The Middling Sort: Commerce, Gender, and the Gamily in England, 1680–1780* (Berkeley, California, 1996).

Hunt, Margaret, 'Wife Beating, Domesticity and Women's Independence in Eighteenth-Century London', *Gender and History*, 4, Spring 1992, pp. 10–33.

Hyde, Ralph, *The A to Z of Georgian London* (Lympne Castle, Kent, 1981).

Ignatieff, Michael, *A Just Measure of Pain: The Penitentiary in the Industrial Revolution, 1750–1850* (1978).

Ingram, Martin, 'Reformation of Manners in Early Modern England', in Paul Griffiths, Adam Fox and Steve Hindle, eds, *The Experience of Authority in Early Modern England* (1996).

Innes, Joanna, 'Managing the Metropolis: London's Social Problems and Their Control, c. 1660–1830', in Peter Clark and Raymond Gillespie, eds, *Two Capitals: London and Dublin 1500–1840* (Oxford, 2001), pp. 53–79.

Innes, Joanna, 'Parliament and the Reshaping of English Social Policy, 1780–1830', in Kazuhiko Kondo, ed., *State and Empire in British History: Proceedings of the Fourth Anglo-Japanese Conference of Historians* (Kyoto, 2003), pp. 81–98.

Innes, Joanna, 'Parliament and the Shaping of Eighteenth-Century English Social Policy', *Transactions of the Royal Historical Society*, fifth series, 40 (1990), pp. 63–92.

Innes, Joanna, 'Politics and Morals: The Reformation of Manners Movement in Later Eighteenth-Century England', in Eckhart Hellmuth, ed., *The Transformation of Political Culture: England and Germany in the Late Eighteenth-Century* (Oxford, 1990).

Innes, Joanna, 'Prisons for the Poor: English Bridewells 1555–1800', in Francis Snyder and Douglas Hay, eds, *Labour, Law and Crime: An Historical Perspective* (1987), pp. 42–122.

Innes, Joanna, 'The "Mixed Economy of Welfare" in Early Modern England: Assessments of the Options from Hale to Malthus (*c.* 1683–1803)', in Martin J. Daunton, ed., *Charity, Self-Interest and Welfare in the English Past* (1996), pp. 139–80.

Innes, Joanna, 'The State and the Poor: Eighteenth-Century England in European Perspective', in John Brewer and Eckhart Hellmuth, eds, *Rethinking Leviathan: The Eighteenth-Century State in Britain and Germany* (Oxford, 1999), pp. 225–80.

Isherwood, Robert M., *Farce and Fantasy: Popular Entertainment in Eighteenth-Century Paris* (Oxford, 1986).

Ivis, Jessica Warner Frank, ' "Damn You, You Informing Bitch", Vox Populi and the Unmaking of the Gin Act of 1736', *Journal of Social History*, 3, Winter 1999.

Jenner, Mark S. R., 'Civilization and Deodorizaton? Smell in Early Modern English Culture', in Peter Burke, Brian Harrison and Paul Slack, eds, *Civil Histories: Essays Presented to Sir Keith Thomas* (Oxford, 2000).

John Wareing, ' "Violently Taken Away or Cheatingly Duckoyed": The Illegal Recruitment in London of Indentured Servants for the American Colonies, 1645–1718', *London Journal*, 26 (2001), pp. 1–22.

Johnson, E. D. H., *Paintings of the British Social Scene from Hogarth to Sickert* (1986).

Jones, Colin and Porter, Roy, eds, *Reassessing Foucault: Power, Medicine and the Body* (1994).

Jones, Gareth, *History of the Law of Charity, 1532–1827* (Cambridge, 1969).

Judge, Roy, *The Jack-in-the-Green: A May Day Custom* (1979).

Kaye, Harvey J. and McClelland, Keith, eds, *E. P. Thompson: Critical Perspectives* (Cambridge, 1990).

Kelly, Veronica and Mücke, Dorothea E. von, eds, *Body and Text in the Eighteenth Century* (Stanford California, 1994).

Kent, D. A., 'Ubiquitous but Invisible: Female Domestic Servants in Mid-Eighteenth Century London', *History Workshop Journal*, 28, Autumn 1989, pp. 111–28.

Kent, D. A., ' "Gone for a Soldier": Family Breakdown and the Demography of Desertion in a London Parish, 1750–91', *Local Population Studies*, 45, Autumn 1990, pp. 27–42.

King, Peter, ' "Press Gangs are Better Magistrates than the Middlesex Justices": Young Offenders, Press Gangs and Prosecution Strategies in Eighteenth and Early

Nineteenth-Century England', in Norma Landau, ed., *Law, Crime and English Society, 1660–1830* (Cambridge, 2002), pp. 97–116.

King, Peter, 'Female Offenders, Work and Life-Cycle Change in Late Eighteenth-Century London', *Continuity and Change*, 11 (1996), pp. 61–90.

King, Peter, *Crime, Justice, and Discretion in England, 1740–1820* (Oxford, 2000).

King, Peter, 'The Rise of Juvenile Delinquency in England 1780–1840: Changing Patterns of Perception and Prosecution', *Past and Present*, 160, August 1998, pp. 116–66.

King, Steven and Tomkins, Alannah, eds, *The Poor in England, 1700–1850: An Economy of Makeshifts* (Manchester, 2003).

King, Steven, 'Reconstructing Lives: The Poor, the Poor Law and Welfare in Calverley, 1650–1820', *Social History*, 22 (1997), pp. 318–37.

King, Steven, *Poverty and Welfare in England, 1700–1850: A Regional Perspective* (Manchester, 2000).

King, Steven, 'Reclothing the English Poor, 1750–1840', *Textile History*, 33 (2002), pp. 37–47.

Kinney, Arthur F., ed., *Rogues, Vagabonds and Sturdy Beggars: A New Gallery of Tudor and Early Stuart Rogue Literature* (Amherst, Massachusetts, 1990).

Klein, Benjamin, '"Between the Bums and the Bellies of the Multitude": Civic Pageantry and the Problem of the Audience in Late Stuart London', *London Journal*, 17 (1992), pp. 18–26.

Konvitz, Josef W., *The Urban Millennium: The City-Building Process from the Early Middle Ages to the Present* (Carbondale, Illinois, 1985).

Kusmer, Kenneth L., *Down and Out, On the Road: The Homeless in American History* (Oxford, 2002).

Landau, Norma, 'Appearance at the Quarter Sessions of Eighteenth-Century Middlesex', *The London Journal*, 23 (1998) pp. 30–52.

Landau, Norma, *Law, Crime and English Society, 1660–1830* (Cambridge, 2002).

Langford, Paul, *A Polite and Commercial People: England, 1727–1783* (Oxford, 1989).

Laqueur, Thomas W., 'Bodies, Details, and the Humanitarian Narrative', in Lynn Hunt, ed., *The New Cultural History* (Berkeley California, 1989), pp. 176–204.

Laqueur, Thomas, 'Bodies, Death and Pauper Funerals', *Representations*, 1 (1983), pp. 109–31.

Lemire, Beverly, 'Peddling Fashion: Salesmen, Pawnbrokers, Taylors, Thieves and the Second-Hand Clothes Trade in England, *c.* 1700–1800', *Textile History*, 22 (1991) pp. 67–82.

Lemire, Beverly, *Dress, Culture and Commerce: The English Clothing Trade before the Factory, 1660–1800* (Basingstoke, 1997).

Linebaugh, P., 'The Ordinary of Newgate and his Account', in J. S. Cockburn, ed., *Crime in England, 1550–1800* (1977).

Linebaugh, Peter, *The London Hanged: Crime and Civil Society in the Eighteenth Century* (1991).

Lis, Catharina and Soly, Hugo, *Disordered Lives: Eighteenth-Century Families and their Unruly Relatives*, trans. Alexander Brown (Cambridge, 1996).

Lloyd, Sarah, '"Agents in Their Own Concerns": Charity and the Economy of Makeshifts in Eighteenth-Century Britain', in Steve King and Alannah Tomkins, ed., *The Poor in England, 1700–1850: An Economy of Makeshifts* (Manchester, 2003).

Lloyd, Sarah, 'Cottage Conversations: Poverty and Manly Independence in Eighteenth-Century England', *Past and Present*, 183 (May 2004).

Lloyd, Sarah, 'Pleasure's Golden Bait: Poverty and the Magdalen Hospital in Eighteenth-Century London', *History Workshop Journal*, 41 (1996).

Lowman, John, 'The Geography of Social Control: Clarifying Some Themes', in David J. Evans and David T. Hebert, eds, *The Geography of Crime* (1989).

M. Dorothy George, *London Life in the Eighteenth Century* (1925; 1966).

Macfarlane, Stephen, 'Social Policy and the Poor in the Later Seventeenth Century', in Beier, A. L. and Finlay, Roger, eds, *London, 1500–1700: The Making of the Metropolis* (1986), pp. 252–77.

MacKay, Lynn, 'A Culture of Poverty? The St Martin in the Fields Workhosue, 1817', *Journal of Interdisciplinary History*, 26 (1995), pp. 209–32.

Malcolmson, Robert W., *Life and Labour in England, 1700–1780* (1981).

Mandler, Peter, ed., *The Uses of Charity: The Poor on Relief in the Nineteenth-Century Metropolis* (Philadelphia, Pennsylvania, 1990).

Markus, Thomas A., *Buildings and Power: Freedom and Control in the Origin of Modern Building Types* (1993).

Marriott, John and Matsumura, Masaie, eds, *The Metropolitan Poor: Semi-Factual Accounts, 1795–1910*, 6 vols (1999).

Marriott, John, ed., *Unknown London: Early Modernist Visions of the Metropolis, 1815–45*, 6 vols (2000).

Marshall, D., *The English Poor in the Eighteenth Century* (1926).

Masters, Betty, R., *The Public Markets of the City of London Surveyed by William Leybourn in 1677*, London Topographical Society, 17 (1974).

Mayhew, Henry, *London Labour and the London Poor* (1861; Dover edn, New York, New York, 1968).

McClure, Ruth, *Coram's Children: The London Foundling Hospital in the Eighteenth Century* (New Haven, Connecticut, 1981).

McConville, Seán, *A History of English Prison Administration*, i, *1750–1877* (1981).

McDowell, Paula, *The Women of Grub Street: Press, Politics and Gender in the London Literary Marketplace, 1678–1730* (Oxford, 1998).

McKellar, Elizabeth, *The Birth of Modern London: The Development and Design of the City, 1660–1720* (Manchester, 1999).

McKendrick, Neil, Brewer, John and Plumb, J. H., *The Birth of a Consumer Society: The Commercialization of Eighteenth-Century England* (1982).

McMullan, J. L., *The Canting Crew: London's Criminal Underworld, 1550–1700* (New Jersey, 1984).

Meldrum, Tim, 'Domestic Service, Privacy and the Eighteenth-Century Metropolitan Household', *Urban History*, 26 (1999), pp. 27–39.

Meldrum, Tim, 'A Women's Court in London: Defamation at the Bishop of London's Consistory Court, 1700–1745', *London Journal*, 19, 1 (1994), pp. 1–20.

Meldrum, Tim, *Domestic Service and Gender, 1660–1750: Life and Work in the London Household* (Harlow, Essex, 2000).

Mitchinson, Rosalind, *The Old Poor Law in Scotland: The Experience of Poverty, 1574–1845* (Edinburgh, 2000).

Morris, Derek, 'Land Tax Assessments for Mile End Old Town, 1741–90', *London Topographical Society Newsletter*, 51, November 2000.

Morrison, Kathryn, *The Workhouse: A Study of Poor-Law Buildings in England* (Swindon, 1999).

Mui, Hoh-cheung and Mui, Lorna H., *Shops and Shopkeeping in Eighteenth-Century England* (1989).

Muldrew, Craig, '"Hard Food for Midas": Cash and its Social Value in Early Modern England', *Past and Present*, 170 (February 2001), pp. 78–120.

Nadelhaft, Jerome, 'The Englishwoman's Sexual Civil War: Feminist Attitudes Towards Men, Women and Marriage, 1650–1740', *Journal of the History of Ideas*, 43 (1982), pp. 555–79.

Naggar, Betty, 'Old-Clothes Men: Eighteenth and Nineteenth Centuries', *Transactions of the Jewish Historical Society of England*, 31 (1992), pp. 171–91.

Nash, Stanley, 'Prostitution and Charity: The Magdalen Hospital. A Case Study', *Journal of Social History*, 17 (1984), pp. 617–28.

Navon, Liora, 'Beggars, Metaphor and Stigma: A Missing Link in the Social History of Leprosy', *Social History of Medicine*, 11 (1998), pp. 89–105.

Nelson, T. G. A., 'Women of Pleasure', *Studies in the Eighteenth Century*, 11, new series, 1 (February 1987), pp. 181–98.

Neuburg, Victor E., *Popular Literature: A History and Guide* (Harmondsworth, 1977).

Outhwaite, R. B., '"Objects of Charity": Petitions to the London Foundling Hospital, 1768–72', *Eighteenth Century Studies*, 32 (1999), pp. 497–510.

O'Connell, Sheila, *London 1753* (2003).

O'Donaghue, Edward G., *Bridewell Hospital: Palace, Prison, School, from the Death of Elizabeth to Modern Times* (1929).

Ogborn, Miles, *Spaces of Modernity: London's Geographies, 1680–1780* (New York, New York, 1998).

Orlin, Lena Cowen, ed., *Material London, ca. 1600* (Philadelphia, Pennsylvania, 2000).

Paley, Ruth, '"An Imperfect, Inadequate and Wretched System"? Policing London before Peel', *Criminal Justice History*, 10 (1989), pp. 95–130.

Paley, Ruth, 'Thief-Takers in London in the Age of the McDaniel Gang, *c.* 1745–1754', in Douglas Hay and Francis Snyder, eds, *Policing and Prosecution in Britain, 1750–1850* (Oxford, 1989).

Palmer, Roy, ed., *The Rambling Soldier* (Gloucester, 1985).

Parry-Jones, William L., *The Trade in Lunacy: A Study of Private Madhouses in England in the Eighteenth and Nineteenth Centuries* (1972).

Patterson, Annabel, '"They Say" or We Say: Popular Protest and Ventriloquism in Early Modern England', in Janet Levarie Smart, ed., *Historical Criticism and the Challenge of Theory* (Urbana, Illinois, 1993).

Paulson, Ronald, *Don Quixote in England: The Aesthetics of Laughter* (Baltimore, Maryland, 1998).

Paulson, William R., *Enlightenment, Romanticism and the Blind in France* (Princeton, New Jersey, 1987).

Payne, Christiana, '"Murillo-Like Rags or Clean Pinafores": Artistic and Social Preferences in the Representation of the Dress of the Rural Poor', *Textile History*, 33 (2002), pp. 48–62.

Pennell, Sara, '"Pots and Pans History": The Material Culture of the Kitchen in Early Modern England', *Journal of Design History*, 11 (1998), pp. 201–16.

Phythian-Adams, Charles, 'Milk and Soot: The Changing Vocabulary of a Popular Ritual in Stuart and Hanoverian London', in D. Fraser and Anthony Sutcliffe, eds, *The Pursuit of Urban History* (1983).

Picard, Liza, *Dr Johnson's London: Life in London, 1740–1770* (2000).

Picard, Liza, *Restoration London* (1997).

Pinchbeck, Ivy and Hewitt, Margaret, *Children in English Society* (1969).

Pincus, Steve, '"Coffee Politicians Does Create": Coffeehouses and Restoration Political Culture', *Journal of Modern History*, 67 (December 1995), pp. 807–34.

Pitt-Kethley, Fiona, *The Literary Companion to Low Life* (1995).

Pollock, Linda A., 'Childbearing and Female Bonding in Early Modern England', *Social History [London]*, 22 (1997), pp. 286–306.

Pope, Norris, *Dickens and Charity* (1978).

Porter, Stephen, 'Order and Disorder in the Early Modern Almshouse: The Charterhouse Example', *London Journal*, 23 (1998), pp. 1–14.

Postle, Martin, *Angels and Urchins: The Fancy Picture in Eighteenth-Century British Art* (1998).

Priestley, Ursula, and Corfield, P. J., 'Rooms and Room Use in Norwich Housing, 1580–1730', *Post-Medieval Archaeology*, 16 (1982), pp. 93–123.

Pringle, Patrick, *Hue and Cry: The Birth of the British Police* (1955).

Pugh, R. B., 'Newgate Between Two Fires', 2 parts, *Guildhall Studies in London History*, 3, part 3, October 1978, pp. 137–63 and 3, part 4, April 1979, pp. 199–222.

Pullan, Brian, *Orphans and Foundlings in Early Modern Europe*, Stenton Lecture (Reading, 1989).

Radner, John B., 'The Youthful Harlot's Curse: The Prostitute as Symbol of the City in Eighteenth-Century English Literature', *Eighteenth-Century Life*, 2 (1976), pp. 59–64.

Reddaway, T. F., *The Rebuilding of London after the Great Fire* (1940).

Reynolds, Elaine A., *Before the Bobbies: The Night Watch and Police Reform in Metropolitan London, 1720–1830* (Basingstoke, 1998).

Ribton-Turner, C. J., *A History of Vagrants and Beggars and Begging* (1887).

Richardson, A. E. and Eberlein, H. Donaldson, *The English Inn: Past and Present. A Review of Its History and Social Life* (1925).

Richardson, John, *London and its People: A Social History from Medieval Times to the Present* (1995).

Roberts, M. J. D., 'Public and Private in Early Nineteenth-Century London: The Vagrant Act of 1822 and its Enforcement', *Social History [London]*, 13 (1988), pp. 273–94.

Roberts, M. J. D., 'Reshaping the Gift Relationship: The London Mendicity Society and the Suppression of Begging in England, 1818–1869', *Intenational Review of Social History*, 36 (1991), pp. 201–31.

Roberts, M. J. D., 'The Society for the Suppression of Vice and its Early Critics, 1802–1812', *Historical Journal*, 26 (1983), pp. 159–76.

Rodgers, Betsy, *Cloak of Charity: Studies in Eighteenth-Century Philanthropy* (1949).

Roger Lonsdale, ed., *The New Oxford Book of Eighteenth-Century Verse* (Oxford, 1984).

Rogers, Nicholas, 'Carnal Knowledge: Illegitimacy in Eighteenth-Century Westminster', *Journal of Social History*, 23 (1989–90), pp. 355–75.

324 DOWN AND OUT IN EIGHTEENTH-CENTURY LONDON

Rogers, Nicholas, *Crowds, Culture and Politics in Georgian Britain* (Oxford, 1998).

Rogers, Nicholas, 'Policing the Poor in Eighteenth-Century London: The Vagrancy Laws and Their Administration', *Histoire Sociale/Social History*, 24 (1991), pp. 127–47.

Rogers, Nicholas, 'Popular Protest in Early Hanoverian London', *Past and Present*, 79 (1978), pp. 70–100.

Rogers, Nicholas, 'Vagrancy, Impressment and the Regulation of Labour in Eighteenth-Century Britain', *Slavery and Abolition*, 15 (1994), pp. 102–13.

Rose, Craig, 'Evangelical Philanthropy and Anglican Revival: The Charity Schools of Augustan London, 1698–1740', *London Journal*, 16 (1991), pp. 35–65.

Rosenthal, Michael and Myrone, Martin, *Gainsborough* (2002).

Rule, John, *The Experience of Labour in Eighteenth-Century Industry* (1981).

Salgādo, Gāmini, *The Elizabethan Underworld* (Stroud, Gloucestershire, 1992).

Saunders, Ann, ed., *The Royal Exchange*, London Topographical Society, 152 (1997).

Schindler, Norbert, *Rebellion, Community and Custom in Early Modern Germany*, trans. Pamela E. Selwyn (Cambridge, 2002).

Schwarz, Leonard, 'London 1700–1840', in Peter Clark, ed., *The Cambridge Urban History of Britain*, ii, *1540–1840* (Cambridge, 2000).

Schwarz, Leonard, *London in the Age of Industrialisation: Entrepreneurs, Labour Force and Living Conditions, 1700–1850.* (Cambridge, 1992).

Scott, James C., *Weapons of the Weak: Everyday Forms of Peasant Resistance* (New Haven, Connecticut, 1985).

Sharpe, J. A., *Crime and the Law in English Satirical Prints, 1600–1832* (Cambridge, 1986).

Sharpe, Pamela, *Adapting to Capitalism: Working Women in the English Economy, 1700–1850* (Basingstoke, 2000).

Sharpe, Pamela, 'Dealing with Love: The Ambiguous Independence of the Single Woman in Early Modern England', *Gender & History*, 11 (1999), pp. 209–32.

Sharpe, Pamela, 'Survival Strategies and Stories: Poor Widows and Widowers in Early Industrial England', in Sandra Cavallo and Lyndan Warner, eds, *Widowhood in Medieval and Early Modern Europe* (Harlow, 1999), pp. 220–39.

Sheehan, W. J., 'Finding Solace in Eighteenth-century Newgate', in J. S. Cockburn, ed., *Crime in England, 1550–1800* (1977).

Sherman, Sandra, *Imagining Poverty, Quantification and the Decline of Paternalism* (Columbus, Ohio, 2001).

Shesgreen, Sean, *Hogarth and the Times-of-the-Day Tradition* (Ithaca, New York, 1983).

Shesgreen, Sean, *Images of the Outcast: The Urban Poor in the Cries of London* (Manchester, 2002).

Shesgreen, Sean, *The Criers and Hawkers of London: Engravings and Drawings by Marcellus Laroon* (Aldershot, 1990).

Shoemaker, Robert, 'Male Honour and the Decline of Public Violence in Eighteenth-Century London', *Social History*, 26 (2001).

Shoemaker, Robert B., *Prosecution and Punishment: Petty Crime and the Law in London and Rural Middlesex, c. 1660–1725* (Cambridge, 1991).

Shoemaker, Robert B., 'The Decline of Public Insult in London, 1660–1800', *Past and Present*, 169 (2000), pp. 97–131.

Shoemaker, Robert B., *The London Mob: Violence and Disorder in Eighteenth-Century England* (London, 2004).

Shoemaker, Robert B., 'The London "Mob" in the Early Eighteenth Century', in Peter Borsay, ed., *The Eighteenth-Century Town: A Reader in English Urban History, 1688–1820* (London, 1990), pp. 188–222.

Shoemaker, Robert B., 'The Taming of the Duel: Masculinity, Honour and Ritual Violence in London, 1660–1800', *Historical Journal*, 45 (2002), pp. 525–45.

Shore, Heather, *Artful Dodgers: Youth and Crime in Early Nineteenth-Century London* (Woodbridge, 1999).

Shore, Heather, 'Crime, Criminal Networks and the Survival Strategies of the Poor in Early Eighteenth-Century London', in King, Steven and Tomkins, Alannah, eds, *The Poor in England, 1700–1850: An Economy of Makeshifts* (Manchester, 2003).

Shore, Heather, 'Cross Coves, Buzzers and General Sorts of Prigs: Juvenile Crime and the Criminal 'Underworld' in the Early Nineteenth Century', *British Journal of Criminology*, 39 (1999), pp. 10–24.

Shurer, Kevin and Arkell, Tom, eds, *Surveying the People: The Interpretation and Use of Document Sources for the Study of Population in the Later Seventeenth Century* (Matlock, 1992).

Sibley, David, *Geographies of Exclusion* (1995).

Sill, Geoffrey M., 'Rogues, Strumpets and Vagabonds: Defoe on Crime in the City', *Eighteenth-Century Life*, 2 (June 1976), pp. 74–78.

Simpson, Antony E., '"The Mouth of Strange Women is a Deep Pitt": Male Guilt and Legal Attitudes Toward Prostitution in Georgian London', *Journal of Criminal Justice and Popular Culture*, 4 (1996), pp. 50–79.

Slack, Paul, *From Reformation to Improvement: Public Welfare in Early Modern England* (Oxford, 1999).

Slack, Paul, 'Hospitals, Workhouses and the Relief of the Poor in Early Modern London', in Ole Peter Grell and Andrew Cunningham, eds, *Health Care and Poor Relief in Protestant Europe, 1500–1700* (1997).

Slack, Paul, 'Perceptions of the Metropolis in Seventeenth-Century England' in Peter Burke, Brian Harrison and Paul Slack, eds, *Civil Histories: Essays Presented to Sir Keith Thomas* (Oxford, 2000).

Slack, Paul, *Poverty and Policy in Tudor and Stuart England* (1988).

Slack, Paul, *The English Poor Law, 1531–1782* (Basingstoke, 1990).

Sloan, Kim, *J. M. W. Turner: Watercolours from the R. W. Lloyd Bequest* (1998).

Smiles, Sam, 'Defying Comprehension: Resistance to Uniform Appearance in Depicting the Poor, 1770s to 1830s', *Textile History*, 33 (2002), pp. 22–36.

Smith, Billy G., *The 'Lower Sort': Philadelphia's Laboring People, 1750–1800* (Ithaca, New York, 1990).

Smith, Bruce R., *The Acoustic World of Early Modern England: Attending to the O-Factor* (Chicago, Illinois, 1999).

Smuts, R. Malcolm, 'The Court and Its Neighbourhood: Royal Policy and Urban Growth in the Early Stuart West End', *Journal of British Studies*, 30 (1991), pp. 117–49.

Snell, K. D. M., *Annals of the Labouring Poor: Social Change and Agrarian England, 1660–1900* (Cambridge, 1985).

Sokoll, Thomas, 'Negotiating a Living: Essex Pauper Letters form London, 1800–1834', *International Review of Social History*, 45 (2000), pp. 19–46.

Spacks, P. M., *Imagining a Self* (Cambridge, Massachusetts, 1976).

Spence, Craig, *London in the 1690s: A Social Atlas* (2000).

Spufford, Margaret, *Small Books and Pleasant Histories: Popular Fiction and its Readership in Seventeenth-Century England* (Cambridge, 1981).

Statt, Daniel, 'The Case of the Mohocks: Rake Violence in Augustan London', *Social History [London]*, 20, May 1995, pp. 179–99.

Steedman, Carolyn, 'Lord Mansfield's Women', *Past and Present*, 176 (2002), pp. 105–43.

Stern, Walter M., *The Porters of London* (1960).

Styles, John, 'Involuntary Consumers? Servants and their Clothes in Eighteenth-Century England', *Textile History*, 33 (2002), pp. 9–21.

Sutherland, James, *Restoration Literature, 1550–1700: Dryden, Bunyand, and Pepys* (Oxford, 1969).

Tadmor, Naomi, 'The Concept of the Household-Family in Eighteenth-Century England', *Past and Present*, 151 (1996), pp. 111–40.

Tanner, Andrew, 'The Casual Poor and the City of London Poor Law Union, 1837–1869', *Historical Journal*, 42 (1999), pp. 183–206.

Taylor, James Stephen, *Jonas Hanway Founder of the Marine Society: Charity and Policy in Eighteenth-Century Britain* (1985).

Te Brake, William H., 'Air Pollution and Fuel Crises in Pre-Industrial London, 1250–1650', *Technology and Culture*, 16 (1975), pp. 337–59.

The Jew as Other: A Century of English Caricature, 1730–1830 (New York, New York, 1995).

Thirsk, Joan, *Economic Policy and Projects: The Development of a Consumer Society in Early Modern England* (Oxford, 1978).

Thomas, Keith, 'Cleanliness and Godliness in Early Modern England', in Anthony Fletcher and Peter Roberts, eds, *Religion, Culture and Society in Early Modern Britain* (Cambridge, 1994).

Thomas, Keith, 'The Meaning of Literacy in Early Modern England', in Gerd Baumann, ed., *The Written Word: Literacy in Transition* (Oxford, 1986), pp. 97–132.

Thompson, E. P., *Customs in Common* (1991).

Thompson, E. P., *Witness Against the Beast: William Blake and the Moral Law* (Cambridge, 1993).

Thorold, Peter, *The London Rich: The Creation of a Great City from 1666 to the Present* (1999).

Trumbach, Randolph, *Sex and the Gender Revolution*, i, *Heterosexuality and the Third Gender in Enlightenment London* (Chicago, 1998).

Turner, John, *Wordsworth: Play and Politics. A Study of Wordsworth's Poetry, 1787–1800* (Basingstoke, 1986).

Valenze, Deborah, 'Charity, Custom and Humanity: Changing Attitudes towards the Poor in Eighteenth-Century England' , in Jane Garnett and Colin Matthews, eds, *Revival and Religion since 17000, Essays for John Walsh* (1993).

Valenze, Deborah, *The First Industrial Woman* (Oxford, 1995).

Vigarello, Georges, *Concepts of Cleanliness: Changing Attitudes since the Middle Ages in France* (Cambridge, 1988).

Voss, Heerma van, ed., *Petitions in Social History, International Review of Social History*, supplement 9 (Cambridge, n.d.).

Voth, Hans-Joachim, *Time and Work in England, 1750–1830* (Oxford, 2000).

Wagner, Peter, *Reading Iconotexts: From Swift to the French Revolution* (1995).

Wall, Cynthia, *The Literary and Cultural Spaces of Restoration London* (Cambridge, 1998).

Waller, Maureen, *1700: Scenes from London Life* (2000).

Walsh, Claire, 'Shop Design and the Display of Goods in Eighteenth-Century London', *Journal of Design History*, 8 (1995), pp. 157–76.

Ward, Joseph, *Metropolitan Communities: Trade Guilds, Identity and Social Change in Early Modern London* (Stanford, 1997).

Wareing, John, '"Violently Taken Away or Cheatingly Duckoyed": The Illicit Recruitment in London of Indentured Servants for the American Colonies, 1645–1718', *London Journal*, 26, 2 (2001), pp. 1–22.

Weatherill, Lorna, *Consumer Behaviour and Material Culture in Britain 1660–1760* (2nd edn, 1996).

Webb, Sidney James and Webb, Beatrice, *English Local Government from the Revolution to the Municipal Corporations Act*, 9 vols (1906–29): vol. i, *The Parish and the County*; vols ii–iii, *The Manor and the Borough* (parts 1–2); vol. iv, *Statutory Authorities for Special Purposes*; vol. v, *The Story of the King's Highway*; vol. vi, *English Prisons under Local Government*; vol. vii, *English Poor Law History*, part 1, *The Old Poor Law*; vols viii–ix, *English Poor Law History*, part 2, *The Last Hundred Years*.

Weinreb, Ben and Hibbert, Christopher, eds, *The London Encyclopedia* (1983).

Weitzman, Arthur J., 'Eighteenth-Century London: Urban Paradise or Fallen City', *Journal of the History of Ideas*, 36 (1975), pp. 469–80.

Wheatley, Henry B., *Hogarth's London: Pictures of the Manners of the Eighteenth Century* (1909).

Whyman, Susan E., *Sociability and Power in Late-Stuart England: The Cultural Worlds of the Verneys, 1660–1720* (Oxford, 1999).

Williams, Carolyn D., '"The Luxury of Doing Good": Benevolence, Sensibility and the Royal Humane Society', in Roy Porter and Marie Mulvey Roberts, eds, *Pleasure in the Eighteenth Century* (Basingstoke, 1996).

Williamson, Tom and Bellamy, Liz, *Property and Landscape: A Social History of Land Ownership and the English Countryside* (1987).

Wilson, Adrian, 'A Critical Portrait of Social History', in Adrian Wilson, ed., *Rethinking Social History: English Society, 1570–1920, and its Interpretation* (Manchester, 1993).

Wilson, Adrian, 'Illegitimacy and its Implications in Mid Eighteenth-Century London: The Evidence of the Foundling Hospital', *Continuity and Change*, 4 (1989), pp. 103–64.

Wilson, Kathleen, 'Empire, Trade and Popular Politics in Mid-Hanoverian Britain: The Case of Admiral Vernon', *Past and Present*, 121 (1988), pp. 74–109.

Wilson, Philip K., '"Sacred Sanctuaries for the Sick": Surgery at St Thomas's Hospital, 1725–26', *London Journal*, 17, 1 (1992), pp. 36–53.

Wiltenbug, Joy, *Disorderly Women and Female Power in the Street Literature of Early Modern England and Germany* (Charlottesville, Virginia, 1992).

Winchester, Hilary and White, Paul, 'The Location of Marginalised Groups in the Inner City', *Environment and Planning D: Society and Space*, 6, (1988), pp. 37–54.

Woledge, H. S. and Smale, M. A., 'Migration in East Yorkshire in the Eighteenth Century', *Local Population Studies*, 70, Spring 2003, pp. 29–48.

Wrightson, Keith, 'The Politics of the Parish in Early Modern England', in Paul Griffiths, Adam Fox and Steve Hindle, eds, *The Experience of Authority in Early Modern England* (1996).

Wrigley, E. A., and Schofield, R. S., *The Population History of England, 1541–1871* (1981).

Index

generally 133, 134, 135–36
number of 132–3
pauper farms 127, 129, 133
reports 236
riots against 138
Sunday routine 135
workhouse families 136

Woty, William 95
Wrigley, Tony 238

Yeats, Ann 145–47
'Young Beggar' (Murillo) 226

Zoffany, Johan 226